THE MONETARY
APPROACH TO
INTERNATIONAL
ADJUSTMENT

THE MONETARY APPROACH TO INTERNATIONAL ADJUSTMENT

Revised Edition

edited by
Bluford H. Putnam
and
D. Sykes Wilford

PRAEGER

PRAEGER SPECIAL STUDIES • PRAEGER SCIENTIFIC

New York   •   Westport, Connecticut   •   London

Library of Congress Cataloging-in-Publication Data
Main entry under title:

The Monetary approach to international adjustment.

Bibliography: p.
Includes index.
1. Foreign exchange—Addresses, essays, lectures.
2. Balance of payments—Addresses, essays, lectures.
I. Putnam, Bluford H. II. Wilford, D. Sykes.
HG3821.M66 1986 332.4'5 85-28314

ISBN 0-275-92024-0 (alk. paper)
ISBN 0-275-92050-X (pbk. : alk. paper)

Library of Congress Catalog Card Number: 85-28314
ISBN: 0-275-92024-0
ISBN: 0-275-92050-x pb.

First published in 1986

Praeger Publishers, 521 Fifth Avenue, New York, NY 10175
A division of Greenwood Press, Inc.

Printed in the United States of America

The paper used in this book complies with the Permanent
Paper Standard issued by the National Information Standards
Organization (Z39.48-1984).

10 9 8 7 6 5 4 3 2 1

DEDICATION

We received our graduate education in economics at Tulane University, and we feel a very great debt to the institution for the training it gave us. We are especially indebted to two faculty members, J. Ernest Tanner and J. Richard Zecher.

Our greatest intellectual debt, however, is to our fellow graduate students. So we dedicate this volume to a special group of classmates who supported us, taught us, learned with us and hobnobbed with us during our years at Tulane University:

Michael Cox, Federal Reserve Bank of Dallas; Donald Kemp, Chase Manhattan Bank; David King, Citibank; Jules LeBon, Xavier University; Frank Martin, Southern University; Charles Smithson, Chase Manhattan Bank; Alden Toevs, Morgan Stanley & Co.

Thank you all,

Bluford H. Putnam
D. Sykes Wilford

ACKNOWLEDGMENTS

The revised edition of this volume benefited greatly from the research and editorial assistance provided by Lynn McFadden of the Chase Manhattan Bank. We especially appreciate her careful research on the compilation of the bibliography.

We would also like to acknowledge the support of our contributors, especially those who prepared new material for this edition.

FOREWORD

J. Richard Zecher

Much of the recent work in international economics, including the studies
in this volume, reflects an evolving theoretical and empirical framework
that has several prominent characteristics. First, there is an emphasis on
market efficiency and rational expectations in both domestic and international markets, in the sense that price or interest rate differences are
quickly eliminated or totally avoided to the extent they can be anticipated,
through the rational behavior of market participants. Second, there is an
emphasis on general equilibrium in the stock markets (bonds and money)
and in the flow markets (commodities and labor). And, of course, there is
the prominent role assigned to the supply and demand for money. This
emphasis follows naturally from interest in issues relating to the balance of
payments, which is the international flow of money, and the exchange rate,
which is the price of one type of money in terms of another.

My reading of the recent and not so recent literature suggests that
most, if not all, of the propositions known as the "monetary approach"
have been around in some form for a long time. Yet it is useful to identify
three modern general equilibrium theorists—Lloyd Metzler, Robert A.
Mundell, and Harry G. Johnson—who brought these propositions together
and developed the general equilibrium outlines of the monetary approach
to international adjustment.

Many scholars have been attracted to work on the monetary approach
by its richness of testable implications. This has led to what is, for the field
of international economics, a large and rapidly growing body of empirical
literature. These studies are too recent to have withstood successfully the
test of time, but they do provide very substantial encouragement for
further work on the monetary approach.

Others have been attracted to the monetary approach mainly because
of its strong policy implications, particularly for those actions of the central
bank and fiscal authorities that affect the dometic supply of money and,
therefore, the balance of payments and the exchange rate. The monetary
approach's general equilibrium nature allows, in a refined form, the
policy-maker to observe and be aware of the key variables determining
international adjustment. Implications of the monetary approach are
applicable equally to the reserve currency-creating country, the United
States, and to the small, open economy. The approach, already being used

to evaluate and promote economic performance in the developing (as well as the industrialized) world, is fast becoming an important tool for the practitioner of economic policy.

Bluford H. Putnam and D. Sykes Wilford made a major contribution with the first edition of this volume by successfully integrating a series of papers that dealt with the broad historical development of the monetary approach, its theoretical and empirical application in a wide variety of circumstances, clarification of previously ambiguous parts of the theory, and refinements in variables in the model and in the statistical tools used to test the model's implications. In this second edition, the coeditors have expanded the book's scope by adding sections on currency substitution and the policy debate over exchange rate regimes and monetary policy. The result is a self-contained volume that provides the reader with a clear picture of where the monetary approach came from, the current state of the art, and the most promising avenues for further research.

PREFACE

With the breakdown of the Bretton Woods international monetary system in the early 1970s and the emergence of a system of managed, floating exchange rates, a number of economic realities have clashed sharply with received economic doctrine. First, the balance of payments problems that undermined the fixed exchange rate system were not those of unsustainable current account or trade account deficits. Instead, the primary problem lay with the very large capital flows from the United States to the rest of the world, fueled by the relatively expansionary monetary policy in the United States. And second, floating exchange rates, managed or not, assure that the foreign exchange market clears, but does not equilibrate nations' current accounts and does not provide an insulated environment in which nations can conduct an independent monetary policy.

The monetary approach to international adjustment goes directly to the heart of these economic realities and has made some impressive strides in providing a consistent framework in which to analyze international adjustment problems under any exchange rate regime. This book is a collection of essays that present the basic theory, trace its historical origins, demonstrate its empirical relevance, and then, in limited ways, extend the basic theories into more sophisticated and complex forms directed toward the many unanswered questions that remain.

This collection is testimony to the complexities and directions of international monetary studies that have developed through the years. In the days of Adam Smith and David Hume, domestic policies geared to acquiring and hoarding monetary wealth—principally gold—were shown to be fallacious at best. Essentially, Hume told us that the price level, the income of a country, and the supply and demand for money were interrelated variables searching for some equilibrium. In his work, the balance of payments or change in holdings of international reserves were part of an automatically adjusting system, determined by market forces. Mercantilistic policies aimed at hoarding reserves were doomed to failure by these forces. The pursuit of mercantilistic policies by various governments would only undermine trade and create a less than optimal level of real trade among nations. Consistent with Hume's view of money and trade were the laissez-faire notions of Adam Smith. His appeal to the "invisible hand" is consistent with modern arguments for market-determined international transactions in goods, services, and assets. Mercantilistic value judgments that trade deficits were bad and supluses good had no meaning to a man who realized a country's wealth was found in its actual output potential and not its stock of gold.

Such arguments as these are strongly embedded in the monetary approach to international adjustment. The emergence of the monetary approach marks a major swing in economic thought back to the concepts of Hume and Smith, and away from the balance of payments theories that emerged from the Keynesian revolution. In particular, economists schooled in the Keynesian tradition tended to focus on the balance of payments, and specifically the current account, as a policy variable. Depreciation policies could be used to make exports more competitive and thereby increase employment at home. Trade account imbalances were viewed as employment problems deserving of protectionist policies if the imbalances could not be corrected with exchange rate changes. In the economic models, capital flows were often ignored and changes in the exchange rate were assumed to cause equal changes in the terms of trade. Partial equilibrium frameworks became the standard for viewing trade imbalances.

The changing reality of the international monetary system, however, began to challenge these approaches. World markets were important for many goods, and capital markets developed internationally at impressive rates. At the same time, domestic monetarism was a rising force, emphasizing the importance of money and the general equilibrium nature of domestic economies. Given that world goods and capital markets were becoming more and more integrated, international theorists were forced to rework their models; simultaneoulsy, the importance of monetary demand and supply relationships on a world level was becoming integrated into this new general equilibrium approach to balance of payments questions. The resultant work is now known as the monetary approach to the balance of payments. In some sense, then, the monetary approach is not a restatement of Hume, but is more properly viewed as the refinements of international adjustment theories prevalent in the 1950s and 1960s, after these theories had been reworked with a view toward global markets in the context of a general equilibrium framework. The basic argument, under fixed exchange rates, became that excess supplies of and demand for money led to changes in international reserves. Trade was viewed as only one portion of the country's international account, as was the capital account. If one viewed trade as representing the goods market and the capital account as reflecting the bond market, the balance of these or the change in international reserves would reflect money market (using Walras' Law) equilibrium or disequilibrium. An excess supply of money implied an outflow of reserves as the country's domestic money stock adjusted to the demand for money with the country.

The development of this literature opened a new chapter in the development of international monetary theory. In the course of changing international monetary relations, this basic theory is leading to new ways of analyzing and forecasting exchange rate movements.

This collection of essays, developed from this heritage, Hume to Mundell, challenges the old theories as well as the new and, it is hoped, contributes to the further understanding of how the international economic system functions.

CONTENTS

Part 2:   FLEXIBLE EXCHANGE RATES

Part 3:   CURRENCY SUBSTITUTION
AND FLEXIBLE EXCHANGE RATES

Part 4: THE POLICY DEBATE

THE MONETARY
APPROACH TO
INTERNATIONAL
ADJUSTMENT

INTRODUCTION

Bluford H. Putnam
D. Sykes Wilford

The modern theory of international adjustment—the monetary approach—has been developing through both the Bretton Woods fixed exchange rate period and the present flexible rate regime, but its genesis is embedded in the history of economic thought. History provides the roots of the theory needed to appreciate fully the flowering of this literature.*

As many authors have noted, the monetary approach traces its roots back to David Hume's classic essay, "Of the Balance of Trade," in his *Essays, Moral, Political and Literary*, published in 1752. The concepts that there is automatic adjustment of the balance of payments, that the existence of expected arbitrage possibilities would in itself lead to speculative arbitrage and then to purchasing-power parity, and that a country's stock of money is determined by demand factors not under the control of authorities—all these are fundamental implications of the monetary approach and are contained in Hume's essay. Indeed, Hume had much more to contribute to balance of payments theory than just the price–specie–flow mechanism so often recounted in economic texts. Thus, before moving on to the present-day extensions of Hume's work, a close

---

*In designing the book, several elements were considered, such as topicality, rigor, level of sophistication, and readability. The layout, however, was constrained by one overriding objective: That the book should be useful to students and scholars, as well as their instructors. Teaching from this text should not be difficult, with learning even easier.

1

look at exactly what Hume said will lead to a fuller appreciation of the monetary approach's debt to him.

After laying the foundation for his analysis of the balance of payments by providing pedagogical illustrations of the price–specie–flow mechanism, Hume takes a general equilibrium view of the world. He states:

> Now, it is evident, that the same causes, which would correct these exorbitant inequalities, were they to happen miraculously, must prevent their happening in the common cause of nature, and must forever, in all neighboring nations, preserve money nearly proportionable to the art and industry of each nation.[1]

Hume is very definite here in his perception of a world in which monetary stocks are consistent with the real income of the nation. He is arguing that the forces that determine the money stock are so strong as to preclude any significant inequalities. To make certain his readers understand this point, Hume likens money to water:

> All water, wherever it communicates, remains always at a level. Ask naturalists the reason: they tell you, that were it to be raised in any one place, the superior gravity of that part not being balanced, must depress it, till it meet a counter-poise; and that the same cause, which redresses the inequality when it happens, must forever prevent it, without some violent external operation.[2]

Hume's statement suggests a perception of the world quite similar to the framework of the monetary approach to the balance of payments. Hume is arguing that the money stock is demand-determined by the "art and industry" of the nation. Furthermore, he is suggesting that prices among countries are also linked. Hume's specific statement on prices is as follows:

> And any man who travels over Europe at this day, may see, by the prices of commodities, that money, in spite of the absurd jealousy of prices and states, has brought itself nearly to a level; and that the difference between one kingdom and another is not greater in this respect, that it is often between different provinces of the same kingdom.[3]

Here, Hume is making the case for the purchasing-power parity doctrine, and his arguments are similar in nature to the monetary approach assumptions of unified world markets.

Building on these basic points contained in Hume's writing, studies of the monetary approach to international adjustment have elaborated these propositions, expressed them in mathematical formulations, and applied modern statistical techniques to evaluate them. The collection of works in this volume is designed to give the reader a broad picture of such studies, from basic theory and historical origins to frontier extensions, new statistical tests and applications to national economic strategy.

This volume has been divided into four parts. The first deals with fixed exchange rates, while the second introduces the flexible rate literature. The third section discusses a most critical development of the monetary approach to flexible exchange rates—currency substitution. Finally the fourth section discusses the present set of national and international economic policy debates brewing in the United States and abroad.

PART 1: FIXED EXCHANGE RATES

The collection is opened by Michael Connolly's "The Monetary Approach to an Open Economy: The Fundamental Theory Revisited." It is an overview of the monetary approach in its basic form, as well as a survey of new developments in theory and empirical work. Following this study is Robert Keleher's extensive investigation of the historical origins of monetary approach concepts titled "Of Money and Prices: Some Historical Perspectives." More than any other historical essay to date, this work documents the thoughts of early economists who grappled with the problems of international adjustments, and refined and extended the theories associated with Hume and his contemporaries.

Initial studies of the monetary approach tended to focus on the small, open economy, but application of the approach to the United States is extremely important given the role of the dollar in international trade and finance. "Money, Income, and Causality in the United States and the United Kingdom," by Bluford H. Putnam and D. Sykes Wilford, analyzes the special case of the large country providing the international system with a reserve currency.

Empirical studies have provided an extensive body of evidence supporting the usefulness of the monetary approach, and two such investigations are in the next entry in Part 1. "International Reserve Flows: Seemingly Unrelated Regressions," by Putnam and Wilford, empirically evaluates the monetary approach for eight European countries and provides evidence on the purchasing-power and interest rate parity assumptions within a reduced-form specification.

Applications of the monetary approach to developing economies are becoming increasing important, as the approach has much to say about the interdependence of these economies and the world financial system. In "The Monetary Approach to the Balance of Payments and Developing Nations: A Review of the Literature," Walton T. Wilford discusses the application of a basic monetary approach model to developing economies, taking care to note the points unique to these countries and embody them in his analysis. His chapter also discusses the empirical evidence to date on using the monetary model in studying developing countries' economies.

The final study in the fixed exchange rate section is by M. A. Akhtar. In "Some Common Misconceptions about the Monetary Approach to International Adjustment," the analytical problems of the monetary approach as noted by its critics and opponents are given special attention. Since many authors of works on the monetary approach concentrate on extending the standard approach rather than on responding to questions and criticism, this study is a valuable contribution to the monetary approach literature.

PART 2: FLEXIBLE EXCHANGE RATES

In the first part of this volume, we addressed the monetary approach to international adjustment under the assumption of fixed exchange rates. Our focus was necessarily on the balance of payments adjustments that take place through changes in a country's holdings of international reserves whenever there is an excess supply or demand for its money. In the second part of this volume, we analyze international adjustment when the equilibrating mechanism is the exchange rate.

Since the breakup of the Bretton Woods system, the international macroeconomist has been challenged by a new and ever-changing economic climate. Although the flexible period is only a few years past its first decade of operation, the system has already managed to generate heated and complex debate in central banks, financial institutions, and universities. Primarily, the debate has been stimulated by the flexible rate system's failure to behave as anticipated. In particular, flexible exchange rates have not guaranteed the independence of national monetary policies, and exchange rates have not moved to fully equilibrate current account balances. Various adaptations of the monetary approach have much to say about these issues.

Also worth noting is that students of the monetary approach do not tend to fall into easily predictable camps when the question of fixed vesus flexible exchange rates is raised. In fact, the monetary approach provides ammunition for both sides of the debate. The first paper in Part 2, "The

Evolution of the Flexible Exchange Rate Debate," by Putnam and Wilford, discusses this dichotomy.

The ease with which the basic monetary model of fixed exchange rates can be converted to a model of exchange rate determination under flexible rates is demonstrated by "Factors Determining Exchange Rates: A Simple Model and Empirical Tests," by Thomas M. Humphrey and Thomas A. Lawler. Besides providing the theoretical transition from fixed to flexible rate models, this study also includes some interesting empirical estimates.

With the basic theory in hand, the next study, "The Monetary Approach to Exchange Rates: Its Historical Evolution and Role in Policy Debates," by Thomas M. Humphrey, takes a close look at three exchange rate controversies in which the monetary approach was forcefully argued. In this study, it is possible to trace the growing sophistication of the approach, as each successive debate produced new thoughts and ideas.

The first monetary approach models of exchange rate determination all assumed that the monetary authorities conducted monetary policy by controlling the money supply. In the final article of this section, "Monetary Policy, Interest Rate Targets, and Foreign Exchange Markets," Putnam assumes that the monetary authorities set interest rates, and derives conclusions about movements in the domestic money supply and the spot exchange rate that are worth the attention of policy-makers.

PART 3: CURRENCY SUBSTITUTION AND FLEXIBLE EXCHANGE RATES

The studies in this section focus upon an important extension of the approach critical to understanding the interdependence of monetary policies under flexible exchange rates. This is the issue of currency substitution or currency mobility. Essentially, currency substitution models assume that residents of a country can hold assets denominated in more than one currency in their portfolios. This allows international adjustment to occur either through price changes (exchange rate movements) or demand-side quantity adjustments (portfolio shifts at existing exchange rates). Demand substitutability among currencies may be considered the counterpart of the perfect supply substitutability imposed by the assumption of fixed exchange rates. "A Currency Portfolio Approach to Exchange Rate Determination: Exchange Rate Stability and the Independence of Monetary Policy," by David T. King, Putnam, and Wilford, redefines the demand for money function of the basic model to encompass currency substitution, providing an introduction to the concept of the interdependence of monetary policies under flexible exchange rates.

"Currency Mobility and Balance of Payments Adjustment," by Russell S. Boyer, ranks as the first modern theoretical statement of the currency mobility concepts. First drafted while Boyer was still a student at the University of Chicago, this study has had a major role in stimulating interest in this topic. Boyer's paper is certainly the cornerstone of this intellectual endeavor.

"Theory and Implications of Currency Substitution," by Lance Girton and Don Roper, is the third selection in this section. It was another of the early breakthroughs in this literature, and was widely circulated before its original publication in 1981. The next article, Marc Miles's "Currency Substitution, Flexible Exchange Rates, and Monetary Independence," was the first empirical piece to provide concrete support for the significance of currency substitution for a country's control of its monetary policy.

"Currency Substitution and Instability in the World Dollar Market," by Ronald McKinnon, is a watershed piece on the theory. This paper not only supported the view that the demand for the individual national monies of industrial countries is affected by international currency substitution, but also noted the implications for a central bank's short-run and long-run control of the money supply.

The last article in Part 3, "Exchange Rates with Substitutable Currencies," by Wilford, provides an example of the empirical application of the theory to an actual exchange rate experience.

PART 4:   THE POLICY DEBATE

Turning theory into practice is never easy. The monetary approach certainly has been misused by both analysts and policy-makers alike. This policy section is not designed to "set the record straight"; this would be a task beyond its scope. The section has a much less ambitious goal; it attempts to illustrate the importance of the monetary approach in current monetary policy debates. The initial paper, "The Policy Consequences of Interdependence," by Putnam and Wilford, illustrates this.

The next chapter, by Krieger and Wilford, "Discretionary Monetary Policy and the Gold Standard," provides a guide to the debate on using a price rule to achieve neutral monetary policy via a gold standard.

The final paper argues a specific point and is included in the policy section to allow the reader to participate in the debate on fixed versus flexible exchange rates. Marc Miles, in "Refocusing Monetary Theory and Policy," argues that price rules are far superior to quantity rules. He argues that discretionary policy is dangerous and unpredictable; moreover, fixed exchange rates are the key to stabilization.

NOTES

1. David Hume, "Of the Balance of Trade," Essays, Moral, Political, and Literary (1752), essay v, part 2, reprinted in *International Trade Theory: Hume to Ohlin*, ed. William R. Allen (New York: Random House, 1965), p. 35.

2. Ibid.

3. Ibid., p. 36.

Part 1

FIXED EXCHANGE RATES

1

The Monetary Approach to an Open Economy: The Fundamental Theory Revisited

Michael Connolly

"Suppose four fifths of all the money in Great Britain to be annihilated in one night," David Hume speculated in 1752 ". . . must not the price of all labor and commodities sink in proportion," giving England a competitive advantage in trade which must quickly "bring back the money we had lost, and raise us to the level (of prices) of all the neighboring nations?"[1] This adjustment process was to be christened the Hume specie-flow mechanism, and is, in a fundamental sense, the earliest known statement of a monetary approach to the balance of payments. Hume's statement also raised specific issues such as the now-controversial, so-called law of one price. This law, apparently contradicted in particular for traded goods by Hume's theoretical adjustment process, was, however, firmly held by him:

> Any man who travels over Europe at this day, may see, by the prices of commodities, that money . . . has brought itself nearly to a level; and that the difference between one kingdom and another is not greater in this respect, than it is often between different provinces of the same kingdom.[2]

(This latter criterion has in fact provided the basis for one of the first modern empirical tests of the law of one price.[3] Hume further noted: "The only circumstance that can obstruct the exactness of these proportions is the expense of transporting the commodities from one place to another."[4])

This is so because "the same causes, which would correct these exorbitant inequalities, were they to happen miraculously, must prevent their happening in the common course of nature."[5] Consequently, price differences would not be an observed part of the specie-flow adjustment process, and the apparent contradiction with the law of one price is resolved.[6]

While the first statements of a monetary approach to the balance of payments stressed commodity trade more than adjustment in asset markets, they nevertheless laid out the fundamental principle of a demand for money that, if not satisfied, led to a surplus to provide the additional money desired or, if exceeded, led to a deficit, thereby depleting the excess balances. This is the basic modern monetary view. It consists of three elements: a theory of the demand for money, a money supply process, and balance of payments surpluses in instances of excess demand for money and deficits in cases of excess supply.

In the context of flexible exchange rates, an excess supply of money would induce an exchange depreciation rather than a loss in foreign reserves, and an excess demand results in an appreciation in lieu of a reserve accumulation. Finally, the monetary model has offered an explanation of both reserve and exchange rate changes in the context of a managed float.[7] Once again, the fortunes of a country's reserves and/or exchange rate depend upon the balance between the supply of and the demand for money.

In what follows, we try to develop somewhat more formally a minimum monetary model for the uninitiated. Modern monetary views are stated more completely elsewhere in a number of articles by Harry Johnson, Robert Mundell, and some of their former students, such as Rudiger Dornbusch and Jacob Frenkel.[8]

A MODERN MONETARY MODEL

The most succinct monetary model is that of the "small, open economy" facing given world prices and interest rates.* We can write a straightforward Cagan demand for money equation:

$$L = kPY \exp(-\alpha i) \qquad (1a)$$

$$= kPY \exp(-\alpha \varrho) \qquad (1b)$$

-----

*Empirically, this model has been fruitfully applied to a number of seemingly large countries, so that it applies to most large ones, if not the United States.

where P is the domestic price level, Y permanent income, i the nominal interest rate, ϱ the expected rate of inflation, and $-\alpha i$ and $-\alpha\varrho$ the interest rate and expected inflation rate elasticities of the demand for money. Note that with the Fisher equation, $i = u + \varrho$, where u is the real rate of interest, assumed to be constant. Consequently $k^* = k \exp(-du)$.

A stable demand for money, no matter what the variant it assumes,* is the cornerstone of the monetary approach to an open economy. If one agrees that the demand for money is stable in the Friedman sense, the monetary approach to the balance of payments is the natural consequence.[9] Put more forcefully, the notion of a stable demand for money and the monetary approach to an open economy are one and the same thing. Harry Johnson put it this way in his nontechnical guide to the monetary approach to the balance of payments: "A proper test of the monetary approach must be essentially a test of the stability of the demand for money (in Friedman's terminology)."[10]

The second essential ingredient of the modern monetary model is a specification of the money supply process. The simplest one, that of Robert A. Mundell,[11] is:

$$M = A(R + D) \tag{2}$$

where R is net foreign reserves in terms of domestic currency of the central bank, D is domestic credit of the central bank, and A the money multiplier. The sum $R + D$ equals H, the high-powered money base. This identity states that changes in the money stock are from foreign or domestic sources or from a change in the money multiplier: that is, from a change in foreign reserves via the balance of payments, dR/dt, or a change in domestic credit extended by the central bank, dD/dt, or a change in the money multiplier, dA/dt.

The third relationship essential to the simple monetary model is the link between domestic and international prices via the exchange rate. It is assumed to hold partly because of arbitrage and partly because of the monetary adjustment process. The purchasing-power parity relationship is shown by

$$P = EP^o \tag{3}$$

where P is domestic prices, P^o is foreign prices, and E is the exchange rate.

---

*An alternative one used in empirical studies is $L = kPY^\varepsilon i^{-\eta}$, where ε and η are income and interest rate elasticities of the demand for money, respectively.

This relationship, while it need only hold in terms of changes (for example $p = e + p^o$, where small letters denote percentage changes), is perhaps one of the more controversial ones in the monetary model. Further, it is an important one in that it is part of the transmission mechanism whereby exchange rate changes and world price movements disturb domestic prices and, consequently, the demand for money. In favor of the purchasing-power parity relationship, one can invoke commodity arbitrage and/or the neutrality of money in an adjustment process. Against it, one can argue that it holds only for purely monetary disturbances. Empirically, the evidence on this law of one price is mixed.* In some instances, the weakness of the evidence on the law of one price has diminished the predictive power of the money model.†

Finally, it simplifies matters greatly to assume that the money stock in existence adjusts rapidly to the quantity demanded, either by a deficit (running down the money stock) or by an exchange depreciation (increasing the demand) or by some combination of the two, so that monetary equilibrium holds:‡

$$L = M \qquad\qquad (4)$$

With fixed exchange rates, the nominal money supply adjusts to the demand via payments imbalances, while with flexible exchange rates the demand for money adjusts to the nominal supply via changes in the

---

*J. M. Keynes was the first to dub purchasing-power parity the law of one price, in his comment on Gustav Cassel's 1916 paper: "The effect of Professor Cassel's interesting calculations . . . seems to me to be that even with the hindrances to free movements of goods which prevail in war time, real price levels in different countries tend to equality. That is to say, the index numbers of local prices corrected by the world-value of local money, as measured by the exchanges, tend to equality."[12] Keynes' later empirical studies in monetary reform, despite his theoretical reticence regarding real disturbances, such as in Germany, found that the "Purchasing Power Parity Theory, even in its crude form, has worked passably well"[13] for the United Kingdom, Italy, and France relative to the United States between August 1919 and June 1923.

†On the side of integrated markets and one-price are H. Genberg, P. Isard, D. McClosky, and R. Zecher, while against is R. M. Dunn. Richardson reports mixed results. M. Connolly and J. da Silveira find that purchasing-power parity predicts well for postwar Brazil where disturbances were frequently monetary.[14]

‡A more sophisticated model allows for less than immediate adjustment. Specifically, in R. Dornbusch's notation, $H = \pi(L - M)$, where H is hoarding, for example, the change in reserves, and π the speed of adjustment. Here we suppose $\pi = \infty$, which implies $L = M$. The Dornbusch model is of interest also because it provides a two-country monetary framework.

exchange rate. In a mixed system, both the demand and the supply of money adjust to achieve equilibrium.

Substituting equation 3 into 1, and equations 1 and 2 into 4, taking logarithms of both sides, differentiating with respect to time, we have after manipulation, $r - e = -a - d + p^o + Y - \alpha\varrho'$, where r is the change in foreign reserves (the balance of payments) as a percent of the money base, d is the increase in central bank credit as a percent of the money base, a is the percentage change in the money multiplier, e is the percentage depreciation of the home currency, p^o the world rate of inflation, Y the rate of growth of permanent income (assumed to be determined exogenously),* and ϱ' the change in the expected rate of inflation.

Two polar cases of the monetary model can be distinguished. First, with fixed exchange rates, e = 0, giving:

$$r = -a - d + p^o + Y - \alpha\varrho' \tag{5}$$

which states that an increase in the rate of growth of domestic credit will cause an equiproportionate loss in reserves, holding other variables constant. Similarly, a rise in the expected rate of inflation causes a loss in reserves. (Parenthetically, the higher income growth is, the more favorable the balance of payments as a result of the increase in the demand for money, contrary to post-Keynesian import demand arguments.) This relationship (or variants of it) has been tested for a good number of countries under fixed exchange rates. The majority of the studies strongly support the negative relationship between domestic credit (for example, monetary policy) and the state of the balance of payments. Put briefly, monetary expansion is at the expense of foreign reserves.

A second polar case is that of fully flexible exchange rates, that is r = 0, with no intervention on foreign exchange markets, giving:

$$e = a + d - p^o - Y + \alpha\varrho' \tag{6}$$

With fully flexible rates any increase in the growth rate of domestic credit causing an excess supply of money results in an equiproportionate depreciation of the home currency. Consequently, the monetary approach

---

*Note that for notational simplicity both the change in reserves and the change in domestic credit are expressed as a proportion of the money base, that is, r = (dR/dt)/H and D = (dD/dt)/H, since d log (R + D)/dt = (dR/dt)(R − D) = (dD/dt)/(R − D) and R = D = H.

provides a theory of exchange rate determination in the event of flexible rates.*

Finally, a mixed case in which exchange market pressure is absorbed partly by reserve losses and partly by exchange depreciation is given by

$$r - e = -a - d + p^o + Y - \alpha\varrho' \tag{7}$$

where, once again, r and d are changes in reserves and domestic credit as a proportion of the money stock, while the other variables are percentage changes.

This model was first proposed by L. Girton and D. Roper for the Canadian-managed float from 1952 to 1962, and is an extremely useful way of viewing the current mixed exchange regime. Basically, the monetary authorities have, for a given rate of growth of domestic credit, world prices, and permanent income, a choice between reserve losses and exchange rate changes that will absorb a given level of pressure on the exchange market. Or it makes clear that an expansionary domestic credit policy will cause a loss in reserves, an exchange depreciation, or a combination of the two.†

For example, with a preannounced rate of depreciation e^*, the path of reserves is given by $r = -(d - e^*) - a + Y - \alpha\varrho'$, so for consistency of monetary and fiscal policy, domestic credit should not grow faster than the rate of crawl in the exchange rate. Put differently, for a given rate of credit growth, d^*, the rate of currency crawl, e, must be greater than or equal to d^* to avoid runs on reserves and a collapse.

When, on the other hand, domestic credit growth is expansionary relative to exchange rate depreciation (the case of Argentina from January 1979 to March 1981), a speculative attack depleting remaining foreign reserves in one fell swoop will occur at t^* and force the country onto a freely floating exchange rate, where:

$$t^* = -\alpha + \frac{\ln(\bar{R}/\bar{D} + 1)}{\varepsilon} \tag{8}$$

where α is the sensitivity of the demand for money with respect to the

---

*This formula applies to freely floating rates, and not to the discrete, discontinuous devaluations of the adjustable peg system of the postwar period until the 1970s. Such one-and-one-for-all exchange rate adjustments are analyzed by M. Connolly and D. Taylor for 18 devaluations that took place in the 1960s.[15]

†Connolly and da Silveira have applied the exchange market pressure model to Brazil.[12]

expected rate of inflation, $\overline{R}/\overline{D}$ is initial central bank reserves as a proportion of initial domestic credit, and ε is the difference between growth in domestic credit and depreciation in the exchange rate, or $\varepsilon = d - e$ (equal to 4.5 percent per month in the case of Argentina).

Consequently, the speculative attack causing a collapse is sooner:

1. the more sensitive the demand for money is with respect to the expected rate of inflation (the larger α);
2. the smaller initial foreign reserves are as a proportion of domestic credit (the smaller $\overline{R}/\overline{D}$); and
3. the greater the inconsistency of monetary and exchange rate policy (the greater $d - e$).

(For a more rigorous treatment, see Connolly and Taylor [1984].[16])

The fundamental monetary model presented here captures, I believe, the essential elements of the monetary approach to an open economy. To sum up, its foundation is a stable demand for money in the Friedman sense coupled with a money stock composed of an external component (foreign reserves) and an internal component (domestic credit). In cases of excess money supply over demand, exchange market pressure results in a loss of foreign reserves, thereby reducing the supply of money, and/or an exchange depreciation which restores equilibrium by increasing the demand for money.

FURTHER ISSUES AND EXTENSIONS

Two-country Model

In the context of a two-country world, the exchange market pressure model can be generalized to:

$$r_1 - r_2 - e_{12} = -(a_1 - a_2) - (d_1 - d_2) + (Y_1 - Y_2) - \alpha_1\varrho'_1 + \alpha_2\varrho'_2 \ (9)$$

where the variables are defined as before.

In the special case where $\alpha_1 = \alpha_2$, the expectations term can also be collected to give $-\alpha(\varrho'_1 - \varrho'_2)$. In terms of interest rate differentials, with no change in the real rates of return in either country, the impact is $-\alpha(i'_1 - i'_2)$. On the other hand, a rise in the real rate of return in, say, country 1, would lead to an improved level of reserves or currency appreciation in an asset model (see Frankel); that is, a positive $\alpha(i'_1 - i'_2)$, which is ruled out by the monetary model.

In short, from equation 9, it is the relative rates of growth of domestic credit, real income, the money multipliers, and the change in the expected inflation rate differential that determine the path of reserves in the two countries and the rate of increase in the price of currency 2 in terms of currency 1: that is, e_{12}.

Expectations

Probably the most important issue regarding exchange rates in particular has to do with expectations. Some recent studies in this area are suggestive of the delicate problems involved. R. Barro, for instance, has devised a scheme of exchange rate dynamics that revolves around individuals and firms distinguishing between a permanent and a transitory component of any exogenous change in the rate of monetary expansion.[18] The greater the permanancy perceived by the public of an increased monetary expansion rate, the more immediate and the greater the exchange depreciation. This raises the quesion of the formation of expectations, which has been explored in a number of interesting papers by John Bilson in the context of rational expectations.[19]

The basic principle is that the spot and forward rates fully incorporate all current information and expectations regarding the future. In this light, J. Frenkel has devised a clever shortcut for measuring expectations in the demand for money by using the forward exchange rate rather than, for example, adaptive expectations.[20] For the German hyperinflation, the forward rate for the mark performs well as an explanatory variable in the demand for money, and has the property of conforming to rational expectations theory, in that spot exchange rates are correlated with the last period's forward rates but not with previous ones. That is, the most recent forward rate incorporates all currently available market information.

A different approach in a monetary context is that of Rudiger Dornbusch.[21] The main interest of his approach is that it provides a "monetary shock" rationale for overshooting of exchange rates. Consider increasing the domestic monetary stock by means of open market purchases in a flexible exchange rate regime. This lowers domestic interest rates instantaneously through a liquidity effect, and immediately depreciates the exchange rate, but by more than its ultimate depreciation. That is, overshooting takes place. The reason for this is the Fisherian relationship:

$$i = i^{o} = \varrho \tag{10}$$

which states that domestic interest rates, i, must equal foreign ones, i^{o}, plus ϱ, the expected rate of depreciation of the home currency. (Irving Fisher puts it succinctly, ". . . two rates of interest in . . . two diverging standards will, in a perfect adjustment, differ from each other by an amount equal to the rate of divergence between the two standards."[22]) Consequently, if monetary expansion depresses domestic interest rates through a liquidity effect, and foreign interest rates remain unchanged, the home currency must initially depreciate more than its eventual decline. Thus the expectation is that it will recover somewhat in value, but not return to its initial value. This satisfies the Fisher rule since it implies $\varrho = 0$. Of course, not all reversible exchange rate swings are necessarily caused by monetary supply shocks; they can also arise from shifts in demands for national monies as assets. This latter view, while admittedly not entirely new, possibly sheds light upon current exchange rate swings. Further, it shifts the emphasis away from relative rates of inflation (or purchasing-power parity) toward an asset or stock market determination of exchange rates. While purchasing-power parity may in the long run (and occasionally in the short run) be a good predictor in instances of widely diverging monetary policies, it cannot account for dramatic, sometimes reversible swings in short periods of time.

Neutralization

In the framework of the monetary approach to the balance of payment under fixed exchange rates it has been suggested that the direction of causation may be from changes in reserves to changes in domestic credit rather than, as the monetarists would have it, the other way around.[23] This occurs with a policy of neutralizing the effects of payments surpluses or deficits upon the high-powered money base via an offsetting credit policy. In the notation of the minimum monetary model:

$$d = a - \beta r \qquad (11)$$

where β, the sterilization coefficient, ranges from zero (no offsetting) to unity (complete sterilization) and a is a constant.

This argument merits further attention. As Pentti Kouri and Michael Porter[24] note, neutralization would tend to bias empirical tests in favor of the domestic credit aspect of the monetary model. (Their study stresses capital outflows in response to monetary expansion. A framework for the analysis of this problem is found in Alexander Swoboda.[25]) In separate tests by Hans Genberg for Sweden, Lance Girton and Don Roper for Canada, and Michael Connolly and Dean Taylor for a cross-section of 27 countries, the evidence suggests that some neutralization takes place, particularly in developed countries, but that even in its presence, the bias in favor of the monetary view is negligible. Further tests would, however, be in order.*

CURRENCY SUBSTITUTION AND
COMPETITION AMONG NATIONAL MONIES

Recent theoretical developments have stressed the importance of currency substitution among asset holders. A number of papers provide a theory of multiple currencies that circulate within the same region (or rather are held by individuals within the same region) and are viewed as substitutes by holders of money. Russell Boyer's early "nickel and dime" paper neatly posed the problem, which, in the context of stability, involves Gresham's Law. Girton and Roper find that the greater the degree of substitution among national monies, the less stable the exchange rate. G. Calvo and E. Rodriguez add rational expectations to the picture, and find that exchange rate responses to monetary shocks exceed price responses but that, with perfect foresight paths, instability does not result. David King, Bluford Putnam, and D. Sykes Wilford examine exchange rate stability and the independence of monetary policy with currency substitution. Finally, John Cuddington has done a complete review recently.[26]

A natural companion to currency substitution is the implied existence of competition among issuers of national monies. (On this, see Benjamin Klein and Gordon Tullock for opposing views.[27]) The situation is similar to the era of state banking in the United States, during which states issued monies and exchange rates between state currencies were flexible (see Friedman and Schwartz.[28]) In principle, there exists an optimal rule for issuing national money, given that competition from other issuers exists. Not surprisingly, currency competition leads to at least a partial internalizing of the well-known negative externality (see Friedman)[29] imposed by overissue in the case of monopoly issue of currency, and imparts a greater degree of price stability to an international monetary system (see Girton and Roper.)[30] Other considerations may well override the competitive one—particularly the debt-financing motive in some instances—but the principle is a sound one, meriting further theoretical and empirical work.

---

*See Chapter 6 of this book for further treatment of this issue.

Marc Miles, using a constant elasticity of substitution (CES) production framework, estimated the elasticity of substitution between U.S. and Canadian dollars and found it greater during floating than during fixed periods, significantly different from zero, but not infinite. (From 1960 to 1975, the elasticity of substitution was estimated to be 5.4.[31])

EXCHANGE RATES AND
THE RELATIVE PRICE OF TRADED GOODS

The minimum monetary model discussed here makes no distinction between traded and nontraded goods: domestic prices of all goods are simply assumed to be kept in line with international prices. This assumption does not hinge upon arbitrage in goods, but rather upon the idea of the long-run neutrality of nominal magnitudes, namely the exchange rate and the money stock, in a monetary system. However, in the short-run adjustment period to, for example, an exchange depreciation, the relative price of traded goods will rise, and consequently there will be not only liquidity effects as outlined in the minimum monetary model, but also substitution effects along the lines of the elasticity approach. The role of such substitution effects between traded and nontraded goods during the adjustment period to monetary shocks is stressed in a monetary framework in a number of papers that build upon the so-called Australian or Swan-Salter model.[32] This model is, once again, one of a small, open economy that produces two composite goods, a traded one (exports and imports) and a nontraded one. In addition, individuals hold domestic money as their sole asset. Exchange depreciation thus has a liquidity effect, increasing the demand for money, and also a substitution effect, as individuals substitute traded goods for nontraded ones. Both effects work toward improving the balance of payments. However, as money flows in during the adjustment period these effects diminish and the system returns to its initial equilibrium. Consequently, real effects due to substitution take place only during the transitional adjustment process, while in the long run there are none. These transitional real effects are highlighted in Dornbusch, while the adjustment process itself has been dealt with by P. D. Jonson and H. Kierzkowski graphically and by Connolly and Taylor (1979) algebraically.[33] The latter model has been extended recently (Connolly and Taylor [1984]) to the problem of speculative attack and collapse models. It is shown that the relative price of nontraded goods rises prior to a dramatic fall at the point of collapse.

A SHORT GUIDE TO EMPIRICAL STUDIES

A masterful survey by S. P. Magee of empirical work on the monetary approach to an open economy appeared in 1976, and another has been written by M. Kreinen and L. Officer.[34] Consequently we need touch upon only a few studies that an interested reader might consult. The considerable amount of empirical work done to date in the area and the rapid rate of appearance of new statistical tests is testimony to the strong empirical thrust of the monetary approach. It is unfortunate that some early reviewers, such as G. Haberler, either neglect the first empirical studies altogether or, as does Marina Von Neuman Whitman, incorrectly dismiss them as "the estimation of an accounting identity rather than a true behavioral relationship," in an otherwise excellent, well-balanced review.[35] (For an empirical rejection of the view that empirical studies of the monetary approach are estimating only an accounting identity, see Putnam and Wilford.[36]) For, as stressed by Rudolf Rhomberg and H. R. Heller in the introduction to an International Monetary Fund volume, the possibility of empirical measurement of monetary and balance of payments aggregates fostered in part the development of the monetary framework.*

Here is a short list of selected empirical studies. (Full references are contained in the bibliography.[37])

1. Surveys
   Magee
   Kreinen and Officer
2. Case Studies
   Fixed exchange rate periods
   Australia: Zecher
   Canada: Cox and Wilford
   Canada: Cox
   Germany: Kouri
   Germany: Porter

---

*In Rhomberg and Heller's terms: "In view of the availability of these two sets of data (on monetary statistics and balance of payments accounts) in a large number of countries for which other statistical information was scarce, the thought naturally presented itself to develop a framework that could take full advantage of this data base." Regarding the IMF studies in that volume, on one hand, it would be too generous to credit the IMF with the empirical, back-of-the-envelope discovery of the monetary approach. On the other, it would be unfair not to note their numerous empirical studies regarding money in an open economy. Further, J. J. Polak's early theoretical essay and the IMF's actual lending practice stress the importance of domestic credit restraint to the state of the balance of payments.[38]

Honduras: Wilford and Wilford
Jamaica: Beals and Collery
Japan: Bean
Mexico: Wilford and Zecher
Mexico: Wilford, Connolly, and Lackey
Mexico: Blejer
Spain: Guitian
Sweden: Genberg
United Kingdom: Jonson
Venezuela: Khan
Eight European countries: Putnam and Wilford
Flexible exchange rate periods:
Afghanistan: Fry
Germany: Frenkel, Frankel
United States–United Kingdom: Putnam and Woodbury,
Clements and Frenkel
United States–Germany: Frankel
Peru: Edwards
Mixed exchange rate periods:
Brazil: Connolly and da Silveira, Blejer and
Leiderman
Canada: Girton and Roper
England: Bilson
3. Cross-section studies
Capital flows offsetting monetary policy (four countries):
Kouri and Porter
Monetary approach to devaluation (18 countries):
Connolly and Taylor
Exchange rate determination with rational expectations
(34 countries):
Bilson
Exchange market pressure model (five countries):
Sargen
Balance-of-payments determination (39 countries):
Aghevli and Khan

NOTES

1. David Hume, "Of the Balance of Trade," in *Essays, Moral, Political, and Literary* (1752), essay V, part II, reprinted in *International Trade Theory: Hume to Ohlin*, ed. W. R. Allen (New York: Random House, 1965), p. 34.

2. Ibid., p. 36.

3. See, for instance, Donald McClosky and J. Richard Zecher, "How the Gold Standard Worked 1880–1913," in Jacob Frenkel and Harry G. Johnson, eds., *The Monetary Approach to the Balance of Payments* (Toronto: University of Toronto Press, 1976).

4. Hume, op. cit., p. 36. See Paul Samuelson, "An Exact Hume–Ricardo–Marshall Model of International Trade," *Journal of International Economics* 1 (February 1971), for further discussion of this matter.

5. Hume, op. cit., p. 36.

6. See J. A. Frenkel and Harry G. Johnson, "The Monetary Approach to the Balance of Payments; Essential Concepts and Historical Origins," in J. A. Frenkel and H. G. Johnson, eds., *The Monetary Approach to the Balance of Payments* (Toronto: University of Toronto Press, 1976), and J. A. Frenkel and Harry G. Johnson, *The Economics of Exchange Rates* (Reading, Mass.: Addison-Wesley, 1978).

7. See L. Girton and D. Roper, "A Monetary Model of Exchange Market Pressure Applied to the Post-War Canadian Experiences," *American Economic Review* 60 (September 1977): 537–48.

8. Standing as two landmarks in the theoretical development of the monetary approach to the open economy are Robert A. Mundell, *International Economics* (New York: Macmillan, 1969); and Robert A. Mundell, *Monetary Theory* (Pacific Palisades, Calif.: Goodyear, 1971). Frenkel and Johnson's *The Monetary Approach to the Balance of Payments*, op. cit., contains a good number of key theoretical articles on the monetary approach, such as R. Dornbusch, "Devaluation, Money and Non-Traded Goods, "*American Economic Review* 61 (December 1973): 871–80. In addition it has a stimulating set of empirical studies. See also Harry G. Johnson, "The Monetary Approach to Balance of Payments Theory," in M. Connolly and A. Swoboda, eds., *International Trade and Money* (London: Allen and Unwin, 1973).

9. The following works are pertinent references: Milton Friedman, "The Optimum Quantity of Money," in the *Optimum Quantity of Money and Other Essays* (Chicago: Aldine, 1969); Milton Friedman, *A Program for Monetary Stability* (New York: Fordham University Press, 1960); and Milton Friedman and A. Schwartz, *A Monetary History of the United States 1867–1960*, National Bureau of Economic Research (Princeton, N.J.: Princeton University Press, 1963).

10. Harry G. Johnson, "The Monetary Approach to the Balance of Payments: A Non-technical Guide, "*Journal of International Economics* 7 (August 1977);263.

11. Mundell, *Monetary Theory*, op. cit.

12. Gustav Cassel, "The Present Situation of the Foreign Exchanges, "*The Economic Journal* (March 1916);62–65.

13. J. M. Keynes, "Theory of Money and the Exchanges," in J. M. Keynes, *Monetary Reform* (London; Macmillan, 1924), p. 111.

14. H. Genberg, "Aspects of the Monetary Approach to Balance of Payments Theory: An Empirical Study of Sweden," in Frenkel and Johnson, op. cit., pp. 198–326; P. Isard, "How Far Can We Push the Law of One Price," *American Economic Review* 65 (December 1977): 942–48; D. McClosky and R. Zecher, "How the Gold Standard Worked, 1880–1913," in Frenkel and Johnson, op. cit.; R. M. Dunn, "Flexible Exchange Rates and Oligopoly Pricing: A Study of Canadian Markets," *Journal of Political Economy* 78 (January 1970): 146–51; M. Connolly and J. da Silveira, "Exchange Market Pressure in Postwar Brazil," *American Economic Review* (June 1979); M. Connolly and Charles Lackey, "Presiones en el Mercado Cambiario de Mexico: 1955–82," in A. Violante and R. Davila, eds., *Mexico: Una Economia en Transición*, (Mexico City: Editorial Limusna, 1984); and D. Sykes Wilford, "Politica Monetaria en Mexico: Examen Retrospectivo y Perspectiva," in A. Violante and R. Davila, eds., *Mexico: Una Economia en Transicion* (Mexico City: Editorial Limusna, 1984).

15. M. Connolly and D. Taylor, "Testing the Monetary Approach to Devaluation in Developing Countries," *Journal of Political Economy* 84 (August 1976): 849–59.

16. Two recent articles containing an analysis of the timing of speculative attacks are M. Connolly and D. Taylor, "The Exact Timing of the Collapse of an Exchange Rate Regime and Its Impact upon the Relative Price of Traded Goods," *Journal of Money, Credit, and Banking* 16 (May 1984): 194–207; and Robert Flood and Peter Garber, "Collapsing Exchange Rate Regime: Some Linear Examples," *Journal of International Economics* 17 (August 1984): 1–13.

17. Connolly and da Silveira, op. cit.

18. R. Barro, "A Simple Flexible Exchange Rate Model with Uncertainty and Rational Expectations." Mimeographed, November 1975.

19. John Bilson, "A Simple Long-Run Model of Exchange Determination." Mimeographed, 1977; and John Bilson, "Rational Expectations and the Exchange Rate," in J. A. Frenkel and H. G. Johnson, eds., *The Economics of Exchange Rates: Selected Studies* (Reading, Mass.: Addison-Wesley, 1978).

20. See J. Frenkel, "A Monetary Approach to the Exchange Rate: Doctrinal Aspects and Empirical Evidence," *Scandinavian Journal of Economics* 78 (1976): 200–24; and J. Frenkel, "The Forward Exchange Rate, Expectations and the Demand for Money: The German Hyperinflation," *American Economic Review* 65 (September 1977): 653–69.

21. R. Dornbusch, "Exchange Rate Dynamics," *Journal of Political Economy* 84 (December 1976): 1161–76.

22. Irving Fisher, *The Theory of Interest* (New York, 1930).

23. See, for example, M. Whitman, "Global Monetarism and the Monetary Approach to the Balance of Payments," Brookings Papers on Economic Activity 3 (1975): 491–556.

24. P. Kouri and M. Porter, "International Capital Flows and Portfolio Equilibriums," *Journal of Political Economy* 82 (May-June 1974): 443–67.

25. A. Swoboda, "Equilibrium, Quasi-Equilibrium, and Macroeconomic Policy Under Fixed Exchange Rates," *Quarterly Journal of Economics* 86 (February 1972): 162–71.

26. See R. Boyer, "Currency Mobility and Balance of Payments Adjustment" (Chapter 12, this book); R. Boyer, "Nickels and Dimes," Federal Reserve Board of Governors manuscript; L. Girton and D. Roper, "Theory and Implications of Currency Substitution," International Financial Discussion Paper (Washington, D.C.: Federal Reserve Board of Governors, May 1976); G. Calvo and C. Rodriguez, "A Model of Exchange Rate Determination Under Currency Substitution and Rational Expectations," *Journal of Political Economy* 85 (June 1977): 617–25; D. King, B. H. Putnam, and D. S. Wilford, "A Currency Portfolio Approach to Exchange Rate Determination: Exchange Rate Stability and the Independence of Monetary Policy" (Chapter 11, this book); and John Cuddington, "Currency Substitution, Capital Mobility, and Money Demand," *Journal of International Money and Finance* 2 (August 1983): 111–34.

27. B. Klein, "Competing Monies: A Comment," *Journal of Money, Credit and Banking* 6 (November 1975): 513–19; and G. Tullock, "Competing Monies," *Journal of Money, Credit and Banking* 6 (November 1973): 491–97.

28. Friedman and Schwartz, op. cit.

29. Friedman, *A Program for Monetary Stability*, op. cit.

30. Girton and Roper, "Theory and Implications," op. cit.

31. Marc Miles, "Currency Substitution, Flexible Exchange Rates, and Monetary Independence," Chapter 14 of this book; and Marc Miles, "Currency Substitution: Perspective, Implications, and Empirical Evidence," in *The Monetary Approach to International Adjustments*, eds., Bluford Putnam and D. Sykes Wilford (New York: Praeger, 1979).

32. W. E. Salter, "Internal and External Balances: The Role of Price and Expenditure Effects," *The Economic Record* 35 (1952).

33. R. Dornbusch, "Real and Monetary Aspects of the Effects of Exchange Rate Changes," in R. Z. Aliber, ed., *National Monetary Policies and the International Financial System* (Chicago: University of Chicago Press, 1974); P. D. Jonson and H. Kierzkowski, "The Balance of Payments: An Analytic Exercise," *The Manchester School of Economic and Social Studies* 43 (June 1975): 105–33; M. Connolly and D. Taylor, "Adjustment to Devaluation with Money and Non-Traded Goods," *Journal of International Economics* 6 (August 1976): 289–98.

34. S. P. Magee, "The Empirical Evidence on the Monetary Approach to the Balance of Payments and Exchange Rates," *American Economic Review Papers and Proceedings* 66 (May 1976): 163–70; and M. Kreinen and L. Officer, "Survey of Empirical Evidence on the Monetary Approach to Open Economies," Princeton Studies on International Finance (Princeton, N.J.: Princeton University Press, 1978).

35. G. Haberler, "The Monetary Approach to the Balance of Payments by Frenkel and Johnson," review in *Journal of Economic Literature* 14 (December 1976): 1324–28; and Whitman, op. cit.

36. B. H. Putnam and D. S. Wilford, "Monetary Equilibrium and International Reserve Flows: An Empirical Treatment of the Money Supply Identity Issue," mimeographed, 1977.

37. Some recent studies focusing on the monetary approach to floating exchange rates are: Kenneth Clements and Jacob Frenkel, "Exchange Rates, Money and Relative Prices: The Dollar-Pound in the 1920's," *Journal of International Economics* 10 (May 1980): 249–62, Jeffrey A. Frankel, "On the Mark: A Theory of Floating Exchange Rates Based on Real Interest Differentials," *American Economic Review*, 69 (September 1979): 610–22, Maxwell Fry, "A Monetary Approach to Afghanistan's Flexible Exchange Rate," *Journal of Money, Credit, and Banking* 8 (May 1976): 219–25, and Sebastian Edwards, "Floating Exchange Rates in Less Developed Countries: A Monetary Analysis of the Peruvian Experience, 1950–54," *Journal of Money, Credit, and Banking* 15, no. 1 (February 1983): 73–81. A recent monetary model of the managed float in Brazil is contained in Mario Blejer and Leonard Leiderman, "A Monetary Approach to the Crawling-Peg System: Theory and Evidence," *Journal of Political Economy* 89 (February 1981): 132–51.

38. R. Rhomberg and H. R. Heller, "Introductory Survey," *The Monetary Approach to the Balance of Payments* (Washington, D.C.: International Monetary Fund), pp. 1–14; and J. J. Polak, "Monetary Analysis of Income Formation and Payments Problems," in IMF, *The Monetary Approach*, op. cit., pp. 15–64.

2

Of Money and Prices:
Some Historical Perspectives

Robert E. Keleher

INTRODUCTION

The monetary approach to exchange rates and the balance of payments is a framework for analyzing open economies within a larger world economy. That is, this approach views the world aggregate as a system of smaller integrated open economies. Recent elaborations of this view have established that different models must be employed in analyzing the small, open economy (SOE) as distinct from the larger, closed aggregate. Moreover, different exchange rate regimes call for the use of alternative frameworks for examining individual small, open economies. Thus, in examining the relationship between money and prices, the monetary approach indicates that three fundamental cases exist that must be clearly distinguished from one another. Accordingly, the relationship between money and prices that has been delineated by the monetary approach for these three cases—the closed economy, the SOE under fixed exchange rates, and the SOE under flexible exchange rates—will be briefly outlined.

Relationship between money and prices in the case of the closed economy is well known. In this case, all the familiar propositions of the conventional monetarist-Patinkin position hold. That is, any increase in the nominal money stock such that actual money balances exceed desired money balances will cause prices to rise. Price level changes, then, serve as the adjusting mechanism to equilibrate discrepancies between actual and desired real money balances. Thus, the quantity theory of money—in the sense of causality running from the stock of money to prices—applies to the case of the closed economy. Advocates of the monetary approach contend that the only purely closed economy is the world economy and, consequently, it is held that the quantity theory applies to the world economy.

In the case of the SOE under a fixed exchange rate regime (where all goods are tradable),* any increase in the nominal money stock such that actual money balances exceed desired money balances cannot increase prices, since tradable good prices are determined in world markets and given exogenously to the SOE. In this case, a balance of payments deficit is created, which, itself, causes the excess supply of money to contract as these excess balances are traded for foreign goods and/or securities. This contraction will continue until actual and desired monetary balances are equated. In this case, then, the quantity theory of money (in the sense described above) does not apply, since prices are invariant with respect to changes in the domestic money supply.

In the case of the SOE under a flexible exchange rate regime, any increase in the nominal money stock such that actual money balances exceed desired money balances will cause an increase in prices via a fall in the exchange rate. This combination of exchange depreciation and price level increase serves as the adjustment mechanism that equilibrates discrepancies between actual and desired real money balances. According to the monetary approach, this depreciation is equivalent to domestic monetary contraction, in that both depreciation and contraction of the money supply bring about temporary real balance effects that operate to bring desired real money balances into equality with actual real money balances. The quantity theory of money, then, applies to this case, since changes in money will precede changes in the price level.

A contribution of the monetary approach is the careful and explicit delineation of these alternative frameworks by which to analyze relations between money and prices. Depending on the relevant circumstances, then, causality may or may not run from money to prices. However, the explicit recognition of these alternative frameworks and their implications for relations between money and prices are by no means revolutionary. Rather, all of the frameworks outlined above and the distinctions among them were well recognized by earlier generations of economists.† The

---

*The various cases are presented here so as to delineate their fundamental differences. Although the cases are admittedly oversimplified, the basic contentions presented here would apply if complicating factors such as the addition of nontradable goods were added to the discussion.

†A good deal of confusion in interpreting historical monetary controversies relates to the fact that some of the authors failed to spell out explicitly the implicit assumptions and contexts of their theoretical formulations. This relates not only to obscurities relating to convertible versus inconvertible currencies but (as will be indicated below) to small, open economies versus large, closed economies as well.

purpose of this study, then, is to demonstrate that all of the essential elements of the various frameworks set out above, as well as their important implications relating to money and prices, were well recognized by earlier generations of economists.* Of these three frameworks, the convertible currency (fixed exchange rate) model of the SOE frequently has been misrepresented by historical interpreters. Among contemporary economists, it is the least understood of the three models and its historical development, unlike that of the other frameworks, has not been adequately documented. Consequently, in this study, emphasis will be given to the fixed exchange rate model of the SOE. Throughout the study, however, it will be shown that various authors clearly recognized the other frameworks and their important (and differing) implications for relations between money and prices.

THE MONETARY APPROACH: HISTORICAL PERSPECTIVES

In discussing the chronological development of the monetary approach, attention will, in general, be given to major monetary writers in English thought, beginning with David Hume.[1] Although some important contributions to this development were made prior to Hume—notably by Isaac Gervaise—these contributions were either subsequently ignored or considered incomplete because of various inconsistencies or errors.† In addition to Hume, particular attention will be given to Adam Smith, David Ricardo, Thomas Tooke (and the Banking School), J. S. Mill, Knut Wicksell, and J. L. Laughlin.

However, before discussing the models employed by these early contributors, a brief discussion of some technical considerations relevant to the analyses of money and prices by economists in the eighteenth and early nineteenth centuries is in order. First, these early classical writers were intimately familiar with the operational aspects of the working of the gold

---

*A secondary purpose of the study is to gain an improved understanding of the historical monetary controversies themselves, both by clearly spelling out the specific frameworks employed by the participating authors and by describing the contexts or circumstances in which the authors wrote.

†Although Hume may not have been the first English writer to set out elements of the fixed exchange rate framework, he set out a consistent, complete model and was by far the most well-known (and widely read) writer prior to Smith recognized by subsequent contributors. In emphasizing the chronological development of the fixed exchange rate model, it seems logical to start with Hume, since it is well known that subsequent contributors were familiar with Hume (but not with Gervaise).[2]

standard. One of these aspects was the fact that under a convertible currency, exchange rates were not absolutely fixed but rather, as modus operandi, varied between relatively narrow bands (between gold import and export points). Secondly, there were no reliable general price indices available to the classical economists.* Consequently, in their discussions relating to money and prices, indirect proxies were frequently employed.[3] To the classical economists, a convenient proxy involved the price of bullion.† That is, the product of the currency price of gold (a fixed rate of exchange when currency is convertible) and the price of goods in terms of gold (determined in world markets for tradable commodities) was employed, albeit implicitly, as a proxy for the level of commodity prices. During periods when currency was convertible, then, the level of domestic prices could vary for one of two reasons: because of changes in the world price of commodities in terms of gold or because of variations in the exchanges between the gold points. During normal periods and within moderate time frames, changes in the former factor were not observed because of large outstanding world stocks of gold (relative to current production possibilities of gold). The latter, although it could be affected by banking and monetary policies, could vary only within relatively narrow bounds. Consequently, sizable amounts of inflation in any single country were regarded as impossible as long as convertibility was maintained. Nonetheless, because of high price elasticities related both to supplies (demands) of foreign exchange at gold export (import) points and to foreign demand (and supply) of tradable products, slight movements in prices could have large influences on commodity and asset flows and thereby could serve as the modus operandi of the system.[6] These considerations have important implications for the interpretation of the classical economists such as Hume, to which we will now turn.

---

*As Jacob Viner has ably pointed out:

Hume wrote before the first attempt in England, that of Evelyn in 1798, to measure price levels by means of statistical averages. Even after 1798, the leading economists until the time of Jevons either revealed no acquaintance with the notion of representing, by means of statistical averages, either a level of prices, or changes in such level, or found it unacceptable for various reasons. ... While a number of crude index numbers were constructed during the first half of the Nineteenth Century, none of the classical economists ... would have anything to do with them.[4]

†Torrens, for example, explicitly asserted that "an increase in the quantity and fall in the value of gold, in relation to commodities, is the same thing as an increase in the quantity and fall in the value of the currency in relation to commodities—is the same thing as a rise of prices."[5]

David Hume

Most interpretations of Hume recognize his natural distribution of specie hypothesis, in which world money is distributed by means of an automatic mechanism according to the relative demands for money balances. That is, the quantity of specie in any one country is a function of real factors normally associated with the demand for money, such as the volume of transactions, population, income, and productivity. On this point, there is virtual consensus. However, certain important implications of this framework for the individual small, open economy have received emphasis in only a few of these interpretations. First, for example, Hume's natural distribution hypothesis implied that money would be distributed *in proportion* to these real variables. Hume indicated that, in each country, money would automatically seek a natural "level" equal to that in other countries:* "It does not seem that money any more than water can be raised or lowered anywhere much beyond the level it has in places where communication is open, but that it must rise and fall in proportion to the goods and labor contained in each state."[7] This equality of level, as Viner has shown, related to *prices* and not to absolute quantities of money:

> The equality of level which Hume posited was not between absolute quantities of money but between the proportions of quantities of money to quantities of commodities, i.e., prices. . . .[8]

Thus, an implication of the natural distribution hypothesis for the SOE is the natural equalization of prices between it and other countries or, in short, the automatic (and exogenous) determination of prices.[10] Another implication of the natural distribution hypothesis relevant to the SOE is that the quantity of money in such an economy is a *dependent* variable, not subject to discretionary manipulation.[11] For this reason, suppositions of large, exogenous changes of the domestic money supply of the SOE are acceptable only for pedagogical purposes and not for practical examinations of the international monetary adjustment mechanism.[12] Most interpreters of Hume would have little difficulty with these propositions.

However, discussions of the adjustment mechanism—the price–specie–flow mechanism—have produced sharp differences in the interpretation of Hume. Specifically, many interpreters of Hume contend that

---

*Hume indicated that "Wherever I speak of the level of money, I mean always its proportional level to the commodities, labour, industry, and skill, which is in the several states."[9]

the price–specie–flow mechanism works such that monetary adjustment proceeds by divergent movements in national price levels.[13] That is, it is contended by these interpreters that variations in the price level serve as the adjustment mechanism.[14] If this were the case, the view would contradict the law of one price, except in long-run equilibrium.[15] On rereading Hume, we prefer to adopt an alternative interpretation of the adjustment mechanism.[16]

According to this alternative interpretation, Hume endorsed the law of one price. He essentially outlined a model of price equalization, which he explicitly stated would make it impossible for the value of money to vary between provinces of the same kingdom. He states, for example:

> How is the balance kept in the provinces of every kingdom among themselves, but by the force of this principle, *which makes it impossible for money to lose its level*, and either to rise or sink beyond the proportion of the labour and commodities which are in each province.[17] [emphasis added]

And further:

> What happens in small portions of mankind, must take place in greater. . . . any man who travels over Europe at this day, may see, by the price of commodities, that money, in spite of the absurd jealousy of princes and states, has brought itself nearly to a level; and that the difference between one kingdom and another is not greater in this respect, than it is often between different provinces of the same kingdom.[18]

Hume repeatedly emphasized the rapid workings of price equalization in his writings.[19] This was particularly apparent after his correspondence with James Oswald (which predated the publication "Of the Balance of Trade"), where he explicitly recognized that prices in an SOE are not necessarily related to changes in the quantity of money but are tied to foreign (world) prices.* Hume, then, held that no important price level differences between countries would in practice be observable.[22] This recognition of the law of one price implied that Hume recognized, albeit implicitly, a high degree of price elasticity for tradable commodities and,

---

*Oswald, after reviewing a preliminary manuscript of Hume's essay, "Of the Balance of Trade," explicitly pointed out that in an SOE, prices were tied to foreign (world) prices rather than to alterations in the quantity of money:

> The increased quantity of money would not necessarily increase the price of all labour and commodities; because the increased quantity, not being confined to the home labour and commodities, might, and certainly would, be sent to

hence, that slight price movements were the modus operandi of the system.

Since Hume recognized that money in an SOE is a dependent variable and not subject to discretionary manipulation (by virtue of his natural distribution hypothesis), he held that any excessive quantity of money could not long persist in a single country. Hume stressed that internal creation of bank credit in one country would result in offsetting outflows of gold rather than in domestic inflation.[23] That is, a trade deficit rather than single-country inflation would result. Accordingly, Hume's supposition of an enormous and exogenous alteration of the quantity of money in an SOE can only be viewed as a pedagogical device.[24]

An implication of Hume's position, then, is that the quantity theory of money—in the sense of causality running from money to prices—does not apply to the SOE. Yet Hume recognized its applicability to a closed economy:

> If we consider any one Kingdom *by itself* . . . the prices of commodities are always proportioned to the plenty of money. . . .[25] [emphasis added]

Hume, then, not only outlined the fundamental model of the SOE under fixed exchange rates but also described the relationship between money and prices in a closed economy. Two of the three cases described above, then, were recognized by Hume.

Adam Smith

Smith was eminently familiar with the writings of Hume and always wrote, as did Hume, in the context of convertible currency.[26] Consequently, Smith endorsed most of the positions relevant to the convertible framework that were set out by Hume. For example, Smith clearly viewed money as a dependent variable:

> The quantity of money . . . must in every country naturally increase as the value of the annual produce increases. The value of the consumable goods annually circulated within the society being greater will require a greater quantity of money to circulate them. A part of the increased

---

purchase both from foreign countries, which importation, unless obstructed by arbitrary and absurd laws, would keep down the price of commodities to the level of foreign countries. . . .[20]

Hume's response indicated that he agreed with Oswald's position and incorporated it into his subsequent analysis of the adjustment mechanism.[21]

produce, therefore, will naturally be employed in purchasing, wherever it is to be had, the additional quantity of gold and silver necessary for circulating the rest. The increase of those metals will in this case be the effect, not the cause, of the public prosperity.[27]

Moreover, Smith explicitly denied the possibility of overissue. That is, Smith contended in a number of passages that the quantity of convertible paper added to the currency is always offset by an equal and direct outflow of specie; or, in short, that "paper money merely changes the form rather than the total of the money supply."[28] The following passage is particularly noteworthy:

The increase of paper money, it has been said, by augmenting the quantity, and consequently diminishing the value of the whole currency, necessarily augments the money price of commodities. But as the quantity of gold and silver, which is taken from the currency, is always equal to the quantity of paper which is added to it, paper money does not necessarily increase the quantity of the whole currency. From the beginning of the last century to the present time, provisions never were cheaper in Scotland than in 1759, though, from the circulation of ten and five shilling bank notes, there was then more paper money in the country than at present. The proportion between the price of provisions in Scotland and that in England is the same now as before the great multiplication of banking companies in Scotland. Corn is, upon most occasions, fully as cheap in England as in France; though there is a great deal of paper money in England, and scarce any in France.[29]

In this denial of overissue, Smith indicates that an increase in convertible paper money will not affect prices and, consequently, will not alter the value of money. An implication of this position, then, is the endorsement of the law of one price. In discussing this passage, for example, J. W. Angell rightly notes that Smith's doctrine of offsetting specie flows "must necessarily presuppose fixity of prices, for the time being at least. It conceives of the 'channel of circulation' as being confined within rigid price walls. . . ."[30] This interpretation is further supported by noting that Smith, in his elaboration of the specie-flow mechanism, clearly placed emphasis on direct specie outflows (or "overflows," as Smith put it) and related import purchases, whereas he never stressed divergent price level movements as an adjustment mechanism in the *Wealth of Nations*.[31]

Another implication of Smith's view of offsetting specie flows is that the quantity theory of money (in the sense of changes in money preceding changes in prices) does not apply to the SOE under a convertible currency regime. This implication was explicitly voiced by Angell, who, in discussing Smith's views on this topic, noted that "Smith adopts what seems to be the exact antithesis of the quantity theory view."[32] Smith, of course, in outlining this position was referring to the open economy. Yet in discussions relating to a closed-world framework, he explicitly adopted a quantity theory view. For example, at one point, in commenting on the world value of the precious metals, he stated that:

> The discovery of abundant mines of America seems to have been the sole cause of this diminution (1570–1640) in the value of silver in proportion to that of corn. ... the increase of the supply had, it seems, so far exceeded that of the demand, that the value of that metal sunk considerably.[33]

That Smith recognized the differing relationship between money and prices in the closed, as opposed to the open, framework is particularly evident in his discussion of specie flows. In one passage, for example, Smith was very careful to make a clear distinction between specie inflows in a single country due to increases in its demand for specie as opposed to autonomous increases in world specie supplies (from new world discoveries of gold and silver mines). Smith clearly showed that specie inflows caused by increases in the domestic demand for specie were not inflationary, since they merely represented a redistribution of world specie supplies, whereas inflows due to new gold and silver discoveries were inflationary. Hence, increases in the domestic money supply (world supplies constant) do not affect prices whereas increases in the world money supply do affect prices; the quantity theory applies to the closed world economy but does not apply to the small, open economy.[34]

Smith, then, like Hume, understood the relationship between money and prices in the context of the SOE under fixed exchange rates, and how this relationship is altered in the closed world framework. Two of the three cases described above, then, were recognized by both Hume and Smith.

David Ricardo

The essentials of the relationship between money and prices in both the case of the SOE on fixed exchange rates and the model of the closed economy, then, were formulated by Hume and Smith. These two authors, it should be noted, wrote during periods when convertible currencies existed and, consequently, had little reason to examine the inconvertible case. The convertible currency model of Hume and Smith was well recognized and endorsed by early bullionist writers. Viner indicates that during the period of early bullionist writings the bullionists "always explained the mode of operation of a metallic standard as if, under given conditions in the world at large, it dictated to a country adhering to it a specific quantity of currency and a specific range of commodity prices."[35]

John Wheatley, for example, explicitly endorsed the natural distribution hypothesis and emphasized specie flows as opposed to price movements in describing the adjustment pricess.[36] Moreover, many of these bullionist writers also recognized basic elements of the closed framework. Wheatley, for instance, noted that whereas single country inflation was impossible under a convertible currency, "universally" high prices could be caused by an excessive amount of "world currency."[37]

The major contribution of the bullionists to the evolution of English monetary thought was the formulation of a model of inconvertible currency. It may be noted here, however, that in view of the fact that they adopted the previously cited convertible and closed models of Hume and Smith, the bullionists were the first group of English economists to recognize all three of the models outlined above (convertible, inconvertible, and closed models). In discussing the bullionists, we will concentrate on the most famous member of the group, David Ricardo.

Although Ricardo may not have been the original architect of the theories he endorsed, they emerged in their most lucid form from his pen.* He presented articulate versions of all three models described above. With regard to the model of the SOE under a convertible currency, Ricardo explicitly endorsed Hume's natural distribution hypothesis:

> Gold and silver, having been chosen for the general medium of circulation, they are, by the competition of commerce, distributed in such proportions amongst the different countries of the world as to accommodate themselves to the natural traffic which would take place if no such metals existed and the trade between countries were purely a trade of barter.[38]

In addition to supporting this central theme, Ricardo also explicitly endorsed its important corollaries. Specifically, he indicated that under convertibility "the circulation could never be overfull," in that any excessive increase of such a currency would result in an offsetting outflow of specie via the balance of payments rather than affecting its purchasing power.[39] Moreover, Ricardo clearly indicated that, when convertible, money acted as a dependent variable and always and everywhere maintained equal value with other convertible currencies.[40] Accordingly, Ricardo supported the law of one price and indicated that the quantity theory of money did not apply to single countries under convertible currency regimes.[42]

---

*In concluding his classic essay, "The High Price of Bullion," Ricardo himself explicitly indicated that he was well aware that he had "not added to the stock of information with which the public has been enlightened by many able writers on the same important subject."[41]

The quantity theory, however, was strongly supported by Ricardo in the context of an inconvertible currency. Indeed, the examination of the inconvertible currency system in Great Britain during the period 1797 to 1821 constituted the major contribution of the bullionists (who included Ricardo and Henry Thornton). In examining this inconvertible currency system, Ricardo (and the other bullionists) demonstrated that the abandonment of the metallic standard removed the constraint of redemption from domestic monetary expansion. As was not the case with a convertible currency, sudden, exogenous changes in the money supply were possible with an inconvertible currency. (Money was no longer viewed as a dependent variable.) Ricardo and the other bullionists showed that any excessive monetary expansion would necessarily lead to both exchange depreciation and commodity price increases (including the price of bullion). In *The Bullion Report*, for example, it was noted that

> a general rise of all prices, a rise in the market price of gold, and a fall in the foreign exchanges, will be the effect of an excessive quantity of circulating medium in a country which has adopted a currency not exportable to other countries, or not convertible at will into a coin which is exportable.[43]

Causal relations, then, were seen as running from changes in money to changes in prices. As such, the Ricardian bullionist model of an inconvertible currency system was rightly viewed as a restated formulation of the quantity theory of money. Ricardo, therefore, held that the quantity theory applied to the SOE on an inconvertible but not on a convertible currency regime.

In examining the relationship between money and prices in Great Britain, Ricardo was led to distinguish between domestic and external sources of inflation. In so doing, he indicated that he understood well the distinction between the open and the closed economies. His analysis indicated that while a currency was convertible any domestic alteration of the quantity of money in a single, open economy would not be inflationary but rather would involve a redistribution of given quantities of the world stock of precious metals. That is, other things being equal, an increase (decrease) in a country's share of the world stock of specie would result if that country's wealth increased (decreased), whereas a decrease (increase) in that share would result with a substantial increase (decrease) in banknote issue.[44] Neither of these alternatives would alter the level of domestic prices as long as world conditions remained unchanged.

On the other hand, Ricardo realised that an increase in the quantity of *world* money would lead to an increase in the price level. That is, he recognized the relationship between money and prices—the quantity theory—in the closed (world) framework:

> If the quantity of gold and silver *in the world* employed as money were exceedingly small, or abundantly great, it would not in the least affect the proportions in which they would be divided among the different nations—the variation in their quantity would have produced no other effect than to make the commodities for which they were exchanged comparatively dear or cheap.[45] [emphasis added]

Ricardo indicated his awareness of the workings of the quantity theory in the closed world framework in another way. He showed that even under a convertible currency, if all countries increased their note issue simultaneously (and in proportion) the total world money supply would increase, causing prices to rise in all countries without any single country necessarily experiencing reserve drains:

> . . . if the circulation of England were ten millions, that of France five millions, that of Holland four millions, etc., whilst they kept their proportions, though the currency of each country were doubled or tripled, neither country would be conscious of an excess of currency. The prices of commodities would everywhere rise, on account of the increase of currency, but there would be no exportation of money from either. But if these proportions be destroyed by England alone doubling her currency, while that of France, Holland, etc., continued as before, we should then be conscious of an excess in our currency, and for the same reason the other countries would feel a deficiency in theirs, and part of our excess would be exported until the proportions of ten, five, four, etc., were again established.[46]

In the particular case in which all countries expand their monetary stocks simultaneously, then, convertibility does not serve as a check to either monetary overexpansion or inflation.* Finally, Ricardo was well aware of the significance of taking into account the size of an economy when examining the relationship between money and prices. In one passage, for example, he indicated that if England were a large enough economy, an English note expansion could influence the world money supply and, hence, not be totally offset by specie drains.[47] In this case, then, a single country's monetary expansion could affect prices, at least to some extent.

In analyzing the relationship between money and prices, then, Ricardo and the other bullionists had a thorough understanding of the distinctions among the alternative monetary frameworks that are essential for such investigations. They demonstrated that, whereas the quantity

---

*This insight had important implications for the currency-banking school debate; see below. It indicated that banks could affect prices either under inconvertibility or under convertibility if all banks adopted similar policies.

theory did not apply to the SOE under a convertible currency regime, it did apply both to large, closed economies and to the SOE under inconvertible currency arrangements.* Ricardo and the other bullionists, then, were the first English writers to understand all three of the frameworks set out above. Their analysis laid the foundations for later writers, including those of both the currency and the banking schools. It is to these writers that we now turn.

Tooke and the Banking School

The writings of Ricardo and the other bullionists served as the foundation from which the positions of both the currency and the banking schools evolved. The analyses of all three of these groups, for example, "took place within the common assumption of the desirability of metallic convertibility."[48] Although the currency and banking schools evolved from the same source and both supported convertibility, they adopted many positions that were diametrically opposed to one another.[50] An important reason that these contrary positions evolved from the same source is related to the fact that these views were based on Ricardian doctrine applicable, albeit implicitly, to differing contexts. An understanding of the currency-banking controversy, then, requires a thorough familiarity with the alternative frameworks employed in Ricardian analysis.

For example, one contention of Ricardo (and the other bullionists) was that convertibility in and of itself was sufficient to prevent any substantial overissuance of bank notes by a single country and, therefore, sufficient to prevent single-country inflation.[51] Convertibility, then, served as a mechanism for monetary (and inflation) control for the SOE. This Ricardian position was endorsed by banking school writers, such as Thomas Tooke, J. Fullarton, James Wilson, and J. W. Gilbart. However, as was shown above, Ricardo also demonstrated that if all countries expanded their note issues simultaneously, overexpansion and inflation would occur despite convertibility. Convertibility, then, was not necessarily a guaranteed safeguard against monetary overexpansion and

---

The Bullion Report, for example, stated that for an inconvertible currency,

An increase in the quantity of the local (inconvertible) currency of a particular country, will raise prices in that country exactly in the same manner as an increase in the general supply of precious metals raises prices all over the world. By means of the increase of quantity, the value of a given portion of that circulating medium, in exchange for other commodities, is lowered; in other words, the money prices of all other commodities are raised, and that of bullion with the rest.[49]

inflation once it was recognized that there is less check to monetary overexpansion by countries or banks when they act in unison than when they act alone.[52] Ricardo had demonstrated, then, that different principles may apply when an analyst shifts emphasis from the context of the individual unit acting alone to the context of an aggregation of these units acting in unison. Different contexts, therefore, require different analytical frameworks. The currency school writers, such as Robert Torrens, Lord Overstone, and George Norman, concluded that, when viewed from the perspective of an aggregate of countries or banks as opposed to a single unit, some form of control over banking and monetary policy in addition to convertibility was necessary.[53] The currency school writers, then, reached their conclusions by carrying out their analysis, albeit implicitly, within the context of a larger, more aggregative framework, whereas the banking school writers were always concerned with the actions of an individual country or bank.* Both schools nonetheless evolved from the Ricardian bullionist framework.

This section will demonstrate that banking school writers recognized all three of the monetary frameworks spelled out above. Moreover, it will be shown that an understanding of these three frameworks easily clarifies various issues of the currency-banking school controversy. Although comparisons between the two positions will be made, emphasis will be given to banking school writers, since these authors not only have been misunderstood but had a broader comprehension of the essentials of all

---

*This contention is further supported by recognizing a related episode of the period. That is, another reason for alternative positions evolving from Ricardian doctrine relates to the controversy regarding the particular banking institutions responsible for overissue during the period of restriction. Since country bank notes were convertible into more widely circulating Bank of England notes, the quantity of notes issued in the various provinces or regions of the country was viewed as being governed by a natural distribution hypothesis (analogous to specie distribution in various countries). Accordingly, the bullionists contended that regional country banks could not overissue and, hence, were not responsible for the rapid rate of note expansion during the period of restriction.[54] On the other hand, Bank of England notes were not convertible during this period and as a consequence were overissued. Therefore, bullionists placed responsibility for overissuance on the Bank of England.[55] However, Ricardo recognized that if all banks, including the Bank of England, expanded notes simultaneously, then convertibility would not serve as a constraint to country bank note issue. Hence, banking and monetary controls were necessary. The view that the Bank of England and the country banks acting together would issue to excess even under convertibility was "adopted by the currency school as one of the elements in their reply to the banking school doctrine that overissue was impossible under convertibility."[56] Implicitly, then, the currency school was employing the entire banking system as a frame of reference, whereas the banking school was focusing on the individual bank.

three monetary frameworks.* In addition, attention will be focused on the most well-known contributor to banking school doctrine, Thomas Tooke.

Banking school writers, and particularly Tooke, clearly recognized the fixed exchange rate model of the SOE, as well as its important implications. In addition, these writers were, in general, careful to emphasize the context to which their doctrines applied. Normally, their analysis pertained to the small individual country (or the small individual bank).[57] These writers emphasized that in a small, open environment, the quantity of a convertible currency was determined by (and passively adapted to) the demands or needs of the public.[58] Any amount in excess of these demands would be immediately traded for other goods or securities. Accordingly, following not only Hume, Smith, and Ricardo but the views of country bankers as well, the banking school writers contended that overissue of a convertible currency was impossible because of offsetting flows of specie (or in the case of the country banks, the offsetting flows of Bank of England notes).† Tooke, for example, indicated that:

> in the case both of the Bank of England and of the country banks, if it were conceivable, which it hardly is, that any addition, beyond the amount of notes required for specific purposes, could be forced into the hands of the public, there is an operation constantly going on which would amost instantaneously reduce the amount within the limits of these purposes. ... The advance by a bank issuing only convertible paper does not ... cause, necessarily, any increase in the circulation. ... [An] increase of the outstanding circulation would be the effect of increased transactions and prices and not the cause of them.[60]‡

Secondly, banking school writers—and especially Tooke—recognized, albeit implicitly, the law of one price (and, consequently, the workings of arbitrage). Tooke, being an empiricist, was familiar with price data for at least the period 1792 to 1856. Most of the data used by Tooke pertained to tradable goods.[61] Tooke analyzed these data and, on the basis of his empirical studies, indicated that prices apparently were independently

---

*Although the currency school, in general, came to dominate British monetary thought, it never achieved a dominant position on the continent, where the banking school received more support.[59]

†Currency school writers contended that overissuance under convertibility could occur at least in the short run and be of a magnitude large enough to threaten convertibility.[62] It was implicit in their writings that to bring this about, all banks would act in unison.[63]

‡Fullarton contends:

> What Mr. Tooke, and those who hold similar opinions, contend for is, that, by the very constitution of a convertible currency, it can never be issued in larger quantities than are required for use and, therefore, can never be redundant.[64]

determined in external international markets and not related to changes in the domestic money supply, even in the short run.[65] This conclusion was in accordance with banker opinion (with which Tooke was familiar) as to the international adjustment mechanism.[66]

The important implication of this, of course, was that the quantity theory of money (in the sense of causality running from changes in money to changes in prices) was not applicable to the individual SOE under a convertible currency. The contention that the quantity theory did not apply to this case was explicitly and repeatedly noted by Tooke:

> In point of fact and historically, as far as my researches have gone, in every single instance of a rise or fall in prices, the rise or fall has preceded and, therefore, could not be the effect of an enlargement or contraction of the bank circulation.[67]

> I believe that the amount of the circulating medium is the effect and not the cause of variations in prices.[68]

> The prices of commodities do not depend upon the quantity of money indicated by the amount of bank notes, nor upon the amount of the whole of the circulating medium, but that, on the contrary, the amount of the circulating medium is the consequence of prices.[69]

In testimony before the Parliamentary Committee on Banks of Issue in 1840 (which he later published in *History of Prices*), Tooke voiced this opinion repeatedly in responses to questions by the committee.* Instead of supporting the quantity theory in the case of the SOE, Tooke (and other banking school writers) endorsed a reverse causation hypothesis. That is, in accordance with their demand-determined view, they inverted the chain of cause and effect of the quantity theorists and argued that increases in the quantity of money were determined by increases in prices and incomes rather than the reverse.[70] Moreover, "They were extremely careful to

---

*This is exemplified by Tooke's answers to the following two questions by the committee:

Question 3303 (by committee): "Suppose . . . the quantity of the precious metals in the world to remain constant, and that the number of deposits in bankers' hands available to the purchase and sale of commodities is doubled, trebled, and so on, will the price of commodities vary in proportion to that increase of deposits in bankers' hands?" *Tooke's Response*: "Not in the slightest degree."

Question 3621 (by committee): "Are the Committee, then, to understand, that so long as the paper is convertible into specie, you cannot attribute any effect whatever upon prices to the variations in the amount of the bank notes in circulation?" *Tooke's Response*: "I am perfectly satisfied that no alteration in the prices can be traced in any way to the amount of the circulation."[72]

confine this proposition to the case of money convertible into specie and, hence, to a case where the arbitrage necessary to preserve the relevant price structure was possible."[71] Furthermore, it is evident in numerous passages that Tooke and other banking school writers emphasized this view to be especially pertinent to small, open economic units.[73] Being particularly relevant to such units, the theory was wholeheartedly accepted by bankers who, by their very nature, deal with money in an open economic environment.*

This banking school view was vigorously criticized by writers of the currency school, who supported the quantity theory, even in the context of the small, open economy with a convertible currency. That is, currency school writers contended that monetary overexpansion was possible in the case of the SOE with a convertible currency and, in describing adjustments to such an overexpansion, placed emphasis on changes in relative price levels rather than on monetary flows.[74] In criticizing writers of the banking school on this issue, currency school writers frequently tried to demonstrate the supposed fallacy of the banking school position by referring to examples of the quantity theory in very large or closed economies. That is, they essentially assumed that an increase in the money supply in a single SOE had an inflationary effect that was analogous to a monetary increase in a large, closed economy.[76] For example, Torrens, in his criticism of Tooke, essentially argued that large increases in the world gold stock and subsequent European inflation demonstrated the fallacy of the banking school position.[77]

The banking school authors, however, had been careful to indicate that their views were applicable to the SOE but not necessarily to the large or closed economy. They clearly recognized a distinction between the large, closed economy and the SOE. Tooke, Fullarton, and Wilson, for example, carefully distinguished between changes in a country's money supply resulting from domestic sources and changes in the money supply due to increases in the world gold stock and, hence, world money supply.[78]

---

*The views of the banking school writers were supported by all of the bankers who testified before various parliamentary committees on the subject. These bankers indicated that (in the words of Fullarton) "The amount of their issues is exclusively regulated by the extent of local dealings and expenditure in their respective Districts, fluctuating with the fluctuations of production and price, and that they neither can increase their issues beyond the limits which the range of such deals and expenditure prescribe, without the certainty of having their notes immediately returned to them nor diminish them, but at an almost equal certainty of the vacancy being filled up from some other source."[75] It is no coincidence, then, that bankers have traditionally been skeptical of the quantity theory of money; they have always operated in the context of an open environment (always constrained from expanding loans and deposits by leakages—as in an open economy).

These authors clearly indicated that increases in the domestic money supply that reflected increases in the world money supply were inflationary whereas increases in the domestic money supply arising from redistribution of the existing world supply (due, for example, to a favorable exchange) would not be inflationary.[79]* That is, domestic (one country) inflation was impossible so long as the currency remained convertible.

Wilson, for example, after demonstrating that Torrens equated an increase in the domestic money supply (due to domestic sources) to an increase in the world money supply, responded in the following manner:

> That this ingenious and accomplished economist should have stated these as two "analogous propositions" is the most striking evidence with which we have yet met of the utter confusion which prevails in men's minds of the very real nature of currency and capital ... some have an idea that in every case of an influx of bullion, a similar effect should be experienced locally that is produced generally by an increase of metals from the mines. The difference is very essential. In the case of an ordinary influx of gold into this country, caused by a favorable state of the exchanges, the general quantity of gold is not changed, nor its relation in value to other commodities: A new distribution of it is all that takes place. To those who received larger quantities of metal from South America ... in consequence of the increased productiveness of the mines, the additional quantity ... would soon increase prices generally in proportion to the new supplies of the metals.
>
> But in the case of an influx of bullion, owing to a favorable exchange, the case is widely different. ... We find that in practice, neither circulation nor prices increase under such circumstances.[81]

After explicitly quoting these comments of Wilson, Tooke clearly voiced his agreement with this view:

> I quite agree with Mr. Wilson in his opinion ... of the difference of the effects on prices between an influx of gold caused by an increase of metals from the mines, and the influx caused by a favorable exchange.[82]

Moreover, Tooke demonstrated his recognition of the distinction between domestic and world monetary expansion in numerous other passages. In his testimony before the Parliamentary Committee on Banks of Issue in 1840, for example, Tooke made it clear that when referring to the case of the SOE, he was assuming that the world money supply was

---

*Fullarton, for example, "went out of his way to make it clear that he did not deny the broad effects on prices of changes in the supply of the precious metals."[80]

held constant. That is, he made note of the differences between the effects on prices of world monetary variations and the effects on prices of variations in the domestic currency, world money held constant.[83] Subsequent questions by the committee were explicitly prefaced by assuming that world money supplies be held constant.* Banking school writers, then, recognized the distinction between the SOE and the large, closed economy and the important implications of this distinction for analyzing causal relations between money and prices. Moreover, banking school writers presented empirical evidence to substantiate their contentions relating to the SOE, whereas the divergent price level adjustment mechanism endorsed by currency school writers never received empirical support.[84] These currency school writers, albeit implicitly, took as the premise for their analysis a larger, more aggregative framework. This is evident not only in their discussion of relations between money and prices but, as pointed out above, in their discussion of the possibility of convertible note overissue.[85]

In addition to their recognition of the distinction between the closed model and the case of the SOE on fixed exchange rates, banking school writers were aware of the inconvertible currency framework. Both Tooke and Fullarton, for example, contrasted an inconvertible to a convertible currency, noting that expansion of an inconvertible currency would have an important impact on prices.[87] Their view of the inconvertible case, then, was essentially a restatement of the bullionist position. Banking school writers, therefore, recognized that the quantity theory would hold in both the case of an inconvertible currency and the case of the closed economy.

In sum, banking school authors recognized all three of the models discussed above. These authors were, in general, practical men who not only were familiar with a good deal of empirical data but understood the views and opinions of bankers. Accordingly, their analysis emphasized the operation of the single, small economic unit in an open environment and indicated that the quantity theory, although valid in other contexts, did not apply to this context. When these alternative theoretical frameworks were not clearly delineated, a good deal of confusion about interpretation resulted.[88] It is for this very reason that many subsequent economists have denigrated the writings of the banking school.

---

*At one point in the testimony, Tooke indicated that he recognized the importance of country size. That is, he indicated that if a country's note issue increased to the extent that the single country specie outflow was large enough to affect world specie values, then prices of commodities in that particular country might still be affected. This, however, could not occur if the relevant economy was small.[86]

J. S. Mill

When one discusses the development of these principles of monetary theory, J. S. Mill looms as an important figure, because he was so widely read even if for no other reason. It has been established, for example, that during the latter half of the nineteenth century, Mill's *Principles of Political Economy* was "the undisputed bible of economists. ... As late as 1900, Mill's work was still the basic textbook in elementary courses in both British and American universities."[89] This observation, together with the fact that Mill endorsed a good many of the banking school propositions, then, makes Mill important in describing the evolution of these monetary principles.

Mill was familiar with the writings of banking school authors such as Tooke and Fullarton and, in fact, supported the banking school position against the Act of 1844.[90] He explicitly supported various propositions of the banking school writers. For example, in addition to explicitly recognizing the natural distribution of specie hypothesis, Mill pointed out that in the normal "quiescent state," the overissue of a convertible currency was impossible, since it would lead to the outflow of specie via the balance of payments.[91] Specifically, Mill noted that in normal circumstances alterations in convertible note issue can have no impact on prices, and that

> there can be no addition, at the discretion of bankers, to the general circulating medium: Any increase of their issues either comes back to them, or remains idle in the hands of the public, and *no rise takes place in prices.*[92] [emphasis added]

Mill explicitly quoted passages from both Tooke and Fullarton in which these banking school authors forcefully stated that because the volume of convertible note issue was determined by demand, it could not possibly increase prices in the SOE.[93] Mill also noted that the unanimous opinion of country bankers examined before various parliamentary committees was in accord with this view.[94] After presenting these views of the banking school, Mill stated that this doctrine appeared to him to be "incontrovertible." He went on to say:

> I give complete credence to the assertion of the country bankers very clearly and correctly condensed ... [by] Mr. Fullarton. I am convinced that they cannot possibly increase their issue of notes in any other circumstances than those which are there stated. I believe, also, that the theory, grounded by Mr. Fullarton upon this fact, contains a large

portion of truth, and is far nearer to being the expression of the whole truth than any form whatever of the currency theory.[95]

In endorsing the view that any expansion of convertible note issue could not affect prices in an SOE, Mill supported, albeit implicitly, the law of one price. He explicitly endorsed it in another passage:

> As soon as the price of cloth is lower in England than in Germany, it will begin to be exported, and the price of cloth in Germany will fall to what it is in England. ... By the fall, however, of cloth in England, cloth will fall in Germany also. ... By the rise of linen in Germany, linen must rise in England also.[96]

In view of these considerations, Mill must be viewed as endorsing the view that, in the case of the SOE with a convertible currency, the quantity theory (in the sense of causality running from money to prices) does not hold. Yet Mill clearly recognized that theory's validity in the case of the large, closed economy. Specifically, Mill described how an increase in the world money supply would have a proportional effect on world prices.[97] Moreover, Mill discussed at length the working of an inconvertible paper currency. He devoted an entire chapter to that discussion in his *Principles*.[98] Mill indicated that, although a convertible currency could not be issued to excess, an inconvertible currency could be overissued and would consequently have a definite inflationary impact, an observation supporting the quantity theory.[99] In short, Mill clearly recognized all three of the fundamental frameworks outlined above. In spite of this recognition, however, in certain passages Mill appeared to lend some support to contrary views, from the currency school.[100] His views with respect to the currency and banking schools, then, were not wholly consistent. Overall, however, his views supported the position of the banking school. Despite these apparent inconsistencies, Mill's support of the banking school principles had important implications. Since Mill's works were so widely read, his endorsement of the banking school served to propagate important elements of that view to make them readily available to later generations of economists.

K. Wicksell

Although Wicksell was not an English economist, he was very familiar with the English authors discussed above. As a consequence, his ideas on monetary theory were, in large part, an extension and propagation of these views. Moreover, Wicksell's writings were available in English in the twentieth century and have been said to have importantly influenced subsequent British and American economists. Wicksell, therefore, represents an important element in any discussion of the evolution of English monetary thought.

In any examination of Wicksell's writings, it is evident that Wicksell fully recognized the important contributions to monetary theory made by the authors discussed above, particularly Ricardo, the banking school writers, and J. S. Mill. These authors are quoted extensively throughout Wicksell's discussions of monetary theory.[101] It is evident, moreover, that from his studies of these earlier authors Wicksell acquired a thorough comprehension of the fundamental frameworks outlined in the present study, as well as an understanding of how the development of these frameworks evolved over time.* As a consequence, he supported the propositions related to the SOE under a convertible currency presented by the authors cited above. His interpretation of these propositions is entirely consistent with the explanations presented in the present study. Moreover, Wicksell stressed that when these considerations pertained specifically to a small, open framework, they should not be applied to other contexts.[103] Consider one of these propositions: there is no doubt that Wicksell understood the law of one price and its important implications. In Wicksell's writings, lucid and forceful statements of this law are presented in several passages:

> No matter how eagerly the products of one country may be demanded by another country . . . no appreciable difference of prices can persist when there is a free interchange of goods.[104]

> If [the obligation to redeem bank notes in metal] exists, . . . then naturally a powerful brake is applied to the banks, simply because commodity prices in such a country can no longer rise materially above the price level in all other countries having the same metal as a measure of value.[105]

Elsewhere, Wicksell contended that if two countries conduct free trade and are divided only by a land boundary, then:

> If these countries were both living under a specie regime, there could not

---

*In addition to understanding the fundamental ideas presented by Ricardo, banking school writers, and Mill, Wicksell also recognized various subtle arguments of these authors. For example, Wicksell recognized the distinction made by Ricardo between the behavior of an individual economic unit and the behavior of a universal set of these units acting in unison. That is, Wicksell had a thorough understanding of the subtle distinctions between an open and a closed economy.[102]

possibly exist different prices of the same commodity on both sides of the frontier; and if we suppose, which of course is not exactly true, that the level of prices in the interior of each country is materially the same as in the boundary districts, there could be no difference of prices at all between them . . . difference(s) of prices in the two countries . . . would be theoretically impossible and practically confined between very narrow limits.[106]

In stressing the validity of the law of one price, Wicksell explicitly recognized its implication that divergent relative price levels could *not* serve as an international adjustment mechanism under a convertible currency regime. He indicated that prices were determined exogenously by direct and rapid arbitrage links that were independent of specie movements.[107] These observations regarding the law of one price have the important implication that the quantity theory of money (in the sense of causality) does not apply to the single SOE under a convertible currency regime. Wicksell recognized well this contention when he demonstrated not only that international adjustments could take place without divergent price level movements but also that domestic prices were determined by international factors independent of domestic monetary considerations.[108]

The distinction between convertible and inconvertible monetary systems and the important implications of this distinction were also recognized by Wicksell. That is, he stated that whereas overissuance and, therefore, single-country inflation were possible under an inconvertible monetary regime, they were not possible under convertibility.[109] The quantity theory, then, although not applicable to the SOE under convertibility, applied to the SOE under an inconvertible monetary system. Finally, Wicksell clearly understood the importance of recognizing the open vis-à-vis the closed economic framework. He explicitly noted in several passages that the only truly closed economy is the world economy.[110] Although he recognized that convertibility ensured the impossibility of single-country inflation, Wicksell restated the Ricardian position that if all countries pursued monetary expansion simultaneously (and, therefore, increased the world money supply), inflation could result despite convertibility.[111] The quantity theory, then, was viewed as applicable to the closed economy.

J. L. Laughlin

Another author who was an important figure in discussions of the evolution of the above frameworks was Laughlin. Laughlin understood well the fundamentals of all three of the frameworks cited above.[112] His understanding of the SOE under a convertible currency was thorough and comprehensive, and his discussion of that model and its important implications was among the most forceful and lucid to be found in the writings of any of the authors discussed here.

Laughlin indicated that the volume of money in an SOE with a convertible currency was demand-determined (endogenous) and noted that a convertible note issue could not be overissued.[113] Consequently, for such an economy he argued that the money stock could not be treated as an exogenous, controllable variable. Any discussion beginning with the assumption of an exogenous change in the money stock (all other things being equal), therefore, was viewed by Laughlin as a fallacious argument.[114]

Laughlin explicitly and repeatedly endorsed the law of one price. For example, in one passage, he noted that

> the action of the international markets, with telegraphic quotations from every part of the world, precludes the supposition that gold prices could in general remain on a higher level in one country than in another (cost of carriage apart) even for a brief time, because, in order to gain the profit, merchants would seize the opportunity to send goods to the markets where prices are high.[115]

Moreover, Laughlin explained the implications of that law for relations between money and prices. In particular, he explicitly recognized that for the SOE with a convertible currency, prices are determined exogenously in world markets by the rapid workings of arbitrage and not by the domestic money stock.

> A rise in the price of any commodity due to local causes (such as deficient harvests, war, etc.) is *instantly* met by importations from other countries; indeed the actual event is more often discounted by shipments of goods. ... The competition between trading countries, as between different parts of the same country, being exceedingly keen, merchants in the leading centres would send the goods themselves to the spot where high prices existed, and by a quick increase of the supply of goods they would reduce prices in the country whose level was artificially high. ... prices would *at once* fall by competition of goods with goods to a normal international level (allowing for differences due to costs of carriage). ... In fact, it has become clear, by the logic of events, that the shipments of gold between commercial countries have little or nothing to do with the level of prices of merchandise in any one country[116]

Accordingly, Laughlin noted that divergent price levels could not be part of the international monetary adjustment mechanism for this type of economy, since such a mechanism would contradict the law of one price.[117] In stating these views, Laughlin made it clear that he was essentially endorsing the view of the banking school writers on this issue and opposing that of the currency school.[118] Unlike some other authors holding similar views, Laughlin very explicitly recognized the implications of this position for the quantity theory of money. In particular, Laughlin—following the views of the banking school—stated repeatedly and forcefully that the quantity theory did not apply to the SOE under a convertible monetary regime.[119]

In addition to examining the relations between money and prices for the SOE with a convertible currency, Laughlin also analyzed those relations for the case of an inconvertible currency. He noted that, in this case, the quantity theory was quite valid.[120]

Laughlin also recognized the distinction between the closed and the open economies and the important implications for money and prices of this distinction. He noted, for example, that for an individual country an inflow of gold reflecting an increase in the world gold stock (and, hence, world money supply) would cause an increase in prices, whereas a gold inflow reflecting a single country's favorable balance of payments (and, hence, manifesting a redistribution of the existing world stock of gold) would not affect the level of prices in that country.[121] Moreover, he explicitly noted that under a convertible monetary regime, an increase in the domestic money supply could affect the domestic price level only if it were large enough to affect world prices.[122] Hence, the quantity theory was valid in the closed world economy and not applicable to the SOE with a convertible currency.

In sum, Laughlin recognized well all three of the frameworks described above, as he demonstrated in the following noteworthy passage:

> If my previous reasoning has been correct, prices would not rise merely from an increase in the media of exchange [of the SOE]; . . . prices could not rise unless there were a serious fall throughout the world in the value of gold—which, owing to its great stock, is quite unlikely to occur in any ordinary period of time. But it is as plain as a pikestaff that a rise of general prices may be brought about by a device that would lower the value of the standard, such as a debasement of the coinage, or any legislative operations which might transfer the standard to a cheaper metal, or which might establish an inconvertible paper as a standard on a depreciating level.[123]

CONCLUSIONS

A contribution of the modern monetary approach has been the careful delineation of three basic monetary models. In this study, after a brief outline of the relationship between money and prices for these monetary models, the historical evolution of the models in English monetary thought was described. This description indicated that all three frameworks and the important distinctions among them were well recognized by earlier generations of economists and, in fact, were clearly delineated in the early nineteenth century by the bullionist writers. Prominent English economists, then, understood the three models and their important distinctions from the early 1800s until well into the 1900s. After that, however, the model of the SOE under a convertible currency and its companion principle—the law of one price—apparently either were forgotten or fell into disfavor until their recent revival in the modern monetary approach. While the reason for this lapse is somewhat enigmatic, some suggestions have been offered in the literature.

One reason for the temporary demise of this model was the endorsement of the currency school version of the international adjustment mechanism under a convertible currency regime given by prominent economists, such as Irving Fisher, J. M. Keynes, A. C. Pigou, and Gustav Cassel. In general, the writings of these authors supported the currency school view that divergent movements in general price levels constituted the adjustment mechanism of a fixed exchange rate (or convertible currency) system—a position that directly contradicted the law of one price. Indeed, this view led these writers to argue that fixed exchange rates and price stability were incompatible.[124]

Another reason for the demise of the fixed exchange rate model of the SOE was the emphasis given by various Harvard neoclassicists (such as Taussig, Viner, Beach, and Williams) to exceptions to the law of one price. As J. G. Witte and B. Henneberry have indicated, this emphasis apparently went unchallenged at the time and, consequently, contributed to the disfavor of the model.[125]

A third reason for the model's temporary demise was the emergence of the macroeconomic analysis of closed systems. That is, the development and analysis of closed models such as the Keynesian and later monetarist models directed the attention of the profession away from the analysis of open economic models. Moreover, by the early twentieth century, the U.S. economy had developed to the extent that, as a first approximation, it was treated as a closed economy.

For these (and probably other) reasons, then, the model of the SOE under a convertible currency and its companion principle—the law of one price—were disregarded after the early twentieth century. It was not until recent detailed analyses of currency devaluation and, consequently, the resurrection of the monetary approach that the model has again found support among economists.

NOTES

1. For contributions by non-English writers, see F. J. De Jong, *Development of Monetary Theory in the Netherlands* (Rotterdam: Rotterdam University Press, 1973); Robert V. Eagly, "The Swedish and English Bullionist Controversies," in *Events, Ideology, and Economic Theory*, ed. Robert V. Eagly (Detroit: Wayne State University Press, 1968); Robert V. Eagly, *The Swedish Bullionist Controversy* (Philadelphia: American Philosophical Society, 1971); and Thomas T. Sekine, "The Discovery of International Monetary Equilibrium by Vanderlint, Cantillon, Gervaise, and Hume," *Economia Internazionale* 26, no. 2 (1973).

2. See, for example, Sekine, op. cit.; J. Frenkel and H. G. Johnson, "The Monetary Approach to the Balance of Payments: Essential Concepts and Historical Origins," in *The Monetary Approach to the Balance of Payments*, ed. J. Frenkel and Harry G. Johnson (Toronto: University of Toronto Press, 1976), p. 37; J. W. Angell, *The Theory of International Prices* (New York: Augustus Kelley, 1965), p. 26 fn, p. 32; I. Gervaise, *The System or Theory of the Trade of the World* (Baltimore: Johns Hopkins University Press, 1954); and J. M. Letiche, "Isaac Gervaise on the International Mechanism of Adjustment," *Journal of Political Economy* 60 (1952).

3. See, for example, Jacob Viner, *Studies in the Theory of International Trade* (New York: Augustus Kelley, 1965), p. 127; O. St. Clair, *A Key to Ricardo* (New York: Kelley and Millman, 1957), p. 298; D. P. O'Brien, *The Classical Economists* (Oxford: Clarendon Press, 1975), pp. 148–49; Johan Myhrman, "Experiences of Flexible Exchange Rates in Earlier Periods: Theories, Evidence, and a New View," *Scandinavian Journal of Economics* 78, no. 2 (1976): 171; and Eagly, "The Swedish and English Bullionist Controversies," op. cit., p. 26.

4. Viner, op. cit., pp. 312–13.

5. L. Robbins, *Robert Torrens and the Evolution of Classical Economics* (London: Macmillan, 1958), p. 125. See also J. L. Laughlin, *The Principles of Money* (New York: Scribner's 1903), p. 417.

6. See Viner, op. cit., p. 333; Robert V. Eagly, "Adam Smith and the Specie-Flow Doctrine," *Scottish Journal of Political Economy* 17 (February 1970): 64; L. Girton and D. Roper, "J. Laurence Laughlin and the Quantity Theory of Money," International Finance Discussion Papers #103, March 1977, Board of Governors of the Federal Reserve System, p. 14.

7. D. Hume, "Hume to Montesquieu," April 10, 1749, in *Writings on Economics*, ed. Eugene Rotwein (Freeport, N.Y.: Books for Libraries Press, 1955) (reprinted 1972), p. 189.

8. Viner, op. cit., p. 313 fn. See also Charles E. Staley, "Hume and Viner on the International Adjustment Mechanism," *History of Political Economy* 8, no. 2 (Summer 1976): 255.

9. D. Hume, "Of the Balance of Trade," in *Writings*, op. cit., p. 66 fn.

10. Hume was explicit that these considerations were subject to the allowance for transportation costs. See Hume, "Of the Balance of Trade," p. 66 fn. See also Viner, op. cit., p. 314.

11. See Barbara Henneberry and James G. Witte, "Variable Gold Parities from a Classical Viewpoint: Hume Versus the Monetarists," unpublished manuscript, Indiana University, November 1974, p. 1. See also Viner, op. cit., p. 376.

12. See Girton and Roper, op. cit., pp. 21, 23.

13. For a critique of this view, see J. G. Witte and B. Henneberry, "A Monetary-Real Approach to Balance-of-Payments Theory: Old-New Synthesis for Old-New Problems," unpublished manuscript, Indiana University, April 1977, p. 2.

14. See, for example, Arnold Collery, *International Adjustment, Open Economies, and*

the *Quantity Theory of Money*, Princeton Studies in International Finance no. 28 (June 1971), p. 26; Harry G. Johnson, "The Monetary Approach to Balance of Payments Theory," *Journal of Financial and Quantitative Analysis* (March 1972): 1555; Harry G. Johnson, "Money, Balance of Payments Theory and the International Monetary Problem," *Essays in International Finance*, International Finance Section, Department of Economics, Princeton University, no. 124, November 1977, p. 5. This view is also implicit in the contention of some contemporary monetarists that fixed exchange rates and price level stability are incompatible. (See Henneberry and Witte, op. cit., p. 7.)

15. See Witte and Henneberry, op. cit., p. 2.

16. This view has been given elsewhere. See, for example, Henneberry and Witte, op. cit.

17. D. Hume, "Of the Balance of Trade," in *Writings*, op. cit., p. 65. See also D. Hume, "Of Money," in *Writings*, op. cit., p. 35. It will be remembered that this equality of level related to prices and not to absolute quantities of money. The view that Hume endorsed the law of one price has also been voiced by Viner. See Viner, op. cit., pp. 316, 317, 319.

18. This hypothesis of Hume—that price differences were no greater between countries than within countries—was empirically supported more than 200 years later by both Genberg, and McCloskey and Zecher. See A. H. Genberg, "Aspects of the Monetary Approach to Balance of Payments Theory," in *The Monetary Approach to the Balance of Payments*, op. cit.; and D. N. McCloskey and J. R. Zecher, "How the Gold Standard Worked, 1880–1913," in *The Monetary Approach to the Balance of Payments*, op. cit., p. 63.

19. See, for example, Hume, "Of the Balance of Trade," op. cit., pp. 63, 69, 72; D. Hume, "Hume to Montesquieu," in *Writings*, op. cit., p. 188; and D. Hume, "Hume to Oswald," in *Writings*, op. cit., p. 197.

20. James Oswald, "Oswald to Hume," in *Writings*, op. cit., pp. 191–92.

21. David Hume, "Hume to Oswald," in *Writings*, op. cit., p. 197.

22. Hume repeatedly recognized the existence of transportation costs and, hence, the possibility of price differences for nontradables. See, for example, Hume, "Of the Balance of Trade," op. cit., p. 66 fn.

23. See Henneberry and Witte, op. cit., p. 2. Also see, for example, Hume, "Of the Balance of Trade," op. cit., pp. 68–70, 72; and Hume, "Hume to Oswald," op. cit., p. 198.

24. See Hume, "Of the Balance of Trade," op. cit., pp. 62–63. See also Girton and Roper, op. cit., p. 23.

25. D. Hume, "Of Money," in *Writings*, op. cit., p. 33.

26. Angell, op. cit., p. 38; J. Hollander, "The Development of the Theory of Money from Adam Smith to David Ricardo," *Quarterly Journal of Economics* (1911): 435; and O'Brien, op. cit., p. 151.

27. A. Smith, *An Inquiry into the Nature and Causes of the Wealth of Nations* (New York: Random House, 1937), pp. 323–24. See also p. 188.

28. Douglas Vickers, "Adam Smith and the Status of the Theory of Money," in *Essays on Adam Smith*, ed. A. Skinner and T. Wilson (Oxford: Clarendon Press, 1975), p. 498.

29. Smith, op. cit., pp. 308–09. See also ibid., pp. 277–78, 284.

30. Angell, op. cit., p. 34. Laughlin also explicitly interpreted Smith in this manner. See, for example, Laughlin, op. cit., p. 238.

31. See, for example, A. I. Bloomfield, "Adam Smith and the Theory of International Trade," in *Essays on Adam Smith*, op. cit., p. 480; O'Brien, op. cit., p. 146; and Vickers, op. cit., p. 484. Although Smith mentioned prices in an earlier description of the adjustment mechanism, he ended that description by emphasizing that prices in different countries will stay in line with one another. See A. Smith, *Lectures on Justice, Police, Revenue and Arms* (New York: Kelley and Millman, 1956), p. 197.

32. Angell, op. cit., p. 34. See also, for example, Laughlin, op. cit., p. 238.

33. Smith, *Wealth of Nations*, op. cit., p. 191.

34. See ibid., p. 188. See also Frank Petrella, "Adam Smith's Rejection of Hume's Price-Specie-Flow Mechanism: A Minor Mystery Resolved," *Southern Economic Journal* (January 1968): 372.

35. Viner, op. cit., p. 205.

36. Hollander, op. cit., p. 465.

37. Ibid., p. 465.

38. David Ricardo, *The Works and Correspondence*, ed. Piero Sraffa (London: Cambridge University Press, 1951), vol. 1, p. 137. See also vol. 3, p. 52.

39. Ibid., vol. 3, pp. 90–92, 57, 64 fn.

40. Ibid., vol. 3, pp. 52, 53, 56.

41. Ibid., vol. 3, p. 99.

42. For evidence that Ricardo supported the law of one price, see Viner, op. cit., p. 315, and Ricardo, op. cit., vol. 9, p. 285. Ricardo recognized that intercountry price differences might exist for some goods, but either he emphasized that these goods were nontradables or the context indicates that this is what he meant. See Viner, op. cit., pp. 315, 323. See, for example, Ricardo, op. cit., vol. 3, pp. 56–57, 64 fn., 90, and vol. 6 (letter to Malthus), p. 90. See also Angell, op. cit., p. 59, where he states, "With respect to metallic currencies, Ricardo emphatically denies that there is any proportional relationship between money and prices."

43. *Report from the Select Committee on the High Price of Bullion*, reprinted in *The Paper Pound of 1797–1821: The Bullion Report*, ed. Edwin Cannan (New York: Augustus Kelley, 1969), p. 17. See also Ricardo, op. cit., vol. 3, pp. 91–92.

44. See, for example, Ricardo, op. cit., vol. 3, pp. 53, 57.

45. Ricardo, op. cit., vol. 3, p. 53.

46. Ibid., pp. 56–57. See also ibid., pp. 218–19. This interpretation of Ricardo was given by K. Wicksell. See, for example, K. Wicksell, *Interest and Prices* (New York: Augustus Kelley, 1965), pp. 81–82; and K. Wicksell, *Lectures on Political Economy*, vol. 2, "Money" (New York: Augustus Kelley, 1971).

47. Ricardo, op. cit., vol. 3, p. 57 fn.

48. Robbins, op. cit., p. 122.

49. *Report from the Select Committee*, op. cit., p. 16.

50. Various analyses of the controversies between the currency and banking schools are given elsewhere. See, for example, Viner, op. cit., and F. W. Fetter, *Development of British Monetary Orthodoxy, 1797–1875* (Cambridge, Mass.: Harvard University Press, 1965).

51. See, for example, Robbins, op. cit., pp. 100, 123; and O'Brien, op. cit., p. 153.

52. Viner, op. cit., p. 240.

53. See, for example, ibid., p. 223.

54. Viner, op. cit., p. 235.

55. Fetter, op. cit., p. 36; and Ricardo, op. cit., vol. 3, pp. 87, 88.

56. Viner, op, cit., p. 240.

57. See, for example, M. Daugherty, "The Currency-Banking Controversy: Parts I and II," *Southern Economic Journal* 9: 151.

58. See, for example, Daugherty, op. cit., p. 150, and D. E. W. Laidler, "Thomas Tooke on Monetary Reform," *Essays on Money and Inflation*, ed. D. E. W. Laidler (Chicago: University of Chicago Press, 1975), p. 214.

59. See D. E. W. Laidler and A. R. Nobay, "International Aspects of Inflation: A Survey," in *Recent Issues in International Monetary Economics*, ed. E. Claasen and P. Salin (New York: North-Holland, 1976), p. 301 fn.

60. Thomas Tooke, *A History of Prices* (New York: Adelphi, 1928), vol. 4, pp. 185, 192, 194.

61. See, for example, T. E. Gregory, "Introduction," Tooke, op. cit., pp. 13–14. It should be noted that the prices employed by Tooke were individual commodity prices and not index numbers.

62. See, for example, Laidler, op. cit., p. 214; Robbins, op. cit., p. 126; and K. Wicksell, *Interest and Prices*, op. cit., p. 83.

63. See Viner, op. cit., p. 240.

64. J. Fullarton, *On the Regulation of Currencies* (1844), p. 58, as quoted in Robbins, op. cit.

65. See, for example, Viner, op. cit., p. 223 fn.; F. Machlup, "Summary of the Discussion on Frenkel," *Recent Issues in International Monetary Economics*, op. cit., p. 50; and Daugherty, op. cit., p. 151.

66. See, for example, Fetter, op. cit., p. 228.

67. Tooke, op. cit., p. 652. From J. S. Mill, *Principles of Political Economy* (London: Longmans, Green, 1926), p. 652. See also Gregory, op. cit., pp. 76, 81.

68. Tooke, op. cit., vol. 4, p. 462. See also ibid., vol. 1, p. 149.

69. Tooke, *An Inquiry into the Currency Principle*, pp. 123–24. From Robbins, op. cit., p. 124. See also O'Brien, op. cit., p. 158, and Daugherty, op. cit., p. 149.

70. See, for example, Gregory, op. cit., p. 81; O'Brien, op. cit., p. 158; and Tooke, op. cit., vol. 4, p. 462.

71. Laidler and Nobay, op. cit., p. 301.

72. Tooke, *History of Prices*, op. cit., vol. 4, pp. 463, 470.

73. See, for example, Tooke, *History of Prices*, vol. 3, p. 191.

74. See, for example, Fetter, op. cit., p. 226, and Daugherty, op. cit., p. 146.

75. Fullarton, op. cit., p. 85, quoted by Mill, op. cit., p. 653. See also Wicksell, op. cit., p. 84; and Tooke, op. cit., vol. 4, p. 232, where he indicates that these bankers also contended that they could not influence prices.

76. See Tooke, *History of Prices*, vol. 4, p. 207.

77. Robert Torrens, *Principles and Practical Operation of Sir Robert Peel's Act of 1844* (3d ed.; London: Longmans, 1858), p. 190, quoted in Robbins, op. cit., p. 124.

78. See Fetter, op. cit., p. 190.

79. See Tooke, *History of Prices*, vol. 4, p. 206.

80. Robbins, op. cit., p. 125.

81. James Wilson, *On Capital, Currency, and Banking*, pp. 85, 87, quoted in Tooke, *History of Prices*, vol. 4, p. 208.

82. Tooke, *History of Prices*, vol. 4, p. 209.

83. Ibid., p. 462.

84. See, for example, Tooke, op. cit., vol. 3, p. 66; Wicksell, *Lectures on Political Economy*, op. cit., vol. 2, p. 173; and Fetter, op. cit., p. 227.

85. See, for example, Viner, op. cit., p. 240.

86. Tooke, op. cit., pp. 462–63.

87. See, for example, Daugherty, op. cit., p. 150; and Tooke, op. cit., vol. 4, p. 463.

88. See, for example, Fetter, op. cit., p. 191; and Wicksell, *Interest and Prices*, op. cit., p. 85.

89. M. Blaug, *Economic Theory in Retrospect* (Homewood, Ill.: Irwin, 1968), p. 180.

90. See, for example, Fetter, op. cit., p. 226.

91. See, for example, Mill, op. cit., Book 3, Chapters 13, 22.

92. Mill, ibid., p. 654. See also Wicksell, *Interest and Prices*, op. cit., p. 86; and Wicksell, *Lectures on Political Economy,* op. cit., vol. 2, p. 174, where Wicksell notes that

"Mill considered that Tooke's view of the innocuousness of the banks as regards price movements was quite correct in normal, tranquil times. . . ."

93. Mill, op. cit., pp. 652–53.

94. Ibid.

95. Ibid., p. 653.

96. Ibid., p. 622 fn.

97. Ibid., p. 630.

98. Ibid., Book 3, Chapter 13.

99. With respect to Mill's analysis of an inconvertible currency, he essentially reproduced the basic arguments of Ricardo. See for example, Blaug, op. cit., p. 200.

100. See, for example, Fetter, op. cit., p. 226. In particular, he mentions price level adjustment as the adjustment mechanism in some passages.

101. See Wicksell's *Interest and Prices*, op. cit., and *Lectures on Political Economy*, op. cit., vol. 2. See also Laidler and Nobay, op. cit., p. 301.

102. See, for example, Wicksell, *Interest and Prices*, op. cit., pp. 81, 82, 85; and Wicksell, *Lectures*, op. cit., p. 171.

103. Wicksell, *Interest and Prices*, op. cit., p. 85.

104. Wicksell, *Lectures on Political Economy*, p. 159.

105. Wicksell, *Lectures on Political Economy*, op. cit., vol. 2, p. 171. See also ibid., p. 177.

106. Wicksell, "International Freights and Prices," *Quarterly Journal of Economics* 32 (1918): 405. See also Laidler and Nobay, op. cit., p. 301.

107. See Wicksell, *Interest and Prices*, op. cit., pp. 157–58. See also Viner, op. cit., p. 305.

108. Wicksell, *Lectures on Political Economy*, op. cit., vol. 2, p. 177; and Wicksell, *Interest and Prices*, op. cit., pp. 157–58.

109. See Wicksell, *Lectures on Political Economy*, op. cit., p. 171.

110. See, for example, Wicksell, *Interest and Prices*, op. cit., pp. 82, 85, 157.

111. Wicksell, op. cit., pp. 81–82; and Wicksell, *Lectures on Political Economy*, op. cit., p. 171.

112. An excellent analysis of Laughlin and his monetary writings was recently presented by Girton and Roper. See Girton and Roper, op. cit. This section does not attempt to expand upon the Girton and Roper paper but rather attempts to place Laughlin among other authors in an evolutionary framework.

113. Laughlin, op. cit., pp. 409, 417; and Girton and Roper, op. cit., p. 15.

114. See, for example, Girton and Roper, op. cit., pp. 13, 15, 23.

115. Laughlin, op. cit., p. 369.

116. Laughlin, op. cit., pp. 380–82. See also, for example, Laughlin, op. cit., pp. 252, 371–72, 375, 377, 379–82, 388, 417.

117. See, for example, ibid., p. 379. See also Girton and Roper, op. cit., p. 24.

118. See, for example, Laughlin, op. cit., pp. 257, 264, 268–69.

119. See, for example, ibid., pp. 247, 263, 371. See also Girton and Roper, op. cit., pp. 13, 21.

120. See, for example, Laughlin, op. cit., pp. 247–48, 285, 314, 400, 407, 510–14, 528–31. See also Girton and Roper, op. cit., pp. 13, 21.

121. See, for example, Laughlin, op. cit., pp. 103, 379, 388–89, 393, 417. See also Girton and Roper, p. 21.

122. See Laughlin, op. cit., pp. 135–37, 388; and Girton and Roper, op. cit., pp. 14, 15.

123. Laughlin, op. cit., p. 393.

124. See, for example, G. Cassel, *Theory of Social Economy* (New York: Augustus

Kelley, 1967), p. 522; I. Fisher, *The Purchasing Power of Money* (New York; Macmillan, 1911), p. 172; J. M. Keynes, *Monetary Reform* (New York: Harcourt Brace, 1924), p. 173; A. C. Pigou, *Industrial Fluctuations*, 2d ed. (New York: Augustus Kelley, 1967), p. 303.

125. See Witte and Henneberry, op. cit., p. 2.

3

Money, Income, and Causality in the United States and the United Kingdom

Bluford H. Putnam
D. Sykes Wilford

Christopher Sims has presented an innovative statistical technique to determine the direction of causality, then applied this methodology to money and nominal income in the United States. He concluded: "The main empirical finding is that the hypothesis that causality is unidirectional from money to income agrees with the postwar U.S. data, whereas the hypothesis that causality is unidirectional from income to money is rejected."[1] In a more recent paper in the *American Economic Review*, David Williams, C. A. E. Goodhard, and D. H. Gowland applied Sims' statistical methodology to the United Kingdom and concluded: "We found for the U.K. some evidence of unidirectional causality running from nominal incomes to money but also some evidence of unidirectional causality running from money to prices. Taken together, this evidence suggests, perhaps, a more complicated causal relationship between money and incomes in which both are determined simultaneously."[2] Furthermore, Williams, Goodhart, and Gowland suggest some general possibilities for the differences between the United States and the United Kingdom, and they are careful to note that: "Because of the various differences in context the finding that in the United Kingdom the relationship between money

The authors wish to thank the *American Economic Review* for permission to reprint this study, which appeared in Volume 68 (June 1978), pp. 423–27. Also, the authors are indebted to David T. King, J. Ernest Tanner, Walton T. Wilford, and J. Richard Zecher for their comments on earlier versions of this paper.

and income appears different from that found by Sims for the United States in no way casts any doubt on the validity of Sims' own results."[3]

The purpose of this note is to present a concise model which draws together the findings of Sims for the United States and of Williams, Goodhart, and Gowland for the United Kingdom. To accomplish this, a fixed exchange rate system is modeled in which one country, the United States, serves as the primary reserve currency country, while other countries, the United Kingdom in this case, hold a substantial portion of their international reserves denominated in terms of the reserve currency.* Particular attention is paid to the asymmetrical nature of the system and the empirical results of Sims and Williams, Goodhart, and Gowland.

The model is couched in a world in which asset reallocations are viewed as adjustments toward maintaining general equilibrium. This equilibrium is based on a stable set of preferences regarding the structure of individual portfolios, broadly defined in terms of holdings of real consumption goods, real interest bearing financial assets, real money balances, and leisure time. The assumption of equilibrium conditions in all markets allows attention to focus directly on the money market to isolate the process of portfolio adjustment in international markets. As in similar models based on the monetary approach to the balance of payments, three equations are specified for each country: a money demand function, a money supply identity, and the condition of monetary equilibrium.[4] The difference between the reserve currency country and all other countries lies in the money supply identity. To follow through the consequences of the differences, the case of the reserve currency country is presented first, and then the case for other countries.

THE RESERVE CURRENCY COUNTRY

The model of the reserve currency country contains three straightforward equations. For simplicity, money demand depends on permanent real income and the price level:

$$M^d(A) = k(A)P(A)Y(A) \tag{1}$$

where the letter 'A' stands for the reserve currency country,

---

*One may note that for the Commonwealth countries the British pound acted as a reserve currency. However, the pound's relative world influence vis-à-vis the U.S. dollar was small during the Bretton Woods period.

k = constant
P = price level
Y = permanent real income
and M^d = quantity of money demanded.

The reserve currency country's central bank has the power to determine the nominal money stock. Thus,

$$M^s = M \qquad (2)$$

This money supply equation does not ignore the fact that the reserve currency country operates in the context of international markets (that is, is an open economy). Equation 2 implies that the domestic money stock of the reserve currency country need not be responsive to its balance of payments. When money flows from the reserve currency country to the rest of the world, that money eventually is purchased by foreign central banks, due to their agreement to buy and sell currency at a fixed price. However, foreign central banks do not hold the major portion of their international reserves in noninterest-bearing form when an alternative exists. In this case, the foreign central banks purchase government securities from the reserve currency country.* Under these conditions, a balance of payments deficit results in an outflow of government securities, but not of money. Thus, the central bank of the reserve currency country maintains control over the nominal money stock. Furthermore, the reserve currency country is the only country with the power to create international reserves, thereby enabling it to remain independent of external influences.

---

*During the Bretton Woods period, when a particular central bank received dollars, which it held as international reserves, a portion of these dollars, that which was not needed for governmental transactions demand, were used to buy U.S. government securities. That is, the dollars returned to the United States, and instead of holding currency, foreign central banks held U.S. government securities. Thus, one may equate the flow of a dollar from a foreign central bank to the United States, not to a loss of international reserves for the United States, but to a securities account transaction between the authorities of the United States and the foreign central bank. As such, this transaction would be counted in the U.S. official settlements balance, since U.S. liabilities to foreign official agencies are affected. But the money supply of the United States is not necessarily affected. For a more detailed explanation of this point see Donald S. Kemp, in *The Monetary Approach to International Adjustment*, eds., Bluford Putnam and D. Sykes Wilford (New York: Praeger, 1979), as well as Lance Girton and D. W. Henderson, "Financial Capital Movements and Central Bank Behavior in a Two Country, Short-Run Portfolio Balance Model," *Journal of Monetary Economics* 2 (January 1976): 33–61; or A. K. Swoboda, "Gold, Dollars, Eurodollars, and the World Money Stock under Fixed Exchange Rates," *American Economic Review* 68 (September 1978).

Finally, the model is closed with the condition of monetary equilibrium:

$$M^d = M^s \qquad (3)$$

Solving this system for the price level and converting to growth terms yields:

$$g(P(A)) = g(M(A)) - g(Y(A)) \qquad (4)$$

where $g(X) = (dX/dt)/X$, for $X = P$, M, and Y.

Growth of the price level is determined by the growth of the money supply relative to permanent real income growth. If permanent real income is growing at a stable rate and is, for the most part, independent of monetary disturbances, then changes in nominal income are caused primarily by changes in the supply of money—the result which Sims obtained for the United States. The essential point is that it is not necessary to postulate that the United States is a closed economy to explain Sims' results. During the Bretton Woods period, the dollar played a leading role in world economic activity. However, by serving as the reserve currency country, the United States maintained control over its domestic money supply.

THE REST OF THE WORLD

The asymmetrical properties of the international monetary system become apparent when examining the nonreserve currency case. For simplicity, the money demand function is changed from the preceding analysis:

$$M^d(j) = k(j)P(j)Y(j) \qquad (5)$$

where j stands for any nonreserve currency country.

With respect to the money supply identity, however, there are major differences between the reserve currency country and other countries. In the process of maintaining fixed exchange rates, central banks will incur inflows and outflows of reserve currency assets (that is, international reserves). Because their monetary base depends on the asset portfolio of the central bank, the balance of payments will directly affect the domestic money supply. That is:

$$M^s(j) = aH = a(R + D) \qquad (6)$$

where a = the money multiplier
  H = high-powered money, or the monetary base
  R = international reserve assets (liabilities of the reserve currency country)
and D = domestic assets held by the bank.

Dividing high-powered money, which makes up the bulk of the liability side of the central bank's portfolio, into international reserves and domestic assets from the asset side of the portfolio, introduces the effects of the balance of payments directly into the money supply identity.[5] This formulation of high-powered money allows one to focus directly upon the sources of high-powered money, foreign or domestic.

The condition of monetary equilibrium completes the model:

$$M^s(j) = M^d(j) \qquad (7)$$

Solving the system for the international reserve flow and converting to growth terms yields:

$$\frac{R}{H}g(R) = g(p(j)) + g(Y(j)) - g(a) - \frac{D}{H}g(D) \qquad (8)$$

In this monetary approach to the balance of payments, the nonreserve currency country's prices are determined on unified world markets and are given exogenously to the domestic economy. The balance of payments reflects attempts by individuals to maintain equilibrium money balances as they adjust their expenditures and receipts. The endogeneity of the international reserve flow thereby implies the endogeneity of the money supply, leading to the conclusion that the nonreserve currency country's monetary authorities cannot determine the domestic money stock.

Two asymmetrical properties of the international system are now apparent. First, the reserve currency country can control its money supply, while other countries cannot. Secondly, the reserve currency country can influence its price level, while other countries must accept prices as determined on unified world markets. This holds true even though the reserve currency country participates in rising price level. Nominal income increases, and there is an inflow of international reserves as individuals seek to maintain equilibrium money balances. The balance of payments surplus reestablishes monetary equilibrium by expanding the supply of money to meet demand. Now suppose that from a position of equilibrium a nonreserve currency country attempts to raise its nominal money supply. As individuals reduce their excess money balances, the central bank experiences an outflow of international reserves due to residents' increased expenditures on foreign goods and assets. The loss of international reserves impacts directly on the monetary base, and the money supply moves back toward its initial level. International reserve flows equilibrate money supply to money demand as determined primarily by permanent real income and the price level. With prices determined on unified world markets and permanent real income not directly affected by the balance of payments, then essentially, nominal income and the money supply are simultaneously determined—a conclusion supported by the empirical findings of Williams, Goodhart, and Gowland for the United Kingdom.*

SUMMARY

A fixed exchange rate system in which one country serves as the reserve currency country has important asymmetrical properties. Indeed, only the reserve currency country can control its money supply. From this property, several implications concerning the direction of causality follow directly. Control of the money supply results in the ability to influence the price level, and thus nominal income in the reserve currency country. Hence, Sims found that causality flows from money to nominal income in the United States. Furthermore, changes in prices and nominal incomes in the reserve currency country will simultaneously affect conditions in world markets. Individuals in other countries, reacting to these changes, adjust their portfolios. This adjustment process prompts simultaneous changes in prices, nominal income, and the money stock in nonreserve currency countries. Thus, Williams, Goodhart, and Gowland found that in the United Kingdom neither money nor nominal income cause each other.

Both Sims' and Williams, Goodhart, and Gowland's investigations covered the Bretton Woods period, during which the world was essentially operating on a dollar standard. Given a model highlighting the asymmetrical properties of such an international monetary system, the apparently

---

*The reader should note that the empirical technique employed by Sims as well as by Williams, Goodhart, and Gowland can only indicate causality when leads and lags exist among the variables studied. For clarity, no attempt has been made to specify these leads and lags mathematically, but as the preceding paragraph indicates, there is a clear presumption as to their existence and direction.

inconsistent findings by Sims for the United States and Williams, Goodhart, and Gowland's for the United Kingdom are, instead, entirely compatible.

NOTES

1. C. A. Sims, "Money, Income, and Causality," *American Economic Review* 62 (September 1972):590.
2. D. Williams, C. A. E. Goodhart, and D. H. Gowland, "Money, Income and Causality: The U.K. Experience," *American Economic Review* 66 (June 1976): 423.
3. Ibid., p. 417.
4. There are several articles that summarize the essentials of the monetary approach to the balance of payments. For particular references see H. G. Johnson, *Further Essays in Monetary Economics* (Cambridge, Mass.: Harvard University Press, 1973), pp. 229–49; H. G. Johnson, "Elasticity, Absorption, Keynesian Multiplier, Keynesian Policy, and Monetary Approaches to Devaluation Theory: A Simple Geometric Exposition," *American Economic Review* 66 (June 1976): 448–52; D. S. Kemp, "A Monetary View of the Balance of Payments," Federal Reserve Bank of St. Louis *Review* 57 (April 1975): 14–22; B. H. Putnam, "Non-traded Goods and the Monetary Approach to the Balance of Payments," Federal Reserve Bank of New York Research Paper #7714, 1976; J. Frenkel and C. A. Rodriguez, "Portfolio Equilibrium and the Balance of Payments: A Monetary Approach," *American Economic Review* 65 (September 1975): 674–88; J. Frenkel and H. G. Johnson, "The Monetary Approach to the Balance of Payments: Essential Concepts and Origins," in *The Monetary Approach to the Balance of Payments*, ed. Jacob Frenkel and Harry G. Johnson (Toronto: University of Toronto Press, 1976), pp. 21–45; D. S. Wilford, *Monetary Policy and the Open Economy: Mexico's Experience* (New York: Praeger, 1977); J. R. Zecher, "Monetary Equilibrium and International Reserve Flows in Australia," *Journal of Finance* 29 (December 1974): 1523–30.
5. A detailed explanation of this view of the money supply process can be found in Zecher, op. cit.; Kemp, op. cit.; or L. Andersen and J. Jordan, "The Monetary Base: Explanation and Analytical Use," Federal Reserve Bank of St. Louis *Review* 50, 8 (August 1968): 7–11.

4

International Reserve Flows: Seemingly Unrelated Regressions

Bluford H. Putnam
D. Sykes Wilford

INTRODUCTION

Much of the recent literature dealing with the balance of payments has centered on the monetary approach to the balance of payments. This new body of literature developed by, among others, Mundell, Komiya, Johnson, and Zecher[1] views on the balance of payments as the result of adjustments in a country's stock of money, while traditional approaches to the balance of payments emphasize adjustments in the current account. An international reserve flow or a payments imbalance is viewed as the mechanism which ensures that the stock of money in a country adjusts to its desired level. That is, international reserve flows are determined by the excess demand or supply of money within a particular country. The monetary approach therefore focuses on the money market for a particular country within the context of a large world.

A number of papers have discussed the usefulness of this approach, and recently some empirical analyses have been undertaken.[2] Most of these discussions are based upon the central set of assumptions that prices and interest rates are determined in world goods, services, and capital

The authors wish to thank *Weltwirtschaftliches Archiv* for permission to reprint this study, which appeared in volume 114 (Summer 1978): 211–26. Also, the authors wish to thank J. Richard Zecher, W. Michael Cox, Walton T. Wilford, M. A. Akhtar, David T. King, and Hubertus Muller-Groeling for their generous discussions of this topic.

markets which are well integrated, thus implying that a small country's domestic price on goods, services, and capital is exogenously determined. The additional assumptions of fixed exchange rates and full employment allow these authors to solve for an international reserve flow equation.* Another factor which the empirical studies have in common is that individual country cases are examined. Although world factors are taken into account through various devices, simultaneous empirical analysis of various countries' reserve flows has not been performed.

This paper extends the empirical analysis of international reserve flows in two ways. First, the study incorporates the interrelationship of several countries' reserve flow equations by utilizing the seemingly unrelated regressions technique. Certain points, heretofore not fully developed in the literature,[3] suggest that these individual countries' international reserve flows are related through various world markets (goods and capital) and institutional arrangements (Bretton Woods) such that shocks to the world system may impact groups of countries simultaneously. We employ seemingly unrelated regression analysis to a group of European countries which are closely tied through capital markets as well as through political constraints for the period 1952–71.[4]

Secondly, in addition to estimating equations specified solely with the domestic price level and interest rate as proxies for the world price level and interest rate, the purchasing-power parity and interest rate parity assumptions are integrated directly into the reduced form tests. Thus, U.S. prices and interest rates, also serving as proxies for world variables, are substituted for domestic variables. This approach allows us to comment directly on certain basic differences between the monetary approach and alternative theories.†

---

*The assumption of full employment can easily be relaxed without disturbing the model. One need only assume that reserve flows do not have an impact upon current period real output.

†This paper is not designed to examine fully the differences among all competing theories of the balance of payments. The interested reader should refer to Donald S. Kemp, in *The Monetary Approach to International Adjustment*, eds., Bluford Putnam and D. Sykes Wilford (New York: Praeger, 1979), Harry G. Johnson, *Further Essays in Monetary Economics* (Cambridge, Mass.: Harvard University Press, 1973), and Harry G. Johnson, "The Monetary Approach to Balance-of-Payments Theory: A Diagrammatic Analysis," *The Manchester School of Economics and Social Studies* 43 (1975): 220–74; as well as S. P. Magee, "Empirical Evidence on the Monetary Approach to the Balance of Payments and Exchange Rates," *American Economic Review* 66 (May 1976): 163–70; or Marina v. N. Whitman, "Global Monetarism and the Monetary Approach to the Balance of Payments," *Brookings Papers on Economic Activity* no. 3 (1975): 491–536.

The analysis upholds the hypothesis that there exists a high degree of integration in capital and goods markets. Empirical results conform to the a priori notions of the monetary approach. And use of the seemingly unrelated regression technique greatly improves the efficiency of our parametric estimates, supporting the hypothesis that balance of payments disturbances are, as would be anticipated, often related.

THE BASIC MODEL

The monetary approach to the balance of payments model can be developed in five basic steps utilizing three assumptions. Following Johnson and Zecher,[5] for the jth country, the three structural equations are:

$$M_j^d = P_j Y_j^{\alpha_1} e^{u_j}/i_j^{\alpha_2} * \tag{1}$$

$$M_j^s = a_j H_j \tag{2}$$

$$M_j^s = M_j^d \tag{3}$$

where M_j^d = the demand for money by country j,

M_j^s = the supply of money in country j,

P_j = the price level in country j,

i_j = the interest rate in country j,

Y_j = the level of output in country j,

u_j = a log normally distributed disturbance term for country j,

a_j = the money multiplier in country j, and

H_j = the stock of high-powered money in country j.

The three assumptions are

---

*This specification of the money demand function assumes no money illusion.

(a) the jth country's price level is world determined,

(b) the jth country's interest rate is world determined, and

(c) the jth country's balance of payments does not affect real output.

By examining the balance sheet of the monetary authorities it can be shown that

$$M_j^s = a_j(R_j + D_j) \qquad (4)$$

where R_j = the stock of international reserves held by authorities and
D_j = domestic credit*

Assuming a fixed exchange rate, one may solve for an international reserve flow equation where the level of foreign reserves held by the monetary authorities is functionally related to excess demand for money over domestically supplied money. Combining equations 1, 3, and 4, placing them in growth terms and rearranging to name the growth in reserves as the dependent variable, one obtains the basic reserve flow equation:

$$(R_j/H_j)gR_j = \alpha_1 gY_j - \alpha_2 gi_j + gP_j - ga_j - (D_j/H_j)gD_j + u_j \qquad (5)$$

where $gX_j = d \ln X_j/dt$ = the rate of growth in country j of X: X = R, Y, P, i, a, and D.

The first three terms on the right hand side of equation 5 determine the growth in money demand while the next two terms capture the growth in the relevant domestic money supply variables. Price and interest rate variables are both assumed to be world determined, thus the price level effect on reserves is positive and the interest rate effect is negative. The inverse relationship between the interest rate and international reserve flows follows from the demand for money specification yielding a result, as Johnson pointed out, which is somewhat contrary to traditional literature.[7] The relationship of the reserve flow equation implies that attempts to

---

*Domestic credit consists to a large extent of the authorities' holdings of domestic assets (both public and private liabilities) minus domestic liabilities other than high-powered money. For most countries, changes in D are closely related to the monetization of treasury debt. See Akhtar, Putnam, and Wilford for a theoretical discussion of the relationship of the change in D to the operation of the United Kingdom's Treasury.[6]

increase the domestic money supply above demand results in a balance of payments deficit since the equilibrium condition (money supply equals money demand) must be satisfied.

RELATED DISTURBANCES

Estimation of the reduced form reserve flow equation for the jth country represented by equation 5, with modifications, has constituted the extent of empirical investigations in the literature.* We do not contend that this is an improper methodology for analyzing an individual country reserve flow. However, participation in world markets allows information to be gained by examining each country in the context of a larger group. The reserve flow equation for the ith country may have an error which is related to the error of the jth country. Thus, if one is investigating the reserve flow equation of n different countries and

$$Eu_j^t u_{j+1}^t = 0$$

t = time and u_j^t = the error in the time t for the jth country, then a proper methodology for examining individual reserve flow equations would involve estimating the equations jointly as one set.

The rationale for the relation of errors among individual country reserve flow equations can be derived from many factors. First, it is evident that a principal relation which may not be captured in the independent variables of the invidual equations is the effect of any shocks directly or indirectly derived from integrated financial systems. During the period of fixed exchange rates, domestic credit creation in the reserve currency country (that is, the United States) had an impact on world international reserves and world money supply. Deviations in credit conditions in the reserve currency country may not be completely reflected in current world prices and interest rates but would still affect the balance of payments of many countries.† Second, real factors which tend to disrupt a major segment of world trade may also lead to correlation of the error terms of

---

*Of course, there are variations on the theme; some taking particular model-building approaches involving portfolio theory such as Kouri and Porter,[8] utilizing rational expectation such as Cox, or including exchange rates as did Girton and Roper. However, these variations have concentrated on a single, small country.

†For a further discussion of the role of the reserve currency country in a fixed exchange rate system see Swoboda, op. cit., Kemp, op. cit., and Putnam and Wilford, op. cit.

reserve flow equations. For instance, a dock strike in the United States or a drought in a major agricultural region of the world might cause shocks in several countries' reserve flows simultaneously.*

This study focuses upon eight European countries characterized by highly integrated traded goods markets and well-developed Eurocapital markets yielding sufficient conditions for the existence of correlation among reserve flow equation error terms. We argue that efficiency is increased through estimating the coefficients of the reserve flow equations in a stacked format utilizing a GLS procedure.† However, it must be noted that the gain in efficiency may be somewhat offset due to any correlation between the explanatory variables' matrices of the different countries.[9]

EMPIRICAL RESULTS

The first set of regressions to be estimated is derived directly from equation 5. The set of eight equations is estimated for Austria, Belgium, Denmark, France, Germany, Italy, the Netherlands, and the United Kingdom, with the jth country's reserve flow regression equation of the form:

$$(R_j/H_j)gR_j = b_1gY_j + b_2gi_j + b_3gP_j + b_4ga_j + b_5(D_j/H_j)gD_j + u_j \quad (6)$$

The second set of estimating equations utilizes the same procedure of estimation except that the jth country's price variable is replaced by the U.S. CPI as a proxy of the movement in world price levels. Thus, the jth country's reserve flow regression equation is of the form

$$(R_j/H_j)gR_j = b_1gY_j + b_2gi_j + b_3gP_{us} + b_4ga_j + b_5(D_j/H_j)gD_j + u_j \quad (7)$$

Since the world is well integrated in the goods market one would, a priori,

---

*A classic example of a simultaneous shock to the international payments system, which occurred outside of the sample period utilized here, was the fourfold increase in oil prices by OPEC in 1973.

†As will be noted later, the increase in estimating efficiency is manifested in a reduction of the standard errors associated with the coefficients of the explanatory variables. The seemingly unrelated regressions technique utilizes the information contained in the correlations of the error terms of the individual equations, and in re-estimating the equation system is able to reduce the portion of error attributed to the explanatory variables. Thus, with simultaneous exogenous shocks accounted for, at least in part, the efficiency of the estimates is enhanced.

expect growth in prices to be very similar or, in a strict sense, equal. In an empirical sense, the use of a consistent proxy provides one with the opportunity to examine the consistency of the theory as well as the stability of the coefficients.

The third set of estimating equations explicitly adds the constraint that the interest rate variable is a proxy for the world rate; therefore, the U.S. interest rate is substituted into the second formulation, (7), for i_j. Thus, the reduced form for the jth equation is

$$(R_j/H_j)gR_j = b_1gY_j + b_2gi_{us} + b_3gP_{us} + b_4ga_j + b_5(D_j/H_j)gD_j + u_j \quad (8)$$

This specification follows from the hypothesis that the world's financial markets ensure interest arbitrage such that movements in any interest rates (the U.S. rate specifically) reflect the underlying real factors which cause a portfolio holder to demand money.

A priori, for all individual country equations in each equation set, the anticipated coefficent for the income variable, b_1, is close to positive unity. This interpretation rests on the role of real income as a determinant of the demand for money. Alternative theories, such as the elasticities or absorption approaches, would postulate a negative coefficient for income. That is, a rise in income would increase imports and, all things being equal, result in a deterioration of the current account. These are primarily theories of the balance on current account, not theories of the combined current and capital accounts or the overall balance of payments, as is the case with the monetary approach. Hence, the direct comparability of the theories is limited without some assumptions concerning capital account behavior in the alternative models.

The sign of the estimated coefficient for the interest rate variable, b_2, should be negative for all equation sets. Again, this interpretation rests on the role of the interest rate in money demand as well as the assumption that world interest rates are linked together. That is, an increase in the world interest rate (or its proxy) implies a decrease in the demand for money and an outflow of international reserves. Conventional theory might argue that an increase in domestic interest rates relative to world interest rates would draw capital from the rest of the world, leading to a reserve inflow. Such an alternative hypothesis suggests a positive sign for b_2 in equations 6 and 7 which use domestic interest rates and a negative sign for equation 8 which uses the U.S. interest rate.*

---

*Of course, a complete specification of the alternative approach is required for an empirical comparison, and this exercise is beyond the scope of this paper.

From the point of view of the theory presented, the coefficient of the price level should be near positive unity. This assumes no domestic money illusion in the demand for money and unified world goods markets, such that world price equal domestic price changes. An alternative hypothesis would be that an increase in domestic prices, with world prices constant, would imply an increase in imports, a decline in exports, a reserve outflow, and a negative sign on the price level in equation 6, while positive in equations 7 and 8 which use U.S. prices.

If the monetary approach is to be supported by the empirical evidence, the price level and the interest rate in each country must serve as determinants of the demand for money and behave as if world goods and capital markets are well integrated. This means that the price level should carry a positive sign and the interest rate a negative sign for each country and in each equation set, regardless of whether a domestic or world proxy is used to represent the relevant variable.*

Coefficients on the sources of domestic monetary influence, both ga and (D/H)gD, are expected to be negative unity. Nonmonetary theories of the balance of payments tend to exclude these variables from the analysis, so no comparisons analogous to the ones given for the demand variables are available.†

The annual data for the fixed exchange rate period 1952–71 are from *International Financial Statistics*. Interest rates are comparable for all countries and the price variables are the individual consumer price indices. The real income variable is nominal GNP deflated by the consumer price index. Money supplies are narrowly defined.

Tables 4.1, 4.2, and 4.3 report the regression results for the eight countries based upon equation forms 6, 7, and 8 respectively. Single equation estimation results (OLS) as well as seemingly unrelated regression (GLS) results are reported for each country. The summary statistics,

---

*Some variation in the size of the coefficient across countries and across equation sets is likely due to the stochastic process.

†In the extreme case where the specified money demand function for a country fits perfectly with zero error in every observation period, equation 6 would also fit perfectly. Then, it would be precisely true that for a given demand for money, any percent change in domestic money (ga + (D/H)gD) would be offset by an opposite change in international reserves ((R/H)gR). In this case, if the domestic money variables, a and D, satisfy the statistical independence properties required by regression analysis, then their estimated coefficients would be precisely negative unity. On the other extreme, where no statistical relationship exists between money demand and the specified explanatory variables (Y, P, and i), then regression equation 6 might yield positive, negative, or even zero coefficients with respect to ga and (D/H)gD. Prior testing has indicated that the underlying money demand functions are relatively stable, but by no means perfect fits.

TABLE 4.1 International Reserve Flows[a]: Domestic Prices and Interest Rates

Country j	Real Income	Interest Rate	Price Level	Money Multiplier[b]	Domestic Credit	Type	R^2
			Explanatory Variables				
Austria	0.76	−0.24	0.93	−0.50	−1.21	OLS	.92
	(5.66)	(−4.19)	(4.53)	(−2.95)	(−8.12)		
	0.69	−0.22	1.05	−0.60	−1.12	GLS	
	(6.07)	(−5.01)	(6.73)	(−5.05)	(−10.35)		
Belgium	0.69	−0.15	0.85	−0.83	−1.08	OLS	.88
	(4.02)	(−2.22)	(1.99)	(−2.34)	(−10.06)		
	0.68	−0.01	0.73	−0.75	−1.11	GLS	
	(4.22)	(−1.76)	(1.80)	(−2.33)	(−11.19)		
Denmark	0.71	−0.27	1.18	−0.99	−0.98	OLS	.91
	(3.58)	(−1.33)	(4.98)	(−4.20)	(−8.93)		
	0.69	−0.12	1.10	−0.99	−0.99	GLS	
	(4.02)	(−0.70)	(5.25)	(−4.89)	(−10.36)		
France	1.22	−0.37	0.17	−0.43	−0.95	OLS	.88
	(5.91)	(−3.98)	(1.10)	(−1.34)	(−9.29)		
	1.32	−0.38	0.15	−0.62	−1.00	GLS	
	(7.45)	(−4.67)	(1.16)	(−2.31)	(−11.57)		
Germany	0.83	−0.04	1.05	−0.54	−1.08	OLS	.98
	(8.34)	(−3.09)	(3.43)	(−3.62)	(−18.07)		
	0.84	−0.05	1.12	−0.54	−1.08	GLS	
	(9.70)	(−4.01)	(4.26)	(−4.67)	(−22.83)		
Italy	1.05	−0.09	1.12	−0.49	−0.82	OLS	.82
	(5.18)	(−1.06)	(2.53)	(−6.22)	(−6.98)		
	1.02	−0.13	1.21	−0.46	−0.83	GLS	
	(5.81)	(−1.88)	(3.17)	(−6.51)	(−8.14)		
Netherlands	0.56	−0.13	0.88	0.52	−1.13	OLS	.97
	(3.69)	(−1.91)	(3.03)	(−3.45)	(−24.51)		
	0.61	−0.06	0.70	−0.59	−1.13	GLS	
	(5.83)	(−1.20)	(3.61)	(−5.80)	(−35.44)		
United Kingdom	0.91	−0.12	0.30	−0.34	−0.82	OLS	.94
	(5.60)	(−2.32)	(2.26)	(−4.45)	(−13.21)		
	0.91	−0.10	0.30	−0.32	−0.84	GLS	
	(6.20)	(−2.20)	(2.48)	(−5.24)	(−16.90)		

[a]Period: 1952–1971; reserves $(R_j/H_j)gR_j$.
[b]Calculated on basis of M1.
Note: t-statistics are in parentheses.
Source: International Financial Statistics (Washington, D.C.: International Monetary Fund).

74

TABLE 4.2   International Reserve Flows[a]: U.S. Prices and Domestic Interest Rates

	Explanatory Variables						
Country j	Real Income	Interest Rate	Price Level	Money Multiplier[b]	Domestic Credit	Type	R^2
Austria	0.76	-0.21	1.00	-0.71	-1.19	OLS	.84
	(3.53)	(-2.64)	(1.98)	(-2.99)	(-5.70)		
	0.69	-0.19	1.09	-0.77	-1.19	GLS	
	(3.62)	(-3.00)	(2.33)	(-4.05)	(-7.17)		
Belgium	0.81	-0.10	0.22	-0.49	-1.08	OLS	.84
	(4.39)	(-1.32)	(0.49)	(-1.24)	(-8.81)		
	0.69	-0.05	0.37	-0.54	-1.04	GLS	
	(4.41)	(-0.94)	(1.00)	(-1.87)	(-11.47)		
Denmark	0.76	-0.03	1.24	-1.01	-0.96	OLS	.80
	(2.36)	(-0.09)	(1.91)	(-2.92)	(-5.94)		
	0.61	-0.04	1.18	-0.72	-0.88	GLS	
	(2.26)	(-0.15)	(1.93)	(-2.58)	-6.71)		
France	1.24	-0.42	0.22	-0.43	-0.94	OLS	.87
	(5.48)	(-3.97)	(0.49)	(-1.28)	(-8.93)		
	1.22	-0.37	1.13	-0.43	-0.88	GLS	
	(6.38)	(-4.17)	(2.75)	(-1.58)	(-10.33)		
Germany	0.88	-0.05	0.85	-0.59	-1.05	OLS	.97
	(8.33)	(-3.44)	(2.86)	(-3.72)	(-16.69)		
	0.84	-0.04	0.89	-0.56	-1.07	GLS	
	(8.44)	(-3.14)	(3.09)	(-3.96)	(-19.26)		
Italy	1.15	-0.03	1.08	-0.52	-0.79	OLS	.80
	(5.95)	(-0.34)	(2.12)	(-6.13)	(-6.56)		
	1.03	-0.02	1.38	-0.45	-0.85	GLS	
	(6.14)	(-0.40)	(3.13)	(-7.31)	(-9.82)		
Netherlands	0.70	-0.13	1.00	-0.57	-1.07	OLS	.97
	(4.74)	(-1.54)	(2.12)	(-3.02)	(-20.39)		
	0.54	-0.09	1.29	-0.74	-1.08	GLS	
	(4.55)	(-1.48)	(3.37)	(-5.61)	(-29.20)		
United Kingdom	0.83	-0.12	0.59	-0.33	-0.79	OLS	.96
	(5.86)	(-2.78)	(3.35)	(-5.12)	(-14.62)		
	0.83	-0.01	0.58	-0.33	-0.80	GLS	
	(5.98)	(-2.61)	(3.33)	(-5.38)	(-15.43)		

[a]Period 1952–71; reserves $(R_j/H_j)gR_j$.
[b]Calculated on basis of M1.
Note: t-statistics are in parentheses.
Source: International Financial Statistics (Washington, D.C.: International Monetary Fund).

TABLE 4.3 International Reserve Flows^a: U.S. Prices and Interest Rates

Country j	Real Income	Interest Rate	Price Level	Money Multi-plier^b	Domes-tic Credit	Type	R^2
Austria	0.64	−0.21	1.27	−0.81	−1.36	OLS	.80
	(2.71)	(−1.46)	(2.11)	(−2.93)	(−6.27)		
	0.60	−0.20	1.30	−0.78	−1.40	GLS	
	(3.25)	(−1.42)	(2.37)	(−4.77)	(−9.61)		
Belgium	0.78	−0.09	0.12	−0.23	−1.01	OLS	.84
	(4.22)	(−1.09)	(0.29)	(−0.75)	(−7.39)		
	0.56	−0.10	0.59	0.41	−0.93	GLS	
	(4.54)	(−1.35)	(1.88)	(−2.49)	(−12.96)		
Denmark	0.73	0.17	1.06	−1.10	−0.99	OLS	.81
	(2.37)	(1.15)	(1.78)	(−4.03)	(−8.04)		
	0.40	0.17	1.33	−0.89	−0.96	GLS	
	(2.05)	(1.13)	(2.51)	(−5.46)	(−13.36)		
France	1.21	−0.34	−0.39	0.35	−0.78	OLS	.85
	(4.95)	(−3.34)	(−0.89)	(1.07)	(−7.06)		
	1.21	−0.03	−0.41	0.36	−0.78	GLS	
	(6.21)	(−3.45)	(−1.00)	(1.53)	(−9.59)		
Germany	0.76	−0.07	1.03	−0.23	−1.10	OLS	.95
	(5.78)	(−0.71)	(2.57)	(−1.49)	(−13.60)		
	0.72	−0.06	1.09	−0.27	−1.11	GLS	
	(6.49)	(−0.65)	(2.89)	(−2.45)	(−19.01)		
Italy	1.34	−0.24	1.38	−0.52	−0.91	OLS	.85
	(7.54)	(−2.53)	(3.12)	(−7.39)	(−8.83)		
	1.13	−0.22	1.67	−0.48	−0.90	GLS	
	(7.27)	(−2.40)	(4.29)	(−8.80)	(−11.44)		
Netherlands	0.74	−0.15	0.84	−0.50	−1.08	OLS	.97
	(5.18)	(−1.78)	(2.07)	(−2.96)	(−22.16)		
	0.58	−0.15	1.22	−0.64	−1.08	GLS	
	(4.83)	(−1.80)	(3.34)	(−4.73)	(−27.82)		
United Kingdom	0.89	−0.07	0.47	−0.30	−0.83	OLS	.93
	(5.28)	(−1.16)	(2.35)	(−3.95)	(−13.55)		
	0.85	−0.05	0.51	−0.31	−0.87	GLS	
	(5.27)	(−0.89)	(2.56)	(−4.42)	(−15.30)		

^{a}Period: 1952–71; reserves $(R_j/H_j)gR_j$.
^{b}Calculated on basis of M1.
Note: t-statistics are in parentheses.
Source: International Financial Statistics (Washington, D.C.: International Monetary Fund).

meaningful for the OLS regressions only, indicated that autocorrelation was not a significant problem, thus averting the necessity of an iterative estimation procedure. All F-values were significant at the 0.05 level.* The R^2's are reported and all are in the .80 to .98 range which is relatively high, given that percentage change specifications are utilized. Summary statistics are not applicable for the seemingly unrelated regressions results, so that the contribution of this technique may be best measured by the consistent drop in the standard errors of the coefficients as reflected in the t-statistics movements. In general, the statistical results are encouraging.

One of the most important results from this exercise is the stability of the money demand coefficients (b_1, b_2, and b_3) as well as the money supply coefficients (b_4 and b_5) over the three separate specifications. In very few cases did the estimated coefficients move significantly when the U.S. price level and interest rate were substituted into the equations for respective domestic variables. The stability as well as the relative size and significance of the coefficients strongly support the integrated markets assumption of the monetary approach to the balance of payments.

The income elasticity of money demand, b_1, is significantly different from 0 and close to its hypothesized value of +1 in *all* cases except Denmark and then only when specification 8 is used. In most cases, especially with respect to specifications 6 and 7, the results for b_1 are not only as anticipated but strongly supported by strong t-statistic values. Since b_1 is the most important elasticity coefficient estimated in the policy sense and given that a stable money demand relationship is necessary to the use of the model for policy, these results are most positive.

The interest elasticity is consistent across all three specifications, being negative and relatively small in all cases, except Denmark. It is significant for the United Kingdom, Germany, France, and Austria and consistently insignificant for the other countries. This result is similar to findings by Zecher and Rutledge.[10] Akhtar notes that the role of the interest rate in a money demand function is not easily interpreted, since the former may influence the latter through either an own price effect or a cross-price effect or both.[11] The use of the U.S. rate as a proxy in Table 4.3 yields results which are poorer overall, but still consistent with those in the other tables. In summary, our results on b_2 conform to a priori expections of the integration of world capital markets.

The coefficient on prices, b_3, is close to +1 for all other countries except France and the United Kingdom. Overall, the results, both OLS

---

*The $\alpha = 0.05$ one-tailed test is used in all discussions in this section unless otherwise noted.

and GLS, conform to the theoretical specification. France and Britain, interestingly, are two of the four countries which exhibit strong interest rate influence on reserve flows, and the inflationary expectations component of interest rate movements may be serving as a proxy for the actual price variable.

The sign of the money multiplier variable coefficient, b_4, in all cases conforms to expectations in both OLS and GLS estimates. The size of the estimated coefficient is different from -1 for most cases, although Denmark and Belgium produced estimates very close to minus unity. The relative stability of this variable for most countries over the period tested could explain the results. When examined in its role as a policy variable our results support the hypothesis that a tightening of monetary policy through reserve requirements, or any other money multiplier control variable, ceteris paribus, will lead to reserve inflows.

The other money supply variable, domestic credit, appears to have a stronger effect on reserves. The coefficient on growth in domestic credit (scaled by its share of high-powered money), b_5, is very close to its hypothesized value of -1 in all cases tested. The t-statistics in the GLS regression range upward to 35.44 in the case of the Netherlands for specification (6) in Table 4.1. Even the OLS results never yield a t-statistic on b_5 less than 5.70.

The performance of both OLS and GLS (seemingly unrelated) results for both the money demand and money supply variables with respect to coefficient size and sign (for most countries) lends credence to the monetary approach. Indeed, the stability of the estimated coefficients when moving from domestic to U.S. price and interest rate variables is impressive. The improved performance of the GLS estimation suggests that the equations are not only stable but are also related over time. In summary, the regression results confirm our a priori notions about the effect of domestic money demand and domestically supplied money on reserve flows, as well as about the validity of the assumptions concerning integrated world goods, services and capital markets.

CONCLUSION

The empirical evidence presented here and developed in the context of the monetary approach to the balance of payments provides useful insights into world monetary adjustment on two counts. First, the use of a seemingly unrelated regressions approach in estimating international reserve flows for eight European nations improved estimating efficiency vis-à-vis standard OLS techniques. This gain in efficiency resulted from a correlation among the error terms in the equation set; thus, factors which are not included in the fundamental determinants, but that jointly affect the balance of payments of a group of countries, are captured in the estimation procedure. Secondly, the use of three specifications of the international reserve flow equation allowed for the examination of assumptions of unified goods and asset markets. In particular, the substitution of the U.S. price level and U.S. interest rate for national price and interest rate variables did not substantially alter the estimation results. This is a particularly impressive result, because it depends so heavily upon a high degree of integration in international goods and financial markets. In sum, the results strongly support the monetary approach views of world payments adjustment and, in addition, point to the usefulness of further research with theoretical and empirical attention to the interaction among countries in the context of highly integrated world markets.

NOTES

1. R. A. Mundell, *International Economics* (New York: Macmillan, 1968); Ryutaro Komiya, "Economic Growth and the Balance of Payments," *Journal of Political Economy* 77 (January-February 1969): 35–48; Harry G. Johnson, *Further Essays in Monetary Economics* (Cambridge, Mass.: Harvard University Press, 1973); and J. Richard Zecher, "Monetary Equilibrium and International Reserve Flows in Australia," *Journal of Finance* 29 (December 1974): 1523–30.

2. For a discussion of theoretical and empirical extensions of the basic money demand and supply relationships as they apply to reserve flows see W. Michael Cox, "Some Empirical Evidence on an Incomplete Information Model of The Monetary Aproach to the Balance of Payments," in *The Monetary Approach to International Adjustment*, ed., Bluford Putnam and W. Sykes Wilford (New York: Praeger, 1978); M. Connolly (this book, Chapter 1); Johnson, op. cit., pp. 229–49; J. Frenkel and Harry G. Johnson, eds., *The Monetary Approach to the Balance of Payments* (London: Allen and Unwin, 1976); Harry G. Johnson, "The Monetary Approach to Balance-of-Payments Theory: A Diagramatic Analysis," *The Manchester School of Economics and Social Studies* 43 (1975):220–74; A. Swoboda, "Gold, Dollars, Euro-Dollars and the World Money Stock and Fixed Exchange Rates," *American Economic Review* 68 (September 1978); and Bluford H. Putnam and D. Sykes Wilford, "Money, Income and Causality in the U.S. and the U.K.: A Theoretical Explanation of Different Findings," *American Economic Review* 68 (June 1978): 423–27.

3. Two papers that have discussed this problem are D. Sykes Wilford and Walton T. Wilford, "Monetary Approach to Balance of Payments: On World Prices and the Reserve Flow Equation," *Weltwirtschaftliches Archiv* 113 (1977): 31–39; and L. Girton and Donald Roper, "A Monetary Model of Fixed and Flexible Exchange Rates Applied to the Post-War Canadian Experience," *American Economic Review* 67 (September 1977): 537–48.

4. This procedure follows from seminal work for grouping equations done by Arnold Zellner, "An Efficient Method of Estimating Seemingly Unrelated Regressions and Tests for Aggregation Bias," *Journal of the American Statistical Association* 57 (1962): 348–68; followed by N. C. Kakwani, "The Unbiasedness of Zellner's Seemingly Unrelated Equations Estimates," *Journal of the American Statistical Association* 62 (1967): 141–42; and Jan

Kementa and R. F. Gilbert, "Small Sample Properties of Alternative Estimators of Seemingly Unrelated Regressions," *Journal of the American Statistical Association* 63 (1968): 1180–1200.

5. Johnson, *Further Essays in Monetary Economics*, pp. 229–49; and Zecher, op. cit.

6. M. A. Akhtar, B. H. Putnam, and D. S. Wilford, "Fiscal Constraints, Domestic Credit, and International Reserve Flows," *Journal of Money, Credit and Banking* 11 (1979).

7. Johnson, *Further Essays*, op. cit., p. 240.

8. Pentti J. K. Kouri and Michael G. Porter, "International Capital Flows and Portfolio Equilibrium," *Journal of Political Economy* 82 (May-June 1974): 443–67.

9. For a more complete discussion see Arnold Zellner and D. S. Huang, "Further Properties of Efficient Estimators for Seemingly Unrelated Regression Equations." *International Economic Review* 3 (1962):300–13.

10. Zecher, op. cit.; and John Rutledge, "Balance of Payments and Money Demand," paper presented to the Southern Economic Association meetings, November 1975, New Orleans, La.

11. M. A. Akhtar, "Demand Functions for High-Powered Money in the United States," mimeographed, Federal Reserve Bank of New York, 1977.

5

The Monetary Approach to
Balance of Payments and Developing Nations:
A Review of the Literature

Walton T. Wilford

The initial theoretical work on the monetary approach to balance of payments (MBOP), which was introduced by Harry G. Johnson and R. A. Mundell[1] and elaborated by a number of subsequent researchers,[2] provided the underpinnings for a growing literature on empirical applications as they relate to the developed industrial Western economies.[3] More recently the approach has been utilized to explain the relationship between monetary policy and the balance of payments adjustments for the economies of a myriad of developing countries whose growth is especially closely linked to international trade. The past ten years have witnessed a wealth of empirical studies that test the influence of domestic credit creation upon price movements.[4]

While the important policy directives that follow from the theoretical literature carry essentially the same relevance for both the developed Western economies and Third World nations, the latter present unique structural characteristics, and this survey focuses upon the contributions of the monetary approach as they relate to the small, open developing economies which are especially vulnerable to the vicissitudes of the international economy. The first section presents a simple monetary model in which world price determination is introduced, and the second section undertakes some observations on the usefulness of the approach as it relates specifically to Third World nations. Finally, some of the growing empirical contributions on Third World applications of the monetary approach are reviewed.

THE THEORY OF THE MONETARY APPROACH

Several models on the monetary approach have been offered.[5] Although not all of them explicitly view the adjustment process as a strictly monetary phenomenon, most models make three basic assumptions, including: (1) country X is a price taker in world goods, services, and capital markets; (2) country X maintains a fixed and stable exchange rate; and (3) the balance of payments does not affect real output. Utilizing these assumptions and knowledge of the monetary authority balance sheet, one may derive the standard reserve flow equation as follows. The explication of the model will provide a point of reference to permit the reader a reference when examining the empirical results discussed later.

The monetary model may be defined in eight basic steps.[6] The stock of high-powered money is related to the money supply in the following identity:

$$M = a \cdot H \tag{1}$$

where M = money supply
a = the money multiplier, and
H = stock of high-powered money.[7]

The monetary authority balance sheet appears as follows:

Monetary Authority Balance Sheet

Assets	Liabilities
R	H
OA	OL

where R = international reserves
OA = assets of monetary authority other than R, and
OL = liabilities other than high-powered money.

OA consists of central bank rediscounts, government bonds, and private notes, while OL includes primarily treasury and bank deposits at the central bank. Therefore,

$$H = R + (OA - OL) = R + D \tag{2}$$

Substituting equation 2 into 1 we derive a new money supply function

$$M = a \cdot (R + D). \tag{3}$$

Postulate a money demand equation in the form

$$M/P = Y^{\alpha_1} e/i^{\alpha_2} \tag{4}$$

where P = price index
Y = real income
i = rate of interest
e = stochastic disturbance term
α_1 = income elasticity of money demand, and
α_2 = interest elasticity of money demand.

Since we have implicitly assumed that money demand is homogeneous of degree one in prices, equation 4 may be rewritten as

$$M = PY^{\alpha_1} e/i^{\alpha_2} \tag{5}$$

and setting money supply equal to money demand

$$a \cdot (R + D) = PY^{\alpha_1} e/i^{\alpha_2} \tag{6}$$

Since we are interested in percentage changes in the variables, a transformation is necessary. Defining

$$gx = (1/x)(dx/dt)$$

where $x = a, R, D, Y, P$, and i

we obtain

$$ga + [R/(R + D)]gR + [D/(R + D)]gD = gP + \alpha_1 gY - \alpha_2 gi + e' \tag{7}$$

Defining $(R/H)gR$ as the dependent variable,

$$(R/H)gR = \alpha_1 Y - \alpha_2 gi + gP - ga - (D/H)gD + e' \tag{8}$$

As is evident from equation 8, the variation in foreign reserve position depends upon the percentage change in income (gY), the percentage change in the price level (gP), the percentage change in the money multiplier (ga), and the percentage change in domestic credit (gD) multiplied by D/H. This follows from equation 3 and shows that changes in the money stock may be related to changes in the amount of reserves.

Therefore, if changes in the money stock are a function of the postulated money demand relationship, movements in foreign reserves depend upon the same factors as do changes in money demand, all other things being equal.

As noted earlier, a positive α_1 is expected, since income is positively related to reserve flow via the money demand equation. Domestic credit is negatively related to reserve flows. Both of these conclusions are at variance with one or more Keynesian theories of balance of payments.

Introducing World Price Determination

Following a strict monetary aproach to price determination one may postulate an equation of exchange for the world. That is,

$$M(w)V(w) = P(w)Y(w) \tag{9}$$

where M = money supply
V = velocity
P = prices
Y = real income
w = world

The identity may be restated in terms of world prices

$$P(w) = \frac{M(w)V(w)}{Y(w)}$$

In growth terms the equation is

$$gP(w) = gM(w) = gV(w) - gY(w) \tag{10}$$

The view of the world as a closed economy permits us to utilize a monetary approach to price determination. Substituting this identity in the reserve flow equation for country X

$$gR\frac{R}{H}(X) = \alpha_1 gY(X) - \alpha_2 gi(X) + gM(w) + gV(w) - gY(w)$$
$$- ga(X) - gD\frac{D}{H}(X) + z \tag{11}$$

Assuming that both gY(X) and gY(w) have the same elasticity of money demand, equation 11 may be rewritten as

$$gR\frac{R}{H}(X) = \alpha_1[gY(X) - gY(w)] - \alpha_2gi(X) + gM(w) + gV(w)$$

$$- ga(x) - gD\frac{D}{H}(X) + z \tag{12}$$

Equation 12 is important to the developing economies because it highlights the impact of nondomestic influences on the level of reserves held by a country. In a sense, the equation shows how dependent the small country is on the rest of the world. More importantly, it highlights what variables are available to the authorities for conduct of policy. As before, the policy alternatives are straightforward: reserve management tools are the money multiplier and domestic credit. But even these tools must be used in conjunction with an acurate assessment of what is happening outside the small country.

Estimating Equations

The two equations relevant for empirical analysis are the equation for the standard reserve flow mechanism of the Zecher model, and the expanded alternative equation based on equation 12. The standard reserve flow equation for country X is

$$gR(\frac{R}{H})(X) = \alpha_1gY(X) - \alpha_2gi(X) + \beta_1gP(X)$$

$$- \beta_2ga(X) - \beta_3gD\frac{D}{H}(X) + z$$

where z = a stochastic disturbance.

The parameter β_1 is introduced to test the assumption of linear homogeneity in prices. The model explicitly asumes that money demand is homogeneous of degree one in prices. An estimated value of β_1 not significantly different from one would lend statistical support to the assumption.

The alternative reserve flow equation incorporating the world equation of exchange is

$$gR(\frac{R}{H})(X) = \alpha_1[gY(X) - gY(w)] - \alpha_2gi(X) + \xi_1gM(w) + \xi_2gV(w)$$
$$- \beta_2ga(x) - \beta_3gD\frac{D}{H}(X) + z$$

and is based upon equation 12.

OBSERVATIONS ON THE MODEL

The monetary approach to analyzing balance of payments (MBOP) and exchange rate issues has its roots in the nineteenth-century English classical school. David Laidler, in noting this fact, observes that the approach is different from the analytical approach utilized during the 1950s and 1960s to address balance of payments issues. He observes several key characteristics of the MBOP. First, the:

> monetary approach is macroeconomic rather than microeconomic in nature. It seeks to explain the behavior either of the overall balance of payments or of the exchange rate, by focusing directly on the interaction of simple aggregate relationships, rather than attempting to build up to such an explanation by way of modeling individually the determination of the various component accounts of the balance of payments.[7]

As Laidler observes, the MBOP asserts that the nonbank public's demand for banking system liabilities is a:

> stable function of a few arguments. In this respect the monetary approach to balance of payments theory represents a working out of the implications for an open economy of the characteristically monetarist proposition that there exists a stable demand for money function. ... It postulates that two of the arguments of such a function—real income and the real interest rate—may be taken as given, and that, under a fixed exchange rate so may the general price level. Given these further propositions, the balance of payments must depend upon the behavior of domestic credit expansion relative to that of the arguments of the demand for money function.[8]

The MBOP accepts (1) the classical assumption that the economy is at full employment, and (2) perfect commodity arbitrage to ensure the "law of one price."

Laidler[9] reconciles the monetarist MBOP long-run model with short-run Keynesian behavior as follows:

> Now there is no doubt that an approach to balance of payments analysis that postulates at the outset the existence of classical long-run equilibrium leaves a lot of questions unanswered, but that is not the same thing as saying that it is irrelevant . . . the academic literature now abounds with dynamic models, whose long-run steady state properties are such as would be predicted by "global monetarism" but whose short-run behavior may be extremely "Keynesian." Such models permit fiscal policy and other real shocks to influence real income and employment, make the interest rate partially a monetary phenomenon, allow devaluation to change the terms of trade, and so on. Such effects are temporary, of course, but that is not to say that they are necessarily of such short duration that they can be ignored.

Are the MBOP assumptions valid for the world economies? Laidler gives a qualified yes by noting that (1) virtually all economies seem to be characterized by a reasonably stable long-run demand for money function; (2) even the United States is sufficiently "open" and well integrated into the international capital markets for long-run linkages between domestic monetary policy on the one hand and the balance of payments/exchange rate on the other to be important; (3) the "law of one price" might operate for a world economy on average over rather long time periods, although in the short run, domestic price levels and exchange rates may diverge from their long-run equilibrium values that are better measured in years than months; and (4) deviations from full employment equilibrium can be of long duration, and can be influenced by traditional tools of Keynesian stabilization policy. That conclusion parallels Jeffrey Frankel's finding that Keynesian short-run effects on exchange rates and liquidity could occur with longer-run monetarist behavior.[10]

Khan and Willett[11] note that, by assuming purchasing-power parity and constant real interest rates, the MBOP models provide two propositions which are at variance with conventional wisdom. First, real income growth creates appreciation rather than depreciation of the exchange rate since the growing real income increases the home demand for money, causing an excess demand for money and currency appreciation. In the traditional Keynesian approach, real income growth increases demand for imports, widens the current account deficit and contributes to currency depreciation. Khan and Willett observe "it has been recognized in the Keynesian literature that higher growth could attract capital inflows which might dominate the deterioration in the trade balance and thus also lead to currency appreciation but at the beginning of 1970s the belief that higher growth would tend to lead to currency depreciation was probably still a majority view."[12]

The second "novel" conclusion of the MBOP, according to Khan and Willett, is that high interest rates are associated with a weak, rather than a strong, currency. In traditional analysis interest rate movements were assumed to reflect changes in real rates, with high rates reflecting tight money and generating capital inflows which strengthen the currency. The MBOP suggests, however, that "high interest rates reflect easy money and inflationary expectations which reduce the quantity of real balances demanded and lead to currency depreciation."[13]

RELEVANCE OF THE APPROACH
TO DEVELOPING ECONOMIES

While the role of demand and supply for money has been an implicit feature in most attempts to analyze balance of payments over the past five decades, more traditional tools of value theory—demand and supply schedules and their elasticities—occupied center stage during the 1920s and 1930s. With the collapse of international fixed exchange rates in the 1930s and mass unemployment, the Keynesian evolution viewed balance of payments adjustment not as an automatic process but as a policy problem for governments. Attention was concentrated on the "elasticity conditions" required for devaluation to have a favorable impact on the balance of payments.[14] Johnson argued that the "so-called 'elasticity approach' to devaluation proved to be demonstrably unsatisfactory for the immediate postwar period of full and overfull employment, owing to its implicit assumption of the existence of unemployed resources that could be mobilized."[15] Rudolf R. Rhomberg and Robert H. Heller noted that:

> as public preoccupation with the insufficiency of aggregate demand and with unemployment gave way in the postwar period to concern about inflation the Keynesian analytical tools were ... replaced by ... instruments of monetary analysis. While there is still controversy about the role of monetarism in solving problems of inflation and unemployment, the monetary approach—all the proponents of which are not "monetarists" in the narrower sense—has come to occupy a central place in the analysis of balance of payments problems.[16]

Donald S. Kemp points out that the so-called elasticities approaches isolated the trade or current accounts, while many times simply ignoring the capital account. One should be careful to differentiate among various definitions of the balance of payments for various discussions.[17]

It is clear that developing countries have experienced widely different inflation rates over time, whether they be on fixed or flexible exchange rate systems. Those on stable fixed exchange rate structures have generally exhibited inflation rates not significantly different from the rest of the world, while others have had inflation rates commensurate with their devaluation—that is, purchasing-power parity appears to hold in numerous empirical tests. Whether or not devaluation generates inflation or the reverse causality exists, domestic credit creation at some level, all other things being equal, requires fixed exchange rate adjustment through devaluation over time. The process has an impact upon the balance of payments. One can point to, for example, the Central American countries which have, in general, maintained relatively stable fixed exchange rates over time and have, in general, observed inflation commensurate with that of the developed nations. Mexico between 1954 and the mid 1970s could also be included in this group of nations that experienced increases in real output and balance of payments stability by controlling the level of domestic credit creation.[18] Other Latin American nations—Brazil, Chile, Argentina, and Uruguay, for example—experienced highly unstable exchange rates and dramatic inflation generated by huge government deficits, accompanied by devaluations over time. Bolivia has observed distinct periods of rapid inflation and devaluation (1952–58 and the 1980s) with little growth, and impressive exchange rate stability (1958–74) and increases in real output. Both the inflation-prone and the relatively stable countries face similar structural bottlenecks, which have been elaborated in the monetarist-structuralist literature on Latin America.

The policy dictates of the monetary approach for developing nations differ from the simple monetarist and structuralist conclusions espoused during the 1960s and, of course, from traditional Keynesian literature. Roberto Campos has noted that "the early controversy between monetarists and structuralists in Latin America has been exaggerated beyond all bounds"[19] and he observes that "we might jocosely define a monetarist as a structuralist in a hurry and a structuralist as a monetarist without policy-making responsibility." The monetary approach as it relates to developing countries does not require the rigidly simplistic monetarist tenets of classical liberalism: strict reliance upon the quantity theory, rigorous free trade, nonintervention by government, and subordination of the structural problems of developing countries to stabilization policies. Indeed, the monetary approach argues that a balanced attack on these structural problems is hindered by misguided monetary and fiscal policies aimed at short-term improvements in the current account, policies that may lead to negative capital account movements and, therefore, obviate the policy goals. The monetary approach argues that resources for dealing with structural problems—including unemployment, supply rigidities, and trade dependence—may be generated through the capital account in an economy with a stable monetary policy and consequent capital inflow. On the other hand, Vijah Joshi concludes that economic theory cannot deal satisfactorily with structural obstacles. He notes that "they are either put into the ceteris paribus clause in which case they are considered 'given'; or they are not, in which case they represent an 'inefficiency' which can be corrected by the price system."[20] In any case, the monetary approach hypothesizes that monetary expansion associated with government borrowing from the banking system is a key factor contributing to both balance of payment deficits and inflation.

The relevance of the MBOP adjustment for developing nations is based on a number of factors. First, it is rooted in the simple premise that the balance of payments is essentially a monetary phenomenon. It therefore places principal responsibility for orderly growth with a developing country's central bank monetary planners, who cannot take a passive position on the matter of expenditure policy goals of government. Second, the MBOP provides a less complicated empirical framework for policy evaluation. Rhomberg and Heller underscore the point, noting that "by focusing directly upon the relevant monetary aggregates, this approach eliminates the intractable problems associated with the estimation of numerous elasticities of international transactions and other parameters describing their interdependence, which are inherent in other approaches."[21] Third, the monetary approach aggregates the current and capital accounts, as opposed to the Keynesian preoccupation with the current account that is implicit in the "elasticities" and "income-absorption" approaches. Through integrating the capital and current accounts and focusing on the demand and supply for money and their consequent influence on reserve positions, the monetary approach argues that a developing country can maintain a negative current account balance yet promote balance of payments stability through attraction of capital inflows. This hypothesis has special relevance for developing countries in that it suggests that they can, through appropriate money management, create a stable climate to attract resources from abroad that may be utilized for development programs. In short, a stable monetary climate may permit attraction of reserves through the capital account, reserves which may be utilized to offset current account imports.

If, as several studies postulate, economic growth and foreign reserve flows are positively related, there follow implications for savings and foreign exchange gap theories. The foreign exchange gap may be reduced if growth accompanied by stable monetary policy permits inflow of foreign reserves to feed the current account import component. Development literature suggests that the internal swings and foreign exchange gaps constitute two separate constraints on the attainable rate of economic growth.[22] Even if savings are mobilized internally, growth may be frustrated by the inability of the system to utilize those resources to purchase requisite imports. As an aside, it is interesting to observe that Joshi notes that the distinction between the savings and foreign exchange constraints is of very limited usefulness and that it may be indeed harmful, since such a distinction lends respectability to the view that developing countries are hampered in their development solely by external foreign exchange factors.

The monetary approach argues that growth with monetary stability contributed positively to the foreign exchange position. D. Sykes Wilford[23] notes that Mexican international reserve flows for the 1954–74 period were:

> as would be predicted by the monetary approach. . . . If money demand grows faster than Mexican authorities wish to expand the money supply via their own resources, then reserves flow inward. Another result is that reserves flow inward, not outward, in response to increases in real income. . . . Mexico experienced rapid growth during the period. Therefore, reserves generally flowed inward, despite a worsening balance of trade. . . . The financial policies of the Central Bank . . . led to a stable reserve position for most of the period.

R. Zecher confirms a similar relationship between output, prices, and output for Australia.[24] He notes that:

> when demand for money grows faster than the supply of money would have grown due to domestic sources alone, international reserves tend to accumulate and to bring actual growth in the money stock closer to desired growth. As implied by the hypothesis, growth in output and the price level are associated with balance of payments surpluses, while growth in the domestically determined portion of the money stock tends to be associated with deficits and reserve outflows.

J. Marcus Fleming and L. Boissonneault noted in an empirical examination of 36 nations that "to the extent that capital is attracted by credit scarcity and high interest rates, an autonomous policy to reduce the expansion of credit would tend to reduce the flow of net capital exports or increase that of net capital imports, thus bringing about a swifter remedial effect on the balance of payments."[25]

In short, if the foreign exchange gap is the critical development bottleneck, it would appear that appropriate management of domestic money stocks can, in a growth economy, encourage foreign reserve inflows.

Fourth, supporters argue that policy prescriptions are more simple and manageable for developing countries, where data on monetary variables from central banks are often more readily available and reliable than are the data from numerous national accounts recording transactions of various goods, services, and capital items that are required in the "elasticities" approach. Indeed, the International Monetary Fund cites as one major reason that it has used monetary approach models for developing countries during the past 25 years the fact that monetary statistics have usually been available, while more detailed national income accounting data for the "elasticities" approach were less available and/or reliable.

Fifth, it is contended that the developing countries typically have simpler financial structures and have, therefore, fewer alternatives to holding funds in monetary form or spending them on domestic or foreign goods and services or on foreign financial instruments. Indeed, the IMF suggests that the MBOP permits a "meaningful approximate analysis of the relevant aggregates with the help of models that are small enough to be calculated with pencil and paper."[26]

Sixth, the MBOP framework is appropriate for Latin American countries where control over domestic credit is utilized as a major instrument of money management and balance of payments control. Further, the approach pinpoints ultimate administrative responsibility for reserve flows in the small, open economy. J. J. Polak[27] notes that:

> it may be difficult—perhaps in some circumstances humanly impossible—for the system to withstand demands for credit from government or from other insistent borrowers; and in such circumstances, the desire to make public development expenditure, or to construct private factories, may be considered the cause of the expansion in the economy. But for purposes of monetary analysis and monetary policy, there is a clear gain in clarity if the responsibility is pinpointed for credit expansion. The economic development could also have been financed by higher taxes or by a foreign loan. In these situations, the desire to spend for a particular purpose would not have led to a payments problem. In a real sense, the credit expansion is the cause of the payments problem.

Seventh, the monetary approach permits monetary authorities to measure more effectively the overall equilibrium adjustment of prices, output, and foreign reserves positions to discretionary policies aimed at influencing domestic credit. D. Lachman[28] reiterates the uniqueness of the MBOP by noting that "in the closed economy . . . the monetary . . . base is regarded as a policy instrument," while in the relatively open economies that generally characterize the Third World, the "monetary base is no longer regarded as being determined solely by policy, since it may be changed by balance of payments surpluses or deficit." D. S. Wilford and W. T. Wilford concluded, based upon evidence for Honduras and Mexico, that "monetary authorities can control the composition of money stock between foreign reserves and domestically created credit," but that they "cannot influence the absolute level of monetary stocks without sacrificing the fixed exchange rate." Further, it can be noted that "restrictive monetary policy by the small economy is rendered ineffectual and central banks of such economies are, by and large, dependent upon movements of world monetary variables beyond their control."[29] Manuel Guitian notes that in "any economy the public determines the *real* quantity of money that it desires to hold . . . the banking community and, in particular, the monetary authorities do not directly control the total money supply but only the part that is made available through domestic credit." Further, he notes that "the attainment of a quantity of money desired by the community is compatible with different movements in international reserves that may not be consistent with the balance of payments objectives of the authorities."[30] The MBOP, therefore, highlights for the developing country the equilibrium adjustment impacts of domestic credit as the control variable for stabilization purposes. It must, however, be viewed as a long-run explanation of adjustment, and a number of those who espouse the MBOP admit to potentially Keynesian short-run policies that could provide temporary balance of payments relief.

In summary, given that most developing countries are small, open systems, the MBOP may permit planners to implement and evaluate development strategies by focusing upon relatively few monetary variables which are more generally statistically reliable than the myriad of national accounts data required by other approaches. Further, the monetary approach requires less discretionary intervention in planning decisions, intervention that is often based upon imperfect knowledge and that, therefore, tends to obfuscate, rather than promote, long-run development objectives.

SOME EMPIRICAL RESULTS FOR THIRD WORLD NATIONS

In this section some results of empirical studies of the monetary approach are reported. Although various models were used by different researchers, the basic formulations can find their roots in the model presented in this chapter's first section. The reader of this survey of results for Third World economies may find it useful to refer back to equations 8 and 12, as well as to their counterpart estimating equations.

Michael Connolly and Dean Taylor: 18 Devaluations in Developing Countries

Michael Connolly and Dean Taylor[31] test the proposition that a devaluation will improve the balance of payments unless accompanied by an "approximately equiproportionate expansion in domestic credit."[32] The sample includes 18 independent devaluations in developing countries over the 1965–70 period. They conclude: devaluation in developing countries is successful in improving payments imbalances, "particularly in light of the fact that it serves the second objective of dismantling exchange controls;"[33] the price adjustment following devaluation involves primarily a substantial increase in the price of traded goods and secondarily a moderate increase in the overall rate of inflation; and, contrary to the findings of Richard Cooper, correlation exists between the change in domestic credit in the banking system in the year following devaluation and the improvement in the goods and service balance for the same year. Connolly and Taylor reconcile their findings with those of Cooper by noting that:

> his [Cooper's] finding differs from ours primarily in that his is for only the merchandise account, while the monetary approach has to do with the overall balance of payments. The monetary argument is basically that one cannot expect devaluation to improve the overall balance of payments unless it lease to an increased demand for money unmatched by an increase in domestic credit.[34]

M. S. Khan: Venezuela

M.S. Khan applies the monetary model to the Venezuelan economy over the 1968–73 period. During this period Venezuela maintained a fixed exchange rate and operated with relatively few restrictions on trade and none on international movement of capital. Khan finds that his 11-equation model, which was estimated on a quarterly basis for Venezuela during 1968–73, gave encouraging results, in terms of both the estimates of the structural equations and the model's ability to track the behavior of key macroeconomic variables. He views the model as "sufficiently general to appear to be relevant to a number of countries."[35]

Maxwell Fry: Afghanistan

Maxwell Fry applies the monetary approach to Afghanistan, a country that has maintained a flexible exchange rate historically.[36] Using the model of

John Rutledge,[37] Fry finds that Afghanistan, with its highly undeveloped monetary sector, fits the reduced-form equation (derived from a conventional demand-for-money function and the purchasing-power parity relationship) very well for the period 1955–72. He noted that the model showed quite remarkable explanatory power, with R^2 = .99, D − W = 2.65, and F = 2705.78. However it must be noted that Fry's results are somewhat tenuous, as pointed out by B. Putnam and J. Van Belle in "A Monetary Approach to Afghanistan's Flexible Exchange Rate: A Comment," *Journal of Money, Credit, and Banking* (February 1978):117–18. Although some of Fry's results were found to be statistically unclear, Putnam and Van Belle confirmed his eventual conclusions supporting the monetary approach.

D. S. Wilford and W. T. Wilford: Honduras

In this analysis an estimation is made of a form of the reserve flow equation as it follows from the assumption of linear homogeneity in prices.[38] The specification below constrains money demand to be free of money illusion and is, therefore, a strict monetarist case. The equation is

$$(\frac{R}{H})gR - gP = \alpha_1 gy - \alpha_2 gi - \beta_2 ga - \beta_3 (\frac{D}{H})gD + u$$

Table 5.1 gives the empirical results for estimating equations utilizing annual data for 1950–74. The results conform closely to the expectations, as all coefficients are significantly different from zero; have the hypothesized signs; and are statistically close to their hypothesized values at the .05 risk level. The size of the interest elasticity coefficients is of interest in that it suggests that changes in interest rates do not significantly affect holding of money vis-à-vis less liquid assets. The results are consistent with those of other studies analyzing less-developed countries.* In less-developed

---

*One almost universal result of Third World empirical balance of payments studies is the lack of significance of the interest variable in the money demand equations. The J. Villasuso, W. T. Wilford, and A. M. Agapos study found interest to be consistently insignificant in Costa Rica.[39] D. S. Wilford and J. R. Zecher find "the signs for the coefficient for the interest variable are consistent with the model though standard errors are high ...[and] could be due to lack of a well-developed capital market ..."[40] Their substitution of U.S. interest rate as proxies yielded insignificant differences. (On the assumption that Mexican reported rates were questionable in accuracy and not representative of market rates, they substituted U.S. interest rates. The results were not significantly improved, however.) D. Lachman notes for South Africa that "the variables included to measure the opportunity

financial markets, the costs of rearranging portfolios on the basis of interest rate movement are higher than they are in developed financial markets, since there are asset alternatives. Thus the estimated $|\alpha_2| < .2$ is entirely consistent with rational behavior in some less-developed capital market economies. The reserve flow equation shows that a 1 percent increase in domestically created money, all other things being equal, will generate approximately a 1 percent loss in foreign reserves. All coefficients are close to predicted values, and the coefficient for gP in regression 3 supports the assumption of the absence of money illusion. The coefficients, as expected, remain stable between regression 3 and 4, with the F-levels for both acceptable at the .01 risk level. The R^2's indicate that about 80 percent of the variation in the dependent variable is explained.

The most important coefficients for the policy-maker, β_2 and β_3, are significantly different from zero and not significantly different from their hypothesized values. Perhaps most important from the policy standpoint is that the coefficients of (D/H)gD are very close to the predicted value of -1 in Table 5.1.

The data show that, as the MBOP hypothesizes, the Central Bank of Honduras cannot control the level of its money stock in the long run. The composition of the stock, however, may be influenced, in that domestic monetary policy can meet the demands for money either through domestically created money stock or through foreign reserves. The implications for monetary policy are, therefore, clear. If the central bank desires a balance of payments position appropriate for maintenance of a fixed exchange rate, it should select a rate of growth in domestic credit and the money multiplier at a rate equal to, or slightly less than, the internal demand for money. Since a stable exchange rate has been one of the major goals of monetary policy in this Central American nation during the past 25 years, it would do well to consider the implications of the MBOP in the implementation of its monetary policy.

B. B. Aghevli: Indonesia

B. B. Aghevli develops a model including four broad areas: demand for real money balances, supply of nominal money, government budget, and

---

cost of holding money although in all cases of the expected sign are not always significantly different from zero."[41] Insignificance of interest rates is probably attributable to a number of factors, including inaccurate reporting of interest rate data for many developing countries, undeveloped financial markets, and interest rate strucures established by nonmarket influences. The rate of inflation might be a better measure of the opportunity cost of capital.

TABLE 5.1 Foreign Reserve Flow Regressions for Honduras: 1950–74* (annual data)

| Regression Number | Dependent Variable | Income Elasticity α_1 | Interest Rate Elasticity α_2 | Elasticity β_1 | β_2 | β_3 | R^2 | DW | F Level |
α_1	α_1								
1	$\frac{R}{H}gR$	1.11 (4.09)	-0.16 (-2.01)	1.12 (3.61)	-0.94 (-3.47)	-0.88 (-6.76)	.81	2.46	19.11
2	$\frac{R}{H}gR - gp$	1.07 (4.42)	-0.149 (-2.16)	— —	-0.968 (-3.85)	-0.88 (-6.99)	.79	2.41	25.24

*Data sources are Central Bank of Honduras and *International Financial Statistics* (Washington, D.C.: International Monetary Fund). The U.S. long-term (as reported by IFS) interest rate is used as a proxy for the world interest rate and therefore the Honduran rate, since no reliable series on the Honduran market rate of interest are available. This U.S. proxy for the world rate follows from the assumption of unified capital markets.

Source: D. Sykes Wilford and Walton T. Wilford, "On the Monetary Approach to the Balance of Payments: The Small, Open Economy," *The Journal of Finance* 33 (March 1978): 322.

balance of payments, with real income considered exogenous; he tests the model for Indonesian quarterly data for 1968–73.[42] The period was characterized by relative price stability and rapid economic growth. He finds that demand for real balances for both the narrow and broad definitions of money, with a R^2 at the .99 level, and that long-run income elasticity for narrow and broad definitions of money demand are 2.18 and 2.29 respectively. The elasticities are "high but by no means unusual for a developing country in which in the absence of other financial assets, the public holds most of its savings in monetary form, and in which, moreover, the monetised sector of the economy is expanding rapidly."[43] Indonesian supply elasticity of exports with respect to income was close to unity (implying that the export sector grows in the same proportion as the rest of the economy), and the coefficient of the relative price term is also significant.

Aghevli estimates the long-run rate of growth of reserve, narrow, and broad money consistent with a 7 percent real growth rate for Indonesia and an 18 percent inflation rate to be a relatively high 30 percent, attributable largely to the high long-run income elasticity of demand for real balances.*

D. Sykes Wilford and J. Richard Zecher: Mexico

D. Sykes Wilford and J. Richard Zecher anaiyze the fixed exchange rate period 1955–75 for Mexico under monetary model assumptions. Mexico throughout the 20-year period experienced negative trade balances. However, in all but six years, there were net inflows of foreign reserves, and the capital account for the 20 years was consistently sufficient to maintain a positive balance of payments. Wilford and Zecher note that "contrary to many standard balance of payments theories, rapid economic growth (averaging 6–7 percent) has been coincidental with the strengthening of Mexico's foreign reserve position."[44] They contend that this was achieved by pursuing deficit financing policies not through excessive increases in domestic credit, but through transference of savings from the private to the public sector by use of financial intermediaries. They further contend that a number of international and internal factors operated together to diminish the ability of the central bank to control injections of

---

*It is becoming increasingly clear that in developing countries where monetization of the barter sector is proceeding at a substantial pace, the demand for money-income elasticity coefficients are higher than those observed for industrialized nations. Further empirical and theoretical research remains to be undertaken in explaining the secular changes in the elasticities over time as nonmarket sectors are monetized.

domestic credit and that these influences contributed to the instability of the peso, culminating in devaluation. Their standard monetary reserve flow equations for the period, equation 8, exhibited low standard errors and consistently high R^2's, ranging from .85 to .92. Interest rates were insignificant in the money demand equations. The model was useful in explaining the data throughout the period until 1975. The authors note that "the experience in 1975 was far different from that predicted by the model. Instead of the implied outflow of reserves sufficient to reduce money growth by about 16 percent, there was an inflow sufficient to increase money growth by 14.5 percent. This whopping error largely reflects the desperate attempts of the Mexican authorities to hold the exchange rate by borrowing from abroad, particularly the fourth quarter of 1975."[45] They conclude that Mexico can again achieve and maintain a fixed exchange with the United States and an approximate zero balance of payments, expanding domestic credit at a rate approximately equal to U.S. inflation plus the rate of growth in real output in Mexico.

N. C. Miller and S. S. Askin: Brazil and Chile

N. C. Miller and S. S. Askin examine the degree to which the balance of payments of

> two small, relatively open economies influences the ability of their monetary authorities to control the money supply . . . and . . . investigate to what extent variations in the domestic component of the monetary base are offset via international payments imbalances, and then to what extent the authorities sterilize the effects of payments imbalances on the monetary base.[46]

They test for the classical payments adjustment for Brazil and Chile, and conclude that monetary authorities "have essentially complete monetary autonomy in the long run as long as international reserves are large enough to finance a payments deficit [and] there is not evidence that the classical adjustment mechanism functions in either country."[47] Although they find that "even if their exchange rates had remained constant, Brazil and Chile would have had almost complete control over their money supplies," such control only extended as long as they were able to finance a payments deficit. One wonders, however, how long international reserves can remain large enough to finance payments deficits and, therefore, the extent to which their findings actually deny monetary predictions. In general, it is the reserve position (precipitated by excessive expansion of domestic credit) that has a direct impact on those resources utilized to sterilize payments imbalances. Recent Brazilian experience suggests that authorities have lost control of reserve positions, and an updated study of the Brazilian experience could well yield conclusions for the MBOP significantly different from Miller and Askin's results.

M. Blejer, Feige and Johannes, and S. Gupta: Domestic Credit and International Reserves

Mario Blejer in 1979 analyzed several developing countries to determine if, as the MBOP predicts, a growth in domestic credit would generate an outflow of foreign exchange reserves.[48] Although MBOP theory assumes causality from domestic credit to foreign reserves, Blejer suggests that it is possible for the reverse causality to exist. Consider a situation in which the central bank sterilizes the impact of exogenous changes in foreign reserves on the domestic money supply, particularly when authorities pursue an interest rate stabilization policy. A second situation in which causality might run from foreign exchange to domestic credit would be when banks borrow from the central bank when confronted with a loss of reserves through an outflow of international reserves. Using the well-known Sims[49] test for causality, he concluded that causality is unidirectional from domestic credit to reserve flow.

Sanjeev Gupta, in a 1984 paper,[50] critiques the Blejer paper by noting that Blejer (1) used only one test of causality instead of three available tests; (2) failed to account for problems associated with potential serial autocorrelation in the residuals of the Sims regressions; and (3) did not disaggregate sufficiently to avoid possible bias (Gupta recommends monthly rather than quarterly data series).[51] Similar criticism of the Blejer paper was made in a 1981 study by Edgar Feige and James Johannes, in which the MBOP was retested for six developed nations after taking account of the three criticisms.[52]

The Gupta study tested for the nature of the relationship between the components of the monetary base for four developing countries: India, Mexico, Malaysia, and Taiwan. He utilizes the Granger,[53] Haugh,[54] and Sims[55] tests for causality. Gupta concludes that, for Granger tests, "causality runs unidirectionally from international reserves to domestic credit for Taiwan, and from domestic credit to international reserves for India. However, for Malaysia, no causality in either direction is observed; in the case of Mexico the relationship is bidirectional. If these relationships held instantaneously then it would seem that in Taiwan, there is either a sterilization of changes in international reserves or borrowing by commercial banks of the nature discussed earlier. However, in India, an exogenous change in domestic credit causes a change in international reserves."[56] He concludes that, "when instantaneous effects are also considered, the relationship between [the change in domestic credit and the change in international reserves] for all countries is bidirectional." This type of relationship is fully consistent with the MBOP. The sterilization and commercial bank scenarios could interact simultaneously with the direction of causality suggested by the MBOP to yield a bidirectional relationship.

W. Khan and T. D. Willett:
Second Thoughts on the Monetary Approach

In a 1984 review of empirical work on the MBOP, Khan and Willett survey the empirical evidence presented by twelve studies.[57] Table 1 in that study compares the results of various monetary exchange rate models for this group of studies which includes work by Bilson (1978 and 1979), Khan (1979), Frankel (1979), Hodrick (1978), Kohlhagen (1979), Driskill (1980), Keran and Zeldes (1980), and Caves and Feige (1980). Khan and Willett conclude that the "first generation of studies reported results favorable to the monetary approach with its 'new' hypothesis that high interest rates would be associated with weak rather than strong currencies, and more rapid economic growth would be associated with appreciation rather than depreciation."[58] However, their analysis of more recent studies suggests that, while the monetary approach model "fits the data quite well for some countries over some time periods, these relationships do not hold up systematically across countries and over time."[59] They point to a number of technical issues of econometric estimation and model specifications, and suggest the need to distinguish between short-run and longer-run applications of the MBOP. Finally, they suggest that the MBOP models appear to have validity in the long run, but are not especially effective for short-run analysis.

Khan and Willett suggest several reasons why the monetary model has not been as robust as earlier thought, including (1) instability in the demand for money, (2) real factors do appear to have a major influence on exchange rate behavior, (3) the coefficients on the real income variable are unstable in magnitude and significance, (4) use of income differentials constrains income elasticities to be equal in both countries when, in fact, if they are not, the estimated coefficients will be biased.[60] They conclude that the statement that "money matters" has more validity than its converse, but they reject the proposition that "only money matters."[61]

SUMMARY

Most of the monetary studies for Third World nations appear to confirm the hypothesis that international reserve levels are positively related to the level of domestic income and the exchange rate, and negatively related to the domestic component of the monetary base. Further, in economies that are highly dependent upon foreign trade as are the developing countries, the money supply should grow at a rate that, over the long run, maintains an equilibrium in the foreign balance. Finally, monetary authorities can influence short-term movements in the money supply, but they cannot indefinitely counteract long-term excess money stocks unless they are prepared to alter the foreign exchange rate from time to time.

Michael Mussa summarizes empirical studies on the MBOP as follows:

> A number of empirical studies have applied the monetary model of the exchange rate to actual data. By and large, these studies conclude that the behavior of exchange rates is consistent with the monetary model and that this model is of assistance in explaining a significant fraction of exchange rate movements. In my judgment, this body of evidence is sufficiently impressive to justify the conclusion that the monetary model of the exchange rate does have empirical content.[62]

That observation appears to be as true in 1985 as it was in 1979, although new questions as to short-run validity of the model have emerged during the past five years. Further country-by-country empiricism is required if the tenets of the MBOP are to be more uniformly accepted within the profession.

NOTES

1. Harry G. Johnson, *Further Essays in Monetary Economics* (Cambridge, Mass.: Harvard University Press, 1973); and Robert A. Mundell, *International Economics* (New York: Macmillan, 1968).

2. See, for example, Mario Blejer, "On Causality and the Monetary Approach to Balance of Payments," *European Economic Review* 12 (July 1979): 289–96; S. Edwards, "The Demand for International Reserves and Exchange Rate Adjustments: The Case of LDCs," *Economica* 50 (1983): 269–80; J. A. Frenkel, "A Monetary Approach to the Exchange Rate: Doctrinal Aspects and Empirical Evidence," *Scandinavian Journal of Economics* 78 (1976): 200–24; J. A. Frenkel and C. A. Rodriguez, "Portfolio Equilibrium and the Balance of Payments: A Monetary Approach," *American Economic Review* 65 (September 1975): 674–88; F. H. Hahn, "The Monetary Approach to the Balance of Payments," *Journal of International Economics* 7 (August 1977): 231–49; Harry G. Johnson, "Money and the Balance of Payments," *Banca Nazionale del Lavoro Quarterly Review* no. 116 (March 1976):

3–18; Harry G. Johnson, "The Monetary Approach to the Balance of Payments Theory," in *International Trade and Money*, eds., M. B. Connolly and A. K. Swoboda (London: Allen and Unwin, 1975); Harry G. Johnson, "The Monetary Approach to the Balance of Payments Theory: A Diagrammatic Analysis," *The Manchester School* (1975); Donald S. Kemp, "A Monetary View of Balance of Payments," *Federal Reserve Bank of St. Louis Review* 57, no. 4 (April 1975): 14–22; David Laidler, "Some Policy Implications of the Monetary Approach to Balance of Payments and Exchange Rate Analysis, *Oxford Economic Papers* (33, Supplement: July, 1981); A. R. Nobay and Harry G. Johnson, "Monetarism: A Historic-Theoretic Perspective," *Journal of Economic Literature* 15 (June 1977): 470–85; M. Obstfeld, "Balance of Payments Crises and Devaluation," *Journal of Money, Credit, and Banking* 16, 2 (May 1984): 208–17; and R. Ramanathan, "Monetary Expansion, Balance of Trade and Economic Growth," *Economic Record* 51 (March 1975): 31–39.

3. W. Michael Cox, "Some Empirical Evidence on an Incomplete Information Model of the Monetary Approach to the Balance of Payments: The Canadian Experience," in *The Monetary Approach to International Adjustment*, eds., Bluford H. Putnam and D. Sykes Wilford (New York: Praeger, 1978); Frenkel, op. cit., Jeffrey Frankel, "On the Mark: A Theory of Floating Exchange Rates based on Real Interest Rate Differentials," *American Economic Review* 69, 4 (September 1979): 610–21; J. Frankel, "On the Mark: Reply," *American Economic Review* (December 1981): 1075–82; Thomas Courchene, "The Price-Specie Flow Mechanism and the Gold Exchange Standard: Some Exploratory Empiricism Relating to the Endogeneity of Country Money Balances," in *The Economics of Common Currencies*, eds., H. G. Johnson and A. K. Swoboda (London: Allen and Unwin, 1973); and R. Zecher, "Monetary Equilibrium and International Reserve Flows in Australia," *Journal of Finance* 29 (December 1974): 1523–30; David Laidler and P. O'Shea, "An Empirical Macro Model of an Open Economy Under Fixed Exchange Rates: The United Kingdom 1954–70," *Economica* 47 (May 1980): 141–58.

4. See, among others, B. B. Aghevli, "Money, Prices and the Balance of Payments Indonesia 1968–73," *Journal of Development Studies* 13 (January 1977): 37–57; B. B. Aghevli, "Experiences of Asian Countries with Various Exchange Rate Policies," in *Exchange Rate Rules: The Theory, Performance and Prospects of the Crawling Peg*, ed., John Williamson (New York: 1981), 298–319; Bijan B. Aghevli and Mohsin S. Khan, "The Monetary Approach to Balance of Payments Determination: An Empirical Test," in *The Monetary Approach to the Balance of Payments* (Washington, D.C.: International Monetary Fund, 1977), pp. 275–90; M. I. Blejer, "The Monetary Approach to Devaluation: A Graphical Presentation," *Weltwirtschaftliches Archiv* 113 (1977): 348–52; M. J. Fry, "A Monetary Approach to Afghanistan's Flexible Exchange Rate," *Journal of Money, Credit, and Banking* 8 (May 1976): 219–25; Manuel Guitian, "Credit Versus Money as an Instrument of Control," in *The Monetary Approach*, op. cit., pp. 227–42; M. S. Khan, "A Monetary Model of Balance of Payments: The Case of Venezuela," *Journal of Monetary Economics* 2 (July 1976): 311–32; Mohsin S. Khan, "The Determination of the Balance of Payments and Income in Developing Countries," in *The Monetary Approach*, op. cit., pp. 243–74; D. Lachman, "A Monetary Approach to the South African Balance of Payments," South African *Journal of Economics* 43 (September 1975): 271–83; N. C. Miller and S. S. Askin, "Monetary Policy and the Balance of Payments in Brazil and Chile," *Journal of Money, Credit, and Banking* 8 (May 1976): 227–38; I. Otani and Y. C. Park, "A Monetary Model of the Korean Economy," *International Monetary Fund Staff* Paper 23 (March 1976): 164–99; Rudolf R. Rhomberg, "Money, Income, and the Foreign Balance," in *The Monetary Approach*, op. cit., pp. 163–84; Rudolf R. Rhomberg and Robert H. Heller, "Introductory Survey," in *The Monetary Approach*, op. cit., pp. 1–14; and D. Sykes Wilford, *Monetary Policy and the Open Economy: Mexico's Experience* (New York: Praeger, 1977).

5. See D. Sykes Wilford and Walton T. Wilford, "Monetary Approach to Balance of Payments: On World Prices and the Reserve Flow Equation," *Weltwirtschaftliches Archiv* No. 1 (1977): 31–39, for empirical tests on Mexico and Honduras using the equations developed in this section.

6. See R. Zecher, "Monetary Equilibrium and International Reserve Flows in Australia," *Journal of Finance* 29 (December 1974): 1523–30; and Harry G. Johnson, *Further Essays*, op. cit.

7. David Laidler, op. cit., p. 70.

8. Ibid., p. 71.

9. Ibid., pp. 71–72.

10. J. Frankel, op. cit.

11. Waseem Khan and Thomas D. Willett, "The Monetary Approach to Exchange Rates: A Review of Recent Empirical Studies," *Kredit und Kapital* 17 (1984): 199–222.

12. Ibid., p. 199.

13. Ibid., p. 200.

14. Stock of high-powered money includes coins, currency, commercial bank deposits at the central bank minus interbank deposits.

15. For short reviews of the evolution of theoretical thought on balance of payments theory, see Johnson "The Monetary Approach," op. cit.; Rhomberg and Heller, op. cit.; and Marina V. N. Whitman, "Global Monetarism and the Monetary Approach to the Balance of Payments," *Brookings Papers on Economic Activity* no. 3 (1975): 491–536. A dissenting view of the monetary approach presented in an historical context is found in D. A. Currie, "Some Criticisms of the Monetary Analysis of Balance of Payments Correction," *Economic Journal* 86 (September 1976): 508–22.

16. Johnson, "The Monetary Approach," op. cit., pp. 208–09.

17. Rhomberg and Heller, op. cit., p. 2.

18. For empirical studies of Central America and Mexico from the monetary approach perspective, see D. Sykes Wilford, op. cit; D. Sykes Wilford, "Price Levels, Interest Rate, Open Economies, and a Fixed Exchange Rate: The Mexican Case, 1954–1974," *Review of Business and Economic Research* 12, no. 3 (Spring 1977); Wilford and Wilford, op. cit.; D. Sykes Wilford and Walton T. Wilford, "On the Monetary Approach to the Balance of Payments: The Small, Open Economy," *The Journal of Finance* 33 (March 1978): 319–23. D. Sykes Wilford and J. Richard Zecher, "Monetary Policy and the Balance of Payments in Mexico, 1955–73," *Journal of Money, Credit, and Banking* 11 (August 1979): 340–48.

19. Roberto do Oliviera Campos, "Economic Development and Inflation with Special Reference to Latin America," in Organization for Economic Cooperation and Development, *Development Plans and Programmes*, OECD Development Center, Paris (1964): 129–37.

20. See Vijah Joshi, "Saving and Foreign Exchange Constraints," in *Unfashionable Economics*, ed. P. P. Streeten (London: 1970).

21. Rhomberg and Heller, op. cit., p. 4.

22. H. B. Chenery and M. Bruno, "Development Alternatives in an Open Economy," *Economic Journal* (1962).

23. D. Sykes Wilford, *Monetary Policy*, op. cit., p. 50.

24. Zecher, op. cit., p. 1530.

25. J. Marcus Fleming and Lorette Boissonneault, "Money Supply and Imports," in *The Monetary Approach*, op. cit., p. 146.

26. Rhomberg and Heller, op. cit., pp. 6–7.

27. J. J. Polak, "Monetary Analysis of Income Formation and Payments Problems," in *The Monetary Approach*, op. cit., p. 27.

28. Lachman, op. cit., p. 272.

29. Wilford and Wilford, "Monetary Approach to Balance of Payments: On World Prices and the Reserve Flow Equation," op. cit., p. 38.

30. Guitian, op. cit., p. 235.

31. Michael Connolly and Dean Taylor, "Adjustment to Devaluation in a Small Country," *De-Economist* 124 (1976): 319–27.

32. Ibid., p. 849.

33. Ibid.

34. Ibid., p. 858.

35. M.S. Khan, "A Monetary Model of Balance of Payments: The Case of Venezuela," *Journal of Monetary Economics* 2 (July 1976): 330.

36. M. J. Fry, "A Monetary Approach to Afghanistan's Flexible Exchange Rate," *Journal of Money, Credit, and Banking* 8 (May 1976): 219–25.

37. John Rutledge, *A Monetarist Model of Inflationary Expectations* (Lexington, Mass.: Lexington Books, 1974).

38. Wilford and Wilford, "On the Monetary Approach to the Balances of Payments: The Small, Open Economy," op. cit.

39. See J.Villasuso, W.T.Wilford, and A. M. Agapos, "The Demand for Money in an Emerging Nation: Costa Rica," *Philippine Economic Journal* (Second Trimester 1974), no. 2: 130–34.

40. D. Sykes Wilford and J. Richard Zecher, "Monetary Policy and the Balance of Payments in Mexico 1955–73," *Journal of Money, Credit, and Banking* 11 (1979).

41. Lachman, op. cit., p. 280.

42. Aghevli, op. cit.

43. Ibid., p. 46.

44. Wilford and Zecher, op. cit.

45. Ibid, p. 346.

46. Miller and Askin, op. cit., p. 227.

47. Ibid., p. 236.

48. Mario Blejer, op. cit., p. 289–96.

49. Christopher A. Sims, "Money, Income, and Causality," *American Economic Review* 62 (September 1972): 540–52.

50. Sanjeev Gupta, "Causal Relationship between Domestic Credit and International Reserves: The Experience of Developing Countries," *Kredit und Kapital* (17,2: 1984): 261–71.

51. Ibid., p. 261.

52. Edgar Feige and James Johannes, "Testing the Causal Relationship between the Domestic Credit and Reserve Components of a Country's Monetary Base," *Journal of Macroeconomics* 3 (Winter 1981): 55–76.

53. C. W. J.Granger, "Investigating Causal Relations by Econometric Models and Cross Spectral Methods," *Econometrica* 37 (July 1969): 428–38.

54. L. D. Haugh, "Checking the Independence of Two Covariance Stationary Time Series: A Univariate Residual Cross-Correlation Approach," *Journal of the American Statistical Association* 71 (June 1976): 378–85.

55. Sims, op, cit.

56. Gupta, op. cit., p. 244–47.

57. Khan and Willett, op. cit.

58. Ibid., p. 221

59. Ibid., p. 221.

60. Using income differentials which constrain the income elasticities to be equal in both countries can lead to bias in the estimated coefficients. This issue was raised by James

Rasul and D. Sykes Wilford in "Estimating Monetary Models of the Balance of Payments and Exchange Rates: A Bias," *Southern Economic Journal*, 47, 1 (July 1980): 136–46.

61. Khan and Willett, op. cit., p. 298.

62. Michael Mussa, "Empirical Regularities in the Behavior of Exchange Rates and Theories of the Foreign Exchange Market," in *Policies for Employment, Prices and Exchange Rates*, eds., Karl Brunner and Allen Meltzer, Carnegie-Rochester Conference Series on Public Policy, vol. 11, Amsterdam, North-Holland, p. 45.

6

Some Common Misconceptions about the Monetary Approach to International Adjustment

M. A. Akhtar

The "monetary approach" to international adjustment is the subject of substantial controversy in international economics. A good deal of the dispute is due to misconceptions concerning the basic features of the approach. The matter has not been helped when in the heat of controversy the proponents of the approach have made unrealistic claims for the revealed truth. While the proponents have, upon occasion, claimed too much, the critics have generally seriously underestimated the contribution of the monetary approach and, in some cases, have failed to understand its widely useful implications for the international adjustment process. In this paper, the general framework of the monetary approach will be outlined, followed by a discussion of some of the common criticisms and misconceptions concerning the approach.

AN OVERVIEW OF THE MONETARY APPROACH

The basic framework of the monetary approach is built on the following relationships:[1]

The author is grateful to Bluford H. Putnam and D. Sykes Wilford for discussions and comments on various aspects of the arguments in this paper.

$$M_s = f(R + D(\ ))\qquad f > 0 \tag{1}$$

$$M_d = g(\ )P^{\alpha} \tag{2}$$

$$P = EwP_F(\ ) \tag{3}$$

$$B = \frac{dR}{dt} \tag{4}$$

$$M_s = M_d \tag{5}$$

where M = nominal money balances (subscripts s and d denote supply
and demand, respectively),
f( ) = supply of money function,
R = foreign exchange reserves,
D( ) = domestic credit function,
g( ) = demand for money function,
P = domestic price level,
P_F( ) = foreign price level function assumed to be related to
the foreign money demand function,
E = exchange rate (units of domestic currency per unit of
foreign currency), and
B = the overall (official settlements basis) balance of payments.

Equation 1 specifies the money supply process; the supply of money is a
stable and increasing function of foreign exchange reserves and the
domestic credit; the latter may be exogenous or endogenous. Equation 2
represents the demand for money, which is a stable function of a few key
variables; specifically, an income or wealth constraint, interest rates, and
probably some other variables such as expectations, exchange risk, and so
on. Note that the money demand function is not necessarily homogeneous
of degree one in the price level. Equation 3 states the relationship between
the domestic price level and the foreign or world price level with w as a
factor that accounts for deviations from the purchasing power parity.
Equation 4 defines the balance of payments, while equation 5 is the stock
equilibrium condition. Inserting 3 into 2 and combining the result with 1
and 5 yields:

$$f(R + D(\ )) = g(\ )[EWP_F(\ )]^{\alpha} \tag{6}$$

Under a fixed exchange rate system, E is fixed and R is endogenous.
A rise in g( ), a rise in P_F( ), or a fall in D( ) will result in a rise in the

overall balance of payments, that is, dR/dt rises. On the other hand, a fall in g( ), a fall in P_F( ), or a rise in D( ) leads to a fall in dR/dt. The process and speed of adjustment, as well as the impact of initial disturbance on the balance of payments, depend upon a number of considerations including institutional arrangements. However, the ultimate result is determined by the equilibrium condition between money supply and money demand. Under freely flexible exchange rates, R is fixed, that is, (dR/dt) = 0. Changes in g( ), P_F( ), and D( ) lead to changes in exchange rates, which in turn may affect the arguments of g( ), P_F( ), and probably D( ). Eventually changes in the exchange rate will bring money demand into equilibrium with money supply. Finally, under a regime of controlled floating the monetary approach to international adjustment is a combination of the alternative theories under fixed and flexible exchange rates. The authorities choose a combination of R and E constrained by (6).

Equations 1 through 6 represent the *basic* structure of the monetary approach, but do not present a *complete* model. They are consistent with any number of formulations ranging from the limiting case where all or most of the determinants of g( ), P_F( ), and D( ) are exogenous, to the more general case where most of the determinants of these functions are endogenous. Moreover, there is no specification of the adjustment to equilibrium; again, any number of ways of specifying the speed and process of adjustment are consistent with the basic framework outlined here. Thus, as noted by M. Mussa, the monetary approach is not embodied in any single theoretical model; rather, it is represented by a large set of models that have certain features in common but differ in many important ways.

Four basic features emerge from the preceding summary view of the monetary approach.[2] First, the balance of payments defined on official settlements basis is an *essentially* monetary phenomenon and balance of payments problems are largely monetary problems that should be analyzed through explicit specification of monetary behavior, and its integration with "real" factors. This does not mean that real forces do not affect the balance of payments (or vice versa), rather that to do so they must affect the demand for and supply of money. This subject is pursued a bit further in the next section.

Second, the monetary approach explicitly recognizes that money is a stock and not a flow, and analyzes international adjustment problems through stock equilibrium conditions and stock adjustment processes. The analysis emphasizes that an adequate theory of the balance of payments must integrate stocks and flows.

Third, money stock is endogenous and can change through changes in domestic credit and/or through international reserve flows. The distinction between domestic origin and foreign origin components of the money stock is important for an analysis of balance of payments problems.

Fourth, the exchange rate is determined in the asset market, and as an approximation it may be taken as the relative price of different national monies, determined by the conditions for stock equilibrium for national monies. However, the exchange rate is not a purely monetary phenomenon; both "real" and monetary factors are important in determining its behavior. Changes in real factors that affect money demand and money supply also affect the exchange rate. In this respect, the monetary approach recognizes the simultaneity between the exchange rate, and the determinants of money demand and money supply.

An Essentially Monetary Phenomenon

This section deals with some of the misconceptions and confusions concerning the monetary approach. The discussion below is a somewhat dispassionate look at the issues involved. It is not intended to be comprehensive in terms of its coverage of the criticisms and misconceptions. Instead, the emphasis is on those issues that have led to confusions about the general framework as presented in the preceding section.

As noted in the previous section, the monetary approach treats the balance of payments as a monetary phenomenon. The view is generally accepted but it is not without its critics. In his review of the theoretical papers in *The Monetary Approach to the Balance of Payments* edited by Frenkel and Johnson, F. H. Hahn has labeled it as a "false scent."[3] Specifically, referring to Mussa's statement that "the balance of payments is an essentially (but not exclusively) monetary phenomenon ... The official settlements balance is in surplus (deficit) when the monetary authorities of a country are purchasing (selling) foreign exchange assets in order to prevent their own money from appreciating (depreciating) relative to other monies,"[4] he argues that "on similar grounds the market for cheese is an essentially monetary phenomenon. Why? Because if some cheese is sold for stock rather than current production then cheese makers must be purchasing money stock from households, etc., etc."[5] While Mussa's rationale is somewhat ambiguous and weak, Hahn's reasoning fails to recognize the nature of exchange rates and misses the whole point. An outline of the rationale for the view that the balance of payments is an *essentially* monetary phenomenon is in order at this point.

Two interrelated points should be made regarding the rationale for the view in question. First, consider the consolidated balance sheet identity of the monetary sector in an open economy (for the sake of simplicity we ignore the money multiplier):

$$M = R + D$$

or

$$R = M - D$$

This identity differentiated with respect to time yields:

$$\frac{dR}{dt} = \frac{dM}{dt} - \frac{dD}{dt} \tag{7}$$

which indicates that the overall balance of payments is identically equal to the difference between the rate of change of money and the rate of change of domestic credit. Both monetary and "real" influences on the balance of payments are reflected in equation 7; however, real influences must appear through monetary factors. Thus, monetary factors have the *primary* role because they transmit the disturbances from the monetary side as well as from the real side. Indeed, it would be impossible to have a balance of payments surplus or deficit in a barter economy. Putting the matter in a somewhat different light, in an open economy excess demands and supplies of goods or bonds may be eliminated by exchanging them for money in the international market.

Second, since there is a direct relationship between the money stock and the overall balance of payments, the latter is approximately analyzed by *explicitly* specifying monetary behavior rather than treating it as a residual of "real" relationships. To say that money is not a residual from the real side is to say much more than what Hahn appears to believe, that is, "money makes an appearance."[6] In the latter sense, money flows can appear as residuals of real flows determined by incomes and relative prices.

Domestic Credit

Domestic credit is usually, but not always, treated as an exogenous variable under the control of the monetary authorities. This has led to the view that the monetary approach ignores the determinants of the money supply and relies too heavily on the money supply identity. The view is most forcefully expressed by D. A. Currie and Max Corden.[7] The monetary approach theorists have, of course, long recognized that the fiscal policy and other "real" variables influence domestic credit creation, but most of them appear to believe that even so the monetary authorities have control over domestic credit. For many cases, the treatment of domestic credit as exogenous may be appropriate. If, however, domestic credit is responding passively to real forces, then the monetary approach should be (and can be) adapted to those forces.

In principle, domestic credit creation may be specified as a function of other variables that are believed to be the major influences or it may be related to the government budget constraint. The latter approach has been taken frequently in the monetary aproach literature.[8] Specifically:

$$\Delta D = G - T - B \tag{8}$$

where ΔD = change in domestic credit, D
 G = government expenditure
 T = fiscal revenue, and
 B = addition to borrowing from the private sector, both foreign and domestic

The introduction of the government budget constraint enables us to treat domestic credit creation as passively responding to the fiscal variables. Thus, fiscal influences on domestic credit can be (and have been) incorporated into the structure of the monetary approach without endangering the internal consistency of the general model.

GENERAL MISCONCEPTIONS
ABOUT THE MONEY DEMAND FUNCTION

The question of exogenous versus endogenous determinants of the money demand function is taken up in the next section. However, before this is done it is important to mention three general misconceptions concerning the role of the money demand function in the monetary approach. First, there appears to be a view that the "specific" form of the money demand function is important for the monetary approach conclusions or results to hold. In a recent article, S. C. Tsiang, while appreciating the importance of the money demand function in the monetary approach, writes that

> there does not yet seem to be general agreement among the proponents of the monetary approach about its [money demand function] precise form ... the actual decision to pick one or the other seems to depend mostly upon expediency in relation to the problem that the author is tackling.[9]

The *general* agreement for the precise form of the money demand function is not important for the monetary approach; what is important is that it should be a stable function of a few key variables over the period of analysis. What those variables are is an empirical question and is likely to differ according to the time period and circumstances.

Second, some authors have criticized the monetary approach by using an extremely restrictive Cambridge form of the money demand function, where money demand is assumed to be interest inelastic. This is the type of function Whitman attributes to the "global monetarists."[10] There are probably no "global monetarists" in Whitman's sense but, if there are any, they probably would include interest rate as an argument in their money demand function.*

Third, sometimes, though not often, critics have ignored the importance of the money demand function in the monetary approach and have criticized it for focusing attention on "the accounting identity between reserves, domestic credit and money" and for confusing accounting identities with causal economic relationships.[11] This type of criticism has also appeared in reference to empirical analyses based on the monetary approach. On the theoretical side, in view of equations 1 through 6 this charge is clearly invalid. On the empirical side, this criticism, as shown in a subsequent section, is due to some confusion about the derivation of estimating equations.

Exogenous vs. Endogenous Variables

Some of the more forceful monetary approach literature makes the assumptions of full employment and "small country" (or alternatively the so-called law of one price in the multicountry context), so that the main arguments of the money demand function become exogenous. This has led to the rather popular impression that the monetary approach is relevant only for small countries or that the exogeneity of the determinants of the money demand function is a necessity for the monetary approach.[12] Neither of these views is correct.†

---

*The "skeleton" model used by Whitman is a slightly modified version of Dornbusch's model in his article in the December 1973 issue of the *American Economic Review*. Apparently, Whitman is cognizant of the fact that Dornbusch is not a "global monetarist" and that he chose a simple model to "emphasize the monetary aspects of the problem," and the Cambridge form of the money demand function so as "not to detract from the main line of argument."[13]

It may be useful to note one other source of confusion in Whitman's conception of "global monetarism." She treats global monetarism as the "full package" and the monetary approach as an extension of it. This is incorrect; global monetarism is a limiting or a polar case of the monetary approach.

†As is obvious from our discussion in the previous sections, on the money supply side R is endogenous except in the case of perfectly flexible exchange rates, and D can be specified as a function of fiscal and other "real" sector variables.

In principle, the proponents of the monetary approach visualize a general equilibrium model of the macroeconomic type with stock and flow variables. But in practice they attempt to reduce the general equilibrium model to manageable proportions by singling out money as the center of analysis. The treatment of the arguments of the money demand function as endogenous is in no way inconsistent with the monetary approach. In fact, some of the recent monetary approach models treat interest rates, prices, or income as endogenous.[14] However, much remains to be done to develop models that determine income and prices simultaneously with the exchange rate and/or the balance of payments within the context of the monetary approach. This is, by far, the weakest area in the monetary approach literature.

In general, two important considerations bear on the issue of exogeneity versus endogeneity of the determinants of the money demand function. The first deals with the length of the time period involved. For very short periods such as days or a few weeks the levels of aggregate real income and prices may be assumed given. However, virtually nothing is known about the stability of the demand for money over such periods. For periods ranging from a quarter to one or two years, the demand for money is generally believed to be fairly stable. But over such periods the simultaneity between the money supply process and the determinants of the money demand may be substantial. In this case, the second consideration becomes important. In other words, whether or not the determinants of the demand for money are exogenous may depend upon the particular circumstances of the country, such as the degree of openness, integration of domestic financial markets with similar markets abroad, and the size of the economy. Thus if the law of one price describes the relevant "reality," interest rates and prices should be treated as exogenous. Obviously, these matters require empirical analysis, which is the subject matter of the next section.

SOME EMPIRICAL CONFUSIONS

Most of the critics have rejected any conclusions based on reduced or quasi-reduced form tests of the monetary approach models. Probably the main reason for this is that they feel the assumptions required to produce reduced or quasi-reduced form models are unduly restrictive or altogether erroneous due to the simultaneous equation bias. This quarrel with reduced form models is not new and, of course, has a great deal of merit. However, as noted above, some of the issues involved are empirical, and cannot be resolved a priori.

The monetary approach can be tested through either direct tests of the models or tests of the models as well as their assumptions.[15] The direct test may be of structural models (which treat some, most, or all of the determinants of the money demand or money supply functions as endogenous) or of reduced and quasi-reduced form models. While the direct tests of structural models are rather rare thus far, though not altogether unknown, such tests for reduced or quasi-reduced form models are very common. However, the latter may appear to be more favorable to the monetary approach than the underlying structural models. This is what makes it necessary to test the key assumptions introduced in order to produce the reduced form version. Tests of the assumptions of reduced form models are fairly common in the empirical literature on the monetary approach.

The empirical tests of the small country assumption (or the law of one price in multicountry models), often made in the limiting case of the monetary approach, indicate that for many countries the assumption or some modified version of the assumption captures the relevant "reality." Similar results have been found for the nonsterilization assumption regarding the balance of payments surplus underlying the money supply process under a fixed exchange rate system. However, neither of the assumptions holds universally. The test of the assumptions combined with the direct tests of the monetary approach suggest that the usefulness of the empirical studies can be determined only on a case-by-case basis, taking full account of the circumstances of the problem as well as the craftsmanship of the researcher. Judged in these terms, many of the empirical tests of the monetary approach can be said to have contributed a great deal to our knowledge.

Some critics have not only rejected empirical findings based on the reduced form models but have gone so far as to argue that "direct estimation of the balance of payments equation implied by the monetary approach involves the estimation of an accounting identity rather than a true behavioral relationship."[16] This appears to be the result of a confusion regarding the derivation of the estimating equation(s). Even in the limiting case of the monetary approach, a single reduced form equation for international reserve flows is obtained by combining the money supply identity with the money demand function under the assumption of monetary equilibrium. Thus, the estimating equation explicitly incorporates the influence of money supply factors as well as the influence of factors underlying the money demand function.[17]

MONETARISM AND THE MONETARY APPROACH

Despite the proponents' claim that the monetary approach is neither entailed by nor entails monetarism,[18] it is commonly believed that the monetary approach is a direct descendant of M. Friedman's restatement of the quantity theory. Presumably this view finds its main support in the fact that the monetary approach largely assumes "normal" full employment in the long run. In this section, some of the distinguishing features of the monetary approach vis-à-vis "monetarism" are noted. The conclusion reached—a rather obvious one—is that the monetary approach does not imply monetarism.

First, the monetary approach treats the money supply as an endogenous variable, whereas it is generally treated as an exogenous variable by the monetarists. As noted elsewhere in this study, R is endogenous under a fixed rate regime as well as under a controlled floating regime. Moreover, D may be exogenous or endogenous regardless of the exchange rate regime.

Second, unlike the monetarists, the proponents of the monetary approach do not consider fiscal policy as impotent, while placing "too much" emphasis on the use of monetary policy. Specifically:

> The monetary approach to the balance of payments asserts neither that monetary mismanagement is the only cause, nor that monetary policy change is the only possible cure, for balance of payments problems; it does suggest, however, that monetary process will bring about a cure of some kind—not necessarily very attractive—unless frustrated by deliberate monetary policy action, and that policies that neglect or aggravate the monetary implications of deficits and surpluses will not be successful in their declared objectives.[19]

As should be evident from the overview of the monetary approach in the first section, the exchange rate problems also have both monetary and nonmonetary causes as well as cures.

Third, the monetary approach, like the modern monetarists' theory, assumes that the aggregate money demand function is a stable function of a few aggregate economic variables. However, in this respect its assumptions are also similar to those of the Keynesian theory. At a more specific level, the monetary approach, unlike that of the monetarists, does not require the assumption that "the demand for money is homogeneous of degree one in all prices and nominal money assets (absence of money illusion)."[20]

Fourth, the monetary approach can be applied to a system in which prices and wages are rigid. In this case, monetary changes affect quantities—employment, output, and consumption—rather than prices and wages. This application has been investigated by, for example, Carlos A. Rodriguez in the context of a Keynesian model.[21]

Fifth, it is worth noting that the proponents of the monetary approach do not have a common stance on the issue of flexible versus fixed exchange rates. In fact, in contrast to the findings of the monetarists, the limiting case seems to favor a fixed exchange rate in that changes in the exchange rate are regarded as unnecessary as well as ineffective for achievement of payments equilibrium.

Finally, an important methodological difference between the monetary approach and the monetarists' theory is evident in the treatment of assumptions. Following Friedman, the monetarists regard the "realism" of their assumptions as unnecesssary to the "correctness" of their models and instead emphasize the predictions the models yield.[22] By contrast, the proponents of the monetary approach attempt to test, as noted above, the assumptions as well as the predictions of their models. In a more general sense, the monetary approach emphasizes the need for general equilibrium methodology and, unlike the monetarists' theory, does not necessarily presume that the private sector is inherently more stable than the public sector or that the monetary impulses dominate in all cases. For example, Johnson warns against "the dangers of the politically popular belief that desirable real results can be achieved by manipulation of monetary magnitudes and maneuvers with the monetary mystique."[23]

NOTES

1. The most relevant contributions to the contemporary revival and development of the monetary approach were made by R. A. Mundell and Harry G. Johnson. See, in particular, R. A. Mundell, *International Economics* (New York: Macmillan, 1968) and *Monetary Theory* (Pacific Palisades: Goodyear, 1971); Harry G. Johnson, *Further Essays in Monetary Theory* (London: Allen and Unwin, 1972). Most of the recent contributions are listed in the bibliography of this book. The presentation of the basic framework of the monetary approach in this study is based primarily, but not exclusively, on R. Dornbusch, "The Theory of Flexible Exchange Rate Regimes and Macroeconomic Policy," *Scandinavian Journal of Economics* 78, no. 2 (1976): 255–75; M. Mussa, "Tariffs and the Balance of Payments: A Monetary Approach," in *The Monetary Approach to the Balance of Payments*, eds., J. A. Frenkel and Harry G. Johnson (Toronto: University of Toronto Press, 1976), pp. 187–221; M. Mussa, "The Exchange Rate, the Balance of Payments and Monetary and Fiscal Policy Under a Regime of Controlled Floating," *Scandinavian Journal of Economics* 78, no. 2 (1976): 229–48; J. A. Frenkel and Harry G. Johnson, "The Monetary Approach to the Balance of Payments: Essential Concepts and Historical Origins," in *The Monetary Approach*, op. cit., pp. 21–45; and A. K. Swoboda, "Monetary Approaches to Balance-of-Payments Theory," in *Recent Issues in Monetary Economics*, eds., E. Classen and P. Salin (New York: North-Holland, 1976), pp. 3–23.

2. The first three features are noted in Harry G. Johnson, "The Monetary Approach to Balance of Payments Theory and Policy: Explanation and Policy Implications," *Economica* 44 (August 1977): 217–29, and Harry G. Johnson, "The Monetary Approach to the Balance of Payments: A Nontechnical Guide," *Journal of International Economics* 7 (August 1977): 251–68. See also Mussa, "Tariffs," op. cit., and Swoboda, op. cit. The last feature emerges from adaptation of the theory to flexible or controlled floating exchange rate regimes. For an emphasis on this aspect see Dornbusch, op. cit.; Mussa, "The Exchange Rate," op. cit., and P. J. K. Kouri, "The Exchange Rate and the Balance of Payments in the Short Run and in the Long Run: A Monetary Approach," *Scandinavian Journal of Economics* 78, no. 2 (1976): 280–304.

3. F. H. Hahn, "The Monetary Approach to the Balance of Payments," *Journal of International Economics* 7 (August 1977): 241.

4. *The Monetary Approach*, op. cit., p. 189.

5. Hahn, op. cit., p. 241.

6. Ibid.

7. D. A. Currie, "Some Criticisms of the Monetary Analysis of Balance of Payments Correction," *Economic Journal* 86 (September 1976): 508–22; and Max Corden, "General Discussion: What Have We Learned? Where are the Fundamental Conflicts of Opinion?" proceedings of a conference on *Flexible Exchange Rates and Stabilization Policy*, published in *The Scandinavian Journal of Economics* 78, no. 2 (1976): 387, 403–05.

8. See, for example, G. H. Borts and J. A. Hanson, "The Monetary Approach to the Balance of Payments," Mimeographed, 1975; P. D. Jonson, "Money and Economic Activity in the Open Economy: The United Kingdom, 1880–1970," *Journal of Political Economy* (October 1976): 979–1012; Johan Myhrman, "Balance-of-Payments Adjustments and Portfolio Theory: A Survey," in *Recent Issues*, op. cit., 203–37; D. Sykes Wilford, *Monetary Policy and the Open Economy: Mexico's Experience* (New York: Praeger, 1977), pp. 21–26; and M. A. Akhtar, Bluford H. Putnam, and D. Sykes Wilford, "Fiscal Constraints, Domestic Credit and International Reserve Flows," *Journal of Money, Credit, and Banking* 11 (1979).

9. S. C. Tsiang, "The Monetary Theoretic Foundation of the Modern Monetary Approach to the Balance of Payments," *Oxford Economic Papers* 29 (November 1977): 321.

10. See Marina v. N. Whitman, "Global Monetarism and the Monetary Approach to the Balance of Payments," *Brookings Papers on Economic Activity*, no. 3 (1975): 491–536.

11. Currie, op. cit., pp. 514 and 516.

12. See, in particular, Joanne Salop, "A Note on the Monetary Approach to the Balance of Payments," in *The Effects of Exchange Rate Adjustment*, eds., P. Clark, D. Logue, and R. Sweeney (Washington, D.C.: U.S. Department of the Treasury, 1976), pp. 23–31; and Whitman, op. cit.

13. R. Dornbusch, "Devaluation, Money, and Non-traded Goods," *American Economic Review* 63 (December 1973): 871.

14. See, for example,Dornbusch, op. cit., and Jonson, op. cit.

15. Some of the recent empirical studies are discussed by S. P. Magee, "The Empirical Evidence on the Monetary Approach to the Balance of Payments and Exchange Rates," *American Economic Review* 66 (May 1976): 163–70. Many others, published and unpublished, are listed in the bibliography of this volume.

16. Whitman, op. cit., p. 525. See also Currie, op. cit.

17. For a detailed discussion of this issue see Bluford H. Putnam and D. Sykes Wilford, "Monetary Equilibrium and International Reserve Flows: An Empirical Treatment of the Money Supply Identity Issue," unpublished paper, 1977. See also Magee, op. cit.

18. See Frenkel and Johnson, op. cit., pp. 24–25. Elsewhere Johnson complained that "there has been a noticeable tendency to dismiss the new [monetary] approach as merely an international economic application of an eccentric and intellectually ludicrous point of view of

a contemporary lunatic fringe referred to as 'monetarism.'" Harry G. Johnson, "The Monetary Approach to Balance-of-Payments Theory: A Diagrammatic Analysis," *The Manchester School* 44 (September 1975): 221.

19. Frenkel and Johnson, op. cit., p. 24.

20. Ibid.

21. Carlos A. Rodriguez, "Money and Wealth in an Open Economy Income-Expenditure Model," in *The Monetary Approach*, op. cit., pp. 222–36.

22. See M. Friedman, "The Methodology of Positive Economics," in his *Essays in Positive Economics* (Chicago: University of Chicago Press, 1953), pp. 3–43.

23. Harry G. Johnson, "Money, Balance-of-Payments Theory, and the International Monetary Problem," *Essays in International Finance*, no. 124 (Princeton, N.J.: Princeton University Press, November 1977).

Part 2

FLEXIBLE EXCHANGE RATES

7

The Evolution of
the Flexible Exchange Rate Debate

Bluford H. Putnam
D. Sykes Wilford

The flexible exchange rate period officially began in 1973 with the complete breakdown of the Bretton Woods agreements. It ushered in a period of intense financial volatility, not seen in U.S. markets since the Great Depression. The degree of exchange rate variability has been associated with high absolute levels of, and great relative movement in, other economic parameters (such as the inflation rate and interest rates), and it has been greater than academicians, policy-makers, or investors anticipated.

Some have stated that this volatility in foreign exchange markets, though unusual, is no greater than that experienced daily in other well-organized markets, such as the commodity or equity markets.[1] Others have argued that this volatility is excessive, imposing high real economic costs which reduce real international trade.[2] Deciding whether or not the benefits of the flexible exchange rate system have outweighed the advantages of the old fixed exchange rate system depends both on the criteria chosen for the assessment and on personal judgment.[3] But the fact remains that the abandonment of Bretton Woods and its replacement with a flexible exchange rate system is a major element in understanding or analyzing the present state of the world's economies.

The authors wish to thank Francisco Comprido and Lynn McFadden for their comments on this manuscript.

This chapter attempts to isolate in which direction—and why—the literature has developed, and to focus on where it will go. It is divided into four parts. First, the international financial situation is briefly reviewed. Second, a discussion of the various schools of thought that have developed to explain how a flexible exchange system should work (or why the present flexible exchange regime has worked as it has) is presented. Third, the recent intellectual and market responses to the experience of floating exchange rates from economists, policy-makers and investors are considered. And fourth, implications for future analysis are drawn. These implications, given recent evidence, are that traditional explanations for exchange rate determination are clearly inadequate. No one model has forecast well. The focus of the literature is shifting toward understanding the effects and implications of risk and volatility. Furthermore, research emphasizing risk management rather than forecasting is becoming increasingly important.

THE INTERNATIONAL FINANCIAL SITUATION

The selection of the fixed exchange rate regime in 1944 by the signatories of the Bretton Woods agreement may be viewed as a belief in achieving an orderly international economy through exchange rate stability. Countries were to maintain a fixed rate of exchange between their currencies and the U.S. dollar, changing this rate only when faced with a fundamental disequilibrium. In turn, the U.S. dollar's price was fixed in terms of gold, ensuring noninflationary monetary policies.

After the United States devalued the dollar twice and President Nixon closed the gold window, the Smithsonian Agreements of 1973 put the world on a flexible exchange rate system, whereby no currency had to maintain any fixed value in terms of the U.S. dollar, other currencies or gold. In other words, the contract between the United States and each and every holder of a U.S. dollar that ensured the price stability of this currency was declared void, and a decision was made not to replace it with any other contract.

The selection of the floating rate system by the participants at the Smithsonian meetings may be viewed as a belief in achieving an orderly international economy through increasing market information, by unfixing one set of prices (that is, exchange rates). The results of this choice are still being analyzed.

First, exchange rate variability is calling into question whether exchange rates are a good insulator against exogenous economic shocks.

And, the flexible exchange rate system has had only very limited success in allowing countries to maintain divergent inflation rates and productivity growth rates. It has proved impossible to resist major changes in world inflation and growth trends.

Second, not only has exchange rate variability been greater than anticipated, but the movement has often been in the "wrong direction," suggesting traditional theories may have been wrong. That is, the exchange rate has deviated substantially from maintaining purchasing-power parity at least over the short term, thus disappointing the expectation that exchange rates would move quickly and smoothly to restore equilibrium, after changes in payments or divergences in growth or prices. On the other hand, the present exchange rate system does allow immediate adjustments to economic imbalances without a waiting for a full-blown exchange rate crisis, as was sometimes the case under fixed exchange rates.

Third, the relationship between current account imbalances (surpluses or deficits) and exchange rate changes (appreciation or depreciation) has not been the strong, corrective one anticipated by some economists. Indeed, current account explanations of exchange rate changes have often pointed in the wrong direction.

Fourth, exchange rate swings based upon demand for a currency due to the safe-haven effect has been a factor not anticipated. This factor, though logical in a rational model that takes a broad perspective on risk-management behavior, may be frustrating to policy-makers, who either benefit or lose as perception of relative long-term financial risks change.

Some have argued that the degree of excessiveness in the movements of exchange rates should be considered in light of other events, such as the oil crises. They suggest that real or monetary shocks such as these may have worsened exchange rate volatility, or that the disruption or inefficiency caused by these shocks may have been even worse under a different type of exchange rate regime. Others argue the experience of the last decade dictates that a new system is needed. The debate is vociferous and heated, and neutral fence sitters have left the field of intellectual combat, but the epitaph of the flexible system is yet to be written.

THE ECONOMIC LITERATURE
ON FLEXIBLE EXCHANGE RATES

Two distinct sets of the literature have developed to explain the mechanics of flexible exchange rates. Both sets had started during the Bretton Woods period, and some would argue that they are merely the international versions of the monetarist-Keynesian debate. Monetary approaches to exchange rates had their roots in the venerable theory of purchasing-power parity (PPP), while the Keynesian strand was related to the elasticities approach to explaining trade balances.

It is noteworthy that both bodies of thought supported flexible exchange rates in the last days of Bretton Woods. The monetarist or PPP School, for the most part, believed that PPP would lead to stable exchange rates because arbitrage would ensure a rapid but smooth adjustment to foreign and domestic price changes. Furthermore, nominal exchange rate adjustment would lead to independent domestic monetary policies, freed from the control of gold. A critical price control—fixed exchange rates—would be ended.*

The elasticities group agreed with the proponents of PPP that exchange rate changes would be few, because their approach suggested that minor adjustments in exchange rates would cause large swings in exports and imports, leading quickly to a payments balance. And once payments were balanced, no change of exchange rates need occur.[4]

Today, the different groups have explained the unanticipated volatility of exchange rates through refinements in their models. However, there is no consensus yet on whether the present exchange rate system should be kept, modified, or discarded.

Historical Approaches

Elasticities Approach

The elasticities approach was originally developed to explain how the balance of trade between two countries would change in response to a currency devaluation or revaluation under a fixed exchange rate regime.

---

*One of the most vocal proponents of flexible rates, Milton Friedman, "The Case for Flexible Exchange Rates," in *Essays in Positive Economics*, ed. Milton Friedman (Chicago: University of Chicago Press, 1953), pp. 157–203, sets the stage for the later monetarist support of floating exchange rates. Out of the early monetarist tradition, another group closely associated with the monetarists on many issues, following Robert Mundell and Harry Johnson (although he was an early supporter of flexible rates), would become supporters of fixed exchange rates. Both groups depended on PPP as a basis for argument. Both would draw different conclusions about the *correct* international financial system, however.

As modified for the floating rate regime, this approach analyzed changes in the exchange rate resulting from changes in the import or export demand for goods and services.

This approach views the exchange rate as the price of foreign exchange that maintains balance of payments equilibrium. The exchange rate moves in response to changes in the demand for imports or exports; the degree to which it moves depends on the sensitivity (or elasticities) of import and export demand to price changes. An increase in domestic demand for imports will cause a trade imbalance, which in turn implies an excess demand for foreign exchange. The home currency must depreciate vis-à-vis the foreign currency to eliminate the deficit. This rise in the exchange rate (measured in units of foreign currency per unit of domestic currency) makes the relative price of imports at home rise, while the relative price of exports falls. If import and export demand is price sensitive (that is, if the price elasticities of import and export demand are large), then small changes in the exchange rate will cause relative import and export price shifts that will greatly affect the levels of demand for imports and exports, and thus quickly bring the balance of payments back into equilibrium.

As Bretton Woods ended, the elasticities approach supporters argued that price elasticities were sufficiently large to ensure that minor exchange rate adjustment would stabilize the balance of payments. Absorptionist theories lended support to the elasticities approach to payments determination; and, while both groups admitted that exchange rate changes *could* be large, massive changes in both exchange rates and payments balances were certainly not foreseen.

Figure 7.1 illustrates the patterns exhibited by the current account balance of the United States and a trade-weighted U.S. dollar index. Current account imbalance has been more common in the past decade than balance. What is more, there have been long periods when the relationship between these two economic variables is exactly opposite to what the Elasticities School predicted; that is, there have been periods where continuing U.S. surpluses (deficits) are associated with a depreciating (appreciating) U.S. dollar.

One characteristic of this approach that may partly explain its inability to foresee big swings in exchange rates is its limited treatment of capital flows; that is, the *trade* balance between two countries is assumed to drive the total balance of payments. Capital flows are passive.

Although the elasticity approach literature still enjoys a following, its impact on modern analysis has been most apparent in how it is used to explain trade flows rather than exchange rates. And, it has little to offer in analyzing exchange rates in a world of highly integrated capital markets.

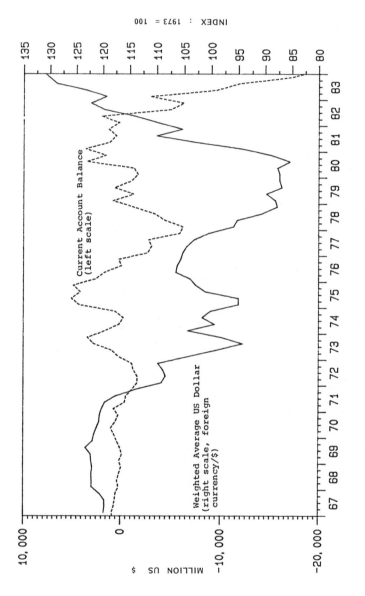

FIGURE 7.1 Weighted Average U.S. Dollar Index and Current Account Balance (1967–83).

Note: The index of the weighted average exchange value of the U.S. dollar is calculated against the currencies of the other Group of Ten countries plus Switzerland. Weights are 1972–76 global trade of each of the 10 countries.

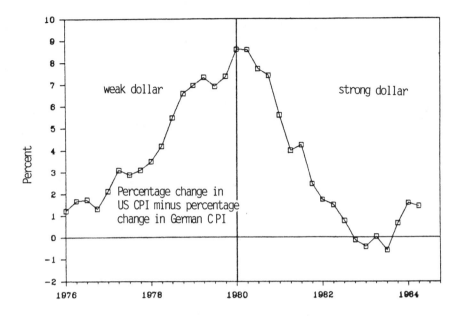

FIGURE 7.2   United States versus German Inflation.

Purchasing-power Parity[5]

Purchasing power parity (PPP), sometimes presented as the law of one price, stipulates that the purchasing power of home currency in the domestic economy must be equal to the purchasing power of home currency abroad, or else arbitrage will occur until parity does exist. The absolute version of PPP regards the exchange rate as the ratio of two countries' general price levels (when the price levels are in terms of the two countries' respective currencies). The relative version of PPP requires, less stringently, that the percentage change in the exchange rate in a certain period equals the difference between the percentage change in the two countries' price levels during this period. The more realistic version merely argues the obvious: economic agents will act to take advantage of arbitrage opportunities whenever and wherever available.

The actual efficacy of PPP in explaining exchange rate movements based on price level differences between countries has been mixed (see Figure 7.2). For example, differences in price levels do not always explain the short-term movement of exchange rates. On the other hand, PPP has been more powerful in explaining exchange rate behavior over the long run. Since PPP can be discussed as both a monetary and a goods phenomenon, discrepancies between the exchange rate changes predicted by PPP and those that actually occur may be explained to some extent by differences in the time it takes the financial asset market and the market for all goods and services to clear. Moreover, if arbitrage is available for traded goods only but sets in motion relative price changes between nontraded goods, then apparent, but only intertemporal, discrepancies occur.

One group observing the frequent disparity between exchange rate movements and changes in divergences in national price levels had suggested that PPP no longer works.[6] This view is based primarily on empirical work in which the estimated coefficients on the price variable in the PPP equation are statistically different from their hypothesized value of unity. Also, the equations often produce very bad fits of the data with poor summary statistics. Alternatively, another group argues that the empirical tests are asking too much. They suggest that the essence of PPP is that arbitragable price differences are eventually arbitraged into extinction. There may well be taxes, tariffs, risks of time, and financing, and so forth, that prevent the PPP equation from explaining actual data, and, yet, no arbitragable price differences exist. PPP works if no one can profit from existing price differences. Thus, the view of PPP originally used in monetary models was too simplistic; these economists argued that this view of PPP was essentially naïve with respect to exchange rate behavior, but essentially correct with respect to the behavior of price arbitragers.[7]*

Modern Approaches

MBOP, Currency Substitution, and Sticky Prices

The Simple Monetary Model The monetary approach strand of literature was inconsistent with many of the views expounded by monetarists on

---

*Interestingly enough, both groups needed a model of exchange rate determination that was not readily available out of traditional monetarist theory, since it was essentially a theory concerned about closed, not open, economies. (*From a policy perspective, of course, closing the economy with respect to the relationship of money and GNP was a goal of the pro-flexible exchange rate camp.*) With no theory of the open economy, however, a rational model of exchange rate behavior was garnered from the Monetary Approach to the Balance of Payments (MBOP) School. See Part 1 of this book as support reading for this argument.

fundamental issues such as the causality of money under the condition of fixed exchange rates.* With flexible rates, many of these inconsistencies would be shoved aside. The MBOP literature yielded the basic monetary model of exchange rate adjustment that many incorrectly describe as the "monetarist model." In fact, it is the simple fixed rate MBOP model modified for flexible rates.[8]

In this "flexible rate MBOP model," PPP, Fisher interest rate parity, and a stable money demand function were necessary. Empirical results have been mixed, and continue to be so.† For all of its robustness, the MBOP basic model was not complete enough to explain many of the seemingly incongruous machinations of the exchange market, particularly in the short run.

Deviations of ex post real exchange rates were large. The simple MBOP model was not sufficently robust to account for these deviations. This was a dynamic problem seemingly unanswerable by the simple MBOP model. Utilizing expectations, later versions would somewhat redress this problem. Albeit not very useful in explaining the short-run dynamics of exchange markets, the basic monetary model is still the basis for most forecasting models now used. Just as importantly, it still provides the starting point for any policy-maker who has to wrestle with the implications of government actions on exchange markets. Some of the lessons derived from working with derivatives of this model remain in good stead and have become accepted doctrine. For example:

---

*See Thomas M. Humphrey and Robert E. Keleher, *The Monetary Approach to the Balance of Payments, Exchange Rates, and World Inflation* (New York: Praeger Publishers, 1982), and Chapter 2 of this book for a complete discussion of this point, since it is key to understanding the policy debates now taking place. In essence, the MBOP literature showed that causality flowed from income to money under a fixed exchange rate regime for all countries except the reserve currency country, quite the opposite of what was proposed by monetarists.

†The early monetary models, as is discussed, were made more complicated. They were changed to allow for sticky process, temporal differences in capital and goods markets, currency substitution, etc. Considering the plethora of the literature that was to follow the early naïve monetary models, two observations are worth noting. First, once rational expectations doctrine is applied to the naïve model it takes many of the characteristics of other more cumbersome asset-based models. Second, the mass of literature generated on the flexible exchange rate literature is, for the most part, in defense of, an attachment to, or simply an extension of this naïve model. The competing theory (elasticities-absorption theory) of exchange rate determination is considered of little challenge to the basic monetary (not only monetarist) model as an explanation of flexible exchange rate determination.

- Real income growth is associated with a net appreciation in the value of a country's currency;
- Interest rates that change because of price expectations are negatively correlated with an appreciating exchange rate; but,
- Interest rate changes which are policy-induced to decrease future domestic credit demand are positively correlated with an appreciating exchange rate;
- The appropriate measure of money, in both definitional and temporal senses, can vary across countries; and,
- A thorough understanding of the reaction function of the monetary authority is necessary if the independent variables are to be utilized correctly for anything except the longest-run forecasting exercise.

Currency Substitution   Many of the earliest attacks on the validity of the basic monetary model came from various international monetary economists who felt a basic assumption of the monetary model was incorrect.[9] Namely, on the margin multicurrency portfolios are extremely important and assuming that residents hold only their own currency is too restrictive. Considering only the issues behind—and not necessarily the implications of—the argument that currencies are substitutable, this offshoot of the literature appeared esoteric and was difficult to support empirically.

The implications of the monetary model assumption of nonsubstitutability of currencies were important, however. If currencies *are* substitutable, then several forces could be at work:

- The empirical assessment and the usefulness of the basic monetary approach (with independent monetary policy) was shown to be fallacious for certain currency relationships; that is, Canada and the United States;
- Extremely large swings in foreign exchange rates could occur if the degree of substitutability between two countries' currencies changed;
- A relatively stable international financial system could only exist if the independent governments' monetary policies converged and if the policies were believed to be inviolate;
- The concept of *independent* monetary policy was, for practical (if not theoretical) purposes, invalidated; that is, an economy could not carry out a monetary policy distinct from other countries, without feeling the effects of the foreign policies on its own economy; and
- The theory helped explain seemingly inexplicable bilateral exchange rate changes between two currencies resulting from third-party actions.

Currency substitution literature continues to play a vigorous role in explaining why foreign exchange markets are so volatile and, by the same token, it continues to restrain those policy-makers who search for the door to independence. The lesson of interdependence was the major one, and due to it, currency substitution was one of the first methodologies to point out the flaws underlying the traditional raison d'être for a flexible rate regime.*

Overshooting: Sticky Prices and Early Portfolio Balance Models During the mid-1970s, the apparent failures of restrictive PPP models to explain observable events led to an alternative development in the literature which, in some ways, revived many of the tenets of earlier Keynesian models. These sticky price models attempted to explain the dynamics of exchange rate behavior by focusing on variables other than simple relative money demands. Current account imbalances were revived as explanations of apparent deviations in exchange rates from long-term PPP.[10] Price rigidity was the key assumption. But even more critical were the implications of differentiation of capital and trade flows, suggesting they responded to different stimuli. These models eventually gave way to portfolio balance models that could take into account investor preferences, a fundamental argument missing from these earlier models.[11]

The portfolio balance models are, in many ways, the natural evolution of the overshooting models, after the failure of the latter to explain much of the movement in rates during the late 1970s. Vicious and virtuous cycles became the slang of the mid-1970s. But the October 6, 1979, monetary policy shock, and the inexplicable strength of the dollar in the early 1980s were unanticipated ex ante and not explained ex post by the overshooting models, as well as by most new portfolio balance models.

Neither model appears to have yet yielded sufficiently robust empirical results to validate many of the policy implications of these models, such as exchange market intervention, which depends on segmented markets. The idea of intervention is somewhat disquieting to a market that has experienced the daily exchange rate variability of 1983 and 1984. Coordinated intervention, such as that experienced in late 1984 and early 1985, can hardly be said to have succeeded in "calming" the market.

---

*One can also make the case that many of the currency substitution arguments can be derived from special cases of the generalized portfolio model suggested by, among others, W. H. Branson, "Asset Markets and Relative Prices in Exchange Rate Determination," *Sozialwissenschaftliche Annalen*, 1 (1977): 69–89. See also, W. H. Branson and Dale W. Henderson, "The Specification and Influence of Asset Markets," *NBER* Working Paper No. 1283 (March 1984).

RESPONSES TO THE EXPERIENCE
OF FLEXIBLE EXCHANGE RATES

The domestic financial systems that were in existence prior to 1973 depended upon the continuation of a fixed exchange rate system, low inflation and financial order. Abandoning Bretton Woods led to volatility and uncertainty in exchange rates and inflation. Domestic markets had to adjust, but of even greater immediate importance was the need to link existing domestic markets, facing different risks, in new ways.

A major bridge has resulted from the growth of the Eurocurrency market.* In this new world of increasingly risky exchange rate exposures, individuals and banks needed instruments that would allow exchange of these risks in an efficient manner. This new financial risk caused by the flexible exchange rate system and heightened by the commodity price boom with its wealth transfer implications, particularly to the Middle East, led to a massive growth in the Euromarket as a vehicle to transform and manage financial risk.

Simultaneously, the current futures markets provided risk mitigation products to groups who did not have cheap access to the interbank foreign exchange forward market. Currency futures became the vehicle most utilized by small corporations to separate currency liquidity (transaction demand) from currency price risk. Following the October, 1979, policy shock from the Federal Reserve, interest rate futures followed the rapid growth pace set by their cousins, currency futures, during the mid-to-late 1970s. By 1984, some estimate that more than three trillion dollars of interest rate futures were traded.

With such a massive market for risk intermediation, interest rate swaps—an interest rate forward market similar to the interbank currency

---

*In part, this market came into existence in order to circumvent various controls that the United States had instituted in the late 1960s or earlier. These controls included banking regulations, such as deposit rate ceilings and noninterest bearing reserve requirements, and tax regulations. Some of these controls had as their primary goal an increase in the U.S. control over its balance of payments while others were intended to allow the United States to earn a revenue from the use of the dollar as the world's currency vehicle. After this market was created, it did not have much of a role to play until flexible exchange rates and oil shocks combined to give it new life. The regulations that existed in many domestic financial markets, including those in the United States, made those markets less efficient in the intermediation of this newfound international financial risk. See Bluford Putnam, "Controlling the Euromarkets: A Policy Perspective," *Columbia Journal of World Business* (Fall, 1979): 25–31.

market—began to develop. Currency swaps and currency options are now providing new avenues to solve the problems created by financial uncertainty. These market responses have been critical to the ability of the financial system to continue to function in the face of the new uncertainties generated during the 1970s and early 1980s.

Individuals, financial institutions, corporations, and governments all have attempted to diversify and manage portfolios of currencies in ways that were never before necessary. The markets have been created to help them by providing less expensive ways to hedge risk. And, no doubt, this has been important in shaping the academic literature as well.[12] We feel two new intellectual responses have begun to develop as a result. First, more simple versions of the portfolio balance models appear to have come to the forefront of the literature, as risk became paramount to any foreign exchange discussion. These models are more similar to those used in analyzing the U.S. stock market than they are to the older, more cumbersome portfolio balance models of the mid-1970s.* Second, there has been a return to the basic tenets of the MBOP model, but with an allowance of nonzero substitutability of currencies as well as nonperfect substitutability of other assets goods, while defining PPP conditions in expectations form with an understanding of the risks involved. The first direction is consistent with the second. A model of how various economic factors affect markets is important in determining the implications of news on individuals' portfolios.

IMPLICATIONS FOR THE LITERATURE

As new markets are developed to allow risk to be priced efficiently, and as individuals, corporations, and governments become more aware of the portfolio implications of foreign exchange risk, the foreign exchange market behaves more and more like equity and commodity markets. Volatility is and will continue to be the norm in these types of markets. This fact will likely reinforce the dichotomy between short-run and long-run analysis now taking place in the literature. Asset-pricing models,

---

*See Richard Roll, "Violations of Purchasing Power Parity and Their Implications for Efficient International Commodity Markets," in *International Finance and Trade*, I, eds., M. Sarnat and G. Szego (Cambridge, Mass: Ballinger, 1979). The issue is less why has PPP failed but more of what are the management implications for market efficiency.

efficient markets, and portfolio balance theory appear to be the issues in the short-run analysis of exchange rates, though the information most apropos to these models is that derived from longer-term PPP model derivatives.

Emphasis on two directions in the academic literature is anticipated. First, much of the work in short-run modeling will continue to adopt finance literature approaches, as the foreign exchange literature comes to grips with risk. Second, the long-run literature will likely begin to return to the basics embodied in the simple MBOP model, adjusted for currency substitution.

We argue that the link between these seemingly different directions of analysis is the substitutability of monetary wealth. Acceptance of currency substitution provides the integration of risk into the basic MBOP model. Expectations and risk assessment are thus integrated fully into the MBOP model while the underlying tenets of MBOP literature provide the key to understanding what long-term factors are important to concentrate upon.

But, why two directions? Market volatility has set in motion economic incentives for financial institutions to create new instruments to deal with new risks. These new products are simply new ways to manage the risk created by volatile markets. And, a premium will be paid to individuals who can understand, create, trade, and utilize these new risk reduction instruments. For this reason—and, more fundamentally, for the reason that economists have been poor forecasters of foreign exchange rates—we believe the next academic response to exchange rate volatility will be more concentrated in *managing* exchange rate risk and the attendant reasons for the risks involved.

Greater concentration on the *basics* should once again dominate longer-term analysis, however. Market participants, will require guidelines to evaluate properly the implied risk characteristics of any new information. Longer-term insight is also needed by policy-makers, who still must deal with the potential liability that the exchange rate system itself imposes on participants. Guides about long-run consequences of policies, not provided by the risk management literature, will continue to be demanded. Heightened financial market risk makes the cost of ignoring information too great for all participants. Better understanding of what information is critical and what is unimportant to exchange rates becomes even more valuable.

Finally, it strikes us that as the emphasis shifts from forecasting to risk management, the scene is set for a revisit to the question of what type of exchange rate system is most desirable. Much of the work of the 1980s will concentrate, once again, on the two extremes, fixed or floating. Less emphasis will be placed on what is *wrong* with floating, and more will be placed upon asking the question of whether or not fixed rates offer a *better* solution. More importantly, it will be asked if a fixed rate solution is even feasible. Are the benefits of a fixed system great enough to offer once again a new version of the "good old days?"

NOTES

1. Jacob A. Frenkel and Michael L. Mussa, "The Efficiency of Foreign Exchange Markets and Measures of Turbulence," *American Economic Review Papers and Proceedings* 70 (May 1980): 374–81.

2. M. A. Akhtar and R. Spence Hilton, "Effects of Exchange Rate Uncertainty on U.S. and German Trade," *Federal Reserve Bank of New York Quarterly Review* 9 (Spring 1984): 7–16.

3. Jacques R. Artus, "Toward a More Orderly Exchange Rate System," *Finance and Development* (March 1983): 10–13. Also see Michael Melvin, "The Choice of An Exchange Rate System and Macroeconomic Activity," Arizona State University (January 1985); and Paul Fabra, "Un Autre Système Monetaire," *Le Monde* (February 16, 1985) no. 12457, p. 1 and p. 16.

4. See J. E. Meade, "The Case for Variable Exchange Rates," *Three Banks Review* 27 (September 1955): 3–27, and Sidney Alexander, "Effects of a Devaluation: A Simplified Synthesis of Elasticities and Absorption Approaches," *American Economic Review* 49 (March 1959): 22–42.

5. See Alan Shapiro, "What Does Purchasing Power Parity Mean?" *Journal of International Money and Finance* (Spring 1983): 295–318. Also see L. T. Katseli-Papaefstration, "The Reemergence of the Purchasing Power Parity Doctrine in the 1970s," Princeton University, International Finance Section, 1979.

6. See Jacob A. Frenkel, "The Collapse of Purchasing Power Parity," *European Economic Review* 16 (May 1981): 145–65, and Peter Korteweg, "Exchange-Rate Policy, Monetary Policy, and Real Exchange Rate Variability," Princeton University, *Essays on International Finance*, no. 140 (December 1980): 1–28.

7. For an excellent discussion of the misunderstanding of PPP, see Don McCloskey and J. Richard Zecher, "The Success of Purchasing Power Parity: Historical Evidence and Its Implication for Macroeconomics," in *A Retrospective on the Classical Gold Standard 1821–1931*, eds., Michael D. Bordo and Anna J. Schwartz (Chicago: University of Chicago Press, 1984).

8. See Chapter 9 of this book; Jacob A. Frenkel, "A Monetary Approach to the Exchange Rate: Doctrinal Aspects and Empirical Evidence," *Scandinavian Journal of Economics* 78 (1976): 200–24; Michael Connolly and J. da Silveira, "An Application of the Girton-Roper Monetary Model of Exchange Market Pressure to Postwar Brazil," *American Economic Review* 69 (June 1979): 448–54; Lance Girton and Don Roper, "A Monetary Model of Fixed and Flexible Exchange Rates Applied to the Postwar Canadian Experience," *American Economic Review* 67 (September 1977): 537–48; Robert J. Hodrick, "An Empirical Analysis of the Monetary Approach to the Determination of the Exchange Rates," in *The Economics of Exchange Rates: Selected Studies*, eds., Jacob A. Frenkel and Harry G. Johnson (Reading, Mass.: Addison-Wesley, 1976), pp. 97–116; and James A. Rasulo and D. Sykes Wilford, "Estimating Monetary Models of the Balance of Payments and Exchange Rates: A Bias," *Southern Economic Journal* 47 (July 1980): 136–146.

9. See Chapters 11, 12, 13, 14, 15, and 16 of this book.

10. See Rudiger Dornbusch, "Exchange Rate Dynamics," *Journal of Political Economy* 84 (December 1976): 1161–76. Also, see John F. O. Bilson, "The Monetary Approach to Exchange Rates: Some Empirical Evidence," *IMF Staff Papers* (March 1978): 48–75.

11. See Jeffrey R. Shafer and Bonnie E. Loopesko, "Floating Exchange Rates after Ten Years," *Brookings Papers on Economic Activity* 1 (1983) for an excellent review of the early literature on sticky price and early portfolio balance models.

12. For example, see John F. O. Bilson, "The Speculative Efficiency Hypothesis," *Journal of Business* 54 (July 1981): 435–51. He uses efficient markets theory as a starting point. A very useful and wide-ranging discussion of statistical research and implications for various theories is found in Michael Mussa, "Theories of Exchange Rate Determination," in *Exchange Rate Theory and Practice*, eds., John F. O. Bilson and Richard C. Marston (Chicago: University of Chicago Press, 1984).

8

Factors Determining Exchange Rates: A Simple Model and Empirical Tests

Thomas M. Humphrey
Thomas A. Lawler

This chapter constructs and tests a simple static equilibrium model of exchange rate determination.[1] The model assumes a regime of freely floating currencies and posits that the exchange rate, by definition the relative price of two national monies, is determined by the basic factors underlying the demands for and supplies of those national money stocks. Besides the money supply itself, these factors include real income and interest rates—the latter reflecting expectational influences that enter into exchange rate determination.

The chapter proceeds as follows. First, it discusses the logic and economic content of the individual equations that constitute the major building blocks of the model. Second, it condenses the model to one reduced-form equation that expresses a functional relationship between the exchange rate and its ultimate determinants. Third, it fits the foregoing equation to the statistical data on several foreign exchange rates, assesses the accuracy of the fit, and discusses some problems involved in testing the model.

This article, in a slightly different form,appeared in the *Economic Review* of the Federal Reserve Bank of Richmond.

THE MODEL AND ITS ELEMENTS

The model itself consists of two hypothetical national economies represented by a set of equations containing the following variables. Let M be the nominal money stock (assumed to be exogenously determined by the central bank) and m the demand-adjusted rate of growth of that stock, that is, the difference between the respective growth rates of the nominal money supply and real money demand, this difference by definition being equal to the rate of price inflation. Furthermore, let D be the real demand for money, that is, the stock of real (price-deflated) cash balances that the public desires to hold, Y the exogenously determined level of real income, and i and r the nomimal and real rates of interest, respectively. Also let X be the exchange rate (defined as the domestic currency price of a unit of foreign currency), P be the price level, and E be the expected future rate of price inflation. Omicrons are used to distinguish foreign-country variables from home-country variables, and the subscript w denotes the entire world economy. The foregoing elements are linked together via the relationships described below.

Monetary Equilibrium Equations

The first part of the model consists of monetary equilibrium equations, one for each country

$$P = M/D \quad \text{and} \quad P^o = M^o/D^o \tag{1}$$

These equations, which can also be written in the form $M/P = D$, state that the price level in each country adjusts to bring the real (price-deflated) value of the nominal money stock into equality with the real demand for it, thereby clearing the market for real cash balances. This market-clearing price adjustment process relies chiefly on equilibrating changes in aggregate expenditure induced by discrepancies between actual and desired real balances. For example, if actual balances exceed desired, cashholders will attempt to get rid of the excess via spending for goods. Given the exogenously determined level of real output, however, the increased spending will exert upward pressure on prices, thereby reducing the real (price-deflated) value of the nominal money stock. Prices will continue to rise until actual real balances are brought down to the desired level. Conversely, a shortfall between actual and desired real balances will induce a cut in expenditure leading to a fall in prices and a corresponding rise in the real value of the money stock. This process will continue until actual real balances are brought into equality with desired balances. To summarize, disequilibrium between actual and desired real balances generates the changes in spending that cause prices to alter sufficiently to eliminate the disequilibrium.

Note that the equations also imply that, given the real demand for money, the price level is determined by and varies equiproportionally with the nominal money supply. This latter result, of course, is the essence of the quantity theory of money. For that reason, the equations could also be called quantity theory equations.

Real Cash Balance Equations

National demand for money functions constitute the second part of the model. Written as follows

$$D = KYi^{-a} \quad \text{and} \quad D^o = K^o Y^o i^{o-a} \tag{2}$$

these equations express the public's demand for real cash balances as the product of a constant K and two variables, namely real income and the nominal interest rate. The income variable is a proxy for the volume of real transactions effected with the aid of money and thus represents the transaction demand for money. By contrast, the interest rate variable measures the opportunity cost of holding money instead of earning assets. The parameter $-a$, which appears as the exponent of the interest rate variable, is the interest elasticity of demand for money. It measures the sensitivity or responsiveness of money demand to changes in the interest rate and is assumed to be a negative number indicating that the quantity of real balances demanded varies inversely with the cost of holding them. For simplicity the numerical magnitude of the interest elasticity parameter is assumed to be the same for both countries. For the same reason the income elasticity of demand for money, as represented by the exponential power to which the income variable is raised, is assumed to possess a numerical value of unity.

The Purchasing-power Parity Equation

The third equation of the model is the purchasing-power parity relationship

$$P = XP^o \tag{3}$$

showing how national price levels are linked via the exchange rate. As indicated by the equation, prices in both countries are identical when converted into a common currency unit at the equilibrium rate of exchange. This means that the exchange rate equalizes such common-currency price levels and, by implication, the buying power of both monies expressed in terms of a common unit. In other words, exchange rate adjustment ensures that a unit of a given currency commands the same quantity of goods and services abroad when converted into the other currency as it commands at home. This condition of equalized purchasing power is of course necessary if the two national money stocks are to be held willingly and monetary equilibrium is to prevail in both countries. For if the purchasing powers were unequal, people would demand more of the high- and less of the low-purchasing power currency on the market for foreign exchange. The resulting excess demand for the former and the corresponding excess supply of the latter would cause the exchange rate between the two currencies to adjust until purchasing power was equalized and both money stocks were willingly held. Note also that the purchasing-power parity equation can be rearranged to read $X = P/P^o$, thus corresponding to the economic interpretation of the exchange rate as the relative price of the two currencies, that is, as the ratio of the foreign currency's internal value in terms of goods to the domestic currency's internal value in terms of goods. Since the internal value of a unit of currency in terms of a composite market basket of commodities is the inverse of the general price level $1/P$, it follows that the relative price of the two monies is simply the ratio of the national price levels as indicated by the equation.

Nominal Interest Rate Equations

The fourth group of relationships in the model are the nominal interest rate equations, one for each country. Written as follows

$$i = r + E \quad \text{and} \quad i^o = r^o + E^o \tag{4}$$

they define the nominal interest rate as the sum of the real rate of interest and the expected future rate of inflation, the latter variable being the premium added to real yields to prevent their erosion by inflation.

Real Interest Rate Parity Condition

The fifth equation expresses the interest-parity condition

$$r = r^o = r_w \tag{5}$$

according to which the real rate of return on capital assets tends to be everywhere the same and independent of the currency denomination of the asset. This equation reflects the model's assumption of a highly integrated efficient world capital market. In such a world, capital is mobile internationally, that is, foreigners can purchase domestic securities and domestic citizens can purchase foreign securities. Given these conditions it follows that real yield equalization is necessary if all asset stocks are to be willingly held. Accordingly, the equation states that real interest rates in both countries are the same and are equal to a given constant world rate r_w. Note that equations 4 and 5 taken together imply that international nominal interest rate differentials reflect differences in expected future national rates of inflation. For example, if the market expects the future rate of inflation to be 12 percent in the United Kingdom and 5 percent in the United States, then the U.K. nominal interest rate will be 7 percentage points above the corresponding U.S. interest rate.

Price Expectations Equations

Completing the model are price expectations equations that describe how the public forms its anticipations of the future rate of inflation. These inflationary expectations constitute the anticipated future rates of depreciation of money holdings. As such, they enter the foreign and domestic demand for money functions via the nominal interest rate variables and thereby play an important role in exchange rate determination. Written as follows

$$E = m \quad \text{and} \quad E^o = m^o \tag{6}$$

the price expectations equations state that the expected rate of inflation E is equal to the demand-adjusted rate of monetary expansion m, that is, the difference between the respective growth rates of the nominal money supply and real money demand.

As written, these equations embody the so-called *rational expectations hypothesis* according to which the public correctly bases its price forecasts on the variable that the model contends actually determines the rate of inflation. This feature ensures that the model is internally consistent, that is, that the equations describing the formation of inflationary expectations are consistent with equations describing how inflation is actually generated. Such consistency is characteristic of the forecasting behavior of rational agents who use knowledge about the actual inflation-generating process in forming expectations of future inflation. Since the model asserts that the actual rate of price inflation is determined by the demand-adjusted growth rate of money (see equation 1), it follows that the expected rate of inflation is determined by that same variable as shown in equation 6.

LINKAGES AND CAUSATION

Taken together, the foregoing relationships constitute a simple six-equation model of exchange rate determination. For convenience the model is summarized below.

$$P = M/D \quad \text{and} \quad P^o = M^o/D^o \tag{1}$$

$$D = KYi^{-a} \quad \text{and} \quad D^o = K^oY^oi^{o-a} \tag{2}$$

$$P = XP^o \tag{3}$$

$$i = r + E \quad \text{and} \quad i^o = r^o + E^o \tag{4}$$

$$r = r^o = r_w \tag{5}$$

$$E = m \quad \text{and} \quad E^o = m^o \tag{6}$$

The foregoing equations imply two unidirectional channels of influence—one direct, the other indirect—running from money and income (both exogenous variables) to prices to the exchange rate. Regarding the former channel, the model implies that both exogenous variables affect prices and the exchange rate directly through the monetary equilibrium and purchasing-power parity equations. As for the indirect channel, the model implies that the rates of growth of the exogenous variables influence prices and the exchange rate indirectly via the price expectations component of the nominal interest rate variable that enters the demand for money function. More specifically, the model postulates the following causal chain:

1. The demand-adjusted money stock growth rate determines the expected rate of inflation.
2. Given the real rate of interest, the expected rate of inflation determines the nominal rate of interest.
3. The latter variable, together with the given level of real income, determines the demand for money.
4. Given the demand for money, the nominal money stock determines the price level.

5. Finally, the two price levels, foreign and domestic, together determine the exchange rate.

In brief, when the demand-adjusted money growth rate rises, price expectations also rise and so too does the nominal interest rate (the cost of holding money). This reduces the quantity of real cash balances that people desire to hold, that is, cashholders will want to get out of money and into goods. The resulting increased spending for goods puts upward pressure on the price level and, via the purchasing-power parity nexus, also on the exchange rate. Clearly the linkages run from money stocks and real incomes to prices to the exchange rate.* Moreover, all variables affecting the exchange rate do so through monetary channels, that is, through the demand for and supply of money. In this sense, money demand and supply may be said to constitute the *proximate* determinants of the exchange rate. The *ultimate* determinants, however, are the variables that underlie and determine the monetary factors themselves.

DETERMINANTS OF THE EXCHANGE RATE

To show the relationship between the exchange rate and its ultimate determinants, simply substitute equations 1–2 and 4–6 into equation 3 and solve for the exchange rate. The resulting "reduced form" expression is

$$X = [K^o/K] [M/M^o] [Y^o/Y] [i/i^o]^a \qquad (7)$$

or, since the nominal interest rate i is the sum of the real interest rate r and the expected rate of inflation E—the latter variable itself being equal to the growth rate of money per unit of money demand m—the equation can be alternatively expressed as

$$X = [\frac{K^o}{K}] [\frac{M}{M^o}] [\frac{Y^o}{Y}] [\frac{r + m}{r^o + m^o}]^a \qquad (7')$$

Disregarding the fixed constants (the Ks), equation 7 (or 7′) collects the determinants of the exchange rate into three groups, namely relative

---

*Note that reverse causality is effectively ruled out by the assumed exogeneity of the money stock and income variables. Therefore, while these variables can affect the exchange rate the exchange rate cannot influence them—at least not within the context of the model.

money supplies, relative real incomes, and relative nominal interest rates comprised of a fixed real rate component and a variable price expectations component. Of these three groups, the first captures purely monetary influences on the exchange rate while the second and third capture real and expectational influences, respectively.

Regarding monetary and real influences, the equation predicts that a country's exchange rate will depreciate (that is, rise) if its demand-adjusted money stock is growing faster than in the other country. Conversely, a nation will find its currency appreciating on the foreign exchanges when its money stock grows slower and its real income faster than in the other country. Note that the model's conclusion that rapid real growth results in currency appreciation contradicts the conventional balance of payments view of exchange rate determination. According to this latter approach, income growth tends to depreciate a country's currency by inducing a rise in imports and a consequent trade balance deficit. By contrast, the present model depicts real growth as stimulating not imports but rather the demand for money. Given the nominal money stock, this increased real money demand necessitates a fall in the price level to clear the market for money balances. With foreign prices given, the fall in domestic prices requires an equivalent appreciation of the exchange rate to maintain purchasing-power parity. In short, the model predicts that growth-induced rises in the real demand for money will raise the internal and therefore also the external value of a currency.

As for expectational influences, the equation predicts that a rise in the expected rate of inflation in one country (as reflected in its interest rate) relative to the other will cause the former's currency to depreciate on the foreign exchanges. The reason, of course, is that when interest rates rise, desired real cash balances fall. Cashholders attempt to get rid of unwanted balances via expenditure for goods thereby putting upward pressure on prices. According to the model, the rise in prices will be relatively greater in the country experiencing the larger rise in interest rates. In this way increasing relative interest rates cause corresponding increases in relative national price levels that must be offset by exchange rate depreciation to preserve purchasing-power parity. Note again that the model's prediction of a direct relation between interest rate movements and exchange rate movements runs counter to the conventional balance of payments view. According to this latter approach, a rising interest rate should lower the exchange rate either by attracting capital from abroad (thereby improving the capital account of the balance of payments) or by reducing domestic expenditure for imports and potential exports (thereby improving the trade balance). This cannot happen in the present model where, instead of strengthening the balance of payments, a rising interest rate induces a shift from cash to goods resulting in domestic inflation and exchange rate depreciation. In short, equation 7 predicts that a country will experience currency depreciation when its relative money stock rises, its relative real income falls, and its relative inflationary expectations rise.

EMPIRICAL APPLICATION

This article has constructed a simple economic model that states that the bilateral exchange rate between any two national currencies is determined by relative money stocks, relative real incomes, and relative nominal interest rates—the last variable reflecting relative expectations regarding national inflationary prospects. All that remains is to illustrate how the model can be applied to empirical studies of exchange rate determination. With this objective in mind, an attempt is made below to estimate the model's reduced-form exchange rate equation (equation 7) and to use it to explain the behavior of the United States/United Kingdom and United States/Italy exchange rates, respectively, over the post-1972 period of generalized floating. To do this, it is necessary to transform equation 7 into linear form by expressing the variables as logarithms. This step is required because equation 7 is nonlinear, and nonlinear equations are difficult to estimate directly. The resulting log-linear version of equation 7 is written as

$$\ln X = a_0 = a_1(\ln M - \ln M^o) + a_2(\ln Y^o - \ln Y) + a_3(\ln i - \ln i^o) \qquad (8)$$

where ln stands for the logarithm of the attached variable and the a's are coefficients to be estimated from the statistical data. Note that according to equation 7 the a priori expected values of the coefficients attached to the money and income variables are unity whereas the coefficient attached to the interest rate variables should lie between zero and unity, consistent with previous empirical estimates of the interest elasticity of demand for money.

Equation 8 was estimated for quarterly United States/United Kingdom and United States/Italy data for the period 1973I to 1977II. The money supply variable used for each country was M1. The income variables used were real gross national product for the United States and real gross domestic product for the United Kingdom and Italy, respectively. As for the interest rate variables, the treasury bill rate was used for each country in the United States/United Kingdom equation and the rate on medium-term government bonds was used for each country in the United States/Italy equation.

The results are shown in Table 8.1.

In general the empirical results are consistent with the theoretical model. According to the estimated equations, fully 94 percent of the variation of both the dollar/pound and dollar/lira exchange rates are explained by variations in the money stock, real income, and interest rate variables. In both cases the coefficients on the explanatory variables have the expected positive signs. All coefficients are statistically significant at the .01 level except for those on the United States/Italy income and interest rate variables. Moreover, the coefficient on United States/Italy money stock variable is close to its expected (theoretical) value of unity, as is the coefficient on the United States/United Kingdom income variable. The interest rate coefficients in both equations are also consistent with previous empirical estimates of the interest elasticity of demand for money.[2] These results are perhaps better than one might expect considering the extreme simplicity of the model, the degree to which floating rates are managed instead of free, the limited number of observations, and the fact that short-run data are used to test a long-run equilibrium model.

TABLE 8.1 Regression Results for U.S./U.K. and U.S./Italy Exchange Rates (quarterly data: 1973 I-1977 II)

Dollar/pound exchange rate

$$\ln X = 3.47 + .55(\ln M_{US} - \ln M_{IT}) + 1.39(\ln Y_{UK} - \ln Y_{US})$$
$$(3.84)^{o} \phantom{5(\ln M_{US} - \ln M_{IT}) + 1.}(4.00)^{o}$$
$$ +.22(\ln i_{US} - \ln i_{UK})$$
$$ (3.47)^{o}$$

$R^2 = .94 \quad DW = 1.63^a$

Dollar/lira exchange rate

$$\ln X = -4.05 + .89(\ln M_{US} - \ln M_{IT}) + .58(\ln Y_{US})$$
$$(4.98)^{o} \phantom{9(\ln M_{US} - \ln M_{IT}) + .}(1.56)$$
$$ +.13(\ln i_{US} - \ln i_{UK})$$
$$ (1.85)$$

$R^2 = .95 \quad DW = 1.03^a$

[a]The reported Durbin-Watson statistics are in the inconclusive region in testing for serial correlation. Correcting for first-order serial correlation using the Cochrane-Orcutt method did not significantly alter the results.

Note: Omicron indicates statistical significance at the 1 percent level of confidence; t-statistics are given in parentheses beneath the estimated coefficients.

Source: Compiled by the author with data from *International Financial Statistics* (Washington, D.C.: International Monetary Fund).

TABLE 8.2 Regression Results for U.S./U.K. Exchange Rates (quarterly data 1920 I-1924 IV)

Dollar/pound exchange rate

$$\ln X = -.17 + .55(\ln M_{US} - \ln M_{UK}) - .16(\ln Y_{UK} - \ln Y_{US})$$
$$(4.48)^o \qquad\qquad (-1.55)$$
$$+.10(\ln i_{US} - \ln i_{UK})$$
$$(2.77)^o$$

$R^2 = .76 \qquad DW = 1.31$

Note: Omicron indicates statistical significance at the 5 percent level of confidence; t-statistics are given in parentheses beneath the estimated coefficients.

Source: Compiled by the author with data from *International Financial Statistics* (Washington, D.C.: International Monetary Fund).

In sum, the equations reported above provide at least modest empirical support for the theoretical model developed earlier in this chapter. One should not make too much of these results, however. Just as one swallow does not make a summer, two regression equations do not prove a theory. In particular, equation 8 may not fit the data well for other countries and other time periods. In fact, an attempt was made to test the equation against recent data for Canada, Japan, and Germany, as well as for data pertaining to the United Kingdom during the early 1920s when that country was off the gold standard. For the first three countries, the equation performed poorly. For the United Kingdom from 1920 to 1924, however, it was at least partly successful. As shown in Table 8.2, the equation performed adequately except for the coefficient on the income variable, which bears the wrong sign.This of course may be due to the unreliability of United Kingdom income data for that period rather than to shortcomings inherent in the model.* Nevertheless, the fact that the equation does not work well for all countries is reason to interpret the results reported here with caution.

---

*Since quarterly national income figures are not available for this period, the Federal Reserve's index of industrial production was used as a proxy for U.S. real income. No such official index is available for the United Kingdom. Therefore a quarterly industrial production index constructed in 1927 by Rowe[3] was used as a proxy for U.K. real income. However, the reliability of this index is open to question.

PROBLEMS IN TESTING THE MODEL

In closing, it may be appropriate to consider why the data did not exactly fit the model like a glove. Regarding this question, at least three likely explanations come to mind. First, the model assumes that exchange rates are permitted to float freely while in fact governments still intervene in foreign exchange markets from time to time in order to achieve a managed float. This suggests that there may be some reverse causality running from exchange rates to money, at least in the short run. In brief, the model may not be a completely accurate description of existing exchange rate regimes.

Second, quarterly data may not be suitable for testing what is essentially a model of long-run equilibrium. Quarterly data are short-run data. As such they may be dominated by transitory dynamic adjustment phenomena that are absent in long-run static equilibrium. Annual (or longer) data are more appropriate for testing an equation that is based on assumptions of purchasing-power parity, interest rate parity, monetary equilibrium, real income exogeneity, and undirectional causality between money and exchange rates—all propositions about long-run equilibrium. Unfortunately, the post-Bretton Woods era of floating rates is only five years old, and the number of annual observations is insufficient to test these propositions. Even the number of quarterly observations is distressingly low.

An alternative solution would be to augment the model with additional equations and variables to represent dynamic adjustment processes. While this might permit the specification of short-run influences affecting the exchange rate, it would unduly complicate the model, contrary to the objective of keeping it simple. Note, however, that this latter feature may constitute a third reason for the model's failure to conform exactly to the data, that is, the model may be far too simple to capture all the influences on the exchange rate. This does not necessarily mean that the model is conceptually unsound. The underlying theory may be correct even though its empirical form is inadequate to fit the facts. Thus the model can be faulted on the grounds that its empirical money demand equations are too simple, that it lacks dynamic adjustment mechanisms, and that it arbitrarily constrains the elasticity coefficients to be the same for each country. These considerations should be kept in mind when interpreting the results of the regression analysis.

SUMMARY

This chapter has developed and estimated a simple model of exchange rate determination. The model states that exchange rate movements are determined by shifts in relative money stocks, relative real incomes, and relative inflationary expectations as manifested in relative interest rate movements. Although the model receives some empirical support from post-1972 data for the dollar/pound and dollar/lira exchange rates, it does not perform well when applied to data for other countries and other time periods. One is therefore advised to take an agnostic attitude regarding the validity of the model until all returns are in. In short, additional experience with floating exchange rates, together with the application of empirical techniques of greater sophistication than those employed here, will be necessary to establish conclusively the validity or invalidity of the model.

NOTES

1. Variants of the model have been employed by a number of analysts to explain recent exchange rate movements. See in particular John F. O. Bilson, "The Monetary Approach to the Exchange Rate: Some Empirical Evidence," Mimeographed, 1976; John F. L. Bilson, "Rational Expectations and the Exchange Rate," Mimeographed, 1976. See also Jacob Frenkel, "A Monetary Approach to the Exchange Rate: Doctrinal Aspects and Empirical Evidence," *Scandinavian Journal of Economics* 78, no. 2 (1976): 200–24; and Bluford H. Putnam and John R. Woodbury, "Exchange Rate Stability and Monetary Policy: A Case Study," Federal Reserve Bank of New York, Mimeographed, 1976. For a survey of much of the relevant work see Peter Isard, "The Process of Exchange Rate Determination: A Survey of Important Models and Major Issues," Federal Reserve Board, International Finance Division Discussion Paper No. 101 (January 1977): 56–60; and Stephen P. Magee "The Empirical Evidence on the Monetary Approach to the Balance of Payments and Exchange Rates," *American Economic Review Papers and Proceedings* 66 (May 1976): 163–70.

2. See John T. Boorman, "The Evidence on the Demand for Money: Theoretical Formulations and Empirical Results," in *Current Issues in Monetary Theory and Policy*, ed. Thomas M. Havrilesky and John T. Boorman (Arlington Heights, Ill.: AHM, 1976). Boorman reports that recent empirical studies of the demand for money suggest an interest elasticity of about −0.2 for short-term rates, quite close to the estimates apearing in Table 8.1.

3. J. W. F. Rowe, "An Index of Industrial Production," *Economic Journal* 37 (June 1927): 186.

9

The Monetary Approach to Exchange Rates: Its Historical Evolution and Role in Policy Debates

Thomas M. Humphrey

One of the oldest debates in economics is that between the monetary and balance of payments approaches to the determination of exchange rates in a flexible exchange rate regime. The monetary approach attributes exchange rate movements largely to actual and anticipated changes in relative money stocks. It stresses a channel of causation running from money to domestic prices to the exchange rate. By contrast, the balance of payments approach holds that autonomous nonmonetary factors affecting individual items in the balance of payments are to blame.* It stresses a causal channel running from real factors through the balance of payments to the exchange rate and thence to domestic prices and sometimes further to the money supply. Both views underlie current discussions of the weakness of the dollar—the monetary approach holding excessive U.S. money growth to blame while the balance of payments view sees excessive oil imports and the sluggish foreign demand for U.S. exports as the culprits. Although the difference between these two rival approaches is fairly well understood, what is not so fully appreciated is that the current debate between them is largely a repetition of earlier disputes going back more than 200 years.

---

*The balance of payments approach is not to be confused with the so-called monetary approach to the balance of payments (MBOP), which is the monetary approach applied to a regime of fixed or pegged exchange rates.

The purpose of this study is to trace the emergence and development of the monetary approach in three of these early controversies, namely the Swedish bullionist controversy of the 1750s, the English bullionist controversy of the early nineteenth century, and the German inflation controversy during and immediately following World War I.[1] These debates are crucial to the evolution of the monetary approach in two respects. First, they establish the analytical foundations of the monetary approach. These foundations consist of a quantity theory relationship linking money to prices, a purchasing-power parity relationship linking prices to the exchange rate, and an expectations theory specifying how anticipations of future money stocks are formed and how they influence the exchange rate. Second, the earlier debates are the origin of current monetarist policy prescriptions for strengthening the dollar. These prescriptions call for the gradual deceleration of the growth rate of the money supply to eliminate the excess supply of dollars alleged to be the basic cause of the fall of the internal and external value of the dollar.

THE SWEDISH BULLIONIST CONTROVERSY (1755–65)

One of the earliest debates in which the monetary approach played a leading role was the Swedish bullionist controversy of the mid-1700s.[2] The events precipitating the debate were as follows. In 1745, Sweden shifted from a metallic monetary system with fixed exchange rates to an inconvertible paper system with flexible exchange rates. The suspension of convertibility was followed by a steady rise in the prices of commodities and foreign exchange. A debate then arose between the two main political parties of the time—known as the Hats and Caps—over the cause of these prices increases.

The Hats and the Caps

The Hats advanced the balance of payments theory, blaming both the external and the internal depreciation of the Swedish mark on Sweden's adverse trade balance. Specifically, they held that the adverse trade balance had produced a depreciating exchange, that exchange depreciation had rendered imported goods more expensive, and that the rise in import prices had spread to the rest of the economy, thereby raising the general level of prices. Here is an early example of the tendency of balance of payments theorists to attribute both domestic inflation and exchange rate depreciation to external nonmonetary shocks and to assert a chain of causation running from the exchange rate to prices, rather than vice versa as in the monetary approach. Consistent with their balance of payments view, the Hats prescribed export promotion and import restriction schemes as remedies for inflation and exchange rate depreciation. Nothing was said about money.

The opposition Cap party emphatically rejected the Hats' balance of payments theory and instead pointed to the importance of the monetary factor. They blamed both domestic inflation and the external depreciation of the Swedish mark on the Riksbank's overissue of banknotes following the suspension of convertibility. They favored a policy of monetary contraction to roll back prices and the exchange rate to preinflation levels.

The Caps also adhered to an evil-speculator theory of exchange rate movements. This conspiracy theory is no part of the monetary approach. For that reason the Caps cannot be considered as full fledged advocates of the monetary approach.

Pehr Niclas Christiernin

One participant who did articulate the monetary view was Pehr Niclas Christiernin, an academic economist at the University of Uppsala, who advanced a quantity theory explanation of the transmission mechanism linking money with the exchange rate. In his *Lectures on the High Price of Foreign Exchange in Sweden* (1976),[3] Christiernin maintained that the chief cause of currency depreciation was an overissue of banknotes by the Riksbank and that causation flowed from money to spending to all prices including the prices of commodities and foreign exchange. He saw monetary expansion as stimulating demand. Part of the demand pressure falls on domestic commodity markets raising prices there. The rest spills over into the current account of the balance of payments in the form of increased demand for imports. The resulting import deficit then puts upward pressure on the exchange rate, which consequently rises to restore equilibrium in the current account. Clearly, money-induced changes in total spending constitute the driving force in Christiernin's version of the transmission mechanism, running from money to the exchange rate. This component has been a hallmark of the monetary aproach ever since.

As for policy recommendations, Christiernin was opposed to the Caps' plan to restore the exchange rate to its original preinflation level via contraction of the note issue. His opposition stemmed from his belief that prices adjusted sluggishly in response to deflationary pressure, so that the monetary contraction required to restore the exchanges to parity would bring painful declines in output and employment rather than the desired price decreases. For this reason he recommended stabilizing the exchange rate at a level established during the inflation level. Unfortunately, his advice was ignored and the Caps enacted a deflationary policy that resulted in the very drop in output and employment that he had predicted.

THE ENGLISH BULLIONIST CONTROVERSY (1797–1819)

The monetary and balance of payments theories clashed again in the famous controversy over the cause of the fall of the British pound following the Bank of England's suspension of the convertibility of banknotes into gold during the Napoleonic wars.[4] As in the earlier Swedish controversy, one side blamed currency depreciation on the central bank's overissue of notes while the other side blamed it on an adverse balance of payments. This time, however, the proponents of the monetary and the balance of payments views were known as the bullionists and the antibullionists, respectively.

The bullionists did more than any group before or since to develop and clarify the monetary view. The so-called strict bullionists crystallized the theory in rigorous form and the moderate bullionists refined and extended it. The strict bullionists included William Boyd, David Ricardo, and John Wheatley, while the moderate bullionists included William Blake, Francis Horner, William Huskisson, and, above all, Henry Thornton.

The Strict Bullionists: Ricardo and Wheatley

The strict bullionists made several major contributions to the monetary approach. They were the first to specify both the quantity theory and purchasing-power parity links in the transmission mechanism connecting money and the exchange rate. In addition, they stated the monetary approach in its most rigid and uncompromising form, asserting that, under conditions of inconvertibility, where money cannot drain out into foreign trade, the exchange rate varies in exact proportion with changes in the money supply. They arrived at this latter conclusion via the following route.

First they assumed that under inconvertibility domestic prices (P) vary in strict proportion with the quantity of money in circulation (M). This of course is the rigid version of the quantity theory, which may be expressed as

$$P = kM \tag{1}$$

where K is a constant equal to the ratio of the circulation velocity of money to real output, both treated as constants by the strict bullionists.

Second, they maintained that under inconvertibility the exchange rate (E) moves in proportion to the ratio of domestic to foreign prices (P/P^o). First enunciated by Wheatley in 1803, this proposition is the famous purchasing-power parity doctrine, so christened by Gustav Cassel, who rediscovered it more than 100 years later in 1918. The Wheatley–Ricardo–Cassel purchasing-power parity condition may be written as

$$E = P/P^o \qquad (2)$$

implying that external currency valuations derive from their real internal values and that the general price level or the purchasing power of money is everywhere the same when converted into a common unit at the equilibrium rate of exchange.

Third, they assumed that the foreign price component (P^o) of the purchasing-power parity ratio was a constant equal to the given world bullion price of commodities, so that exchange rate movements reflected corresponding movements in domestic paper money prices only. Given this assumption, the exchange rate is a good proxy for domestic prices and may be expressed as

$$E = P \qquad (2')$$

assuming the constant foreign price level is "normalized" and set equal to unity.*

Finally, they substituted the exchange rate proxy for the price variable in the quantity theory relationship, obtaining the result

$$E = kM \qquad (3)$$

which states that the exchange rate varies in exact proportion with the money supply. On this basis they were able to conclude that a rise in the exchange rate above its gold parity constituted both proof and measure of overissue of inconvertible currency. In other words, if the exchange rate stood 5 percent above its gold parity, then this was prima facie evidence that the note issue was 5 percent above what it would have been under convertibility. This was most clearly stated by Ricardo:

---

*Due to the unavailability of reliable general price indices, the classical economists also used the paper money price of bullion as an empirical proxy for the commodity price level. Accordingly, they interpreted a rise in the market price of gold above its mint price as both a sign and a measure of the fall of the internal purchasing power of money.

If a country used paper money not exchangeable for specie, and, therefore, not regulated by an fixed standard, the exchanges in that country might deviate from par *in the same proportion* as its money might be multiplied beyond that quantity which would have been allotted to it by general commerce, if . . . the precious metals had been used.[5]

Wheatley extended the analysis to the case where both countries are on an inconvertible paper standard. He simply substituted quantity theory relationships for both the domestic and foreign price variables in equation 2. This gave him the result that the exchange rate varies in proportion with relative money supplies, that is

$$E = kM/k^o M^o = K(M/M^o) \qquad (4)$$

where K is the ratio of the constants k and k^o. Wheatley stated this result when he declared that "the course of exchange is the exclusive criterion [of] how far the currency of one [country] is increased beyond the currency of another."[6]

Another contribution of the strict bullionists was their assertion that exchange rate movements are purely a monetary phenomenon. They rejected the antibullionist argument that real disturbances to the balance of payments—such as harvest failures, wartime disruption of trade, and military expenditures abroad—were responsible for the fall of the paper pound during the Napoleonic wars. Regarding supply shocks and foreign remittances, they denied that such factors could influence exchange rates even in the short run. Their position was that the slightest real pressure on the exchange rate would, by making British goods cheaper to foreigners, result in an instantaneous expansion of exports sufficient to eliminate the pressure. In their view, an adverse exchange was solely and completely the result of an excess issue of currency. Ricardo even went so far as to argue that even if foreign transfers and domestic crop failures *did* affect the exchanges by reducing real income and hence the demand for money, the cause of exchange depreciation is still an excess stock of money, albeit one arising from a reduction of money demand rather than an expansion of money supply. Ricardo's point was simply that real factors could affect the exchange rate only through shifts in money demand not offset by corresponding shifts in money supply. In such cases the latter was to blame for exchange rate movements. The notion that all factors affecting the exchange rate must do so through monetary channels, that is, through the demand for or supply of money, is of course central to the modern monetary approach.

Finally, the strict bullionists prescribed monetary restraint as the *only* cure for a depreciating currency. They held that a rise in the prices of foreign exchange constituted an infallible sign that the currency was in excess and must be contracted. Ricardo even defined an excess issue in terms of exchange depreciation, thus implying a single unique correct money stock, namely one associated with the exchange being at its former gold standard parity.[7]

The Moderate Bullionists: Blake and Thornton

The moderate bullionists modified the strict bullionists' analysis in three respects. First, they pointed out that it applies to long-run equilibrium situations but not necessarily to the short run. Second, while acknowledging that long-run (persistent) exchange depreciation stemmed solely from note overissue, they were willing to admit that real shocks could affect the exchanges in the short run. Their position is best exemplified by William Blake's distinction between the Real and the Nominal exchange.[8] According to Blake, the real exchange or real barter terms of trade R are determined by nonmonetary factors—crop failures, unilateral transfers, structural changes in trade, and the like—that affect the balance of payments. The nominal exchange N, however, reflects the relative purchasing powers of different currencies as determined by their relative supplies (M/M^o). Blake's analysis can be summarized by the equation

$$E = RN \tag{5}$$

which expresses the actual exchange rate as the product of its real and nominal components, both of which contribute to exchange rate movements in the short run. Blake maintained, however, that in the long run the real exchange (R) is self-correcting (that is, returns to its original level) and that only the nominal exchange (N) can remain permanently depressed. Therefore, persistent exchange depreciation is a sure sign of an excess issue of currency.

The third modification was made by Henry Thornton, whose analysis of the money–price–exchange rate nexus was much more subtle and sophisticated than that of the strict bullionists. In particular, he argued that interest rates and the velocity of money enter the nexus, that velocity is extremely variable in the short run owing to shifts in business confidence, and that this variability invalidates the rigid money–price–exchange rate linkage postulated by the extreme bullionists.[9] In terms of equation 3 he argued that k is a variable determined by the interest rate (i) and the state of business confidence (c). That is,

$$k = k(i,c) \tag{6}$$

Since k varies in the short run, the exchange rate and money do not exhibit exactly equiproportional movements. A given change in the money stock affects k as well as the exchange rate. In the long run, however, k is a constant and the equiproportionality proposition holds.

The Antibullionists

Except for an expectations mechanism, the bullionists had assembled and integrated all the elements of the monetary theory of exchange rate determination. Compared with this accomplishment, the contributions of the antibullionists appear quite meager indeed. They attributed exchange depreciation and domestic inflation solely to real factors—crop failures, overseas military expenditures, and the like—operating through the balance of payments. They correctly asserted that the exchange rate is determined by the supply and demand for foreign exchange arising from external transactions. But they fail to see that an important factor influencing supply and demand might be relative price levels, as determined by relative money stocks. In fact, they rejected all monetary explanations, claiming that banknote expansion could not affect the exchanges in the slightest. They thought the price of foreign exchange could rise indefinitely without indicating the existence of an excess note issue. As for policy recommendations, they urged curtailment of imports and overseas expenditures to improve the balance of payments and to strengthen the pound. They doubted that any conceivable reduction in the banknote issue could restore the exchanges to parity.

Their main analytical tool was the real bills doctrine, which they employed in an unsuccessful attempt to refute the charge that the Bank of England had overissued the currency. The real bills doctrine states that money can never be issued to excess as long as it is tied to bills of exchange arising from real transactions in goods and services. Henry Thornton, however, exposed the fallacy of this doctrine when he pointed out that rising prices would require an ever-growing volume of bills to finance the same level of real transactions. In this manner inflation would justify the monetary expansion necessary to sustain it and the real bills criterion would not effectively limit the quantity of money in existence. Thornton's demonstration of the invalidity of the real bills doctrine constituted a victory for the bullionists and for the monetary approach to the exchange rate. The victory, however, was not definitive. For when the debate erupted again in World War I, the balance of payments approach was the dominant view.

THE GERMAN INFLATION CONTROVERSY (1918–23)

The debate reopened in 1918 when Gustav Cassel used his purchasing-power parity doctrine, together with the quantity theory, to attack the official balance of payments explanation of the wartime fall of the German mark. Whereas the policy-makers blamed the currency depreciation on real disturbances to the balance of payments—for example, obstructions to German shipping, wartime disruption of trade, and the like—Cassel blamed it on excessive monetary expansion in Germany compared with that of her trading partners.

Cassel's Critique of the Balance of Payments Approach

Cassel's criticism of the balance of payments theory was virtually the same as that of his strict bullionist counterparts, Wheatley and Ricardo. Like them, he argued that the exchange rate is automatically self-correcting in response to real shocks to the balance of payments. Therefore the theory is incapable of accounting for persistent exchange rate depreciation.

Regarding the operation of the self-correcting mechanism, he noted that when balance of payments disturbances push the external value of a currency below its internal value, the currency becomes undervalued on the foreign exchanges, that is, its domestic purchasing power is greater than that indicated by the exchange rate. Such undervaluation, he held, will immediately invoke forces returning the exchange rate to equilibrium. For as soon as a country's currency becomes undervalued relative to its purchasing-power parity, foreigners will find it profitable to purchase the currency for use in procuring goods from that country. The resulting increased demand for the currency will bid its price back to the level of purchasing-power parity. In short, deviations of the exchange rate from purchasing-power parity generate corrective alterations in the trade balance that eliminate the deviations. Both the balance of payments and the exchange rate return swiftly to equilibrium. Thus, contrary to the balance of payments view, external nonmonetary shocks have no lasting impact on the exchange rate.[10] It follows that any persistent depreciation must be due to excessive monetary growth that raises domestic prices and thereby alters the purchasing-power parity or equilibrium exchange rate itself. In this connection he repeated Ricardo's dictum that an excess supply of money, whether stemming from a rise in money supply or stemming from a fall in money demand, is always and everywhere the cause of exchange rate movements.

Cassel also criticized the proposition that exchange depreciation causes domestic inflation rather than vice versa. He acknowledged that currency depreciations relative to purchasing-power parity produce import price increases. But he denied that these import price increases could be transmitted to general prices provided the money stock and hence total spending were held in check. He maintained that, given monetary stability, the rise in the particular prices of imported commodities would be offset by compensating reductions in other prices, leaving the general price level unchanged. In short, he denied that, as proponents of the balance of payments approach contended, causation ran from the exchange rate to domestic prices.[11]

Hyperinflation and the Reverse Causality Argument

Despite Cassel's forceful and vigorous attack, the debate did not go into high gear until the postwar hyperinflation episode of the early 1920s.[12] During this episode the price of foreign exchange rose to fantastic multiples of its prewar level and everybody wanted to know why. Advocates of the monetary approach, including Cassel and his followers, pointed to the explosive growth of the money supply as the obvious answer. But proponents of balance of payments approach dismissed the monetary factor and instead attributed exchange depreciation to the adverse balance of payments caused by the burden of reparations payments combined with Germany's alleged "fixed need for imports" and "absolute inability to export." In their view money had nothing to do with the fall of the mark. On the contrary, they claimed that causation ran from the exchange rate to money rather than vice versa. They specified the following causal order of events: depreciating exchanges, rising import prices, rising domestic prices, consequent budget deficits, and increased demand for money requiring an accommodative increase in the money supply.

Regarding the increase in the money supply, they contended that the exchange-induced rise in prices created a need for money on the part of business and government, that it was the Reichsbank's duty to meet this need, and that it could do so without affecting prices.* Far from seeing currency expansion as the source of inflation, they argued that it was the solution to the acute shortage of money caused by skyrocketing prices.

---

*Balance of payments theorists placed the blame for government deficits financed by new money issues squarely on inflation rather than on the actions of the policy authorities. Inflation, they said, caused government expenditures, which were largely fixed in real terms and thus rose in step with prices, to rise faster than revenues, which were fixed in nominal terms in the short run and thus adjusted sluggishly in inflation. The result was an inflation-induced deficit that had to be financed by money growth. The authorities had

Here is the familiar argument that the central bank must accommodate supply-shock inflation in order to prevent a disastrous contraction of the real (price-deflated) money stock. German proponents of the balance of payments view, however, pushed this argument to ridiculous extremes. In 1923, when the Reichsbank was already issuing currency in denominations as high as 100 trillion marks, Havenstein, the president of the Reichsbank, expressed hope that the installation of new high-speed currency printing presses would help overcome the money shortage. Citing the real bills doctrine, he refused to believe that the Reichsbank had overissued the currency. He also flatly denied that the Reichsbank's discount rate of 90 percent was too low although the market rate on short-term loans was an astronomical 7,300 percent per year.[13]

Characteristics of the Balance of Payments School

It is instructive at this point to identify the chief characteristics of the German balance of payments school if only because some of these characteristics survive in vestigial form in popular discussions of the fall of the dollar. First, members of the school tended to adhere to superficial supply-and-demand explanations of the exchange rate. Some merely asserted that the exchange rate is determined by supply and demand without saying what influences supply and demand. Others specified certain autonomous real factors affecting the balance of payments as the underlying determinants of foreign exchange supply and demand. None recognized that relative price levels and/or relative money stocks might also play a role. These variables were effectively excluded from the balance of payments school's list of exchange rate determinants.

The school's second characteristic was its tendency to identify exchange depreciation with one or two items in the balance of payments. In particular, members singled out raw material imports as the culprit, just as some analysts currently blame petroleum imports. Third, they tended to treat the items in the balance of payments as predetermined and independent, when in fact they are interdependent variables determined by prices and the exchange rate. For example, they asserted that Germany's import requirements were irreducible regardless of price and that her exports were likewise fixed. They then extended this reasoning to

---

nothing to do with the deficit. The monetary school rejected this argument on the grounds that the government possessed the power to reduce its real expenditures and, moreover, that the authorities had deliberately engaged in deficit spending for several years before the hyperinflation, thus establishing the monetary preconditions essential to that episode.

the other accounts of the balance of payments. Fourth, they denied the operation of a balance of payments adjustment mechanism. This denial followed from their assumption that both the balance of payments and the exchange rate are exogenously determined by factors that are independent of money, prices, and the exchange rate itself. This assumption permitted no equilibrating feedback effects from the exchange rate to the balance of payments. M. J. Bonn, a prominent balance of payments theorist, expressed the point as follows.[14] Suppose, he said, that import contraction is impossible given Germany's dependence on imported raw materials and foodstuffs. Likewise export expansion is impossible because of tariff barriers and economic depression abroad. Now assume a disturbance that produces a deficit in Germany's trade balance, thereby causing an exchange rate depreciation of the mark relative to its purchasing-power parity equilibrium. According to Cassel and his school, the depreciation, by lowering the foreign currency price of German goods and raising the mark price of foreign goods, should spur exports and check imports, thereby restoring equilibrium in the trade balance. But these price-induced readjustments in trade are impossible when imports and exports are independent of exchange rate changes. In such a case, an adverse trade balance may persist in the face of an undervalued currency, contrary to the conclusion of the monetary school. Finally, the fifth characteristic of the German balance of payments school was its categorical rejection of the proposition that money influences prices and the exchange rate. As previously mentioned, this antimonetarist view was implicit in the school's reverse causation, money shortage, and real bills doctrines.

The Monetary School's Critique

Members of the monetary school had little trouble exposing the fallacies in these views. They noted that supply and demand constitute only the *proximate* determinants of the exchange rate, that the *ultimate* determinants are the factors underlying supply and demand themselves, and that these factors include the relative levels determined by relative money stocks. They pointed out that the components of the balance of payments are variables, not constants, that they are determined simultaneously by prices and the exchange rate, and that exchange rate movements reflect primarily monetary pressure on the entire balance of payments, rather than nonmonetary disturbances to particular accounts. Regarding the reparations account, they noted that the depreciation of the mark was not caused by these payments themselves but rather by the inflationary way they were financed, that is, by fresh issues of paper money. As for

Germany's alleged need for a fixed physical quantity of imports regardless of prices, they argued that needs are not incompressible and that even the import demand for absolute necessities possesses some price elasticity. Moreover, they pointed out that exports too are responsive to changes in relative prices and that the exchange rate mechanism would therefore tend to equilibrate exports and imports were it not continually frustrated by inflation. They maintained that had domestic prices stopped rising, a further depreciation of the mark, by making German goods cheaper to foreigners and foreign goods dearer to Germans, would have stimulated exports and restrained imports until new equilibrium was reached. In their view, it was only the rise in domestic prices consequent upon the increase in the money supply that prevented the expansion of exports and the contraction of imports. Otherwise current account equilibrium would have been restored by the exchange-induced shift in relative prices of exports and imports.

Most important, advocates of the monetary approach argued convincingly that exchange depreciation originated in excessive money growth and that the monetary authorities could have stopped the depreciation had they been willing to exercise control over the money stock. In short, they showed that the price of foreign exchange could not have risen indefinitely unless sustained by inflationary money growth. Had the latter ceased, the exchange rate would have stabilized.

The Expectations Element

The German inflation controversy contributed the last of the three major elements to the monetary approach. The English bullionist writers had already established the quantity theory and purchasing-power parity elements. All that remained was the statement and development of the expectations channel, linking anticipations of future money supplies with the current exchange rate. This step was taken during the hyperinflation debate when the monetary school sought to explain why the dollar/mark exchange rate actually rose faster than the German money supply. According to the strict quantity theory and purchasing-power parity hypotheses, the two variables should rise at roughly the same rate. Their failure to do so was taken by the balance of payments school as constituting evidence of the invalidity of the monetary approach. Advocates of the monetary approach, however, rescued it from this criticism by explaining the exchange rate/money growth disparity in terms of market expectations. In a nutshell, they contended that in disequilibrium, the exchange rate is influenced by the expected future exchange rate (that is *anticipated* purchasing-power parity), which depends on prospective price levels, governed by expected money stocks. Howard Ellis, in his *German Monetary Theory 1905-1933* (1934),[15] cites several economists, notably Gustav Cassel, Walter Eucken, Fritz Machlup, Ludwig von Mises, Melchior Palyi, A. C. Pigou, and Dennis Robertson, who claimed that exchange rate movements reflected anticipated increases in the money stock, and argued that the external value of the mark varied in proportion to the expected future quantity of money rather than to the actual current quantity. In sum, observers watching the money supply accelerate month after month came to expect future money growth to exceed present money growth; these expectations caused the exchange rate to outpace the money supply.

Similar explanations were advanced to account for disparities between the rate of domestic price inflation and the rate of currency depreciation in Germany. Eucken, Machlup, and von Mises argued that the exchange rate embodies inflationary expectations and that exchange rate movements parallel movements in expected future prices, not actual current prices. For this reason, they claimed, the exchange rate may deviate from the purchasing-power parity computed from current price levels. Cassel perhaps put the matter most clearly when he wrote:

> A depreciation of currency is often merely an expression for discounting an expected fall in the currency's internal purchasing power. The world sees that the process of inflation is constantly going on, and that the condition of State finances, for instance, is rendering a continuance of the depreciation of money probable. The internal valuation of the currency will, then, generally show a tendency to anticipate events, so to speak, and becomes more an expression of the internal value the currency is expected to possess in a few months, or perhaps in a year's time.[16]

As this passage suggests, members of the monetary school explained not only how expectations affect the exchange rate, but also how expectations themselves are determined. In essence, they said that people base their exchange rate expectations on observations of the behavior of the policy authorities, especially the latter's monetary and fiscal response to large budgetary commitments such as reparations payments. These observations yield information about the authorities' policy strategy, and people use this information in predicting future policy actions affecting the exchange rate. As Dennis Robertson put it in his famous textbook *Money* (1922), "the actual rate of exchange is largely governed by the *expected* behavior of the country's monetary authority. ..."[17] In the case of Germany, the authorities were already demonstrating a pronounced tendency to finance reparations payments with budget deficits and excessive monetary growth. People expected this policy to continue and these expectations were embodied in the exchange rate.*

CONCLUSION

This study has surveyed the development of the monetary approach to the exchange rate in three historical controversies with the rival balance of payments approach. The study offers some support for Sir J. R. Hick's argument that monetary theory, unlike other branches of economic theory, tends to be influenced by historical events and episodes, notably severe monetary disturbances and institutional change that alter the character of the monetary system.[18] In the case of the monetary theory of the exchange rate, at least, Hicks's argument seems validated. For, as discussed above, the main elements of the monetary approach emerged from controversies triggered by currency, price, and exchange rate upheavals following the suspension of metallic parities. Specifically, the study argues that the monetary approach originated in the Swedish bullionist controversy of the 1750s, that its quantity theory and purchasing-power parity components were thoroughly established during the English bullionist controversy of the early 1800s, and that the expectations component was added during the German inflation debate of the early 1920s. Thus all the elements of the modern monetary approach were firmly in place by the mid-1920s.

NOTES

1. For another treatment of the role of the monetary and the balance of payments approaches in these debates see John Myhrman, "Experiences of Flexible Exchange Rates in Earlier Periods: Theories, Evidence, and a New View," *Scandinavian Journal of Economics* 78, no. 2 (1976): 169–96.

2. On what follows, see Robert V. Eagly, *The Swedish Bullionist Controversy* (Philadelphia: American Philosophical Society, 1971).

3. Pehr Niclas Christiernin, *Lectures on the High Price of Foreign Exchange in Sweden*, 1761.

---

*Expectations were not the only factor cited by the monetary school as causing the exchange rate to lead prices and money. Another was currency substitution, that is, the substitution of stable dollars for unstable marks in German residents' transactions and asset money balances.

4. On the English bullionist controversy see Denis P. O'Brien, *The Classical Economists* (London: Oxford University Press, 1975), pp. 147–53; and Jacob Viner, *Studies in the Theory of International Trade* (New York: Augustus Kelley, 1965), pp. 119–70.

5. David Ricardo, *The Principles of Political Economy and Taxation* (London: J. M. Dent and Sons, 1917), p. 151, quoted in James W. Angell, *The Theory of International Prices* (New York: Augustus Kelley, 1965), p. 69, n. 3.

6. John Wheatley, *Remarks on Currency and Commerce* (London: Burton, 1803), p. 207, quoted in Angell, op. cit., p. 52.

7. Regarding the policy implications of the Ricardian definition of excess, see O'Brien, op. cit., p. 148.

8. On Blake, see O'Brien, op. cit., pp. 150–51.

9. Thornton's contribution is discussed in O'Brien, op. cit., pp. 149–50.

10. Gustav Cassel, *Money and Foreign Exchange After 1914* (New York: Macmillan, 1922), pp. 149, 164–65.

11. Ibid., pp. 145, 167–168.

12. What follows relies heavily on Ellis' classic survey of the German inflation controversy. See Howard S. Ellis, *German Monetary Theory, 1905–1933* (Cambridge: Harvard University Press, 1934), Chapters 12–16.

13. Leland Yeager, *International Monetary Relations: Theory, History, and Policy*, 2nd ed. (New York: Harper & Row, 1976), p. 314.

14. Bonn's views are discussed in Paul Einzig, *The History of Foreign Exchange* (London: Macmillan, 1962), pp. 271–72, and Ellis, op. cit., pp. 248–52.

15. Ellis, op. cit.

16. Cassel, op. cit., pp. 149–50.

17. Dennis Robertson, *Money* (London: Cambridge University Press, 1922), p. 133.

18. Sir John Hicks, *Critical Essays in Monetary Theory* (London: Oxford University Press, 1967), pp. 156–58.

10

Monetary Policy,
Interest Rate Targets,
and Foreign Exchange Markets

Bluford H. Putnam

The interaction between domestic monetary policy and foreign exchange markets has been analyzed only from the perspective of an exogenous change in the money supply causing a change in the exchange rate of the domestic currency vis-à-vis the currency of a specific trading partner. Studies such as those by Jacob Frenkel or by Thomas Humphrey and Thomas Lawler always assume that monetary policy is conducted through changes in the money supply, and conclude, all other things being equal, that increases in the domestic money supply *cause* a depreciation of the domestic currency in terms of foreign currency.[1] Monetary policy, however, is not always conducted through the money supply, particularly in the very short run. For instance, U.S. monetary authorities set targets for the growth of monetary aggregates, but day-to-day and week-to-week policy actions follow federal funds interest rate targets. Furthermore, the central bank discount rate is a very active policy tool for many foreign countries.

   If central banks conduct monetary policy in the short run with respect to interest rate targets, then variations in the money supply may be caused by events in the foreign exchange markets, particularly changes in expectations of future exchange rates. The argument is developed in the following manner. Should some exogenous event result in reformulation by exchange market participants of their expectations of future exchange rates, the market forward exchange rate would not reflect the change in expectations, because central banks in adhering to an interest rate target are implicitly fixing the interest rate differential between assets denominated in different currencies. International arbitrage will ensure that the market forward exchange premium (or discount) will correspond quite closely to this interest rate differential. Since the forward exchange rate does not shift when exchange rate expectations do, market participants have an incentive to increase their liabilities in the depreciating currency and increase their assets in the appreciating currency. This change in the demand for certain monies will be validated by the central banks if they maintain constant interest rates. Substantial shifts in exchange market expectations, then, result in swings in the money supply, and, as will be apparent later, changes in the spot exchange rate, too.

The study is organized as follows. First, a behavioral relationship is postulated between the demand for domestic liabilities and differences between forward exchange rates and expected future spot rate. Second, the supply of domestic liabilities is specified by assuming that central banks set interest rate targets and meet them. Third, with the supply and demand for domestic liabilities already specified, an examination of the foreign exchange markets completes the model, determining the equilibrium spot and forward exchange rates and the domestic money stock. In the final section, the conclusions of the model are reviewed with particular attention to their policy implications.

DEMAND FOR DOMESTIC LIABILITIES

In well-integrated international capital markets the mechanism known as international arbitrage serves to guarantee that the interest rate differential between comparable assets denominated in different currencies will be nearly equal to the forward exchange premium or discount. Ths arbitrage assumption can be expressed as follows:

$$(F - S)/S = rd - rf \tag{1}$$

where F = the forward exchange rate (in terms of foreign currency units per unit of domestic currency)
S = the spot exchange rate
rf = the interest rate on foreign assets
rd = the interest rate on domestic assets, and
F, rf, and rd are all quoted with respect to the same time dimension (maturity date)

If international markets function efficiently they will reflect some aggregate forecast of the future spot exchange rate and provide an expected return to the bearer of the foreign exchange risk.[2] In equation form,

$$F = F^e + v \qquad (2)$$

where F^e = market forecast of the future spot exchange rate, and
v = expected return due to foreign exchange risk

For the purposes of this analysis, the expected return due to foreign exchange risk, v, will be set equal to zero. While this need not be the actual case, recognition of a risk return is unnecessary in the context of this study.

Equation 2 is essentially an equilibrium condition. For if market expectations of the future spot exchange rate do not equal the forward rate ($F \neq F^e$), then some market participants have an incentive to borrow in one currency and lend in another. Such portfolio-optimizing actions would cause movements in the spot exchange rate, the domestic interest rate, and the foreign interest rate until equilibrium values were reached.

Expanding on the adjustment process noted in the preceding paragraph, one can focus initially on the demand for liabilities denominated in the currency that is expected to depreciate in excess of that predicted by the forward exchange rate.* In equation form,

$$\Delta DL^d = f(\Delta K, (F - F^e)/S) \qquad (3)$$

where DL^d = the demand for liabilities denominated in the domestic currency
K = all other demand factors, which are held constant in this analysis, and
$\partial((F - F^e)/S)/\partial DL^d > 0$

Whenever actual market expectations differ from the market forward exchange rate, there will be a demand for liabilities in the currency that is expected to depreciate in excess of the forward rate. This demand for liabilities in the currency expected to depreciate is matched by a demand for assets denominated in the currency whose expected appreciation is greater than that indicated by the forward rate.

———

*The text assumes that the domestic currency is also the currency expected to depreciate with respect to some particuar foreign currency. To analyze the reverse case, in which the domestic currency is expected to appreciate, one need only substitute "domestic" for "foreign" and vice versa.

Without being specific concerning the type of liabilities being discussed here, a reasonable assumption is that a stable set of these liabilities will be included in standard definitions of the money supply for any particular country. Thus, money supply changes should be in the same direction and of similar relative magnitude as changes in domestic liabilities. Explicitly,

$$\Delta M^d = h(\Delta DL^d) \tag{4}$$

where M^d = the domestic money supply demanded.

CENTRAL BANK POLICY

Turning now to the supply of domestic liabilities, the key factors are the private banking system and the monetary authorities or central bank. The private banking system is assumed to supply credit (liabilities) to demanders for some market-determined spread over the interest rate at which the banking system can acquire the funds to lend. The interest rate on the "wholesale" funds market is determined by the central bank. That is, the central bank conducts monetary policy by fixing some interest rate, and in this case, the interest rate fixed by the authorities is the interest rate on the interbank market for loanable funds.*

The assumption that the central bank fixes the interest rate is expressed as follows:

$$rd = \overline{rd} \tag{5}$$

The banking system is essentially passive and loans funds at some spread over the wholesale interest rate. This spread is set equal to zero for simplicity, and it can be noted that the supply of domestic liabilities will expand to meet demand. That is,

$$\Delta DL^s = \Delta DL^d \tag{6}$$

---

*For the United States, this compares with the federal funds markets.

Editor's Note: This study was written originally in 1972, and was the product of research done while the author was a graduate student at the University of Chicago. Minor revisions were made in the process of editing this manuscript to make it suitable for publication in this volume.

And, correspondingly, the money supply will also accommodate the quantity of money demanded:

$$\Delta M^s = \Delta M^d \tag{7}$$

By assuming that the banking system is passive, that is, that banks do not change their net position, the analysis focuses directly on the monetary policy of the central bank. And, instead of assuming that the money supply is the control variable, the analysis assumes that the interest rate is the control variable. While this assumption is certainly anything but new to large segments of the economic literature, it provides a different focus in the context of recent developments in international monetary theory, such as the monetary approach to the balance of payments literature. In any case, the assumption has two implications. First, the supply of money will accommodate changes in the demand for money, as the central bank acts to fix prices in the bond market. Secondly, in terms of practical applications, the model is essentially short-run in nature, for two reasons. First, many central banks use interest rate targets only for short-run policy and adjust these targets over the course of a year to control certain monetary aggregates, and second, to preserve the simplicity of the argument this model does not allow for feedback effects of central bank policy into any real variables affecting money demand (see equation 3, the constant K).

On the foreign side, the foreign central bank acts to fix the interest rate on foreign assets, hence,

$$rf = \overline{rf} \tag{8}$$

Coupling these two central bank policy assumptions, equations 5 and 8, with the international arbitrage assumption, equation 1, the market forward exchange premium or discount is determined. This implies that the demand for domestic liabilities is also determined, equation 3, given the spot exchange rate and expectations of its change.

FOREIGN EXCHANGE PRESSURES

At this stage, the process generating an expansion in domestic liabilities is clear, but the model contains no mechanism for reaching any kind of equilibrium. Looking at the demand for domestic liabilities, equation 3, one can identify three areas for further attention. First, nothing has yet been said about the determination of the expectations of the future spot rate (F^c). Second, the spot exchange rate is also undetermined. And third, the counterpart of the demand for domestic liabilities, that is, the demand for foreign assets, has yet to be discussed.

With respect to the formation of expectations concerning the future spot exchange rate, only the briefest of specifications is required here. Thus,

$$F^c = \overline{F^c} \tag{9}$$

which is to say that expectations of the future spot rate are determined outside the scope of this model.*

The determination of the spot exchange rate and the discussion of the demand for foreign assets are intertwined. In this analysis, the change in demand for domestic liabilities is desired specifically for use in acquiring foreign assets. That is, when the forward exchange rate does not equal the markets' expectations of the future spot rate ($F \neq F^c$), there is a demand for domestic liabilities to finance the purchase of foreign assets. The price of foreign assets is fixed in foreign currency terms by the foreign central bank's policy of fixing the interest rate (equation 8). But the price of a foreign asset is not fixed in terms of the domestic currency price. In other words, the exchange rate can change in response to pressures in the foreign exchange market, and changes in the spot exchange rate effectively change the domestic value of any foreign assets bought or sold. With respect to the foreign exchange market, the demand for foreign currency is, thus, established as directly related to the change in demand for domestic liabilities. Or simply,

$$FC^d = g(K, 1/S, \Delta DL) \tag{10}$$

where FC = foreign currency, and
$\partial \Delta DL / \partial FC^d > 0$
K = other relevant factors (held constant here), and
$\partial (1/S) / \partial FC^d < 0$

---

*A more sophisticated specification might include feedback effects from changes in the money supply to changes in expectations of the future spot exchange rate. While such a specification would affect the dynamic path of this model, it would not alter the basic conclusion concerning the direction of change in the money supply and spot exchange rates that are derived later in this section.

The supply function is held constant with respect to changes in the demand for domestic liabilities since there is no incentive to borrow funds denominated in the appreciating currency. So,

$$FC^s = h(K, 1/S) \tag{11}$$

where $\partial 1/S/\partial FC^s > 0$

and for equilibrium,

$$FC^s = FC^d \tag{12}$$

Equations 10, 11, and 12 describing foreign exchange market pressures indicate that the domestic currency will depreciate whenever there is a demand for domestic liabilities due to differences between the forward exchange rate and the market's expectations of the future spot rate.

The spot rate can be solved from equations 10, 11, and 12, plus the interest arbitrage assumption, 1, and the central bank policy assumptions, 5 and 8, given the expected future spot rate, 9. That is, the spot exchange rate will adjust to equilibrate the actual forward exchange rate and the expected future spot rate.* Substituting the interest rates from 5 and 8 into the arbitrage equation 1 yields the actual market forward discount, $(F - S)/S$. When equilibrium conditions 2, 7, and 12 hold, $F = F^e$, and $(F - S)/S = (F^e - S)/S$. This uniquely determines the spot exchange rate.

A numerical example is useful. Initially, the domestic and foreign central banks set interest rates such that the forward exchange discount is 5 percent on the domestic currency. Also, the spot exchange rate is 100 units of foreign currency per unit of domestic currency. Starting from equilibrium in which $F = F^e$, the forward exchange rate can be calculated from equation 1 and equals 95 units of foreign currency per unit of domestic currency. Now, some exogenous event causes market expectations of the future spot rate to change such that now $F^e = 92$. Since $(F - F^e)/S$ is now a positive value, the demand for domestic liabilities and foreign assets increases. This results in the spot foreign exchange markets in a depreciation of the domestic currency until $F = F^e$. With no change in the forward discount of 5 percent, since central banks have not altered interest rates, the spot exchange rate must fall to 96.84 foreign currency units per unit of domestic currency. At this rate, $F = F^e = 92$. The actual increase in

---

*This was alluded to earlier in the discussion of equation 2.

domestic liabilities and the money supply is determined by the elasticity of the demand for foreign assets in terms of the domestic currency price, but the direction is clear. Furthermore, the greater the difference between the forward exchange rate and the expected future spot rate, the greater the equilibrating increase in the money supply.

CONCLUSION

Essentially the model indicates that the decision by central banks to fix interest rates (stabilize local bond prices) implies a willingness to accept deviations in both the money supply and the spot exchange rate when exogenous events occur that shift foreign exchange expectations. Central banks often fail to admit this and on occasion can be observed intervening in exchange markets to resist downward spot exchange rate changes and intervening in the domestic bond markets to resist upward interest rate movements. One of these operations is doomed to failure.

NOTES

1. See Jacob Frenkel, "A Monetary Approach to the Exchange Rate: Doctrinal Aspects and Empirical Evidence," in *Flexible Exchange Rates and Stabilization Policy*, ed. Jan Herin, Assar Linbeck, and Johan Myhrma (Boulder, Colo.: Westview Press, 1977), pp. 69–92; Thomas M. Humphrey and Thomas A. Lawler, "Factors Determining Exchange Rates: A Simple Model and Empirical Tests," Federal Reserve Bank of Richmond *Economic Review* (May-June 1977): 10–15 also reprinted in this volume (Chapter 8).

2. While this risk premium is not critical to this study, it is worth noting that it does exist. For related papers, see B. Cornell, "Spot Rates, Forward Rates and Exchange Market Efficiency," *Journal of Financial Economics* 5 (1977): 55–65; F. Modigliani and R. Sutch, "Innovations in Interest Rate Policy," *American Economic Review* 56 (May 1966): 178–97; and J. R. Hicks. *Value and Capital* (Oxford: Clarendon Press, 1946), p. 138 in particular.

Part 3

CURRENCY SUBSTITUTION AND FLEXIBLE EXCHANGE RATES

11

A Currency Portfolio Approach to Exchange Rate Determination: Exchange Rate Stability and the Independence of Monetary Policy

David T. King
Bluford H. Putnam
D. Sykes Wilford

The strongest argument traditionally made in favor of flexible exchange rates has been that they allow countries, not committed to buying and selling currencies at fixed prices, to pursue independent monetary policies according to their own welfare criteria. Actual experience with floating rates, however, has called into question the meaningfulness of monetary autonomy even under these conditions. Moreover, recent developments in the literature, specifically those adopting monetary approaches to international finance theory, have suggested that monetary independence may be illusory even in a positive sense. From R. Dornbusch,[1] it can be concluded (among other things) that independent monetary policies ultimately affect only nominal variables, simply altering (equivalently) inflation and exchange rate paths. J. Frenkel,[2] in underlining the money–expectations–exchange rate linkage, suggests that monetary independence in any real sense may be largely chimerical, even in the short run.

The Frenkel study is based on a generalization to a flexible exchange rate system of the "monetary" or "assets" view of balance of payments adjustment under fixed exchange rates.[3] The substitutability of currencies in the *supply* of credit that explains international reserves flows and

This study benefited from comments by Richard Zecher, Richard Levich, William Gasser, Marc Miles, Alden Toevs, Ed Frydl, and M. A. Akhtar.

connects monetary policies under fixed exchange rates in turn determines exchange rate fluctuations under flexible rates. As he observes,

> Being a relative price of two assets (moneys), the equilibrium exchange rate is attained when the existing *stocks* of the two moneys are willingly held. It is reasonable, therefore, that a theory of the determination of the relative price of two moneys could be stated conveniently in terms of the supply of and demand for these moneys.[4]

In this model, then, exchange rates are equilibrium solutions at which the existing stocks of the set of highly liquid financial assets—the world's currencies—are contentedly held.

The assets approach, through emphasis on the role of supply substitutability among the various monies, shows that the same fundamental force that induces monetary integration under fixed rates—optimizing international reallocation of credit demand in response to changing relative credit supply conditions—still creates pressures tending to frustrate monetary independence under flexible rates. The potential short-run benefits of divergent monetary policies quickly evaporate as the process of arbitrage among internationally substitutable credit sources chokes off incipient short-term changes in real interest rates. Monetary deviations are consequently pushed into nominal adjustments of prices and exchange rates.

However, this approach to exchange rate determination stops short of being wholly analogous to other monetary models of assets pricing—for example, the assets approaches to bond price determination of James Tobin or Karl Brunner. In particular, in these other models all transactors generally hold some or all of the assets under consideration, so that bond prices are determined by a process of portfolio balancing among assets substitutable in both supply and demand. In the assets approach to exchange rate determination, on the other hand, economic agents are implicitly viewed as holding only *one* asset (one money), in that the ultimate demand for a particular currency stock implicitly arises only from *domestic* sources. Monetary services can be provided only by the domestic currency, so that, though one optimizes over the set of currencies in obtaining the cheapest source of credit, the transactor always converts the proceeds of his acquisitions into domestic currency. In effect, the elasticity of substitution in demand among the various monies is, in the received monetary approach to exchange rate determination, assumed to equal zero. Any one agent's "portfolio" of highly liquid assets therefore consists of only one currency. Consequently, all other things being equal, incipient changes in the domestically determined supply of money inevitably generate exchange rate movements. Clearly, however, multinational trade and investment firms, as well as banks and foreign exchange market speculators, maintain money holdings denominated in several currencies. Insofar as their particular institutional framework and the ability of the various assets to provide similar monetary services allow, these transactors optimize through substitutions among their money balances as expectations concerning the value of the currency portfolio change. Recent literature has developed the concept of currency substitution in the demand for money. Concentrating on potential differential return to the various monies and exogenously stipulating various degrees of substitution, Lance Girton and Don Roper[5] show how currency substitution can moderate exchange rate movements. Marc Miles[6] has attempted empirically to identify parametric indicators of the degree of currency substitution in money demand.[7] Emphasizing the theoretical development of demand-side substitutions, however, these authors abstract from substitution in supply, so that a comprehensive currency portfolio approach to exchange rate determination remains to be enunciated. Moreover, a theory of the degree of currency substitution itself has not been fully developed.*

To assess better the questions of exchange rate stability and the independence of monetary policy under flexible exchange rates, the initial purpose of this study is to extend the assets or monetary approach to a balance of payments-exchange rates model into a more general (portfolio adjustment) model of exchange rate determination. This is done by taking explicit account of substitution among currencies in *both* the demand for and supply of money. To this end, first the money demand function is generalized to include foreign monies. A theory of the degree of currency substitution is obtained at the same time. Then, the portfolio approach to exchange rate determination—an assets model that includes currency substitution in demand—is developed. The study concludes with a discussion of the implications of the general model for the efficacy of international monetary policy divergence.

Summarizing, the application of this monetary synthesis to the question of policy independence strongly implies the meaninglessness of monetary autonomy under flexible exchange rates. Optimizing demanders of monetary services react in a manner that reinforces stable and harmonious policies but magnifies the undesirable effects of unstable and digressive policies.

———

*Associated with the literature on currency substitutability are issues addressed by F. A. Hayek and Gordon Tullock on competition between monies.[8]

CURRENCY SUBSTITUTION AND
THE DEMAND FOR MONETARY SERVICES

Generalizing Money Demand

Casual observation suggests that a large proportion of exchange market transactions are conducted by banks and corporations that regularly deal in foreign exchange and hold balances of several currencies simultaneously. Foreign currencies perform monetary services for these transactors as they conduct their daily business of buying and selling goods and assets on an international scale. These transactors are the first to feel any wealth effects due to the change in exchange rates, and consequently are continually optimizing at the margin in the foreign exchange market to the extent that institutional constraints allow.

Thus, for an open economy, a general money demand specification must take into account transactors who utilize several currencies in order to fulfill desired monetary services. Such a money demand function can be simply stated as follows:

$$M^d/p = \Phi \cdot f(y, i, u) \tag{1}$$

where M^d = quantity of *domestic* money (currency) demanded
   P = the domestic price level
   Φ = proportion of monetary services provided by domestic money
     $(0 < \Phi < 1)$
   y = permanent real income
   i = opportunity cost of holding money, and
   u = stochastic disturbance (log normally distributed)

In this function, the total demand for real monetary services, given by $f(\cdot)$, depends on a traditional set of determinants—permanent real income and the opportunity cost of holding money. This total demand is adjusted by Φ to yield the demand for domestic money.

In this function, residents' (domestic transactors') demand for money can be partly satisfied by foreign currency holdings ($1 - \Phi$ gives the proportion of monetary services provided by foreign money). Residents' allocations of their money holdings between foreign and domestic currencies will depend on the degree of substitutability between monies. In the extreme case of perfect substitutability, transactors would be indifferent between domestic and foreign currencies. Excess demand for domestic money would tend to be satisfied simply by increased private holdings of foreign money, with no change in the exchange rate.* This is the counterpart to the fixed exchange rate case in which currency substitution is perfect on the supply side. Alternately, the assumption of zero substitution among monies, implied in nearly all existing models of exchange rate determination, requires that exchange rates fully reflect all relative changes in excess money supply. Of importance from this brief discussion, then, is that the existence of a set of transactors able to substitute among currencies, even imperfectly, directly affects how exchange rates will adjust following events that change relative excess demands for money. Thus, the currency substitution question has important implications for the independence of monetary policy under flexible exchange rates.

Currency Substitution: The Fundamental Scope

What, then, are the determinants of the substitution among currencies in the demand for money—that is, of the proportionality factor, Φ, in equation 1, which reflects the shares of foreign and domestic currencies held in real money balances? Basically, currencies are substitutes in demand to the extent that they provide similar monetary services to *any* transactor. Alternatively, the extent to which the monetary services rendered to the representative individual by any set of currencies differ is reflected in the degree to which the two assets are not perfect substitutes in demand. Thus, the fundamental scope for currency substitution is determined in a macroeconomic sense by the integration of world goods and capital markets. The state of global market integration in turn affects the allocation of the currency portfolio through both transactions and speculative reasons for demanding money.

Currencies are ultimately imperfect substitutes because domestic trade is denominated in domestic currency. Thus, for a large part of their usual transactions for goods and services, individuals acquiring foreign currencies must first go through the exchange markets to obtain the required domestic currency. However, increased integration of world markets for goods and services—making foreign goods and services more readily accessible (more effectively substitutable) to domestic residents— would tend to provide a wider role for foreign currencies in satisfying transactions demands for money. Indeed, the transactions demand for

---

*This assumes appropriate foreign monetary expansion. Otherwise, relative holdings remain the same; the attempt to increase holdings simply raises interest rates everywhere.

various forms of money for use in international trade is substantial. Transactors trading internationally have the opportunity to choose from a broad variety of substitutable goods and services denominated in a variety of currencies. Optimizing over changing costs of money balances, they substitute among currencies in their transactions demand portfolios as they reallocate demands for *goods* among substitute sources. Moreover, international corporations, incurring large flows of receipts and expenditures in several currencies, have wide latitude in deciding whether to convert to domestic currency or to hold foreign currencies for possible future international transactions.

Currency substitution in "speculative" money demand is determined by world capital market integration. In this context, utility-maximizing individuals—especially through nonbank intermediaries—can distribute their financial wealth among all available currencies and currency denominations of bonds, instead of just between domestic money and domestic currency-denominated bonds as in the traditional closed economy case. The high degree of world capital market integration and the ease of acquiring foreign deposits and foreign currency-denominated bonds suggest that "speculative" money demand portfolios are well diversified among the various currencies.

Generalizing, then, it is the integration of world markets for goods and financial assets that allows different currencies to perform similar monetary services and thus provides the institutional framework within which currency substitution is possible. Formulating this concept more rigorously, the elasticity of currency substitution is given by

$$\sigma = g(I) \tag{2}$$

where σ = elasticity of currency substitution in real money demand
 I = the intensity of integration of global goods and capital markets, arising from that institutional structure, and $d\sigma/dI > 0$

that is, an increase in world market integration increases currency substitutability.*

To simplify the analysis, we take the intensity of world market integration as constant for the relevant period of analysis. However, market integration can change as a result of secular forces and official

---

*Miles estimated the elasticity of currency substitution in money demand between U.S. and Canadian dollars, showing it to be significantly greater than unity.[9]

policies. The primary institutional factors determining the level of I for any time period are the set of tariffs, quotas, and other barriers to trade of goods; the set of controls on international movements of capital, transportation, and other transactions costs; and the availability of information concerning external sources of and markets for goods, services, and financial assets. The first two sets of factors are officially determined, while the latter two change secularly over time. Symbolically,

$$I = h(T, C; \theta, \phi) \tag{3}$$

where T = barriers to trade
     C = capital controls
     θ = transportation and transactions costs, and
     ϕ = information availability;
and where $\partial I/\partial T < 0$
        $\partial I/\partial C < 0$
        $\partial I/\partial \theta < 0$, and
        $\partial I/\partial \phi > 0$

Increases in official barriers to trade or restrictions on capital movements decrease global market integration, while decreases in transportation costs or increases in information availability enhance it.

As the world market becomes more integrated, different currencies become more acceptable as payment for goods or assets, since any currency more readily provides monetary services to the transactor. Thus, increased world economic integration reduces the ultimate institutional rigidity making for nonsubstitutability—the acceptability on the part of sellers of goods and assets of only the domestic currency in their marketing operations.

According to the theory outlined in this section, then, those factors that tend to enhance market integration also expand the fundamental scope for currency substitution by improving the extent to which different currencies can provide similar monetary services. In the context of well-integrated world markets, currency substitution is therefore an increasingly important issue in international finance theory and policy. Empirical indications of substantial integration of world markets for goods, services, and financial assets—as reflected in the existence of a sizable Eurocurrency market heavily involved in financing international flows of goods and services, and in the rapid growth of world trade, which now accounts for some 25 percent of world output—constitute a strong a priori case for taking account of currency substitution in exchange rate models and domestic monetary policy formulation.

Portfolio Substitution

Optimization over incipient changes in the relative cost of credit stimulates substitution in credit demand among the various currencies. Traditionally, these acquired balances were seen as always being fully converted back into domestic currency, in effect assuming that domestic money alone could supply monetary services to the transactor. The previous section shows that, in fact, monetary services are provided to individuals by several currencies in an integrated world economy. Consequently, transactors have reason to accept and hold both domestic and foreign monies in optimizing their money holdings, while continuing to substitute among these portfolio assets in order to minimize the overall opportunity cost of holding money balances. On this basis, optimizing shifts in demands for currency stocks tend to eliminate deviations in relative excess supplies of these monies. These adjustments tend to obviate changes in both interest rate differentials and exchange rates.

However, the transactor is now faced with a new optimization problem arising from the fact that currency substitution, though significant, is not perfect. That is, given the opportunity cost structure of holding the set of currencies, he must be alert to possible changes in the relative real values of the currencies he or she holds.* These potential changes arise from the possibility of differential rates of growth in the prices of goods and assets that the various currencies will purchase. To the extent that currencies are to any degree unique in their control over goods, with respect to their country of origin, the problem of adjusting balances of a currency expected to depreciate in real value arises.† This institutional characteristic or residual imperfection in world economy, caused by the absence of perfect integration, represents the fundamental nonsubstitutability among currencies.

Under floating rates, capital gains and losses to holding currency stocks, if anything, tend to occur *ahead* of actual changes in differential inflation, because possible future changes in the relative purchasing power of currencies over goods or financial assets tend to be quickly reflected in current exchange rates.[10]

---

*Throughout the discussion we abstract from the money-bond portfolio decision. Attention is concentrated on substitution among currencies aimed at maintaining the overall real value of the *money* portfolio.

†Thus, for example, incipiently higher inflation rates in New York do not provoke the running down of Second Reserve District notes in individuals' domestic currency portfolios, since Second District notes control Third, ... District goods. It is the fact that Second District notes control other district goods—currency substitutability is perfect—which guarantees that speculative arbitrage will lead to similar inflation rates in both districts.

Given the structure of relative opportunity costs of holding money and the basic scope for currency substitution, changes in the real value of currency portfolio holdings are most immediately brought about by exchange rate changes. Thus, possible exchange rate changes are of continuing concern to holders of currency portfolios as they attempt to maintain the overall real value of their money balances. It therefore seems clear that given the basic institutional factors determining the intensity of world market integration that allows substitution, the actual share of foreign currency in residents' real money balances will also depend on exchange rate expectations. Furthermore, an increase in uncertainty associated with the set of exchange rate expectations, all other things being equal, will encourage a portfolio shift away from domestic currency—now a relatively more risky asset in the currency portfolio—by risk-averse transactors.*

Formally, the share of foreign currencies in the total real money holdings of residents for any given set of relative credit conditions depends upon exchange rate expectations and the confidence with which these expectations are held, conditional upon the institutional structure determining currency substitutability.

$$\Phi = j(E^{o}, V|I) \tag{4}$$

where E^{o} = the expected exchange rate, in units of domestic currency per unit of foreign currency, relative to the current spot rate
V = the uncertainty associated with exchange rate expectations

and where $\partial\Phi/\partial E^{o} < 0$
$\partial\Phi/\partial V < 0$

Expectations of exchange rate appreciation unambiguously tend to increase domestic money holdings. The effects of increased uncertainty on the share of domestic money in the currency portfolio result in a shift away

----

*The presentation we are using illustrates the implications of portfolio substitution in a model in which the covariances of returns on all other assets are held constant. Thus, we can represent the portfolio optimization decision by looking at the behavior of the exchange value of only one currency vis-à-vis an unspecified foreign currency. As the uncertainty (taken as originating only from domestic sources) associated with the set of home currency-foreign currency exchange rates rises, the fundamental scope for currency substitution encourages a marginal shift into the foreign currency, whose exchange value, though simultaneously becoming more uncertain with respect to the *domestic* currency, is unchanged in its perceived variability with respect to all other currencies. Thus, the total variance of the portfolio is reduced by moving out of the home currency, even as (given the basic scope for substitution) money demand services are maintained.

from the risky asset. That is, if the exchange risk of holding the domestic money increases, then, all other things being equal, the marginal transactor alters the composition of his currency portfolio in favor of the less risky asset, toward foreign money.*

Following the rational expectations approach, market participants are assumed to use information efficiently, including information about the underlying economic structure.[11] Given foreign inflation, exchange rate expectations would therefore be based first on expectations concerning future domestic and foreign inflation rates,[12] which depend primarily on their perceptions about relative monetary policies and real growth prospects.[13] For simplicity, taking permanent real income growth as the more stable component, these expectations generally result from changes in transactors' perceptions of current and future domestic monetary policies, given foreign monetary policy. Thus,

$$E^o = m(M^o | M^o_w, I) \tag{5}$$

where M^o = expected domestic monetary expansion, and
M^o_w = expected foreign monetary expansion (considered given),

and where $\partial E^o / \partial M^o > 0$

That is, given a state of world market integration that fundamentally allows currency substitution, expectations of "loose" domestic monetary policies relative to given foreign monetary policies provoke expectations of exchange rate depreciation.

In turn, the uncertainty associated with exchange rate expectations will depend on the perceived variability of domestic and foreign policies:

$$V = V[Var(M^o) | M^o_w, I] \tag{6}$$

where Var (M^o) = the variance associated with expectations about domestic monetary policy

---

*We can cite as an example the recent (1976) Mexican experience. Prices in the tourist industry (an internationally traded and highly substitutable service) in Mexico have traditionally been denominated in both dollars and pesos, with a certain level of dollars to pesos held individually in the industry. The uncertainty surrounding the peso and its possible further depreciation changed this ratio dramatically as people moved toward dollar-denominated transactions much more heavily. Similarly, in border towns where most retail goods are, in effect, internationally traded, prices became widely quoted in dollars during the period of uncertainty following the initial de facto devaluation.

and where $\partial V/\partial$ Var $(M^o) > 0$

Increased variance raises the level of exchange uncertainty associated with portfolio holdings of domestic currency.

Substituting the specifications for exchange rate expectations, 5, and the associated uncertainty, 6, into the determination of the share of foreign currency holdings in residents' money balances, 4, yields

$$\Phi = k [M^o, \text{Var} (M^o) | M^o_w, I] \tag{7}$$

where $\partial\Phi/\partial M^o < 0$
$\partial\Phi/\partial$ Var $(M^o) < 0$

All other things being equal, an expected increase in the domestic money supply increases the portfolio share of real foreign money balances, to the extent that the domestic currency is expected to depreciate relative to foreign currencies. With respect to the variance of expectations, increased uncertainty concerning the real value of domestic money leads to a portfolio shift away from that asset. Increased domestic monetary policy variability requires a more careful monitoring of exchange rates, raising the relative cost of holding the domestic currency and reducing its usefulness for international transactions.

A GENERALIZED MODEL
OF EXCHANGE RATE DETERMINATION

The exchange rate model presented here is based on the demand and supply of money, monetary equilibrium, and assumptions concerning the integration of world markets for goods and assets. Thus, the model is a descendant of the monetary models of Harry G. Johnson, Robert A. Mundell, Arthur Laffer, Jacob Frenkel, Rudiger Dornbusch, and others.[14]

The money demand function is given a specific form,

$$M^d/p = \Phi y^a e^{\gamma_i} e^u \tag{7a}$$

The demand for domestic real money balances depends on the traditional determinants—permanent real income and the opportunity cost of holding money—and a factor of proportionality representing the shares of real monetary services provided by domestic and foreign monies. Converting this equation to growth terms yields,

$$g(M^d) - g(p) = g(\Phi) + \alpha g(y) + \gamma d(i) + u \tag{8}$$

where α = the real income elasticity of the demand for
real money balances $(\alpha > 0)$,

and where $g = (dx/dt)/x$ for all x (that is, the notation $g(x)$ represents
the percentage change form of the relevant variable),
γ = the (semilog) interest parameter of the demand for
real money balances $(\gamma < 0)$.

The supply of money is determined by the monetary authorities and is expressed here in growth terms:

$$g(M^s) = g(M) \tag{9}$$

Monetary equilibrium is maintained such that

$$g(M^d) = g(M^s) \tag{10}$$

As the earlier discussion of currency substitution outlines, the analysis is based on the assumption of well-integrated and efficient world goods, services, and assets markets. The tendencies linking domestic and foreign price levels and interest rates are reflected in the equilibrium conditions of purchasing-power parity and interest rate parity:

$$g(p) = g(p_w) + g(E) \tag{11}$$

and

$$i = i_w + g(E^o) \tag{12}$$

where the subscript w indicates a world market variable, and

E = the exchange rate expressed in units of domestic currency
per unit of the foreign currency, and
E^o = exchange rate expectations

Solving this five-equation system—that is, equation 8 to equation 12—yields:

$$g(E) = -g(p_w) - \alpha g(y) - \gamma d(i_w) - g(\Phi) - \gamma dg(E^o) + g(M) + u \tag{13}$$

In this formulation, all other things being equal, factors increasing net money demand tend to cause exchange rate appreciation, while factors causing expansion in domestic money cause exchange rate depreciation. The inclusion of the share variable, Φ, follows from the demand for money specification. Thus, portfolio shifts in the currency compositions of transactors' money balances influence the exchange rate in a direct manner.*

To complete the model, the equation specifying the form of exchange rate expectations, 5, and the determinants of the domestic and foreign currency shares in real money balances, 7, are expressed here in growth terms and then substituted into equation 13. Thus, from equation 5,

$$dg[E^{\varrho}|M^{o}_{w}, I] = mdg(M^{\varrho}) \tag{14}$$

where $m = \partial E^{\varrho}/\partial M^{o} > 0$

From equation 7,

$$g(\Phi|I) = k_1 g(M^{\varrho}) + k_2 g[Var(M^{\varrho})] \tag{15}$$

where $\Phi = k(M^{o}, Var(M^{\varrho}), |M^{o}_{w}, I)$

showing how monetary policies affect the composition of the currency portfolio. Substituting these equations in 13 yields the final reduced-form equation,

$$g[E|g(M^{o}_{w}),I] = -g(p_w) - \alpha g(y) - \gamma d(i_w) - k_1 g(M^{\varrho}) - \gamma mdg(M^{\varrho})$$
$$- k_2[Var(M^{\varrho})] + g(M) + u \tag{16}$$

where k_1, γm, $k_2 < 0$.

This expression is a generalized version of the monetary approach to exchange rate determination. As in the latter, a decrease in world prices,

---

*Put another way, the inclusion of a share variable more fully specifies the exchange rate equation. For example, an excess demand for money may be partly met through portfolio shifts; the effect of an excess demand (of domestic currency) need not be fully reflected in an exchange rate change. On the other hand, an outside shock affecting Φ would imply an exchange rate change, all other things being equal.

an increase in world interest rates, or a decrease in domestic real permanent income leads to exchange rate depreciation as the demand for domestic money rises, all other things being equal. Moreover, as in the received literature, actual or expected relatively expansive domestic monetary policy tends to depreciate the exchange rate, all other things being equal. In addition, however, equation 16 captures the effects of currency substitution in the demand for money. The coefficients on anticipated domestic monetary policy show clearly that transactors' capacity to change the composition of currency portfolios between domestic and foreign monies aggravates depreciation pressures (or the converse), pushing exchange rates beyond what would be implied by the model in the absence of currency substitution in money demand.* Furthermore, an increase in the variability of domestic monetary policy tends to depreciate the exchange rate, as transactors, able to substitute among currencies according to the given state of world market integration, shift their portfolio holdings toward less risky foreign monies.

Finally, equation 16 should be discussed in light of the recent literature dealing with the efficacy of monetary policy.[15] Recent studies show how monetary authorities can avoid the nominal implications of their policies only by conducting "innovative"—variable or uncertain—monetary policies. Real effects are possible only to the extent that nominal variables—wages, prices, interest rates, and, in this case, the exchange rate—do not quickly offset the change in the nominal money stock. When variability and uncertainty surround the course of monetary policy, transactors are hindered in their attempts to anticipate nominal money changes, resulting in such lags in the adjustment of the dependent nominal variables and, consequently, temporary real effects.

In the context of a currency portfolio approach to exchange rate determination, the increase in monetary variability makes the formation of exchange rate expectations more difficult, so that these expectations adjust to any fundamental policy shift more slowly than they otherwise would. In equation 16, then, increased variability serves to mask true changes in policy temporarily, and changes in expectations on monetary growth $[g(M^c)]$ will lag actual monetary changes. Monetary authorities can

---

*That is, the coefficients associated with expected domestic monetary growth (γm and k_1) are absolutely larger than for the case of no currency substitution. Further, it is shown that a move toward greater than expected money creation, $dg(M^c)$, aggravates the problem. Empirical tests of this hypothesis would presumably be based on sets of time series data, segregated in some manner according to the state of world economic integration.

therefore elect to suffer the initial exchange rate depreciation associated with increasing the variability of their policies in order to gain some flexibility for achieving short-run effects in policy deviations. The situation, then, is analogous to the conditions discussed in recent closed-economy literature: the nominal implications of monetary divergence in an open economy can be escaped only insofar as the policy is innovative—but this capacity for innovation is "bought" with an initial depreciation of the exchange rate.

THE INDEPENDENCE OF MONETARY POLICY AND THE CURRENCY PORTFOLIO APPROACH

This analysis is conditional upon the state of world market integration. On one hand, the integration of international markets constrains the independence of monetary policies by dissolving distinctions among the world's monies. Thus, for example, an expansionary monetary policy in any individual country simply expands the *world* money supply and has no country-specific effects. This has been the message of the received currency substitution literature.

On the other hand, if the possibility of monetary autonomy exists at all, it is due to the residual absence of integration of the world economy. But the above analysis shows that the capacity for altering the composition of portfolios of money holdings tends to frustrate even this potential. That is, the *apparent* scope for independent monetary policy—suggested by the extent to which control over substitutable goods and assets remains currency-specific—is eroded by the optimizing reactions of economic agents substituting among currencies in money demand. Indeed, consistent with recent literature on monetary policy in a closed economy, the monetary authorities can postpone the inevitable off-setting exchange rate effects of their policies only by making the policies variable and uncertain.

But currency portfolio substitution thus has further clear implications for monetary autonomy under flexible exchange rates. Since transactors can substitute from one currency to another, they are quick to reallocate their portfolios in response to any exchange rate changes that can be anticipated. Exchange markets can therefore be expected to reflect immediately the potential inflationary implications of divergent monetary policies, once perceived by holders of currency portfolios. These implications are thereby rapidly communicated to the public through the prominence of exchange rate changes, thus frustrating any real effects of the "independent" policy. Exchange rate stability among countries following predictably harmonious monetary policies naturally tends to be maintained by profit-maximizing commercial and professional speculators. On the other hand, the actions of these same transactors, who are able to adjust quickly the shares of foreign and domestic currencies in their portfolios, increase the exchange rate instability of currencies of countries following inharmonious monetary policies: countries following "independent" policies quickly reap the consequences of their actions in the exchange markets. Under a fixed exchange rate system, countries can maintain inconsistent monetary policies for however long they are willing to bear the implied reserves flow problems or are able to have these policies financed by international transfers of funds. Since the central bank carries the burden of adjustment under fixed exchange rates, the consequences of divergent policies can be hidden or ignored, at least temporarily. In a flexible exchange rate system, with private transactors bearing the burden of adjustment, the market acts swiftly, reflecting inharmonious policies in highly visible exchange rate changes. It is, perhaps, a sterner taskmaster than the self-imposed discipline of Bretton Woods.

The general model of exchange rate determination presented in this study, concentrating on currency portfolio adjustments in the face of changing conditions of costs and returns to holding various currencies, shows that private optimization in an increasingly integrated world economy severely compromises the ability of flexible exchange rates to provide countries with a scope for conducting meaningfully autonomous monetary policies. The implications of the model are consistent with increasing evidence that the attempts undertaken since 1973 to use flexible rates as a shield for attempting independent monetary policies have been, in any real sense, largely futile.

NOTES

1. Rudiger Dornbusch, "Expectations and Exchange Rate Dynamics," *Journal of Political Economy* 74, 6 (December 1976): 1161–76.

2. J. Frenkel, "A Monetary Approach to the Exchange Rate," *Scandinavian Journal of Economics* (May 1976): 200–61.

3. See, for example, Harry G. Johnson, "The Monetary Approach to the Balance of Payments," in *Further Essays in Monetary Economics* (Cambridge: Harvard University Press, 1973), pp. 229–49; Harry G. Johnson, "The Monetary Approach to the Balance of Payments Theory: A Diagramatic Analysis," *The Manchester School* 43 (1975): 220–74; Arthur Laffer, "The Anti-Traditional General Equilibrium Theory of the Rate Growth and the Balance of Payments under Fixed Exchange Rates," manuscript, University of Chicago (1968); J.

Richard Zecher, "Monetary Equilibrium and International Reserve Flows in Australia," *Journal of Finance* 29, 4 (December 1974): 1322–30; John R. Rutledge, "Balance of Payments and Money Demand," manuscript, 1975; and Alexander K. Swoboda, "Monetary Approaches to the Balance of Payments Theory," in *Recent Issues in International Monetary Economics*, ed. E. Claassen and P. Salin (New York: North Holland, 1976), pp. 3–24.

4. Frenkel, op. cit.

5. Lance Girton and Don Roper, "Theory and Implications of Currency Substitution," *International Finance Discussion Papers*, Federal Reserve Board, No. 86, 1976.

6. Marc Miles, "Currency Substitution, Flexible Exchange Rates and Monetary Independence," *American Economic Review* 68 (June 1978).

7. For other literature that utilizes this concept of substitutability, see R. Boyer (this book, Chapter 12); Arthur Laffer, "Optimal Exchange Rates," paper presented at The American Economic Association Meeting, Atlantic City, September 1976; Guillermo Calvo and Alfredo Rodriguez, "A Model of Exchange Rate Determination Under Currency Substitution and Rational Expectations," *Journal of Political Economy* 85 (May-June 1977): 617–25; and W. Michael Cox, "The Impact of Substitute Currencies on International Monetary and Exchange Market Equilibrium," manuscript, Virginia Polytechnic Institute, 1976.

8. See Gordon Tullock, "Competing Monies," *Journal of Money, Credit, and Banking* (November 1975): 491–97; and F. A. Hayek, *Denationalization of Money* (Hobart Special Papers, 1976).

9. Miles, op, cit.

10. See Dornbusch, op. cit.; and David T. King, "Monetary Autonomy and Flexible Exchange Rates," mimeographed, January 1977.

11. See, for example, John Rutledge, *A Monetarist Model of Inflationary Expectations* (Toronto: Lexington Books, 1974).

12. See David T. King, "The Performance of Exchange Rates in the Recent Period of Floating: Exchange Rates and Relative Rates of Inflation," *Southern Economic Journal* 43, no. 4 (April 1977): 1582–87.

13. See Cox, op. cit; Frenkel, op. cit.; Lance Girton and Don Roper, "A Monetary Model of Exchange Market Pressure Applied to the Post-War Canadian Experience," *American Economic Review* 67 (September 1977): 537–48; Bluford H. Putnam and John Woodbury, "Exchange Rate Stability and Monetary Policy: A Case Study," Federal Reserve Bank of New York Research Paper No. 7718 (1976); and Nicholas Sargen, "Exchange Rate Stability and Demand for Money," paper presented at the meeting of The American Finance Association, Atlantic City, N.J., September 1976.

14. Johnson, "The Monetary Approach to the Balance of Payments," op. cit., and "The Monetary Approach to the Balance of Payments Theory: A Diagramatic Analysis," op. cit.; R. A. Mundell, *International Economics* (New York: Macmillan, 1968); Laffer, "Anti-Traditional General Equilibrium Theory," op. cit.; Frenkel, op. cit.; Dornbusch, op. cit.; Girton and Roper, op. cit.; Sargen, op. cit.; *Studies in the Monetary Approach to the Balance of Payments*, eds. J. Frenkel and Harry G. Johnson (London: Unwin, 1976); Donald S. Kemp, "A Monetary View of the Balance of Payments," *Federal Reserve Bank of St. Louis Review* 57, no. 4 (April 1975): 14–20; Harold Fry, "A Monetary Approach to Afghanistan's Flexible Exchange Rate," *Journal of Money, Credit and Banking* 8 (May 1976): 219–25; Bluford H. Putnam and John J. Van Belle, "A Monetary Approach to Afghanistan's Flexible Exchange Rate: A Comment," *Journal of Money, Credit and Banking* 10, no. 1 (February 1978): 117–18; Rutledge, op. cit.; D. Sykes Wilford and Walton T. Wilford, "Monetary Approach to the Balance of Payments: On World Prices and the Reserve Flow Equation," *Weltwirtschaftliches Archiv* vol. 113, no. 1: 31–39; "A Note on the Monetary Approach to the

Balance of Payments: The Small, Open Economy, *Journal of Finance* vol. 33, no. 1 (March, 1978): 319–22; and Zecher, op. cit.

15. See R. J. Barro, "Rational Expectations and the Role of Monetary Policy," *Journal of Monetary Economics* 2 (1976): 1–32; R. J. Barro and Stanley Fischer, "Recent Developments in Monetary Theory," *Journal of Monetary Economics* 2, no. 2 (April 1976): 133–68; E. S. Phelps and J. B. Taylor, "Stabilizing Powers of Monetary Policy under Rational Expectations," *Journal of Political Economy* 85, no. 1 (January 1977): 163–90; and T. J. Sargent and Neil Wallace, "'Rational' Expectations, the Optimal Monetary Investment, and the Optimal Money Supply Rule," *Journal of Political Economy* 83, no. 2 (April 1975): 241–54.

12

Currency Mobility and
Balance of Payments Adjustment

Russell S. Boyer

Most of the literature on balance of payments theory assumes that national currencies are held only by domestic residents.[1] The usual postulate is that citizens place any foreign exchange they accumulate through exports on the foreign exchange market in order to obtain domestic currency. This is in sharp contrast with the extensive analysis of financial capital mobility, in which foreigners can acquire interest-bearing assets from abroad, so that foreign assets are substitutable for domestic ones.[2] It is also at variance with the analysis of pure trade theory, in which foreign and domestic goods are often assumed to be perfect substitutes. This study attempts to ascertain some of the consequences of the relaxation of this restrictive assumption on currency mobility within the framework of the monetary approach to exchange rate determination.

Editors Note: This study was written originally in 1972, and was the product of research done while the author was a graduate student at the University of Chicago. Minor revisions were made in the process of editing this manuscript to make it suitable for publication in this volume.

Earlier versions of this study were presented in workshops at the University of Western Ontario, at Purdue University, at the Federal Reserve System, Board of Governors, and in a session of the University of Western Ontario's conference on *International Monetary Problems*, April 1972. The author would like to thank R. A. Mundell, J. R. Melvin, and J. C. Leith for comments on a previous draft. They are, of course, not responsible for the views contained herein.

Currency mobility, or trading in money, seems to be an important phenomenon in recent international financial dealings, as the extraordinary growth of the Eurodollar market in Canada, Europe, and Japan demonstrates. In addition, one can surmise from Canadian data that foreign-currency holding was important even before resident banks offered such deposits. This substitutability arises from asset demands and therefore does not depend on a particular exchange rate regime (as can be gathered from the continued growth of U.S. dollar holdings by residents of Canada since the decision to float).

This analysis is important because economists should attempt to fortify or dismiss the distinction central bankers have drawn between currency and capital markets: between currency mobility and capital mobility. The possibility of destabilizing speculation, which has received substantial attention in the discussion of flexible exchange rate regimes, has not been discussed as seriously applicable to domestic bond or equity markets.[3] This study shows that, while capital mobility tends to stabilize international relations with fixed exchange rates, currency mobility causes instability in a world of flexible exchange rates, thus adding theoretical weight to the central bankers' distinction.

THE ADJUSTMENT PROCESS
WITHOUT CURRENCY MOBILITY

This section of the study develops a simple diagrammatic model of the balance of payments in order to describe the determination of the exchange rate in the monetary approach and to demonstrate the usual conclusions of international financial theory.[4] Throughout this section it is assumed that currencies are immobile (not substitutable), so that money of a particular denomination is held only by residents of the corresponding geographical currency area. The basic framework divides the world into two regions, A and B, of equal size and with different currencies. The totality of economic goods in the world is aggregated, for convenience, into these two currencies and all other things (AOT).* Currency is taken to be a financial asset without value in alternative uses, which provides some nonpecuniary service.

---

*This aggregation can be justified formally through the use of Hicks' composite good theorem.

Equilibrium is attained in the world economy when excess demand in each market is equal to zero. By Walras' Law, when two of these markets clear, the third does as well. Therefore, the analysis can concentrate upon only two market-clearing conditions; for simplicity, this study investigates the equilibrium conditions only in the two money markets. The model consists merely of the two demand functions for money equated to the supply of real balances:

$$\frac{M_i}{P_i} = \ell_i(y_i, \frac{M_i}{P_i}) \qquad \begin{array}{l} 0 < \ell_{i1} \\ \\ 0 < \ell_{i2} < 1 \end{array} \tag{1}$$

where M_i, P_i, ℓ_i, and y_i are the nominal money supply, the money price of nonmonetary items (AOT), the demand for real balances, and the level of real income, respectively, in each region, with i = A, B. Conspicuous for its absence from these functions is the rate of interest, measuring the opportunity cost of holding money. The reason is that this discussion deals only with problems for which this cost can be viewed as constant. Real balances are taken as arguments in these demand functions to represent the short-run wealth effects that such holdings have.[5] In order to ensure stability of the model, it is assumed that a unit increase in actual real balances increase on the demand for them by less than a unit. This is shown in the constraints on ℓ_{i2}.

This model is represented diagrammatically in Figure 12.1. The values of real balances are measured along the axes, and excess demands for these monies are shown within the graph. In particular, along the E_i locus the excess demand for currency i is equal to zero. The extreme slopes of these loci, vertical and horizontal, indicate that the two currencies are not substitutable for each other, in the sense that the demand for either does not depend upon the supply of the other. To the right of E_A, there is excess supply of money A; to the left, there is excess demand. Similarly, above E_B, there is excess supply for that currency; below there is excess demand.

When there is excess supply of one currency, but an equal excess demand for the other, the third market is in equilibrium. The locus of points for which this is true is shown in Figure 12.1 as E_{AOT}. It must pass through point Q, since here two of the three markets clear; as a consequence, the third must clear as well. Furthermore, its negative slope is dictated by the fact that only in the southeast and northwest quadrants is there an excess demand for one currency and an excess supply of the other.

Prices in the two regions must be consistent with the exchange rate so that no arbitrage profits can be made by transacting in those goods that face no important trade barriers or transportation costs. Even in the case where nontraded goods exist, in the steady state prices satisfy relative

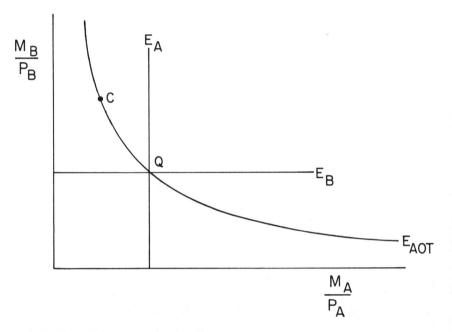

FIGURE 12.1   Currency Immobility.

Source: Constructed by the author.

purchasing-power parity for the monetary experiments considered here. Thus, the exchange rate defined in the conventional way from the point of view of the A region (as the number of units of A currency required to purchase a unit of B currency) is equal to

$$\varepsilon = \frac{P_A}{P_B} \tag{2}$$

Figure 12.1 shows the determination of the real quantity of money held in the two currencies, under the assumption of zero substitutability between them. The method by which these real quantities are attained depends upon the exchange rate regime.

If the exchange regime is one of fixed exchange rates, then the authorities must supply whatever quantity of money is needed to keep the exchange rate at its par value. Thus, an excess demand for a particular currency is satisfied automatically by an increase in its quantity as a consequence of the authorities' pegging operation. In this way the desired level of real balances is achieved through the appropriate adjustment of the quantity of nominal balances.

In contrast, if the authorities pursue a regime of flexible exchange rates, the quantitites of the two monies are exogenous, since movements in prices and exchange rates do not alter the stance of financial policies. Under these circumstances, changes in the supplies of or demands for various monies cause alterations in these prices relative to other goods so as to re-equilibriate their markets. Desired real balances are attained under this exchange rate regime through the adjustment of these prices, rather than through the adjustment in quantities.

This figure has an interpretation also in terms of balance of payments analysis using a monetary approach. According to this view, the regions of excess demand for a particular money are the regions also of balance of payments surplus in an ex ante sense. The excess demand for money is satisfied through a surplus in the external sector. Similarly, deficits in the balance of payments, ex ante, exist for those points where there is an excess supply of money.

Whether these ex ante surpluses and deficits appear as imbalances in the balance of payments depends upon the exchange rate regime. Under flexible exchange rates, that there is no trade in money implies that the balance of payments ex post is zero. Instead prices and the exchange rate adjust to assure balance of payments equilibrium. In contrast, under fixed exchange rates, the surpluses and deficits ex ante are not eliminated by price movements, so that the balance of payments for each region can differ from zero.

To establish the mechanism behind this diagram, consider a situation in which the supply of money A is decreased by 10 percent; at the same time the supply of money B is increased by 10 percent. At unchanged prices, this shock puts the world economy at a point like C, where the market for all other things remains in equilibrium. The reason is that this experiment creates an excess demand for one currency and an equal excess supply of the other, leaving the state of excess demand for currency in total unchanged. However, there are distribution effects between the two regions.

The movement back to steady state, point Q, requires a decrease in real balances in economy B and an increase in real balances in economy A. In the case of fixed exchange rates, this is accomplished in the following way: The two economies trade money with each other, with the central banks acting as intermediaries altering the supplies of these currencies in the process of pegging the exchange rate. The balance of payments surplus of economy A is just equal to the deficit for B, so that the plans of agents in both countries are fulfilled. In this way, the economies move from point C to point Q over time, traversing along the E_{AOT} loci. For flexible rates, if prices can move rapidly, the readjustment is not a time-consuming process. The insufficient supply of A balances is eliminated through a fall in P_A; the excessive B balances cause inflation in B, which restores real balances to their desired levels. In this way, point Q is rapidly reattained.

THE WORLD ECONOMY WITH CURRENCY MOBILITY

The discussion so far has assumed that the world can be divided into two regions distinguished by their demands for different currencies. This was done to analyze the behavior of the balance of payments of regions, from both an ex ante and an ex post perspective. The purpose of this section is to eliminate these distribution effects, to permit citizens of any country to hold either currency; thus the concept of currency mobility can be modeled. In the absence of distribution effects, the important consideration for the determination of equilibrium is the excess supplies and demands for various assets in the world as a whole.

The analysis of the previous section is valid for such a model as long as the assumption that currencies have no substitutability is maintained. Under these circumstances, the fact that a particular currency is held worldwide does not alter the model except that now the concept of balance of payments must be applied to those agents holding a particular currency rather than to a grouping made according to geographical or political considerations. Now the polar slopes of E_a and E_B give evidence that the holdings of either currency do not affect the demand for the other, because of the assumption on demands for these currencies.

On an intuitive level, the meaning of substitutability between two currencies is quite clear. As financial assets, the relevant variable that, in the first instance, is crucial to determining the amount of each held is the rate of return on that asset as compared with other substitutable assets. For assets without pecuniary yield, their relative rate of return is just the rate of appreciation of one in terms of the other.

In this view, to say that the Canadian and U.S. dollars are perfect substitutes, or that either is a good substitute for pound sterling, means that none of these currencies is expected to change in value relative to any of the others. If this expectation were not held, then agents would accumulate the asset that was appreciating in value, while going short in market instruments denominated in the depreciating currency.

This analysis can be made more specific by widening it to include interest-bearing assets, with the assumption that capital mobility is perfect. In such a world, all expected real rates on interest-bearing assets are equated in accordance with the interest rate parity theorem. Therefore, differences in nominal rates of return must be associated with differences in inflation rates, and expected changes in exchange rates must be consistent with these. The population of currency substitutability forces changes in exchange rates to be zero, so that expected inflation rates must be equal. This implies that nominal rates of interest are the same when high capital mobility is combined with substantial currency mobility.

The argument so far has failed to mention the level of the exchange rates themselves, but, instead, considers the first derivative of exchange rates with respect to time. The reason for this is clear: Exchange rates themselves are irrelevant to the problem of currency substitution. Thus, the fact that U.S. and Canadian dollars are good substitutes implies nothing about which is more valuable. If individuals wish to hold a given quantity of real balances and are indifferent to whether they hold these real balances in Canadian or in U.S. dollars, for given expectations this indifference should be just as valid at an exchange rate of (C\$/US\$)1.08 as it is at (C\$/US\$).92. Clearly the fact that in one case the Canadian dollar is "cheaper" is not a valid reason for holding that currency. When a currency is less valuable relative to other currencies, it is less valuable relative to goods as well as by purchasing-power parity. Thus, more of it is needed to provide the same real balances.

Although it is true that exchange rates are not directly relevant to the question of currency substitution at a micro level, this analysis should model their role at a macro level. The reason for this is that the central concern here is to establish how currency substitution alters the process of exchange rate determination. In particular, this study is concerned with the nature of the equilibrium that exists for a world characterized by such substitution.

To focus attention on the determination of equilibrium exchange rates, it is postulated that expected changes in them are equal to zero. Thus, agents willingly hold nonzero quantitites of currencies with different denominations, even when currencies are close substitutes.

When currencies are substitutes for each other, an increase in the real quantity held of one, all other things being equal, reduces the desired holdings of other currencies. There is a full offset only if the two currencies are perfect substitutes, since then agents are completely indifferent as to their holdings in real terms. With imperfect substitution, the offset is somewhat less. Thus a unit increase in real balances of a particular denomination causes less than a unit increase in desired real balances held in another denomination.*

This mechanism can be represented by modifying the equations in 1. Those equations now have the form:

---

*Throughout this analysis it is assumed that demand for real balances has a wealth elasticity less than one with respect to both monies. In the case of perfect substitutes, the other-currency elasticity is equal to one minus the own-currency elasticity, so that an increase in money holdings of one form reduces demand for the other money by an equal amount.

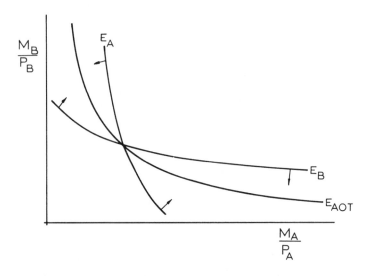

FIGURE 12.2 Currency Mobility.

Source: Constructed by the author.

$$\frac{M_A}{P_A} = \ell_A \left(y_A, \frac{M_A}{P_A}, \frac{M_B}{P_B} \right)$$

$$\frac{M_B}{P_B} = \ell_B \left(y_B, \frac{M_B}{P_B}, \frac{M_A}{P_A} \right)$$

(3)

where $0 \leq \ell_{i3} \leq 1 - \ell_{i2}$. Equations 1 are the special case of these specifications for which $\ell_{13} = 0$. Under those circumstances, increases in real balances denominated in B have no influence on the demand for real A balances, and vice versa. However, in the present context $\ell_{i3} > 0$, and the higher the degree of substitutability the larger the value of this partial derivative.

The modification of Figure 12.1 caused by this substitution is shown in Figure 12.2. The vertical locus of points for which the market currency A clears was based on the assumption of zero substitutability, so that the demand for that currency was independent of holdings of other currencies. With nonzero substitution, desired holdings of this currency are negatively related to those of other currencies, since the two serve the same purpose. In this way, the E_A locus rotates about the steady-state equilibrium in a counterclockwise direction. A similar argument for currency B shows that it rotates clockwise. Thus both E_A and E_B rotate toward the E_{AOT} locus. That locus does not shift with the exogenous increase in substitution. The reason is that it is the degree of substitution between currencies only that is being investigated here rather than the degree of substitution between money and all other things.*

A Comparison with Mundell's Definition of Currency Mobility

Robert A. Mundell has considered the problem of currency mobility in a number of papers written during the late 1960s.[6] Indeed, Figures 12.1 and 12.2 are based largely upon the diagrammatic tools that he developed. These tools figure prominently in his later research but were presented earlier, when the concept of currency substitution was first mentioned.

The reader of that analysis will note the similarity between Mundell's diagrams and those presented here. Nonetheless, there is one striking difference between his framework and the present one. He finds that the loci E_A and E_B are positively rather than negatively sloped. This is disconcerting, since his model is trying to represent currency substitution in the same way as is this analysis. Mundell argues that E_A and E_B "have positive slopes . . . if all currencies are gross substitutes. . . ." For the case of two specific currencies, the reasoning is that "appreciation of the franc must be associated with appreciation of the pound to maintain equilibrium"[7] in each country's balance of payments.

It is clear that the Mundell definition of "gross substitutes" does not refer to a definition of the relationship between currencies so much as it refers to the substitutability in demand of the outputs of various economies. The reasoning is that if the domestic-currency price of exports is fixed, then the domestic-currency price of imports varies with the exchange rate. In this way the terms of trade for each country are tied to the value of the exchange rate.

Thus, Mundell's model must be seen as one describing substitutability among goods; this is inconsistent with the stated intention of modeling substitution among currencies. Furthermore, the Mundell analysis requires a good deal more structure to ensure that it is immune to the criticism that

---

*In order for E_{AOT} not to rotate, one must assume, in particular, that the influence of actual B-balances on desired A-balances equals the influence of actual A-balances on desired B-balances. In a linear model, E_{AOT} has a slope of -1 with this assumption.

it is based on money illusion in the form of disregarding the effects of movements of the exchange rate on the levels of the real values of wages and profits. As the model stands, workers are apparently willing to take cuts in real incomes when they come in the form of devaluations, but may not be willing to take them when they occur through changes in domestic-currency wages.

It is of interest to note that Mundell's diagrammatic tools are applicable to the discussion of substitutability among interest-bearing assets when they are denominated in the same currency. This topic is considered next.

Substitutability of Bonds

It is important to distinguish between substitutability of assets denominated in the same currency and substitutability of those denominated in different currencies. In order to do this, consider two bonds that promise to pay one unit of currency per period indefinitely. Thus the price of these bonds is just equal to the inverse of their rate of return.

Assume initially that these two bonds, denoted again by A and B, are not substitutable for each other. Then a diagrammatic framework similar to that used in the previous section represents equilibrium in the economic system. Define the units of A and B bonds so that each has a fixed supply of one. Then the real quantity of each bond, equal to the unit supply multiplied by the price of the bond in terms of money, and divided by the exogenous unit price of goods in terms of money, is equal to the inverse of the rate of return on each bond. These real quantities are measured along the axes in Figure 12.3.

The E_{AOT} locus in Figure 12.3 has the same position and slope as it did in previous figures and serves a similar function here. Curves E_A and E_B, the loci of points for which there is zero excess demand for bonds A and B respectively, have their polar positions for the same reason as in sections above: the two financial assets are viewed as not substitutable for each other. Thus, for example, the E_A curve is completely vertical because the demand for A bonds depends positively upon its own rate of return, but is independent of the return on B bonds. This stringent assumption, of zero substitutability, must now be modified.

In relaxing this assumption, we employ the usual definition of substitutability among financial assets: a rise in the rate of return on either causes an excess supply of the other.[8] Thus, the demand functions for these assets are:

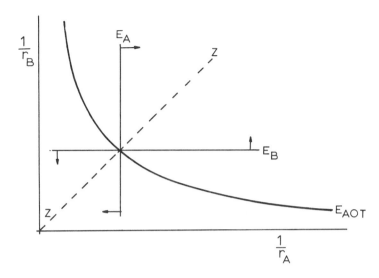

FIGURE 12.3   Bond Substitutability.

$$K_A^d = K_A^d (r_A, r_b)$$

$$K_B^d = K_B^d (r_B, r_A) \tag{4}$$

$$K_{i2}^d \leqslant 0 \leqslant K_{i1}^d \quad i = A,B$$

As they become substitutes, K_{i2}^d becomes negative, becoming larger in absolute value without limit as substitutability increases.

The process of becoming substitutes of higher and higher degree can be represented as in Figure 12.3. Take A bonds to establish the diagrammatic consequences of this process. Zero excess demand for A bonds can be maintained (with a given nominal supply) if any rise in their rate of return is matched by a larger increase in the return on B bonds. Thus, E_A must have a positive slope, following the direction of rotation shown by the arrows in that figure. A similar argument shows that E_B rotates in a counterclockwise direction. That an increase in either rate of return must be more than matched by the increase in the other asset's return in order to keep each asset market cleared can be varified by the following argument: an equal increase in the two rates of return does not alter their relative rates, and therefore should not change portfolio balance decisions between the two bonds; rather it should create an excess demand for them both, and an excess supply for all other goods. This shows that E_A has a slope greater than one, while E_B has a slope less than one.

As these assets become closer substitutes for each other, the curves E_A and E_B rotate toward one another and away from E_{AOT}. Once again E_{AOT} does not need to rotate, because we are considering changes in substitutability between the two bonds, rather than between each of them and all other things.

In the limit when these bonds are identical in agents' utility functions, there are only two curves describing economic behavior in the economy. (1) E_{AOT}: this curve shows that the excess demand for the aggregate asset, A and B bonds together, varies directly with the average rate of return on these assets: and (2) ZZ, the 45° line: this line shows that there cannot be any substantial deviation in the rates of return of two assets that are perfect substitutes for each other.

The reader will note that the diagram derived for substitutability between bonds is quite different from that representing a similar relationship between currencies. Furthermore, these differences become more important as the degree of substitutability becomes higher.

Perfect Substitution and Destabilizing Speculation

The discussion so far has shown that the analysis of substitution between financial assets denominated in different currencies is in marked contrast to that between assets of similar denomination. In particular, substitution between bonds leads to a diagrammatic analysis consistent with the tools used for goods that are gross substitutes; substitution between currencies yields a quite different diagram (Figure 12.2). This section continues the analysis of currency mobility, focusing on the limiting perfect mobility case.

Increasing substitution causes E_A and E_B in Figure 12.2 to rotate toward E_{AOT}. Indeed, in the limit of perfect substitutability, all these loci coincide. Thus, in the case where a unit increase in real A balances matched by a unit decrease in real B balances leaves both money markets in equilibrium, clearing of all markets occurs along the locus E_{AOT}. This shows that the static analysis of currency mobility leads to the conclusion that perfect substitutability yields a neutral equilibrium.

This conclusion is quite obvious in the case of fixed exchange rates. If Chicago dollars and New York dollars are perfect substitutes, then the total stock of either is indeterminate since agents at whim move their monies between these locations. A similar argument can be applied to Toronto dollars (that is, Canadian dollars) and Chicago dollars during a period of fixed exchange rates only.

It is during a period of flexible exchange rates that the theory of currency mobility yields interesting conclusions. The argument above shows that the supplies of Toronto dollars and Chicago dollars are indeterminate with perfect currency mobility (even though their real sum is constant). Under flexible exchange rates, the way in which agents in aggregate alter the supplies of real balances held is through the exchange rate and the price levels in different currencies, with these variables always satisfying purchasing-power parity. Thus, this argument shows that the price levels in Canadian and U.S. dollars and the exchange rate are indeterminate. This conclusion is based on the argument that as currencies become substitutable, the expected opportunity cost of holding them is the dominant variable, more important than the exchange rate. Unless this expected opportunity cost is tied to it, the equilibrium exchange rate may become indeterminate.

Thus far the argument has been entirely static. However, this indeterminacy of equilibrium exchange rates assumes more importance when dynamic considerations are included in the discussion. For example, it is well known that adaptive expectation models of asset markets yield unstable solutions when the elasticity of demand and the coefficient of expectations become large.[9] The indeterminacy demonstrated here would modify this rule to make the stability condition even more stringent. Furthermore, the elasticity of demand with respect to opportunity cost becomes very large for such assets. Thus, there are no forces arising from static analysis to propel the exchange rate toward equilibrium, whereas dynamic considerations appear to force the model to be unstable.

The position of perfect currency mobility is a polar case toward which the world economic system appears to have moved recently. There do seem to be certain financial institutions and other multinational corporations for which monies of different denomination are very close substitutes. If these groups represent even a minor proportion of the total money supply of a particular denomination, their behavior can be destabilizing for the country as a whole. Furthermore, the analysis suggests that potential instabilities arise when less than perfect substitutability is combined with dynamic considerations.

CONCLUSIONS

The growth of Eurodollar markets has been so rapid that it has come upon international financial experts unawares. This study suggests that these markets do not represent a minor new phenomenon that is to be explained within the confines of existing theoretical structures. Instead, it finds that currency mobility must be analyzed using new techniques, since substitutability of financial assets denominated in different currencies has substantially different effects from substitutability of financial assets of the same denomination. In particular, exchange rates between currencies become indeterminate as the currencies become close substitutes; similar bonds, however, must have the same price if they have the same denomination.

Both the growth of currency mobility and the diminution of money illusion argue for a substantial degree of exchange rate fixity in the world economy. If this policy is carried out according to the rules of the gold standard, gearing monetary policy to external balance, then the system is completely viable. A serious commitment to such a regime would effectively create large unified currency areas in which speculative capital movements caused by expectations of parity changes would be eliminated. The resulting international financial system would be much more stable than are the present arrangements.

NOTES

1. See, for instance, the analyses of the foreign exchange market by Joan Robinson, "The Foreign Exchanges," in her *Essays in the Theory of Employment*, 2d ed. (Oxford: Blackwell, 1947), part 3, Chapter 1; F. Machlup, "The Theory of Foreign Exchanges," *Economica* 6 (November 1939): 75–97; and G. Harberler, "The Market of Foreign Exchange and the Stability of the Balance of Payments: A Theoretical Analysis," *Kyklos* 3 (fasc. 3, 1949); 193–218.

2. A detailed analysis of international capital mobility is contained in R. A. Mundell, *International Economics* (New York: Macmillan, 1968). See also L. Metzler, "The Process of International Adjustment Under Conditions of Full Employment: A Keynesian View," in *American Economic Association Readings in International Economics*, eds., R. Caves and H. Johnson (Homewood, Ill.: Irwin, 1968), pp. 465–86.

3. Modern discussion of this subject originated with Milton Friedman in his "The Case for Flexible Exchange Rates," in his *Essays in Positive Economics* (Chicago: University of Chicago Press, 1966). For examples that counter Friedman's contentions, see W. J. Baumol, "Speculation, Profitability and Stability," *Review of Economics and Statistics* 39 (August 1957): 263–71; and G. Telser, "A Theory of Speculation Relating Profitability and Stability," *Review of Economics and Statistics* 41 (August 1959): 295–301.

4. An extensive treatment of the theory supporting this approach is contained in Harry G. Johnson, "The Monetary Approach to the Balance of Payment Theory," *Journal of Financial and Quantitative Analysis* 7 (March 1972): 1555–72.

5. Such a specification for money demand is employed by D. Patinkin, in his *Money Interest and Prices* (New York: Harper & Row, 1965).

6. Mundell, op. cit.; and *Monetary Theory: Inflation, Interest and Growth in the World Economy* (Pacific Palisades, Calif.: Goodyear, 1971).

7. Mundell, *International Economics*, op. cit., p. 52. Also, an early discussion of

competing monies may be found in F. von Hayek, *Monetary Nationalism and International Stability* (London: Longmans, Green, 1939).

8. Such a definition is used in S. Royama and K. Mahada, "Substitution and Complementarity in the Choice of Risky Assets," in D. Hester and J. Tobin, eds., *Risk Aversion and Portfolio Choice* (New York: Wiley, 1967).

9. The stability condition is derived in P. Cagan, "The Monetary Dynamics of Hyperinflation," in *Studies in the Quantity Theory of Money*, ed. M. Friedman (Chicago: University of Chicago Press, 1956).

13

Theory and Implications
of Currency Substitution

Lance Girton
Don Roper

Thus if currency notes were to be deprived of their liquidity-premium by the stamping system, a long series of substitutes would step into their shoes—bank-money, debts at call, foreign money, jewelery and the precious metals generally, and so forth. (John M. Keynes [18, p. 358])

Monetary theory has traditionally assumed that one currency circulates in each country. The relaxation of the one-currency-per-country assumption allows currency questions to be separated from questions dealing primarily with international and interregional trade. Just as the pure theory of international trade abstracts from monetary phenomena, the pure theory of multiple currencies can be investigated independently of the number of countries or regions.

This paper has benefited from helpful suggestions from Dale Henderson, Tom Grennes, George Moore (for material in Appendix B), Stephen Turnovsky, and two anonymous referees. The authors appreciate the comments and support from members of the IIES (Institute for International Economic Studies) at the University of Stockholm, where the first draft of the paper was completed in 1974. Helpful discussions over subsequent drafts followed seminars at ANU, Chase Manhattan Bank, University of North Carolina, Monash University, Princeton University, and UCLA. Our work was stimulated by conversations with Russell Boyer at the Federal Reserve Board in the summers of 1972 and 1973. An earlier version of the paper was circulated under the same title in 1976.

Lance Girton and Don Roper are professors of economics at the University of Utah. This article originally appeared in the *Journal of Money, Credit, and Banking* 13 (February 1981). Permission to republish this article here is greatly appreciated.

The theory of substitutable monies developed here is applicable to several monies circulating in one country and to several monies circulating internationally. Consideration of issues involving CS (currency substitution) cuts across the usual distinction (based on political or governmental jurisdictions) between "domestic" and "international" monetary economics. Consequently, the literature on substitutable monies comes from domestic monetary economics (for example, notes 2, 4, 20, 25, 32) and international monetary economics (for example, notes 3, 5, 15, 16, 19, 21, 22, 23, 24, 28, 33). A brief survey is given in 6.

The paper is organized as follows: In the first section a two-currency model of the exchange rate is developed under the assumption that (the paths of) the quantitites of monies are exogenous. The exchange rate between monies is shown to be "unstable" in the sense that movements in the exchange rate necessary to maintain monetary equilibrium become larger without limit as CS increases. In addition, the exchange rate is indeterminate with perfect CS. In contrast with CS, an increase in substitution between bonds does not produce an "unstable" bond-exchange rate and perfect bond substitution does not produce indeterminancy. CS is different from substitution between other financial assets because the yield on money is independent of the value of money. This independence, is, as argued in the second section, due to the choice of units in which financial contracts are specified. The fact that the interest payment on money is denominated in terms of itself (money) and that the interest payment on bonds is not denominated in terms of bonds provides a distinction between money and bonds which, we argue, is more fundamental than the usual view of the money-bond distinction. In the third section the behavior of money issuers in response to CS is characterized as the choice between fixing exchange rates or competing in the production of monies. It is shown that there is no externality in the production of money such that the usual implication of competition, allocative efficiency, is as applicable to money as to other commodities. When the behavior of money issuers is endogenized, the presence of CS is found to eliminate rather than cause exchange rate instability. In the summary it is concluded that the usual fixed money-growth rule will lead to an inferior, depreciating money if the public is offered competitively produced substitutes.

AN ASSET DEMAND MODEL OF CURRENCY SUBSTITUTION

The model of CS developed here contains two money-demand functions which, together with exogenous money supplies, are used to analyze the money exchange rate. A third nonmonetary asset is implicit in the model, but the balance sheet constraint makes the market equilibrium condition for this asset redundant.

CS can be modeled by the inclusion of real return on both monies in both money-demand functions. Defining r_1 and r_2 as the anticipated real returns on monies one and two, the demands for real balances can be expressed as

$$M_k/P_k = L_k(r_1, r_2, r, w) \qquad (k = 1,2) \tag{1}$$

where M_k is the nominal quantity of currency k, P_k is the price of goods in terms of currency k, r is the anticipated real return on the nonmonetary asset, and w is a scale variable such as real wealth. w and r are taken as exogenous. Money holders are assumed to hold both monies so the same scale variable, w, is used in both L_1 and L_2.*

In keeping with standard specifications, money-demands are assumed to depend on differential returns:

$$L_1(r_1 - r, r_1 - r_2, w) \qquad \text{and} \qquad L_2(r_2 - r, r_2 - r_1, w) \tag{2}$$

To simplify the argument, the demand functions are assumed to have exponential specifications. The equilibrium condition for currency one is,†

$$M_1/P_1 = \theta_1(w) \exp[\alpha_1(r_1 - r) + \sigma_1(r_1 - r_2)] \qquad (\alpha_1, \sigma_1 > 0) \tag{3}$$

where σ_1 is a coefficient of substitution between monies one and two and

---

*The money-demand functions L_1 and L_2 are defined by currency, not by country. Most BOP (balance of payments) models are based on the assumption of one currency-per-country and therefore do not distinguish between money demand defined by country of residence and money demand defined by currency. When defined by country, money-demand functions are appropriate for explaining the multiregional or interregional BOP. When defined by currency, they are appropriate for explaining the multicurrency concept of exchange market pressure, defined as that combination of reserve and exchange rate changes that is independent of central bank intervention. A measure of EMP with equal weights is given in note 11.

Standard BOP accounting does not distinguish between these two concepts of the BOP. Data are collected for above-the-line-entries on the basis of country residency. The offical settlements definition of the BOP, a measure (when the exchange rate if fixed) of exchange market pressure, is entered below the line.

†$\alpha_1(r_1 - r)$ is the usual interest rate term found in money-demand functions. This becomes clear if r_1 is expressed as the difference between the market or nominal interest rate on money one, i_1, and the anticipated rate of inflation in terms of money one, π_1. Substituting $i_1 - \pi_1$ for r_1 converts $\alpha_1^i(r_1 - r)$ to $-\alpha_1(r + \pi_1) + \alpha_1 i_1$, where $\alpha_1 i_1$ is usually assumed constant and therefore suppressed. Equation 3, therefore, is a typical LM equation with the addition of the substitution effect between the two monies.

CURRENCY SUBSTITUTION / 215

α_1 is a coefficient of substitution between money one and the nonmonetary asset.

The monetary equilibrium conditions in logarithmic form are

$$\ln M_1 - \ln P_1 = \ln \theta_1 + \alpha_1(r_1 - r) + \sigma_1(r_1 - r_2) \tag{4a}$$

$$\ln M_2 - \ln P_2 = \ln \theta_2 + \alpha_2(r_2 - r) + \sigma_2(r_2 - r_1) \tag{4b}$$

Implications of CS can be obtained by focusing on the relative values of the two monies. To find the expression determining the relative value of the monies, subtract 4b from 4a and rearrange terms to obtain

$$\ln(P_1/P_2) = \ln[(M_1/\theta_1)/(M_2/\theta_2)] - \alpha(r_1 - r_2) - 2\sigma(r_1 - r_2) \tag{5}$$

where the following symmetry conditions have been imposed: $\alpha_1 = \alpha_2 = \alpha$ and $\sigma_1 = \sigma_2 = \sigma$. The assumption $\sigma_1 = \sigma_2$ identifies CS with the single parameter, σ, and the condition $\alpha_1 = \alpha_2$ makes the relative value of monies invariant to changes in r, the yield on the nonmonetary asset.

Equation 5 can be used to determine the exchange rate between the two monies if some relation between P_1/P_2 and E (the exchange market price of money two in terms of money one) is imposed. The obvious condition to use is that $E = P_1/P_2$. This looks like and might well be regarded as purchasing-power parity, but it is not based on the usual arbitrage assumption associated with PPP. Rather than the usual condition that arbitrage takes place across space or between regions, the multicurrency version of PPP requires that arbitrage take place between currencies. This condition means that neither money is discriminated against, or discounted relative to the other, when used as a medium of exchange. When two prices are quoted for the same good, the ratio of the prices must equal the rate at which the currencies are traded in the exchange market.

Defining $e = \ln E$ and imposing the condition that $e = \ln(P_1/P_2)$, equation 5 can be expressed as

$$e = \bar{e} - \eta \delta$$

where $\bar{e} - \ln[(M_1/\theta_1)/(M_2/\theta_2)]$, $\eta = \alpha + 2\sigma$, and $\delta = r_1 - r_2$. Exogenous money supplies and demand factors are contained in the term $\bar{e}$.* CS is

---

*We are assuming that $\bar{e}$ is independent of e. A sufficient condition to assure this independence is that any exchange-rate induced wealth effects have proportion impacts on θ_1 and θ_2. In contrast to an arbitrage version of PPP, we could have assumed the neutrality version

reflected in the σ-parameter such that η will vary from α to infinity as CS ranges from zero to infinity.

The differential anticipated real return on monies is equal to the differential nominal return minus the differential anticipated rate of inflation:

$$\delta = r_1 - r_2 = (i_1 - \pi_1) - (i_2 - \pi_2)$$

$$= (i_1 - i_2) - (\pi_1 - \pi_2) \tag{7}$$

Assuming anticipations are formed in a manner consistent with (the multicurrency version of) PPP, the anticipated rate of exchange in the exchange rate, x, will equal the difference between the anticipated inflation rates such that equation 7 can be expressed as

$$\delta = i_1 - i_2 - x \tag{7'}$$

Substituting this expression for δ into the exchange rate equation 6 produces

$$e = \bar{e} - \eta(i_1 - i_2 - x) \tag{8}$$

Since equation 8 will be used to derive implications of CS, it is worth summarizing the assumptions used in the derivation of this relationship. First, the nominal interest rates on monies, i_1 and i_2, are assumed fixed. This assumption will be discussed in the second section. Second, the money supplies are taken as exogenous and are contained in $\bar{e}$. The assumption of exogenous money supplies will be relaxed in the third section. Third, the anticipated rate of change of the exchange rate x is taken as exogenous. When x is endogenized using rational expectations in Appendix A or using adaptive expectations in note 10, the results are consistent with the conclusions of this section.

There are two basic implications of CS, given the assumptions of this section. One implication relates directly to a policy issue and the other concerns the foundations of monetary theory. First, CS will cause exchange rate "instability" in the sense that shifts in the anticipated rate of change of the exchange rate lead to larger exchange rate movements with

---

of PPP, namely, the real exchange rate is independent of nominal variables. This would complicate the definition of $\bar{e}$ but leave the conclusions unaffected.

greater degrees of CS. Second, perfect CS implies that the exchange rate is indeterminate.

Consider first the impact of a shift in the anticipated rate of change of the exchange rate x. Taking the derivative of expression 8,

$$\partial e/\partial x = \eta = \alpha + 2\sigma \qquad (8')$$

The greater the degree of CS (that is, the larger the value of σ), the larger the change in e needed to satisfy monetary equilibrium for a given shift in x. The movement in the exchange rate needed to satisfy the monetary equilibrium conditions approaches infinity as substitution becomes perfect (that is, as η approaches infinity).

From equation 8, the impact of $\bar{e}$ on e, given by $\partial e/\partial \bar{e} = 1$, holds for all finite value of CS. Since money supplies are included in $\bar{e}$, changes in the supplies or composition of monies have a proportional impact on the exchange rate for all finite degrees of CS. CS increases the impact of x (or δ) on e but leaves the impact of money supplies on e unaffected, so exchange market intervention becomes a relatively less effective instrument for offsetting shifts in x. The fact that e is more sensitive to i_1 and i_2 as CS increases motivates the assumption in the third section that, when money issuers compete for larger market shares, they do so by offering more attractive rates on their liabilities.

The second implication concerns the theoretical question of exchange rate determination under perfect CS.* In order for both monies to circulate, their values (in terms of goods) must be finite. This means the exchange rate must be nonzero and finite. In order for the exchange rate to be finite and greater than zero, the rate of return δ must be zero. But equal real returns do not impose any condition on the exchange rate because δ is independent of P_1 and P_2 and, therefore, of the exchange rate. The remaining condition to which one might appeal is $e = \bar{e}$. But with perfect CS, the individual money-demands in $\bar{e}$ are no longer defined. Consequently, any exchange rate is an equilibrium rate when CS is perfect.†

---

*The implications of perfect CS for exchange rate determination are also found in notes 2, 3, 10, 15, 16. We assume that monies (like other financial assets) are distinguished by issuer and counterfeiting is effectively prohibited. (See notes 20, 33, 12.) Perfect substitution does not imply indistinguishability.

†It should be noted that there is no inconsistency in the proposition that, when CS is perfect, the exchange rate is both unstable and indeterminate. Instability does not presuppose determinacy as can be seen with the following argument: Suppose that two perfectly substitutable currencies have the same initial real yields and are exchangeable at some initial finite exchange rate, e^0. Now suppose that δ is changed from its initial zero value. This shock

To see that these implications of CS are peculiar to money, per se, we will contrast CS to bond substitution. With slight changes in the expression for δ, equation 8 can be used to examine substitution between two bonds, A and B. The only assumption that makes the preceding specification of δ unique to money is that the market yields i_1 and i_2 have been taken as exogenous. Rather than being fixed, bond market yields vary inversely with the values of the bonds. For convenience, the bonds are assumed to be perpetuities paying a constant and continuous stream of interest denoted as C_a and C_b. The market yields on the bonds are

$$i_a = C_a/Q_a \quad \text{and} \quad i_b = C_b/Q_b$$

where Q_a and Q_b are the bond prices. Both bond prices and their stream of interest payments are measured in terms of a single background numeraire needing no further specification for our purposes.

Retaining the symbols η and x from the money equation 8, the counterpart bond equation is

$$R = \bar{R} - \eta(C_a/Q_a - C_b/Q_b - x) \tag{8b}$$

where R is the (log of the) bond-exchange rate, $\ln(Q_b/Q_a)$, and x is the anticipated rate of change of R. Supply and demand factors are embedded in $\bar{R}$ exactly as they were in $\bar{e}$ such that $\bar{R}$ is the value of R when the anticipated differential return is zero.

It is clear from the construction of the money equation 8 and the bond equation 8b that the only difference between the determination of the money-exchange rate (e) and the bond-exchange rate (R) is that the values of bonds affect the differential bond yield whereas the values of monies do not influence the differential money yield.

Equation 8b can be used to contrast the implications of CS to the implications of bond substitution. First, we found that the change in e necessary to accommodate a change in the anticipated rate of change of e, as given by $\partial e/\partial x$, approaches infinity as CS becomes perfect. In contrast, the change in R necessary to accommodate a change in the differential bond return is

---

will cause e to go to plus or minus infinity (E will go to plus infinity or to zero). The infinite movement in e reflects instability under perfect CS. But e^0 was completely arbitrary. It is not necessary to determine the initial value of e to determine that the (limit of the) derivative $\partial e/\partial x$, is infinite.

$$\partial R/\partial x = \eta/(1 + \eta i) \tag{9}$$

where the derivative has been simplified by evaluating it at the point where $C_a/Q_a = C_b/Q_b = i$. The derivative $\partial R/\partial x$ approaches $1/i$ as bond substitution becomes perfect. Thus, changes in x have a limited impact on the bond-exchange rate. If, for example, bondholders suddenly expect bond B to appreciate relative to bond A, their effort to sell A and purchase B increases the yield on A and decreases the yield on B until holders are satisfied with the existing quantitites of bonds. This is not the case for two monies since values of monies have no influence on the market yields on monies.

Finally, consider the determination of the bond-exchange rate, R, when bonds A and B are perfect substitutes. Just as individual money demands are no longer defined ($\bar{e}$ is undefined) when CS is perfect, individual bond demands are no longer defined ($\bar{R}$ is undefined) when bond substitution is perfect. But in the case of perfect bond substitution, R is determined by the requirement that the differential return is zero. Setting the parenthesis on the right-hand side of 8b to zero constrains the bond-exchange rate since Q_a and Q_b are determinants of the differential yield. In contrast, P_1 and P_2 did not appear in the differential yield formula for monies. For perpetuity bonds with continuous interest payments, the bond-exchange rate equals the ratio of interest payments, that is, $Q_b/Q_a = C_b/C_a$.* Perfect bond substitution rigidly fixes the bond-exchange rate whereas perfect CS leaves the money-exchange rate indeterminate.

Although indeterminancy is a logical implication of a model that utilizes widely accepted money-demand functions, we regard it as a consequence of abstracting from transactions costs and not of immediate concern for policy. The macro model used in this section abstracts from the costs of posting multiple prices or converting prices stated in one money to another money. Examples of *perfect* substitution of which we are aware, such as Federal Reserve notes of different districts, exhibit *unitary* exchange rates. This suggests that transactions costs at exchange rates

---

*With perfect substitution between bonds A and B, their anticipated real yields will be equal, which implies that

$$C_a/Q_a + g_a = C_b/Q_b + g_b$$

where g_a and g_b are the capital gains. If capital gains are equal, the equality of real yields immediately implies that the bond-exchange rate equals the ratio of the interest payments. This solution is also derived in Appendix B, where the capital gains are not assumed equal.

other than unity (or perhaps multiples of ten) may be an important constraint on the rate of exchange between perfectly substitutable currencies.

THE DISTINCTION BETWEEN MONEY AND BONDS

In the preceding section the implications of CS were contrasted with the implications of bond substitution. It was emphasized that the peculiarity of the CS implications is due to the invariance of the market yields on monies with respect to their values. The economic rationale for this distinguishing characteristic of money will be examined in this section.

It will be sufficient to focus on only one bond and one money. The analysis is simplified with the assumption of perfect foresight. With this assumption, r_m and r_b are used to represent both the anticipated and actual real returns on the money and the bond, respectively. The procedure will be to examine the yield formulas for r_b and r_m to determine exactly why r_b depends on the value of the bond and why r_m does not depend on the value of money.

The formula for the instantaneous real return on a bond can be expressed as

$$r_b = C_b/Q_b + g \tag{10}$$

where g represents the capital gain against goods (which could be decomposed into the appreciation of the money price of the bond minus the rate of change of the money price of goods). Using π to represent the rate of inflation, the instantaneous real yield on money is

$$r_m = i_m - \pi \tag{11}$$

To understand why i_m is "constant" requires explicit recognition of the difference between the interest *payment* and the interest *rate* on money.*

---

*In this section we assume that the interest *payment* on money is fixed and use the fixed interest payment to explain the fixed interest rate i_m. In a broader analysis in which other variables are endogenized, neither the interest rate nor the interest payment would need to be fixed. i_m could vary but, if the model were neutral (with respect to the level of nominal variables), then r_m and, therefore, i_m would be independent of P. The invariance of i_m with respect to P is consistent with the observable, positive relation between bank deposit rates (that are not subject to ceilings) and the *rate of exchange* of P.

By denoting the money value of the interest payment as C_m, formula 11 can be expressed as

$$r_m = C_m/1 - \pi \qquad (12)$$

where $-\pi$ is, like g in equation 10, the capital gain against goods. C_m is the (fraction of) units of money paid per time period per unit of money. The price of money that must be used to deflate C_m is, as the dimensions indicate, the price of money in terms of itself, namely, unity.

A comparison of the yield formulas 10 and 12 reemphasizes the earlier argument that the yield on a bond depends inversely on its value Q_b, whereas the yield on money does not depend on its value (whether measured in terms of goods P^{-1}, or in terms of bonds Q_b^{-1}). To explain the difference between money and bonds, we will briefly consider how the yield formulas would be written if the interest payments on both bonds and money were tied to the price level or indexed against inflation. Suppose that the interest payment on a bond were indexed against inflation such that the real interest payment were constant. Then the appropriate expression for the real bond return would be

$$r_b = c_b/q_b + g \qquad (10')$$

where $c_b = C_b/P$, $q_b = Q_b/P$, and P is the money price of goods. If c_b is constant, then 10' shows that r_b depends not on Q_b per se, but on q_b.

Similarly, if the coupon or interest payment on money were fixed in real terms, then the appropriate real return formula for money would be

$$r_m = c_m/P^{-1} - \pi \qquad (12')$$

where c_m is the constant real payment. The denominator P^{-1} is the goods value of money. Equation 12', in contrast to 12, shows that the yield on money *does* depend on the (goods) value of money when the interest payment is contracted in terms of goods. When contrasted with 10 and 12, equations 10' and 12' show that the yield on an asset depends inversely on the value of the asset measured in the units in which the interest payments are fixed.

One observes that most contractual obligations are specified in terms of the units in which the medium of exchange is measured. Escalated contracts and other forms of indexation are the exceptions, not the rule. Interest payments on money, when they are nonzero, are specified in terms of money units.* Interest payments on bonds are not specified in bond units. As Keynes pointed out, "it is the essence of debt [in contrast to what Keynes called "money proper"] to be enforceable in terms of something other than itself."[17] Conversely, it is the essence of money that its own return be contracted in the same units used to measure the asset itself. And this defining characteristic of money explains the differences in the implications generated by CS and those generated by bond substitution.

The distinction developed here between money and bonds contrasts sharply with the current view in the theoretical literature. A widely accepted statement of the money-bond distinction is given by Tobin.[30,31] According to Tobin, the nominal interest rate on money is "exogenously fixed." But the only items fixed are the coupons or interest payments on both money and bonds. And the interest *rate* on money is "fixed" (that is, invariant to the value of money), not because the interest payment is fixed, but because interest on money is specified in terms of itself. It is not the fixity of the interest payment but the units in which it is fixed that makes i_m invariant to the value of money. If the interest payment on money were fixed in terms of any other commodity or asset, then money, like other assets, would have a market yield dependent on its value and the implications of CS would be similar to the implications of substitution between other financial assets. Further research should provide more insight into why contracts are specified in units in which the medium of exchange is measured.† But it is unnecessary to accept the invariance of i_m as an institutional datum.

---

*We have thus far considered only the pecuniary yield on money. To determine the relation between the value of money and its *total* return, it is necessary to consider the nonpecuniary yield on money and payments in kind (for example, bank services to large depositors). As long as real behavioral functions are homogeneous of degree zero in nominal variables, these considerations do not alter the invariance of money's return to the value of money.

†Opinions differ over priority of the unit-of-account and medium-of-exchange properties of money. We conjecture that the medium-of-exchange property is fundamental to the unit of account because creditors can be paid off in any exchange medium as long as the market value of the medium satisfies the contract. If this is true, then, contrary to prevailing opinion, the medium-of-exchange property *is* embedded in models of the financial sector through the standard assumption that i_m is fixed. If the medium-of-exchange property is fundamental, then it is both the source of indeterminancy (through its determination of the units in which interest-payment contracts are specified) and a source of resolution of the indeterminancy issue (through the transactions costs of using more than one exchange media without unitary exchange rates).

Other authors (for example, Keynes[17]) have argued that the unit-of-account property is fundamental to the medium-of-exchange property. Resolution of this question is outside the scope of this paper.

IMPLICATIONS OF CS
FOR THE BEHAVIOR OF MONEY ISSUERS

In the first section, CS was associated with instability in the sense that, for a given shift in anticipated exchange rate movements, greater CS produced larger exchange rate fluctuations. One of the crucial assumptions underlying the model in the first section was that money issuers were assumed to alter neither the nominal quantity of money, M, nor the nominal yield on money, i_m, in response to exchange rate fluctuations. By altering either the explicit interest paid on money or the quantity of money (and imposing a capital gain or loss on money holders), a money issuer could alter the real return (r_m) and induce the changes in currency demand necessary to eliminate or at least dampen fluctuations in the exchange rate. It is particularly appropriate for an issuer of substitutable money to use the real money yield as the monetary control variable because, as was shown in the first section, the impact of a change in r_m on the exchange rate becomes greater as CS increases. In this section, the behavior of money issuers is endogenized and their response to demand shifts is shown to eliminate the instability associated with CS in the model of the first section.

There are a multitude of objectives leading money issuers to respond to exchange market pressure. With an increase in CS, the role of profit or seigniorage considerations should become more important in the determination of monetary policy. Central banks with policies more expansionary than the average would find their monetary control seriously eroded if they acted as if their seigniorage position was unimportant when their liabilities are substitutes with other currencies. The model developed in this section will, consequently, assume profit-maximization.

With substitutable monies, market pressure will force individual money issuers to make their monies attractive relative to alternative monies available to money holders. But the implications of CS will depend on the market structure in which substitutable monies are issued. Of particular interest are a competitive market structure and a cartel market structure.*

---

*Rather than compete or form a cartel, money issuers could be protected through the institution of currency controls. The absence of such controls was implicitly assumed in the first section when (the multicurrency version of) purchasing-power parity was introduced, and that assumption is continued here. If governments protect central banks' monopoly position by prohibiting the use of "foreign" monies, then the arbitrage condition underlying PPP will be violated.

Money issuers may cooperatively determine a joint monetary policy through a cartel agreement to retain market shares.* To reduce the incentive for money holders to shift between monies, a formal cartel would likely include a fixed exchange rate agreement to help ensure that cartel members properly coordinate their policies. If, for example, one member bank attempted to pursue a less inflationary policy (and pay a higher real yield), the demand for its currency would increase. In order to keep its currency from appreciating against member currencies, the bank would have to reverse its tight policy and create money against the purchase of the weaker currencies. Similarly, commercial banks' traditional commitment to maintain a fixed exchange rate between their deposit liabilities and central bank money restrains competition between the central and commercial banks. A cartel would stabilize exchange rates without providing money holders lower inflation rates or higher real yields.

A primary purpose of this section is to develop the implications of competitively supplied money.† Authors such as Friedman[7] and Pesek and Saving[26] have argued that competition in the production of money is not viable because the value of money will be driven to its marginal cost of physical production. If this occurred, a commodity money would be the result and the advantages of a fiduciary system would be lost.

Since the marginal cost of paper and ink or maintenance of accounting entries necessary to produce physically other debt instruments (for example, bonds) is, like money, near zero, we should ask why a similar conclusion has not been deduced for the supply of other financial instruments. The primary cost of producing a bond is, obviously, the interest and principal obligation, not the trivial cost of paper and ink. But the contractual payments represent a cost to a bond issuer only because the coupons are fixed in terms of another asset, usually money. On the other hand, the physical cost of production appears as the only cost for a monopoly issuer of fiat money because money holders must accept interest payments determined by contracts expressed in units of money issuers own liability, if interest is paid at all. The fact that contracts are traditionally specified in money units explains why it is frequently argued that competitively supplied money will be issued until it becomes worthless and why a similar argument is not (to our knowledge) generally made for competition in the supply of other debt instruments.

---

*As we have argued[13] the European Monetary Union is an example of monetary cooperation facilitated through the use of a fixed-exchange-rate regime.

†Monetary competition has been introduced in a general neoclassical framework by Thompson.[29]

Money holders choose between monies on the basis of anticipated real rates of return and, consequently, banks compete through their offers of real returns. Since the real return on money is $r_m = i_m - \pi$, a bank can change its real return by altering either the nominal yield i_m or the capital gain or loss on money, π. The theoretical results of this section are independent of the particular way a money issuer chooses to offer a given real return. But the institutional arrangements for rate-of-return competition are interesting in their own right. A brief discussion of possible arrangements will motivate a key assumption in the model that follows.

Under existing institutional arrangements, the monetary liabilities of commercial banks are convertible into the liabilities of a national central bank. But if commercial banks were not required to link their deposits to central bank liabilities, they could make their deposits convertible into any assets or goods they might choose. A bank concerned with seigniorage would choose assets that would have the greatest appeal to money holders. Since money holders are presumed interested in real rather than nominal values, they would prefer convertibility into real assets or assets with stable purchasing power. If the bank were able to, in effect, hold a portfolio of real assets, then the convertibility of the bank's deposit liabilities into real assets would insure depositors against real capital loss.* In short, profit considerations would induce banks to offer monetary liabilities convertible into assets with stable real values. This would be a return to a real (but not necessarily gold) standard.

At the abstract level of the model developed here the assets available for the banks of issue to hold are limited to capital goods paying a real yield of r. The assumption that banks maintain convertibility of their deposit liabilities into bank-held assets implies that the bank's monetary liabilities are fixed against (capital) goods. This implies that the value of bank liabilities are guaranteed against capital loss in terms of goods.†

---

*Banks would presumably hold correspondent balances at other banks and deposit withdrawals could take the form of checks on other banks rather than convertibility into the actual assets of the first bank. The convertibility arrangement would be like a modern open-ended mutual fund or money market fund.

†According to Friedman,[8] it is not feasible for monetary policy to stabilize a price index given the current state of economic knowledge; hence, a stable rate of monetary growth is preferable to an active policy to stabilize P. Friedman is implicitly assuming that money issuers hold nominal assets. As we argue in the text, a bank that is serious about controlling the real value of its monetary liabilities would hold real, not nominal, assets. Just as money issuers once maintained the gold value of their liabilities by holding gold assets, they can maintain the real value of their liabilities by holding real assets. This would allow for price stabilization at the present state of economic knowledge.

To make our model compatible with previous work on the revenue from inflation, we assume the nominal interest payment on money is zero ($i_m = 0$) such that the entire real return r_m is paid through deflation. This is equivalent to the institutional arrangement described above (in which money issuers maintain convertibility of their liabilities into assets with stable real purchasing power) if the convertibility feature is modified. Rather than maintaining a fixed parity between its liabilities and its (real) assets, a bank maintains convertibility at a price changing at a constant rate, $r_m = -\pi$. The bank of issue stands ready to redeem its liabilities at a price path whose slope is (minus) the real return that the bank offers on its monetary liabilities.*

A profit-maximizing model for the behavior of a single money issuer will be developed for all degrees of CS. We depart from earlier literature on the revenue from inflation by dividing the flow of earnings into two parts. The first is the flow of net real income from issuing new money. The gross flow is $\dot{M}/P$. Part of the new money issued is used to purchase and hold real assets to provide a redemption fund to back the liabilities being created. Thus, the flow of net real income is $\dot{M}/P - m = \pi\dot{m}$ where $\dot{m} = d(M/P)/dt$. The second part of the bank's earnings is the return on the redemption fund, rm. Total net real revenue at time t, measured as an instantaneous rate is, therefore,

$$\pi m + rm = im \tag{13}$$

where im is the area under the usual liquidity preference schedule. The area is a maximum (or minimum) where the elasticity of the demand for real balances with respect to the market rate on the alternative asset is (minus) unity.† The elasticity, $m'(i)[i/m]$, is unitary when

---

*The assumption that the bank of issue guarantees a price path is equivalent to Auernheimer's[1] concept of an "honest" bank.

The question of the honesty or deception of money issuers in a competitive market has been given detailed attention by Klein.[20] He treats money as a consumer durable and argues that a long-run profit maximizing bank will limit current deception and hold down the current inflation rate in order to not erode consumer confidence in its money. Banks will act to create (what Klein calls) "brand name capital." In Klein's model with costly information it will be profitable, even under conditions of perfect competition, to have nonzero deception. We differ from Klein in that we assume banks can costlessly write binding contracts if they so desire, these contracts can be costlessly enforced, and default can be insured against. Under these conditions only firms that offer a goods-back guarantee (along a price path) will be able to attract money holders.

†The present value of a bank offering a return $r_m = -\pi$ and facing an initial money demand, $m(i, w(O))$, is $\int im(i, w(\tau))\exp(-r\tau)d\tau$, where integration is from zero to T, w is real

$$i = m/m' \ (i) \quad \text{or} \quad \pi = m/m' - r \tag{14}$$

A maximum is assured (that is, $\partial^2[im(i)]/\partial i^2 < 0$) when an exponential specification for the demand for money is used. Assuming market interest rates on other monies are unchanged, the exponential specification used in the first section (equation 3) implies the relation $m'(i) = -(\alpha + \sigma)m$. Substituting this relation into 14 yields

$$i = 1/(\alpha + \sigma) \quad \text{or} \quad \pi = 1/(\alpha + \sigma) - r \tag{15}$$

Several implications of CS follow immediately from equation 15. Beginning from a position in which each bank has a complete monopoly ($\sigma = 0$), equation 15 implies $\pi = 1/\alpha - r$, a result which has been derived by Phelps[27] and Auernheimer.[1]

With substitution between the liabilities of money issuers, their ability to maintain monopolies in segmented markets is undermined. As inspection of equation 15 shows, the profit-maximizing inflation rate falls with larger values of σ. The greater the degree of CS, the more easily a money issuer can capture a larger share of the market by offering a lower rate of inflation. As substitution between monies becomes perfect ($\sigma \to \infty$), a competitive money issuer engineers a deflation equal to the alternative real return, r. Another way to express the condition is that the alternative asset's nominal yield is zero, that is, $r + \pi = 0$. With perfect CS, therefore, the opportunity cost of holding money becomes equal to the

---

wealth growing at an exogenous rate γ, and r is assumed greater than γ to assure convergence. Auernheimer[1] has a similar present value formula for the limiting case, $T \to \infty$. As long as $m(i,w)$ is "separable" in I and w as in equation 3 of the first section, then the maximization of the flow, $im(iw(t))$, at every point in time will assure the maximization of its present value. The discussion in the text is based on this assumption.

The upper limit of integration, T, is the date at which the bank is assumed to retire all of its liabilities outstanding. The preceding present value expression equals

$$m(0) + \int(M/P)\exp(-r\tau)d\tau - m(T)\exp(-rT)$$

where integration is from 0 to T, $m(T)$ is short hand for $m(i,w(T))$, and the last term is the present value of the cost of converting $M(T)$ into $m(T)$ goods at the price $P(T) = P(0)\exp(\pi T)$. When the partial derivative of the present value is taken with respect to π and set to zero, the result is equation 14, which is independent of the value of T.

The assumption of an explicit redemption fund is expositionally convenient but not logically necessary. Regardless of the resources a bank might or might not retain in order to be able to maintain convertibility along the announced price path, the discounted value of the monetary liability, $m(T)\exp(-rT)$, must be subtracted out to correctly ascertain the firm's net worth.

(assumed) zero marginal cost of production. This condition was introduced by Friedman[9] for an optimal quantity of real money balances.* Resource allocation between money creation and other activities should be efficient when money issuers compete and their liabilities are perfect substitutes in demand.†

The solution found for no CS or for a monopoly bank, namely, that $\pi = 1/\alpha - r$, is also applicable to a cartel of money issuers whose liabilities are linked with fixed rates. A cartel produces money with a low or negative real return and suboptimal real balances.

The results of this section can be cast in more general terms by relaxing the assumption that the bank pays no explicit interest on its liabilities. The market or nominal yield on the alternative nonmonetary asset can be represented by $i = r + \pi$. If no interest is paid on money, then i is equal to the differential real yield. In symbols,

$$r - r_m = (i - \pi) - (i_m - \pi) = i - i_m \tag{16}$$

is equal to i if i_m is zero. If the more general expression $r - r_m$ is substituted for i in the profit-maximizing condition 15, the result is

$$r_m = r - 1/(\alpha + \sigma) \tag{15'}$$

---

*Literature on the optimum quantity of money is usually expressed in terms of *the* optimum quantity of money. But the marginal conditions for Pareto efficiency can hold for different levels of real balances if other variables, such as the distribution of wealth, are considered. Consequently, it is more accurate to refer to the marginal conditions for *an* optimum quantity of money. The marginal condition ($i = 0$) assures efficiency in the production of money if efficiency conditions are not violated elsewhere, and, in particular, if other sources of government revenue are nondistorting. These issues are dealt with in an optimal tax framework by Phelps.[27]

†Competition does not produce efficiency if, as has been argued, there is an externality involved in the holding of money. The usual argument (for example, Freidman[9]) is that an individual who increases his cash balances must forgo consumption. Given a fixed nominal quantity of money, others in the community are able to temporarily consume more than their income as the value of their real balances is increased. Thus, the person who acquires more real balances confers an external benefit on others in the community for which he receives no compensation. This argument is based on the assumption of an exogenous money supply.

When money is endogenized with the assumption that the bank of issue accommodates any changes in real demand, it becomes clear that an externality is not inherent in the holding of money. The bank issues more fiduciary currency in return for the goods (or equities) that the first person sells to acquire more cash balances. The individual must consume less only if the bank is not competitive. If the bank is competitive, the money holders receive the real rate of return, r, and the individual's consumption does not fall. In short, there is no externality involved in the holding of money. What has appeared as an externality is due to the fixed money supply assumption. (A similar point has been developed in note 33.)

If the interest payment on money is not taken as exogenous, then i_m and π can take on an infinity of values without violating the competitive profit-maximizing condition (15') (cf. also note 20). When there are no exogenous nominal rates, a homogeneous model such as ours determines the difference in nominal rates but not their absolute levels.*

If the nominal returns on monies are equal, whether at zero or otherwise, then the equality of real returns assures equal inflation rates and secularly stable exchange rates.† The regime of fixed rates imposed by a cartel bears only a superficial resemblance to the stable rates under competition. While the real returns on monies will be equal in either situation, the level of the returns will be very different.

SUMMARY

Two fundamental implications of CS were derived in the first section. CS was found to produce instability in the sense that shifts in the anticipated rate of exchange rate change produce larger movements in the exchange rate and these movements are unbounded as CS increases. The second implication was that, if two monies are perfect substitutes in demand, their rate of exchange is indeterminate.

The indeterminancy of the exchange rate between two perfectly substitutable monies is a logical consequence of an asset-demand model

---

*The original revenue function 13 can be redeveloped under the assumption that i_m is nonzero. The gross revenue is $M/P = i_m$ and the net flow of real revenue is $M/P - i_m m - m$ which equals $-r_m m$. The stream of real returns from the redemption fund remains $r \cdot m$ such that the total net flow of real revenue is

$$-r_m m + rm = [r - r_m] \cdot m(r - r_m) \tag{13'}$$

Maximization of 13' with respect to the differential real return yields equation 15'.

Our results are consistent with Hayek's[14] argument that competition in the provision of currencies (that he calls "concurrent currencies") will produce a stable price level if it is assumed that i_m is equal to r. If there is no explicit interst on money, then competition should produce deflation rather than stable prices.

†With only one real asset in our model, the banks offer the same real return on their monetary liabilities and hold only the single real asset. An extended model would allow for many goods and diversity of tastes among money holders. In the more complex model, banks might offer monies with different characteristics and hold different assets. With the possibility of banks holding different asset bundles and offering real returns measured against different bundles of goods, the exchange rate between monies would vary as the relative price indices of the different bundles of goods changed.

utilizing standard money-demand assumptions. But we suspect that the exchange rate would be determinate (probably at the value of unity) if transactions costs were developed more fully in aggregate money-demand functions. Further research appears necessary before policy prescriptions can be based on the finding of indeterminacy.

The instability found in the first section was eliminated when the behavior of money issuers was endogenized in the third section. The original instability was implied by a model with exogenous nominal returns and exogenous nominal money supplies. When the response of money issuers to CS is incorporated in the analysis, the nominal returns and/or nominal supplies change in response to demand shifts. The pressures of CS induce coordination of monetary policies or rate-of-return competition. In either case, the exchange rate should be stable or follow a stable path. In the absence of CS, money issuers can engage in independent monetary policies resulting in fluctuating exchange rates. It is the absence of CS, not its presence, that allows for unstable exchange rates.

Boyer[3] and Kareken and Wallace[15] have argued, and some of the remarks by Mundell[23,24] suggest, that the instability associated with CS should be countered with fixed exchange rates. But as was shown in the third section, fixing exchange rates is a method whereby money issuers agree to coordinate monetary policies to avoid market pressure and maintain market shares. The chief disadvantage of the cartel solution is that it allows money issuers, by collective action, to frustrate money holders' search for superior monies and is consistent with the high inflation rates experienced with the demise of the gold standard.

It is widely believed that one solution to the problem of inflation is to replace discretionary monetary policy with a rule for a fixed money growth rate. In the absence of CS, such a rule might eliminate exchange rate instability. But in the presence of CS, money-growth rate rules (in conjunction with fixed nominal yields on monies) would, as shown in the first section, cause exchange rate instability. Moreover, monies with fixed growth rates would be seen as inferior to competitively supplied currencies. Interestingly enough, these rules have come from economists (for example, Milton Friedman and Henry Simons) who have been staunch advocates of the free market. The fear of eliminating government supported monopolies in the production of money stems from the view that competitively supplied money would be issued in such quantitites that it would become valueless. But to attract ultimate wealth holders faced with a choice in monies, banks would have to issue monies convertible into real assets to assure money holders against capital loss. Rather than the competively supplied money becoming worthless, it would be convertible into real goods such that risk against capital loss would be minimal. A fixed money growth rule can be applied to a monopoly or a cartel. But a money supplied at a fixed rate of growth would be driven from circulation if the public is offered substitutable convertible currencies.

APPENDIX A:
The Exchange Rate with Rational Expectations

In the text the expected rate of change in the exchange rate x is taken as exogenous. In this appendix the expected rate of change of the exchange rate is endogenized using the assumption of rational expectations, that is, the expected rate of change in the exchange rate is equal to the rate of change in the exchange rate determined in the model. It will be demonstrated that if dynamic stability is assumed, the rational expectations assumption is a special case of the model developed in the text.

The assumption of rational expectations can be imposed by substituting e for x in equation 8 of the text:

$$e(t) = \bar{e}(t) - \eta(i_1 - i_2) + \eta\dot{e}(t) \tag{A1}$$

where e and $\bar{e}$ are written as explicit functions of time. In order to solve the differential equation A1 we need to specify how $\bar{e}(t) = \ln[(M_1(t)/\theta_1(t))/(M_2(t)/\theta_2(t))]$ moves over time. We assume that $\bar{e}(t)$ is a linear function of time,

$$\bar{e}(t) = \bar{e}(0) + kt \tag{A2}$$

Substituting A2 into A1 we obtain

$$e(t) = \bar{e}(0) + kt - \eta(i_1 - i_2) + \eta\dot{e}(t) \tag{A3}$$

which is a nonautonomous, linear differential equation with constant coefficients.

The general solution of (A3) is

$$e(t) = [\bar{e}(0) - \eta(i_1 - i_2) + \eta k] + kt + C\exp(t/\eta) \tag{A4}$$

where

$$\dot{e}(t) = k + (C/\eta)\exp(t/\eta)$$

The characteristic root is positive, $1/\eta > 0$, so the autonomous part of the solution for $e(t)$ (A4) is unstable unless $C = 0$. The initial condition implies $C = e(0) - [\bar{e}(0) - \eta(i_1 - i_2 - k)]$. Thus for the exchange rate to be on a nonexplosive time path $e(0) = \bar{e}(0) - \eta(i_1 - i_2 - k)$. That is, stability requires that the level of the exchange rate jump instantaneously to its equilibrium value, $e(0)$, folowing any shock to the system. Dynamic stability implies the time path of e is given by

$$e(t) = [\bar{e}(0) + kt] - \eta(i_1 - i_2 - k) \tag{A5}$$

where

$$\dot{e}(t) = k$$

Equation A5 produces the same implications as equation 8 in the text, with the proviso that x is equal to k, rather than being set arbitrarily, and where $\bar{e}(t)$ is separated into the level of $\bar{e}(t)$ at time zero, $\bar{e}(0)$, and the growth of $\bar{e})(t)$ after $t = 0$, $kt = (\bar{e}(t) - \bar{e}(0))$. Monetary changes are then separated into jumps in the levels of money supplies (and exogenous components of money demands), and changes in the rate of growth of $\bar{e}(t)$:

$$de(t) = d\bar{e}(t) - \eta d(i_1 - i_2) + \eta dk \tag{A6}$$

As in the text, jumps in $\bar{e}$ (exogenous changes in money supplies and demands) produce proportional changes in e independently of the degree of CS. Changes in the anticipated relative rate of return (changes in the is and in k) produce effects on e in proportion to the CS parameter η. In particular higher degrees of CS require larger jumps in e for given changes in the anticipated differential rate of return.

APPENDIX B:
Determination of the Bond-Exchange Rate

The bond-exchange rate is the ratio Q_b/Q_a, where Q_a and Q_b are found as the capitalized values of the streams of future interest payments. Since the instantaneous bond yields may vary over time, a variable-yield capitalization formula must be used to determine Q_a and Q_b.

The instantaneous capital gain on bonds A and B will be denoted as $\hat{Q}_a$ and $\hat{Q}_b$, where $\hat{\ }$ indicates the percent change or instantaneous logarithmic time derivative. By definition, $x = (\hat{Q}_b - \hat{Q}_a)^*$ and we assume that the latter term is equal to $\hat{Q}_b^* - \hat{Q}_a^*$, where * represents an anticipated magnitude. The condition that $\delta = 0$ for all t therefore implies that $C_a/Q_a + \hat{Q}_a^* = C_b/Q_b + \hat{Q}_b^*$ for all t. The instantaneous yields are inclusive of capital gains and will be denoted as

$$\hat{\phi}_j(t) = d\ln\phi_j/dt = C_j/Q_j + Q_j^* \quad (j = a,b)$$

where ϕ_j is the discount factor used in the capitalization formula, and

$$Q_j(t) = \int C_j\phi_j(\tau)\, d\tau \,/\, \phi_j(t) \quad (j = a,b)$$

where integration is from t to infinity and the discount factor has the initial condition $\phi_j(0) = 1$. Perfect bond substitution implies that $\phi_a(t) = \phi_b(t)$ holds for all t. Consequently, the ratio of $Q_b(t)$ to $Q_a(t)$, both found from the capitalization formula, equals C_b/C_a. Were the bonds not perpetuities, the bond-exchange rate would not generally equal the ratio of the interest payments, but it would nevertheless be fully determinate.

NOTES

1. Auernheimer, Leonardo. "The Honest Government's Guide to the Revenue from the Creation of Money." *Journal of Political Economy* 82 (May/June 1974): 598–606.
2. Boyer, Russell S. "Nickles and Dimes." Unpublished manuscript, Federal Reserve Board, 1972.
3. _____ . "Currency Mobility and Balance of Payments Adjustment." In *The Monetary Approach to International Adjustment*, eds., Bluford H. Putnam and D. Sykes Wilford (New York: Praeger, 1978), pp. 184–98.
4. Bronfenbrenner, Martin. "The Currency-Choice Defense," *Challenge*, 22 (January/February 1980): 31–36.
5. Calvo, Guillermo A., and Carlos A. Rodriguez. "A Model of Exchange Rate Determination Under Currency Substitution and Rational Expectations." *Journal of Political Economy*, 85 (June 1977): 617–25.
6. Connolly, Michael, "The Monetary Approach to an Open Economy: The Fundamental Theory." In *The Monetary Approach to International Adjustment*, eds., Bluford H. Putnam and D. Sykes Wilford (New York: Praeger, 1978), pp. 6–18.
7. Friedman, Milton. *A Program for Monetary Stability* (New York: Fordham University Press, 1959).
8. _____ . "The Role of Monetary Policy," *American Economic Review* 58 (March 1968): 1–17.
9. _____ . "The Optimum Quantity of Money." In *The Optimum Quantity of Money and Other Essays*, ed. Milton Friedman (Chicago: Aldine, 1969), pp. 1–50.

10. Girton, Lance, and Don Roper, "Theory and Implications of Currency Substitution." *International Financial Discussion Papers*, Federal Reserve Board, 1976.

11. _____ . "A Monetary Model of Exchange Market Pressure Applied to the Post-War Canadian Experience." *American Economic Review* 67 (September 1977): 537–48.

12. _____ . "Substitutable Monies and the Monetary Standard." In *The Political Economy of Policy Making*, eds., Michael Dooley, Herbert Kaufman, and Raymond Lombra (Beverly Hills, Calif.: Sage, 1979), pp. 233–46.

13. _____ . "A Theory of Currency Substitution and Monetary Unification," *Economie Appliquée*, 1980.

14. Hayek, Frederick A. *Denationalization of Money: An Analysis of the Theory and Practice of Concurrent Currencies* (London: Institute of Economic Affairs, 1976).

15. Kareken, John, and Neil Wallace. "Samuelson's Consumption-Loan Model with Country-Specific Fiat Monies." *Staff Report*, No. 24, Federal Reserve Bank of Minneapolis, July 1978.

16. _____ . "International Monetary Reform: The Feasible Alternatives." *Quarterly Review*, Federal Reserve Bank of Minneapolis, Summer 1978.

17. Keynes, John Maynard. *A Treatise on Money: The Pure Theory of Money* (London: Macmillan, 1930).

18. _____ . *The General Theory of Employment Interest and Money* (New York: Harcourt, Brace, 1936).

19. King, David, Bluford H. Putnam, and D. Sykes Wilford. "A Currency Portfolio Approach to Exchange Rate Determination: Exchange Rate Stability and the Independence of Monetary Policy." In *The Monetary Approach to International Adjustment*, eds., Bluford H. Putnam and D. Sykes Wilford (New York: Praeger, 1978), pp. 119–214.

20. Klein, Benjamin. "The Competitive Supply of Money." *Journal of Money, Credit, and Banking* 6 (November 1974): 423–53.

21. Miles, Marc A. "Currency Substitution, Flexible Exchange Rates, and Monetary Independence." *American Economic Review* 68 (June 1978): 428–36.

22. _____ . "Currency Substitution: Perspective, Implications, and Empirical Evidence." In *The Monetary Approach to International Adjustment*, eds., Bluford H. Putnam and D. Kykes Wilford (New York: Praeger, 1978), pp. 170–83.

23. Mundell, Robert A. *International Economics* (New York: Macmillan, 1968).

24. _____ . *Monetary Theory: Inflation, Interest, and Growth in the World's Economy* (Pacific Palisades, Calif.: Goodyear, 1971).

25. Parkin, Michael. "Price and Output Determination in an Economy with Two Media of Exchange and a Separate Unit of Account." In *Recent Issues in Monetary Economics*, eds., Emil Claassen and Pascal Salin (Amsterdam: North-Holland, 1976), pp. 74–98.

26. Pesek, Boris P., and Thomas R. Saving. *Money, Wealth, and Economic Theory* (New York: Macmillan, 1967).

27. Phelps, Edmund S. "Inflation in the Theory of Public Finance." *Swedish Journal of Economics* 75 (March 1973): 67–82.

28. Takayama, Akira, and Y. N. Shieh. "Flexible Exchange Rates Under Currency Substitution and Rational Expectations—Two Approaches to the Balance of Payments." Texas A&M University, manuscript, 1980.

29. Thompson, Earl. "The Theory of Money and Income Consistent with Orthodox Value Theory." In *Trade Stability and Macroeconomics*, eds., George Horwich and Paul A. Samuelson (New York: Academic Press, 1974), pp. 427–51.

30. Tobin, James. "Commercial Banks as Creators of Money." In *Banking and Monetary Studies*, ed. Deane Carson (Homewood, Ill.: Irwin, 1963), pp. 408–19.

31. ———. "A General Equilibrium Approach to Monetary Theory." *Journal of Money, Credit, and Banking* 1 (February 1969): 15–29.

32. Tullock Gordon. "Competing Monies." *Journal of Money, Credit, and Banking* 7 (November 1975): 491–97.

33. Vaubel, Roland. "Free Currency Competition." *Weltwirtschaftliches Archiv* 113 (October 1977): 435–59.

14

Currency Substitution, Flexible Exchange Rates, and Monetary Independence

Marc A. Miles

In the persistent fixed vs. flexible exchange rate debate, one of the most common arguments in favor of flexible exchange rates is that they insulate a country's money supply from monetary developments in the rest of the world (see, for example, Milton Friedman, 1953; Robert Mundell). Under fixed rates such monetary independence is impossible because, by pegging the value of domestic currency to foreign currency, the central bank makes foreign currency a perfect substitute for domestic currency on the supply side. Should the monetary authorities in country *A* increase the money supply once and for all, the domestic money supply would exceed domestic money demand, and money would immediately flow out through the balance of payments. The domestic balance-of-payments deficit must be matched by a balance-of-payments surplus abroad. Thus money supplies abroad must also increase, and a common rate of inflation would be observed among countries. But perfectly flexible exchange rates are assumed to eliminate this source of monetary interdependence. Under flexible rates the balance of payment is always zero, that is, there is no net

*The author is affiliated with Rutgers College. I would like to thank John Van Belle, Arthur Laffer, and William Gasser for their help in developing this paper. Useful comments were also provided by an anonymous referee. Sarah Biser provided research assistance. This article originally appeared in The *American Economic Review* 68 (June 1978). Permission to republish this article here is greatly appreciated.

money flow between central banks. Central banks are no longer allowed to intervene to guarantee the value of their currencies. Thus flexible rates make currencies perfect nonsubstitutes on the supply side.

The lack of intervention by the central banks and the accompanying elimination of the substitution of currencies on the supply side in turn is assumed to result in no net movements of money among countries at all and thus complete monetary independence. But this monetary independence argument makes the implicit assumption that currencies are also nonsubstitutes on the demand side, that is, Frenchmen hold only francs and Germans only deutschemarks. It is assumed that no foreign currency is held by domestic transactors for either transactions, speculative or precautionary purposes. However, in the context of the existing international economic environment this assumption appears quite dubious. Multinational corporations have strong incentives to diversify the currency composition of their cash balances in order to facilitate their endeavors in various countries. Even individuals and businesses that are clearly domiciled in a particular country often have transactions or precautionary or even speculative motives for diversifying the currency composition of their money holdings. Anyone who consistently makes purchases from foreign countries has at least the same transactions motives for demanding foreign currency balances as for demanding domestic currency balances. Importers and exporters, businesspersons who travel abroad, tourists, and residents of border areas all have incentives to diversify their currency balances. By holding foreign money, the transactions costs of the foreign purchases are reduced. With a significant subset of a country's citizens and businesses maintaining diversified currency portfolios, the conclusion of independent monetary policy no longer appears valid. A change in a country's monetary policy can generate an adjustment in the currency composition of cash balances and thus an intercountry movement of currencies which can offset at least part of the policy change.

In this paper the question of currency substitution is examined. In the first section the possible mechanisms through which the substitution can occur are discussed. Two mechanisms are presented, corresponding to whether an increase in the money supply causes a drop in the interest rate or a rise in inflationary expectations. The second section shows the implications of currency substitution on the existence of independent monetary policies under perfectly flexible exchange rates. The conclusion is that where currency substitution exists, even perfectly flexible rates may not guarantee monetary independence. In the next section a constant elasticity of substitution (*CES*) production function for the services of money is used to derive a testable model of currency substitution. This model is then tested on Canadian data. It is found that a high degree of currency substitution exists in Canada, especially during floating rate periods. The paper concludes with a summary of the implications.

THE MECHANISM OF CURRENCY SUBSTITUTION

The mere ownership of foreign currency-denominated balances by domestic residents is not a sufficient condition for currency substitution to occur. A given amount of foreign currency balances may exist within the country for institutional or historical reasons. For currency substitution to exist, not only must there be foreign currency balances, but the level of these balances must change in response to changes in other economic variables. Furthermore, it is not a necessary condition for currency substitution that each individual within the country hold foreign currency balances. Currency substitution requires only that there exist a group of individuals who, given the current value of economic variables, hold both domestic and foreign currency balances and are indifferent at the margin between holding more domestic or more foreign balances.

In order to discuss the mechanism of currency substitution, assume that such a group of individuals exist. These individuals may be foreign traders, border residents, or even multinational corporations. The important characteristic of each, however, is that they hold a diversified portfolio of real money balances. While the overall size of the real cash balance portfolio will vary with the level of real income and the returns on other types of assets, the composition of the portfolio will vary with the relevant opportunity costs of holding real balances of the various types of currencies. If the opportunity cost of holding real balances denominated in currency A rises relative to the opportunity cost of holding those denominated in currency B, all of these individuals will be assumed to reduce their real balances denominated in currency A and to increase their holdings denominated in currency B.

The particular aspect of currency substitution that is of interest here is its effect on monetary policy. The discussion of the mechanism of currency substitution will therefore be in terms of the interaction of monetary policy and currency substitution. Specifically we will examine whether changes in monetary policy change relative costs of holding currency and thus induce offsetting inflows or outflows of money.

The model will be assumed to consist of two countries A and B, each supplying its own domestic currency-denominated money asset, C_A and C_B, respectively. Both countries are assumed to have a group of individuals who hold real balances denominated in both C_A and C_B in their cash balance portfolios. The ratio in which the jth individual holds real balances of the two currencies can be described by

$$m_j(r) = (c_A/c_B)_j \tag{1}$$

where $c_A = C_A/P_A$ is the level of real balances denominated in currency A, and $r = i_B/i_A$ is the ratio of the opportunity costs of holding real balances in C_B and C_A. As R rises, m_j is also assumed to rise. The model is assumed initially at equilibrium, so that each individual's total demand for real balances precisely equals his holdings. Also, given the prevailing opportunity costs of holding c_A and c_B, each individual is assumed to have adjusted his cash balance portfolio so that he is just indifferent between holding a little more c_A or a little more c_B.

Now suppose that the monetary authorities of A increase the supply of C_A, the supply of C_B remaining constant. Following Friedman (1969) there are two possibilities for this increase, a once-and-for-all increase or a change in the rate of increase from zero to a positive number. The two possibilities will be considered in turn. In both cases it will initially be assumed that the entire adjustment to the change in the quantity of C_A occurs through a change in P_A. This assumption will be subsequently relaxed.

A Once-and-for-all Increase in C_A

Assume, as does Friedman, that the monetary authorities of country A unexpectedly decide to perform a once-and-for-all increase in the quantity of C_A by dumping from a helicopter additional units of C_A. For ease of exposition it will be assumed that each individual's cash balances increase in proportion to his initial holdings. If the economy was initially at equilibrium, this monetary shock will require adjustments in order to return the economy to equilibrium. In terms of the present model possible adjustments of four variables are of interest. First, how does the monetary shock affect the rate of interest i_A? Second, how does the change in i_A affect desired ratios of real balances m? Third, what change in P_A is required to achieve equilibrium? Finally, do changes in the preceding three variables cause a redistribution of C_A between the two countries? Each of these questions will be answered in turn.

If there is a once-and-for-all increase in C_A, the real quantity of money assets denominated in C_A increases relative to the real value of other assets denominated in C_A. In order for the additional relative amounts of c_A to be absorbed, the cost of borrowing c_A balances must fall. Thus the increase in

C_A causes i_A to fall. However, since it is assumed that the real value of C_B and all other assets denominated in C_B remain constant, the cost of borrowing c_B balances remains unchanged. The value of r is observed to rise.

The rise in r makes holding relatively more c_A suddenly more attractive. Thus m will also rise. But m does not rise only in country A. Since individuals anywhere in the world are assumed to face the same opportunity cost of holding real balances denominated in a particular currency, r rises in both countries. Thus the new equilibrium must be characterized by a higher value of m in both countries as compared with the initial equilibrium.

Two other conditions must also hold in the new stock equilibrium. First, in each country the supply of C_A must be equal to the demand for C_A. This condition will be satisfied when supply of c_A equals the demand for c_A in each country. Second, if money demand equals money supply in each country, then total world demand must equal total world supply. These two conditions will determine the final rise in P_A and the distribution of C_A among countries.

For example, for total world money demand to equal money supply, the excess world supply of real balances denominated in C_A must be eliminated. One possibility is for P_A to rise sufficiently to eliminate completely the excess supply in country A. This is the solution suggested by flexible exchange rate models. The derivation of this solution is the fact that all the increase in the supply of C_A occurs in country A. But while all the increase in supply occurs in A, all the increase in demand does not. The desired value of m rises in both countries, implying that at even a constant P_A there is excess demand for C_A in country B. Thus while such a rise in P_A will eliminate the excess supply in A, it will only increase the excess demand in B. Since such a price rise does not completely eliminate the world excess demand for C_A, it cannot be the equilibrium price rise. Obviously world equilibrium requires a smaller rise in P_A. But with a smaller price rise, there will be excess supply of C_A in country A. The final equilibrium rise in P_A will therefore be determined by where the excess supply of C_A in A is precisely equal to the excess demand for C_A in B.

While the rise in P_A is sufficient to determine world equilibrium in the C_A market, it has not equated the markets within the two countries. The inability for changes in P_A to equate both world and domestic markets is caused by the distribution effect that demand has risen in both countries while supply has risen in only one. The only way for domestic markets to clear, given the P_A that creates world equilibrium, is for units of C_A to flow from country A, where there is excess supply, to country B where there is excess demand. Thus a once-and-for-all increase in C_A in country A has caused units of C_A to flow between countries.

An Increase in the Rate of C_A: Increase from Zero to a Positive Number

Now assume that the monetary authorities of country A decide to send the helicopter over the country at regular intervals. The monetary authorities inform the public of this decision and that each trip of the helicopter will increase the amount of C_A by a constant percentage. Again, the changes in r, m, P_A, and the distribution of C_A between countries will be of interest.

In contrast to the once-and-for-all increase, the decision to increase the supply of C_A at a constant rate will create expectations of inflation which will cause i_A to rise. The rise in i_A will cause r to fall. The fall in r will cause the desired m to fall in both countries as individuals try to reduce the share of real balances denominated in C_A.

The ensuing rise in P_A in each period can be divided into two parts, the rise in P_A necessary to maintain the initial level of relative real balances in each country and the rise in P_A that reduces m from its initial level. The second source of a rise in P_A will have a positive value in the first period, and a zero value in subsequent periods. For example, consider the first period. The supply of C_A has been increased in country A. Ignoring for a moment any change in desired m, the analysis is very similar to the once-and-for-all increase case. The level of P_A must rise in order to equilibrate the world supply and demand for C_A. But in order for the supply of C_A to equal demand in both countries, units of C_A must flow from A to B. Again the increase in C_A causes a flow of currency between countries.

But the expectation of inflation causes i_A to rise, and m will not remain constant. The value of m must fall in both countries. Assuming symmetrical responses, the desired level of m will fall by the same percentage in the two countries. This adjustment can be accomplished by a once-and-for-all rise in P_A equal to the percentage fall in m. Such a rise will reduce c_A in both countries by the desired amount and will not require further flows of C_A between the countries.

So only one of the two rises in P_A causes net flow of C_A in the first period, and the flow is again from country A to country B.* Furthermore,

---

*The analysis has concentrated exclusively on the substitution effect of inflationary expectations. However, there is another effect, the change in the total demand for real balances relative to the total portfolio supply. Inflationary expectations on the one hand reduce the total demand for real balances by raising the weighted average of the cost of holding real balances, a point emphasized in the description of the empirical model. On the other hand, inflation reduces the real supply of C_A in any country holding it. Naturally those countries holding c_A in the greatest proportion will find their supply of real balances reduced

once the level of m adjusts to the level consistent with the expected inflation, there will no longer be any force creating a second source of a rise in P_A. In subsequent periods P_A will adjust only to maintain real balances at the initial m level, and as has been shown, this adjustment requires a movement of C_A from A to B. So a continuous increase in C_A produces offsetting outflows of C_A in each period.

Until now it has been assumed that when C_A increases all the adjustment in the level of real balances occurs through a rise in P_A. However, if currencies are substitutable, it is quite possible that at least some of the adjustment can occur through a rise in P_B. When C_A is increased by the monetary authorities in A, the overall level of real balances in the world is increased above the level of world demand. To this point it has been assumed that the overall level is reduced back to an equilibrium level by lowering only c_A. But lowering c_B through a rise in P_B also has this desired effect. In addition lowering c_B can also have the desired effect on m. For example, in the case of the once and for all rise in C_A, a rise in P_B will help to cause m to rise to the desired level and P_A will not have to rise as much as in the previous case.

IMPLICATIONS FOR FLEXIBLE EXCHANGE RATES AND MONETARY INDEPENDENCE

Once the assumption of currency substitution on the demand side is introduced, the conclusion that perfectly flexible exchange rates imply independent monetary policy begins to evaporate. As shown above, currency substitution in demand produces flows of money and changes in price levels that are not consistent with the traditional flexible exchange rate model. When the monetary authorities of A increase the supply of C_A, rather than the entire increase remaining within country A and P_A adjusting to eliminate the domestic excess supply of real balances, some units of C_A are redistributed through private markets to country B. The effects of the monetary policy are no longer internalized within A. Without

---

by the largest percentage. It is at least conceivable that this change in total real balance demand relative to supply could cause the opposite type of money flow to occur. For example, with hyperinflation in country A, the large rise in P_A will reduce the total value of real balances in country A more than any other country. If that supply is falling faster than demand, country A will have to be a net importer of money, and there will be a net flow of money from country B to country A, the opposite of the flow described above. In this particular case the overall demand for balances will dominate the substitution effect. However, while this case is possible, in most cases the substitution effect should dominate.

any intervention by governments of either country A or country B, the nominal money supply also rises in B.

Once possible changes in P_B are introduced, the implications become even more obvious. As long as c_A and c_B are substitutes in demand, a rise in C_A can cause not only P_A to rise, but also P_B. Thus inflation is transmitted between countries without having to assume any government intervention in the foreign exchange market. Yet transmission of inflation is precisely the type of phenomenon from which flexible rates are assumed to insulate a country.

The degree to which inflation will be transmitted between the countries will of course be proportional to the degree of substitution between currencies. The limiting case is where c_A and c_B are perfect substitutes. In that case there is the equivalent of one world currency, just as when central banks make currencies perfect substitutes on the supply side by fixing exchange rates. In that case no distinction can be drawn between either c_A or c_B, or between P_A or P_B. An increase in the nominal money supply in either country will increase the real balances used in both countries and cause the price level in both countries to rise by precisely the same amount. The degree of substitution in demand between currencies therefore becomes an important empirical question.

AN EMPIRICAL MODEL
OF CURRENCY SUBSTITUTION

For the most part the concepts of currency substitution and the diversification of cash balances have been ignored in the literature. Two exceptions, however, are Ronald McKinnon and Chow-Nan Chen. McKinnon argues that under a system of floating exchange rates, in order to facilitate the international flow of commerce, the demand for dollars and all other currencies in which international transactions are conducted would increase. Chen goes even further. He has a model which explicitly incorporates the demand for more than one currency and recognizes that the relative demand depends on the relative opportunity costs. Furthermore, he understands the basic implication of currency substitution, concluding that flexible exchange rates may no longer provide a cushion against foreign shocks. The problem with the Chen model, however, is in the demand for money function. Chen assumes a Cobb-Douglas demand function, which unfortunately constrains the elasticity of substitution to equal one. From the above discussion it should be obvious that a very important empirical question is the precise value of this elasticity. The

Chen model, therefore, cannot be accepted without considerable empirical investigation.

Instead the functional form to be estimated is derived from a procedure similar to one employed by V. Karuppan Chetty. Real balances, denominated in terms of both domestic and foreign currencies, from an individual's cash balance portfolio are combined in a production function for money services. Given the relative efficiencies of domestic and foreign currencies in producing money services (defined by the production function) and the relative opportunity costs of holding different currencies (reflected in the asset constraint), the individual tries to maximize the production of money servives.

More specifically, if a *CES* production function is assumed, the level of money services produced by M_d/P_d domestic currency real balances and M_f/P_f foreign currency real balances is

$$\frac{MS}{P_d} = \left[\alpha_1 \left(\frac{M_d}{P_d} \right)^{-p} + \alpha_2 \left(\frac{M_f}{P_f} \right)^{-p} \right]^{-(1/p)} \tag{2}$$

where

MS = level of money services

M_d, M_f = the domestic and foreign currency-denominated cash balances held

P_d, P_f = domestic and foreign currency prices indices

α_1, α_2 = weights reflecting the efficiency of domestic and foreign real balances in producing money services.

This production function directly relates the level of real balances to the level of money services. Notice that since real balances in both currencies are in goods units, there is no need for an exchange rate. However, for empirically estimating this relationship, it is desirable to express the production function in terms of nominal cash balances and exchange rates. Defining the exchange rate as $e = P_d/P_f$ from purchasing-power parity, and since P_d and P_f are indices, after defining $P_d = 1$, equation 2 becomes

$$MS = (\alpha_1 M_d^{-p} + \alpha_2 e M_f^{-p})^{-(1/p)} \tag{3}$$

The asset constraint for money balances is constructed to reflect two factors: (a) that there is an opportunity cost to holding real balances, and (b) this opportunity cost may differ between the two types of real balances. The overall portfolio of the nonbank private sector of the country is assumed to consist of holdings of all types of real assets, only one of which is money. In constructing that portfolio, desired amounts of each of these assets are determined. Once the demand for each individual asset has been determined, asset constraints for each asset can be constructed. The asset constraint in this paper reflects such an asset demand. It is assumed that in determining the composition of the overall portfolio, the private sector decides to hold M_o real cash balances. These cash balances are then divided between M_d/P_d domestic currency-denominated real balances and M_f/P_f foreign currency-denominated real balances on the basis of the relative cost of holding these different types of balances (reflected in the asset constraint) and their relative efficiencies in providing money services (reflected in the production function).

The asset constraint is the form

$$\frac{M_o}{P_d} = \frac{M_d}{P_d}(1 + i_d) + \frac{M_f}{P_f}(1 + i_f) \tag{4}$$

where i_d and i_f are the interest rates on domestic and foreign currencies balances, respectively. In terms of nominal balances and exchange rates, equation 4 becomes

$$M_o = M_d(1 + i_d) + eM_f(1 + i_f) \tag{5}$$

The asset constraint reflects the fact that M_o is the total money assets that must be held to provide the money services of M_d and eM_f money assets. If for example the money balances are borrowed each period, since it costs $M_d \cdot i_d$ and $eM_f \cdot i_f$ to borrow M_d and to compute the ratio of the efficiency coefficients from the estimated coefficients. This procedure will provide a measure of whether 5.4 is sufficiently close to infinity. If U.S. and Canadian dollars are equally efficient in providing monetary services to Canadians, the ratio should equal one.

The initial test on the ratio of the coefficients is to examine the t-statistic on the constant term of the regression. If α_1/α_2 equals one, the logarithm of the ratio will equal zero and the constant term should not be significantly different from zero. However, the significant t-statistic indicates that the value of the ratio is not precisely one. An actual estimate of the value of the ratio is obtained by substituting values from equation 12 into 11, yielding $\alpha_1/\alpha_2 = 1.60$. From this value it can only be concluded that U.S. and Canadian dollars are not perfect substitutes for the entire period.

This estimating procedure is repeated for three subperiods. For the purposes of this analysis it is fortunate that Canada has experienced periods of both fixed and floating rates. The values of the elasticities of substitution under the different exchange rate regimes can now be estimated. Two possible hypotheses concerning these values arise. One hypothesis states that the only reason that the elasticity of substitution was high for the period as a whole was that for a significant subperiod the exchange rate of Canada was fixed. The Bank of Canada was willing during this subperiod to exchange Canadian dollars for U.S. dollars, and all the elasticity of substitution was measuring was the substitution on the supply side during this subperiod. This hypothesis would be consistent with high values of elasticities of substitution during fixed rate periods and low values during floating rate periods.

The second hypothesis has just the opposite conclusion. It states that during periods of fixed rates the public does not have to substitute between currencies in private markets since the government is already making currencies perfect substitutes on the supply side. Alternatively, during floating rate periods the public will have to resort to performing all of its substitution through private markets. This hypothesis would be consistent with low or insignificant estimates of the elasticity of substitution during fixed rate periods when the substitution mechanism is not needed, but large estimates during the floating rate periods.

Canada was on floating rates until May 2, 1962, and returned to floating rates on June 1, 1970. The subperiods examined were therefore 1960IV–1962II (floating), 1962III–1970II (fixed), 1970III–1975IV (floating). The results are presented in Table 14.1. The most striking difference between the subperiods is that in subperiods where the exchange rate was floating the estimate of the elasticity of substitution is larger and statistically significant, while in the subperiod where the exchange rate was fixed, the estimated coefficient is smaller and insignificantly different from zero. For example, in the first subperiod where the exchange rate was floating the estimated value of σ is 12.8, and that value is significantly different from both zero and one at the 95-percent level (one-tailed test). Similarly, in the final subperiod where the exchange rate was again floating, the estimated value of σ is 5.8, and that value is significantly different from zero at the 95-percent level and from one at the 90-percent level. In contrast the estimated value of σ for the subperiod where the exchange rate was fixed is less than half the value in any other subperiod or the period as a whole. In addition, the coefficient is not significantly different from zero at even the 90-percent level. Not surprisingly the ratio of the efficiency parameters exhibit a similar pattern with estimates of 1.2 and 1.6 in the first and second floating rate periods and 2.4 in the fixed rate period.

The results from analyzing the subperiods are therefore consistent with the second hypothesis and not the first. The large significant elasticity of substitution for the period as a whole does not seem to be the result of substitution during the fixed rate subperiod, but rather during the floating rate subperiods. The concept of substitution between U.S. and Canadian

TABLE 14.1 Estimates of the Elasticity of Substitution During Subperiods of Fixed and Floating Exchange Rates

Subperiod	Exchange Rate Regime	Type of Equation	Constant Term	Elasticity of Substitution	R^2	D.W.	F	Rho
1960IV–1962II	Floating	OLSQ	2.78 (50.8)	12.8 (2.54)	0.48	1.66	6.47	
1962III–1970II	Fixed	CORC	2.31 (12.7)	2.66 (0.79)	0.78	1.41	107.4	0.9
1970III–1975IV	Floating	CORC	2.79 (16.1)	5.78 (1.83)	0.79	1.27	74.0	0.8

Note: *t*-statistics in parentheses.
Source: Treasury Bulletin and Statistical Summary, Annual Supplement.

dollars by private Canadians appears to be statistically valid when the Canadian government is not performing that service for them. The results are even more impressive when one considers that the above data have not even included holdings of U.S. dollar-denominated Eurodollars, whose elasticity of substitution with respect to Canadian dollars could quite possibly be even higher.

SUMMARY AND IMPLICATIONS

In this paper it has been argued that there exists a group of individuals within a country who diversify their real cash balance holdings between domestic and foreign currency-denominated balances. These diversified portfolios imply that monetary policy will produce changes in the interest rate that induce offsetting money flows even under perfectly flexible exchange rates. The importance of these offsetting flows will be directly proportional to the degree of substitution between currencies. In the case where currencies are perfect substitutes monetary independence is impossible, even where central banks do not intervene in the foreign exchange markets.

Thus the argument that flexible exchange rates imply monetary independence is brought into question. Only to the extent that individuals do not substitute between currencies will the argument be valid. As the empirical tests show, the elasticity of substitution in at least one major country is quite high. The proper model for analyzing monetary policy may, therefore, be one of monetary dependence, not monetary independence, even when perfectly flexible exchange rates are assumed.

REFERENCES

C.-N Chen, "Diversified Currency Holdings and Flexible Exchange Rates," *Quart. J. Econ.*, Feb. 1973, 87, 96–111.

V. K. Chetty, "On Measuring the Nearness of Near-Moneys," *Amer. Econ. Rev.*, June 1969, 59, 270–81.

Milton Friedman, "The Case for Flexible Exchange Rates," in his *Essays in Positive Economics*, Chicago 1953.

_____ , *The Optimum Quantity of Money and Other Essays*, Chicago 1969.

Ronald McKinnon, *Private and Official International Money: The Case for the Dollar*, in *Essays in International Finance*, Princeton Univ. No. 84, Apr. 1969.

Robert A. Mundell, *International Economics*, New York 1968.

Bank of Canada, *Statistical Summary*, Annual Suppl., Ottawa 1960–69.

_____ , *Review*, Ottawa 1971–76.

U.S. Treasury Department, *Treasury Bull.*, Washington 1960–76.

15

Currency Substitution and Instability in the World Dollar Standard

Ronald I. McKinnon

Should foreign exchange considerations or observed growth in the money supplies of other industrial countries significantly influence the domestic monetary policy of the United States? The received wisdom of both monetarist and Keynesian economists and the revealed preferences of U.S. policy-makers has been to try—often unsuccessfully—either to suppress international influences or to ignore them. Both groups define policy targets in terms of growth rates in purely *domestic* monetary aggregates, or in terms of domestic (dollar) rates of interest.

Indeed one of the main objectives of Milton Friedman's persuasive advocacy (1953) of floating exchange rates was to secure, without the use of exchange controls or other trade distortions, national monetary autonomy for all countries—whether they be the United States, Germany, or Canada, or Brazil. This point of view has been vigorously espoused by both Keynesians such as James Meade (1955) and monetarists such as Harry Johnson (1972); it was influential in persuading policy-makers to accept (albeit under pressure) an advent of floating exchange rates among industrial countries in 1973—followed by formal legal ratification through amendment of the IMF's Articles of Agreement in 1976. And monetarists

*The author is professor of economics, Stanford University. I would like to thank John Cuddington and James Powell for helpful comments. This article originally appeared in *American Economic Review* 72 (June 1980). Permission to republish this article here is greatly appreciated.

have a strategy for exercising this autonomy: each country pursues its own fixed monetary growth rule as if the demands for national monies were stable and independent of one another.

In contrast, the admittedly casual empirical evidence presented below suggests a radically different view: the national (convertible) monies of an inner group of industrial countries are highly substitutable in demand according to anticipated exchange rate movements. This international currency substitution destabilizes the demand for individual national monies so that one can't make much sense out of year-to-year changes in purely national monetary aggregates in explaining cycles in purely national rates of price inflation.

However, all is not necessarily lost for the monetarist view. The world demand for money seems relatively stable. By considering a crude index of a "world" money supply (confined to the convertible currencies of industrial countries), the two great outbreaks of international price inflation in the 1970s become explicable. The world money supply exploded in 1971–72 and again in 1977–78 (well before the two oil crises of 1973 and 1979). Speculation against the U.S. dollar was combined with exchange interventions by foreign central banks (to prevent the dollar from falling) that directly expanded money supplies in Europe and Japan. How this inflationary pressure was divided among countries depended on relative exchange rate movement in each case, but the impact on the world price level was unambiguous. Even for the United States itself, this tentative measure of changes in the world money supply explains the great (dollar) price inflations of 1973–74 and 1979–80 much better than does any domestic American monetary aggregate.

But why didn't the American money supply decrease as people shifted out of dollars into foreign monies? First, the American monetary authorities were operating myopically under a fixed domestic money growth rule over a monthly or quarterly time horizon. Secondly, in the very short run, the U.S. money stock did not contract automatically in response to official exchange intervention. Because the United States is the reserve-center country under the world dollar standard, even massive dollar interventions by foreign central banks are usually sterilized of any impact on the American monetary base—as described in the theoretical model given below.

But the sterilization appropriate for the strong dollar standard under the fixed exchange rates of the 1950s and 1960s is less benign under today's managed floating and volatile exchange rate expectations. I conclude by briefly discussing how American monetary policy should be suitably "internationalized" in order to stabilize better both the international and American price levels.

THE EVIDENCE

The usual procedure would be to present an ostensibly complete structural model of the international macroeconomy, and then estimate the individual parameters by using elaborate econometric techniques only loosely related to the theoretical model. The nature and quality of the data would not be discussed, but the unprocessed statistical series might be available from the author upon special request.

Here, I follow a different strategy. First unprocessed but standardized data on the industrial countries' national money supplies, price levels, and foreign exchange reserves are compiled from the *International Financial Statistics* of the International Monetary Fund. Without trying to build a comprehensive model of income, employment, or price levels in the world economy, two extreme cases where international currency substitution seemed to lead to a loss of monetary control are identified. Then a very short-run and highly simplified analytical model is developed to explain what happened in those two episodes and, possibly, in other less easily identified cases.

The money supplies, whose rates of change appear in Table 15.1 are defined narrowly to include currency and mainly noninterest-bearing checking accounts—although some countries do include deposits bearing fixed rates of interest in this M1 category. Precisely which of these convertible currencies are the strongest substitutes for one another, and which should enter with the heaviest weights in any index of world money, is not addressed. Nevertheless, Table 15.1 includes the principal monies that are used for invoicing world trade and for denominating internationally liquid wealth in the Euromarkets. But Eurocurrency deposits per se are omitted because they are more like bonds in bearing an equilibrium market rate of interest and in not being usable by nonbanks for making payments to third parties (Helmut Mayer, 1979). In short, I am interested in a narrow definition of money in the spectrum of financial assets, but one which has effective potential as an international medium of exchange and standard of value.

Annual percentage growth rates in the nominal money supplies of the ten industrial countries in Table 15.1 are then averaged using weights corresponding to their nominal GNP in 1970—the last year of more or less fixed exchange rates and the midpoint of my 20-year data series. This aggregation procedure for measuring the growth in world money neatly avoids incorporating continual exchange rate fluctuations, (Harold Van Cleveland and Bruce Brittain, 1976), and ignores national differences in GNP growth and in growth in real money stocks. The United States enters with a heavy unchanging weight of .5174. More importantly, no eco-

TABLE 15.1 World Money Supply Increases: Ten Industrial Countries (percentage changes between year-end stocks)

	U.S.	Canada	Japan	U.K.	Germany	France	Italy	Nether-lands	Belgium	Switzer-land	Weighted World Average
(GNP weights 1970)	(.5174)	(.0432)	(.1042)	(.0648)	(.0989)	(.0804)	(.0491)	(.0167)	(.0137)	(.0115)	
1960	0.6	4.0	36.6	0.4	7.2	14.1	13.6	6.7	1.9	5.0^a	7.03
1961	3.3	12.7	18.4	2.0	14.5	15.5	16.0	7.7	7.7	15.3	8.18
1962	2.5	4.3	16.6	-5.0	6.8	18.1	17.6	7.5	7.2	11.3	6.23
1963	3.2	7.3	34.6	14.5	7.2	14.5	13.6	9.3	9.6	7.3	9.43
1964	4.7	9.4	13.0	3.2	8.5	8.3	7.5	8.0	6.6	6.5	6.57
1965	4.8	14.3	18.2	3.9	7.7	9.4	16.4	10.0	7.1	3.8	7.88
1966	2.4	7.3	13.9	0.0	1.9	7.8	13.3	6.8	6.6	3.8	4.72
1967	7.5	4.0^a	14.1	7.6	10.0	4.8	15.7	6.2	3.2	6.7	8.38
1968	8.1	0.6	13.3	3.9	7.6^a	8.0	11.9	11.4	7.2	11.9	8.26
1969	3.3	-4.2	20.6	0.0	5.3	-2.5	15.9	8.1	-6.0	11.0	4.96
1970	4.3	1.8	16.8	9.3	8.6	11.4	27.4	11.8	7.0	11.0	8.19
1971	6.5	13.1	29.7	15.2	12.8	11.8	19.0	15.0	11.1	18.4	11.77
1972	9.1	12.2	24.7	14.0	14.1	14.9	17.3	17.6	15.2	5.7	12.73
1973	5.7	8.8	16.8	5.1	1.7	9.8	24.3	0.0	7.5	0.0	7.65
1974	3.0	1.5	11.5	10.8	10.7	15.2	9.4	12.2	6.2	-3.3	6.51
1975	5.5	19.0	11.1	11.0^a	14.3	12.6	13.4	19.7	15.7	4.4	9.22
1976	5.9	1.5	12.5	11.3	3.3	7.5	18.8	8.2	7.0	10.5	7.36
1977	8.2	10.4	8.2	21.5	12.0	9.3^a	21.4	13.2	8.3	0.6	10.27
1978	8.2	7.0	13.4	16.4	14.2	11.1	26.6	4.1	5.9	19.7	10.98
1979	8.0	1.4	3.0	9.1	3.2	11.9	23.7	2.8	2.5	-1.3	7.60
1980	5.3	10.7	-2.1	3.9	4.0	6.4	12.9	6.0	0.3	-0.5	4.88

Source: All data are noninterest bearing M1 and are taken from line 34 of the *International Financial Statistics:* 1975–80 data from the February 1982 issue, and 1960–72 data from the 1981 yearbook.
^{a}Implies a discontinuous series where arbitrary averaging was used.

252

nometric attempt is made to distinguish the international moneyness of, say, the Italian lira from that of the German mark.

Nevertheless, the weighted average of world money growth appearing in the right-hand column of Table 15.1—with a trend rate of about 8 percent per year—clearly reveals the monetary consequences of the two major episodes of "bear" speculation against the dollar:

(1) 1971–72: the anticipated collapse of official dollar parities under the Bretton Woods and then the Smithsonian agreements; and

(2) 1977–78: the attempt by officials in the Carter administration to talk the dollar down, culminating in the massive stabilization program of November 1, 1978.*

During both these major episodes (and in a host of minor ones), foreign central banks were heavily intervening—but to varying degrees—to prevent their currencies from appreciating against the dollar. Because of passive sterilization by the Federal Reserve (as explained below), the American money supply was undiminished even as foreign money supplies rose substantially above their trends. Thus, the world money supply rose unusually rapidly to between 10 and 13 percent per year in 1971–72 and again in 1977–78: the far right column in Table 15.1.

These international losses of monetary control were followed—with lags of uncertain duration—by inflationary explosions in 1973–74 and 1979–80, as one can see from the price level data in Table 15.2. Using the same 1970 GNP weights, one can aggregate wholesale price levels internationally to get a weighted world average price index in the right-hand column of Table 15.2. In measuring international inflationary pressure, wholesale indices come closer than consumer price indices to providing a common denominator of tradable goods.

Were foreign exchange interventions responsible for this loss of monetary control? Those increases in the (gross) foreign exchange reserves of different countries that are associated with increases in their domestic monetary bases are hard to identify. Table 15.3 presents data on the direct dollar liabilities of the U.S. government—almost all in the form of U.S. Treasury bonds and bills—to the governments of Canada, Japan, and Western Europe. (Rather arbitrary valuation changes in monetary gold stocks have nothing to do with foreign exchange intervention, and the

---

*This unfortunate official perception that the dollar was overvalued was based on an emerging U.S. trade deficit in 1977. However, one can explain (see my 1981 article) the deficit on fiscal grounds rather than an exchange rate or price level disalignment. The initial tendency for the dollar to fall led to a loss of monetary control in the United States, and a much bigger dollar devaluation than the authorities wanted.

TABLE 15.2 World Price Inflation: Ten Industrial Countries (percentage changes from past year's period average)

	U.S.	Canada	Japan	U.K.	Germany	France	Italy	Netherlands	Belgium	Switzerland	Weighted World Average
(GNP weights 1970)	(.5174)	(.0432)	(.1042)	(.0648)	(.0980)	(.0804)	(.0491)	(.0167)	(.0137)	(.0115)	
1960	0.1	0.1	0.1	1.3[a]	1.1	3.6[c]	0.9	-2.5[d]	1.1	0.6[d]	0.6
1961	-0.4	1.1	0.1	3.8	1.5	3.0	0.1	-1.2	-0.1	0.2	.5
1962	0.2	2.8	-1.6	2.1	3.5	0.5	3.1	1.2	0.7	3.5	.7
1963	-0.4	1.9	1.7	1.2	0.4	2.8	5.3	2.5	2.5	3.8	.8
1964	0.2	0.4	0.2	2.9	1.1	3.6	3.2	6.2	4.7	1.3	1.1
1965	1.3	2.1	0.7	3.7	2.4	0.7	1.6	3.5	1.0	0.5	1.5
1966	3.3	3.5	2.4	2.8	1.8	2.7	1.6	4.5	0.6	1.9	2.9
1967	.2	1.8	1.8	1.2	-1.0	-0.9	-0.1	0.0	0.0	0.3	.3
1968	2.4	2.2	0.9	3.9	-0.7	1.7	0.3	1.1	1.2	0.1	1.5
1969	4.0	4.7	2.1	3.4	1.8	10.7	3.9	0.0	3.4	2.9	4.0
1970	3.6	1.4	3.6	7.1	4.9	7.5	7.3	6.4	6.0	4.1	4.4
1971	3.3	1.2	-0.8	9.0	4.3	2.1	3.4	1.0	1.9	2.2	3.1
1972	4.5	7.0	0.8	5.3	2.6	4.6	4.1	4.0	4.1	3.6	4.1
1973	13.1	21.5	15.9	7.3	6.6	14.7	17.0	12.4	7.4	10.7	12.9
1974	18.9	22.1	31.3	23.4	13.4	29.2	40.7	13.6	20.1	16.2	21.9
1975	9.2	6.7	3.0	24.1	4.7	-6.1	8.5	7.5[e]	4.5	-2.3	7.5
1976	4.6	5.1[a]	5.0	17.3	3.7[b]	7.4	23.8	7.8	7.1	-0.7	6.6
1977	6.1	7.9	1.9	19.8	2.7	5.6	16.6	5.8	2.4	0.3	6.6
1978	7.8	9.3	-2.5	9.1	1.2	4.3	8.4	1.3	-2.0	-3.4	5.6
1979	12.5	14.4	7.3	12.2	4.8	13.3	15.5	2.7	6.3	3.8	11.1
1980	14.0	13.4	17.9	16.3	7.5	8.8	20.1	8.2	5.8	5.2	13.5

Source: All data are wholesale price indices from *International Financial Statistics* (various issues), line 63.

[a]Series based on industrial output prices.

[b]New series based on industrial product prices.

[c]Series based on industrial goods prices (tax included).

[d]Series based on home and import goods prices.

[e]New series based on final product prices.

physical quantitites of gold held by industrial countries have been relatively stationary. Hence gold positions as well as Special Drawing Rights are ignored in Table 15.3.) Because the industrial countries (unlike LDC's) tend *not* to diversify their official reserves into Eurodollar deposits or foreign exchange assets other than dollars, the buildup of direct dollar claims on the U.S. government is a good approximation of their cumulative intervention in the foreign exchanges. Of course, under the asymmetrical world dollar standard, the U.S. government itself has negligible net accumulations of foreign exchange reserves.

Fortunately, in interpreting the crude data in Table 15.3, the very sharp run-ups of foreign exchange reserves by Western Europe and Japan

TABLE 15.3 Dollar Liabilities of the United States Government to Foreign Central Banks and Official Agencies (in billions of U.S. dollars; year-end stocks)

	Canada[a] (1)	Japan[c] (2)	Western[b] Europe (3)	Total (1) to (3)	Annual Percentage Change (5)
1963	1.79	1.59	8.51	11.89	
1964	1.81	1.50	9.32	12.63	+6.2
1965	1.70	1.57	8.83	12.10	−4.4
1966	1.33	1.47	7.77	10.57	−14.5
1967	1.31	1.45	10.32	13.08	+23.7
1968	1.87	2.26	8.06	12.19	−7.3
1969	1.62	2.61	7.07	11.30	−7.9
1970	2.95	3.19	13.61	19.75	+74.8
1971	3.98	13.78	30.13	47.89	+142.0
1972	4.25	16.48	34.20	54.93	+14.7
1973	3.85	10.20	45.76	59.81	+8.9
1974	3.66	11.35	44.33	59.34	−0.8
1975	3.13	10.63	45.70	59.46	+0.2
1976	3.41	13.88	45.88	63.17	+6.2
1977	2.33	20.13	70.75	93.21	+47.6
1978	2.49	28.90	93.09	124.48	+33.5
1979	1.90	16.36	85.60	103.86	−19.9
1980	1.56	21.56	81.59	104.71	+0.8

Source: All data from *International Financial Statistics.*
[a]Line 4aad, *IFS* (United States).
[b]Line 4abd, *IFS* (United States).
[c]Because direct U.S. liabilities to the Japanese government were not available, the virtually identical series on total Japanese reserves in foreign currency was used—line 1 d.d. *IFS* (Japan).

in 1970–72 and 1977–78 are so striking that one need not quibble about whether or not direct dollar claims on the United States are an inclusive measure of foreign exchange intervention. From virtually zero growth in the 1960s, the rate of foreign exchange accumulation rose to about 70 percent per year in 1970–72. After another quiescent period of zero growth, foreign exchange accumulation again rose to about 40 percent per year in 1977–78—before falling back to zero net growth. These marked increases in foreign reserves are sufficient to explain the sharp increases in money supplies in Europe and Japan that dominated world money growth in 1971–72 and 1977–78, as portrayed in Table 15.1.

To be consistent with the idea of a stable aggregate demand for "world money," the resulting world price inflation—after a one- or two-year lag—should be quite general in 1973–74 and again in 1979–80 as seems to be true in Table 15.2. By comparison, individual rates of growth in national money supplies are—by themselves—quite puzzling as explanations of national inflation rates. For example, in 1978 Switzerland's money growth was 19.7 percent and the American money growth was "only" 8.2 percent; yet the United States experienced price inflation at about 13 percent in 1979–80, whereas Switzerland's rate was only about 4.5 percent. *In general, growth in the world money supply is a better predictor of American price inflation than is U.S. money growth.* Switzerland avoided the same inflationary pressure by letting its currency appreciate.

While not conclusive, the data are at least consistent with the idea that national monies are substitutable to the extent of making national money demand functions appear quite unstable if foreign exchange considerations are ignored. In the 1980s, it seemed highly questionable for even the center country, the United States, to pursue a purely nationalistic monetary rule irrespective of whether money supplies of other convertible currency countries were sharply expanding or contracting—or irrespective of whether the dollar was falling or rising in the foreign exchange market.

A MODEL OF THE WORLD DEMAND FOR MONEY

Following Alexander Swoboda (1978), consider only two countries: the United States issues dollars and the rest of the world (ROW) issues a single convertible currency called *rowa*. The ROW is an analytical abstraction only for industrial countries other than the United States. However, demand for either of these two noninterest-bearing monies could well originate, in part, with third countries whose own currencies are inconvertible and which are not formally part of the analysis. Nevertheless, dollars are mainly demanded for monetary circulation in the United States, and *rowa* for monetary circulation in ROW. The margin of substitutability between the two remains to be described.

A complete picture of international inflation would link money creation to realized price and possibly output increases—with differing variable lags. Such a complex process cannot be captured within a simple analytical framework. Focus instead on the much narrower problem of how changing exchange rate expectations immediately influence the demand for *rowa* relative to dollars and the total supply of world money. In analyzing these monetary disturbances in the very short run, assume that national price levels, real incomes, and the spot exchange rate are all given. Fixing the spot exchange rate between dollars and *rowa* roughly reflects the current propensity of ROW government to intervene by "leaning against the wind" to prevent any immediate sharp changes. (Prior to 1973, it would have represented an attempt to maintain an official parity.) This presumed short-run stability in the spot exchange rate under managed floating allows us to aggregate the two national money stocks, and define the world's nominal money stock, M^w, to be

$$M^w = M + SM^*$$ (1)

where M is U.S. money stock (dollars), M^* is ROW money stock (*rowa*), and S is dollars/*rowa*.

Although the spot exchange rate is stable within a very short time horizon of a few days, private expectations of future exchange rate movements may be quite volatile from time to time. Let s represent the expected change in S, averaged into the near future of "several weeks." The parameter s is equal to the discount on the dollar in the forward exchange market, which reflects anticipated dollar depreciation,

$$s = E\{dS/dt\} = (F - S)/S$$ (2)

where F is the forward exchange rate.

Fluctuations in s are given *exogenously* to the model. They may reflect pure foreign exchange disturbances as when the U.S. Treasury secretary suggested early in 1977 that the dollar was overvalued; or they may vary simultaneously with changing assessments of future American monetary policy vis-à-vis ROW monetary policy. Indeed, historical evidence suggests that exchange rate movements (beyond the very short-run official commitment to managed floating) are highly sensitive to perceived or actual changes in monetary policy (Peter Bernholz, 1981). Without spelling out all the mechanisms by which s could change, the analysis begins rather arbitrarily with an expectations shock in the form of a discrete change in s.

Perfect Capital Mobility

With free Euromarkets and the absence of sustained exchange controls that separate national markets in interest-bearing securities, for analytical purposes suppose the international bond market is "perfect." After taking expected exchange rate changes, s, into account, investors are indifferent between investing in short-term dollar or *rowa* bonds. Define this common nominal world yield on bonds to be i^w: the opportunity cost of holding money in the demand function for world money.*

$$M_d^w/P = L(i^w, Y^w) \tag{3}$$

where $Y^w = Y + Y^*$ is given world income, and P is the given world price level.

With P and Y^w given in the very short run, the demand function describes how i^w must vary to accommodate any changes in the world's money supply. The function L describes Keynesian liquidity preference on a global scale.

As a first approximation, we shall ignore any direct effect that changes in s might have on i^w or on the *world* demand for money. This would require a more complete macro-model specifying how s influences expected world price inflation. Hence s does not appear in world money demand—equation 3. But s directly affects individual money demands and the rates of interest on dollar bonds and on *rowa* bonds. Assume that

$$i = i^w + (1 - \alpha)s \tag{4}$$

$$i^* = i^w - \alpha s \tag{5}$$

where 4 is interest rate on dollar bonds and 5 is interest rate on *rowa* bonds.

Suppose $\alpha = B/B^w$ is the financial weight of the United States in the world capital markets as measured by the (given) ratio of dollar to total bonds outstanding. For the single term to maturity in equation 4, a rise in s (the expected dollar depreciation) will force up the dollar rate of interest by $(1 - \alpha)s$. In the 1950s and early 1960s, during the "strong" dollar standard and American financial predominance, α was likely close to

---

*Throughout the analysis, the subscript d represents demand. The M_d^w is the ex ante world money demanded at the going interest rate, where M^w is the actual stock of world money in existence.

unity: as $\alpha \to 1$, $i \to i^w$ for any given s. The interest rate on dollar bonds dominates our hypothetical world rate of interest, and changes in s have a negligible impact on interest rates in the American money market.

In the 1980s, on the other hand, the financial importance of the United States in the world's bond market has been reduced so that α may be closer to, say, one-half. In this latter case, an increase in s leads to a more symmetrical adjustment: the (short-term) rate of interest on dollar bonds is forced up by $s/2$ and that on *rowa* bonds is forced down by $s/2$. In this more symmetrical situation, nominal rates of interest in U.S. money markets are no longer determined solely by domestic influences. The dollar rates of interest on federal funds or U.S. Treasury bills become even more treacherous as short-run indicators of monetary ease or tightness.

Finally, consider two strong implications of the perfect capital mobility assumption embedded in equations 4 and 5:

$$i - i^* = s \qquad (6)$$
(Fisher Open Condition)

$$i^w = \alpha i + (1 - \alpha)i^* \qquad (7)$$
(Integrated Capital Market)

The short-term interest differential accurately reflects expected exchange rate movements, and the world interest rate is simply a weighted average of the two national interest rates. Clearly, these are very strong implications of the perfect capital markets assumption, and this dominance of the foreign exchanges in domestic interest rate determination may not be valid during much of the 1960–80 period. Nevertheless, in the two extreme episodes of 1971–72 and 1977–78 when expectations of dollar depreciation were highly developed, this simplifying assumption gives insight into how currency substitution actually occurred and is consistent with interest rate movements actually observed (see my 1981 article).

A Two-stage Money Demand Function

This consistent weighting of the United States and ROW in the international bond market makes the world demand for money independent of s. However, the *distribution* of demand between dollars and *rowa*, for any given M_d^w, will be highly sensitive to expected changes in the exchange rate. Let β be the dollar share of world money such that

$$M_d = \beta(s; Y/Y^w)M_d^w \qquad (8)$$

$$SM_d^* = (1 - \beta)M_d^w \tag{9}$$

where 8 is demand for dollars and 9 is demand for *rowa*.

In effect we have a two-stage money demand function. The first stage—equation 3—describes the world demand for money, and the second stage—equations 8 and 9—divides that demand between the two currencies. In the short run, the share of dollars in M_d^w declines with s and the share of *rowa* increases commensurately so as to keep the total demand for world money constant for any given world interest rate. Hence $\partial\beta/\partial s < 0$ is a convenient measure of pure *currency substitution* between dollars and *rowa*. On the other hand, in the short run, α is insensitive to s because interest rates on bonds adjust to compensate their owners.

The first channel through which an increase in s raises M_d^w and reduces M_d is when large commercial banks, and possibly some nonfinancial multinationals, shift their noninterest-bearing working balances from dollars into *rowa* to reduce direct losses from anticipated dollar devaluation. Ordinarily, a rather small proportion of each country's noninterest-bearing money stock would be owned by such trade-oriented institutions. Hence this direct form of currency substitution, Channel One, may well be significant without being dominant.*

Instead, the indirect route, Channel Two, which utilizes our strong assumption of perfect mobility in the international bond market, is likely to lead to greater substitution between the two monies and to create a larger capital outflow from the United States. Let us take a simple example. In a situation where $\alpha = 1/2$, suppose s increases from zero to 6 percent because the U.S. secretary of the treasury opines that the dollar is overvalued. The "perfect" international bond market quickly adjusts to these new exchange rate expectations: the incipient arbitrage pressure to move out of dollar bonds into *rowa* bonds causes interest rates to adjust immediately: i rises by three percentage points, and i^* falls by three points. At this stage, significant capital outflows need not occur if expectations are commonly

---

*Bruce Brittain (1981) provides some independent evidence that the velocities of money in Germany and the United States are inversely related according to the interest differential between dollar and deutschemark bonds. Marc Miles (1978) concludes that currency substitution exists between Canada and the United States, also based on the interest differential that incorporates expected changes in exchange rates. Whereas Arturo Brillembourg and Susan Schadler (1979) compute semielasticities of substitution between the dollar and a number of other currencies.

held, and interest rates adjust immediately so as to eliminate the incentives for profiting from international arbitrage in interest-bearing securities.*

Currency substitution induced by these interest rate changes occurs indirectly. American transactors naturally try to sell noninterest-bearing dollar cash balances and buy dollar bonds when i jumps by three percentage points—and foreign transactors sell *rowa* bonds and buy *rowa* cash balances. But this arbitrage from money to bonds tends to decrease i and increase i^* so as to reduce $i - i^*$ below s, thus creating temporary pressure in the international bond market. In our example, the interest differential falls incipiently below six percentage points. Then international bond arbitragers do the rest: they sell dollar bonds and buy *rowa* bonds to preserve $i - i^* = s$. This additional capital outflow from the United States is exactly equal to the reduced demand for dollar cash balances and to the augmented demand for *rowa* cash balances. Because most domestic transactors (money owners) in the United States and in ROW are influenced by these interest rate changes, this indirect form of currency substitution may well be the most important quantitatively. *Massive capital flows can easily be induced even when the interest differential remains "correctly" aligned to reflect accurately the change in expected exchange depreciation.*

Throughout the above analysis of money demands, I have assumed that the authorities maintain the spot exchange rate at S. Indeed, this provided part of the analytical basis for our world money demand function—equation 3. The next step is to look more explicitly at the short-run supply mechanism arising out of this foreign exchange intervention.

THE SUPPLY OF INTERNATIONAL MONEY

The supply of world money is under the joint control of the U.S. Federal Reserve system and ROW bank, which is the single hypothetical central bank representing the other convertible currencies. Because the United States is the reserve center, only the ROW bank directly enters the foreign exchange market to smooth the spot exchange rate, S. How such intervention may, in turn, influence the money supply (monetary base) of

---

*Notice that the forward discount on the dollar would instantaneously go to 6 percent to match the interest differential. Our assumption of perfect capital mobility eliminates the need to consider the forward market separately.

either country is important to spell out—as has been done by Lance Girton and Dale Henderson (1976), Robert Heller (1976), Swoboda (1978), and Richard Marston (1980). However, none of these authors has focused on my main theme: how currency substitution potentially destabilizes the world's money supply even when the world's aggregate demand for money is stable.

For simplicity, I ignore fractional reserve banking and the separate existence of commercial banks: at this level of abstraction no significant conclusions would change from building them into the model. Hence, the *rowa* component, M^*, of the world's money supply held by nonbanks is simply direct claims on ROW bank; and M is dollar claims of nonbanks on the Federal Reserve. The sum of these central bank liabilities is world money as defined by equation 1.

Reflecting the workings of the international dollar standard, 10 is a simple balance sheet equation showing both the domestic and foreign assets upon which ROW bank expands the *rowa* money supply:

$$M^* = A^* + M_r/S + B_r/S \tag{10}$$

where A^* is domestic (*rowa*) assets, M_r is dollar deposits with the Fed, and B_r is U.S. Treasury bonds.

Equation 11 is the balance sheet identity showing the assets and liabilities of the Federal Reserve system:

$$M + M_r = A \tag{11}$$

where A is domestic (dollar) assets.

From 10 and 11, the world's monetary base is simply the sum of domestic assets held by each central bank plus nonmonetary U.S. Treasury bonds held by ROW bank.

$$M + SM^* = M^w = A + SA^* + B_r \tag{12}$$

The important asymmetry in the world system hinges on how ROW bank (with the concurrence of the Fed) chooses to hold its dollar reserves. If as a result of foreign exchange intervention, ROW bank purchases U.S. Treasury bonds B_r in the open market, then the world money supply increases—according to equation 12—as long as the domestic asset positions of each central bank are fixed. This closely corresponds to actual practice as shown by foreign holdings of U.S. Treasury bonds in Table 15.3. However, if ROW bank chooses to build up and hold direct depository claims on the Fed, M_r, the world's money supply would remain unchanged because the reduction in dollar holdings by nonbanks (the dollar money supply) is offset by a rise in the *rowa* money supply. How ROW bank holds its dollar reserves is important, and the consequences of each alternative are explored below.

The Nonsterilization of Exchange Interventions

If a central bank purchases foreign exchange, the domestic monetary base initially expands and the foreign monetary base potentially contracts. Under the present system of managed floating, should governments remain free to influence their exchange rates directly without accepting their immediate monetary consequences? Central banks often take offsetting actions—through open-market operations, changed reserve requirements, or rediscounting—to sterilize the domestic monetary impact of these official interventions.

Within its own simple model of the world dollar standard, ROW bank would have to contract its domestic assets consciously in order to sterilize the influence of a buildup in its foreign assets. Clearly, sterilization would make it much more difficult for ROW bank to meet its exchange rate target. Moreover, Hans Genberg and Swoboda (1981) provide evidence that when sterilization occurs in Europe and elsewhere, it is only partial. Hence, let us assume for analytical purposes that ROW bank does not sterilize: A^* is constant as foreign exchange intervention takes place.

To impose a nonsterilization rule on the Federal Reserve system (in response to ROW bank's interventions) requires more than keeping domestic assets A constant—or on a predetermined Friedman growth path. Dollar claims accumulated by ROW bank should be allowed to contract the American money supply in the hands of the nonbank public. And having ROW bank build up dollar claims M_r—perhaps interest bearing—on the Federal Reserve system would be the simplest technique. Although in practice, the direct deposits of foreign central banks with the Fed are only transitory, let us provisionally assume that ROW bank holds all its exchange reserves in this form, that is, assume that $B_r = 0$ and $M_r < 0$.

What then are the monetary consequences of discretionary shifts in either central bank's domestic asset position (A or A^*) or in exogenous changes in the relative attractiveness of dollars versus *rowa* as denoted by the parameter s? From equation 12 and the assumption that $B_r = 0$, the relevant money multipliers are

$$dM^w/dA = dM^w/d(SA^*) = 1$$

$$(13)$$

$$dM^w/ds = 0$$

By varying its domestic assets by one dollar, each central bank has exactly the same impact on the world's money supply: one dollar. From our world money demand function, equation 3, each has an equal impact on the world rate of interest, i^w. In addition, the world's money supply is independent of s—any changes in the expected rate of dollar devaluation. The nonsterilization procedure prevents flights from one currency to another from upsetting the world's stock of money—while allowing the authorities to track automatically this changing demand for each national money. This last result can easily be seen by computing the multiplier effect of a change in s for each national currency:

$$dM/ds = (d\beta/ds)M^w = -\Delta M_r < 0 \qquad (14)$$

The stock of dollars changes according to our currency substitution parameter $d\beta/ds$ weighted by the world's money stock: a change which in turn is equal to the international flow of capital, ΔM_r. The American money stock changes dollar for dollar according to the reduced demand for it—neither more nor less. Similarly the stock of *rowa* increases symmetrically by as much as the stock of dollars decreases.

$$dM^*/ds = (d\beta/ds)M^w/S = \Delta M_r/S > 0 \qquad (15)$$

In response to open-market operations in domestic assets by either central bank, the individual money multipliers are:

$$dM/dA = dM/d(SA^*) = \beta(s) \qquad (16)$$

$$dM^*/d(A/S) = dM^*/dA^* = 1 - \beta(s) \qquad (17)$$

Domestic credit expansion by either central bank has exactly the same effect on national money supplies, as well as on the world money supply. However, when A increases, capital flows out of the United States by $(1 - \beta)\Delta A$ and when A^* increases, capital flows into the United States by βA^*. The M_r adjusts by the amount of each capital flow.

What room then does our stabilizing rule of no sterilization leave for discretionary monetary policy on the part of our two countries? Although each national money supply changes endogenously with official foreign exchange intervention, the monetary base for the world as a whole still depends on the domestic components of each country's monetary base, A and A^*. Without generating net international capital flows, secular rates of growth in A and SA^* could be designed roughly to equal the increase in demand for world money at a constant price level (see my 1974 article).

Whereas, random short-run shifts in demand between national monies by private speculators would be fully accommodated by official intervention in the foreign exchanges *without* losing control over the world's money supply.

Passive Sterilization and Increasing Currency Instability

Our short-run analysis simply assumed that ROW bank intervenes to maintain S, the spot exchange rate. I am not necessarily advocating such intervention, although a carefully delimited case can be made for it (see my 1981 article). More important is to ensure that intensive official intervention of the kind that occurred in the 1970s does not result in further inadvertent losses of international monetary control in the 1980s. Under the workings of the dollar standard, however, foreign official interventions have been conducted so as to leave the supply of dollars relatively unchanged while foreign money supplies—and the weighted world average money supply—have fluctuated erratically (see Table 15.1).

To demonstrate what happens when sterilization occurs, suppose foreign exchange interventions result in only transitory and negligible changes in M_r—deposits of ROW bank with the Federal Reserve—such that $M_r \cong 0$. Instead such deposits are used immediately to buy U.S. Treasury bonds, B_r. In practice, foreign central banks from industrial countries hold almost all their foreign exchange reserves in nonmonetary U.S. government bonds or bills as indicated in Table 15.3. These may be purchased directly with dollar demand deposits in U.S. commercial banks (which are not represented in the model) or the Federal Reserve itself simply acts as a broker by immediately buying U.S. Treasury bonds on account for ROW bank in response to incipient increases in M_r. Either method results in *sterilization* because the dollar money supply in the hands of the nonbank private sector is insulated from foreign official transactions.* It is *passive* because the Federal Reserve is not consciously sterilizing with offsetting changes its own domestic asset position. Rather, the U.S. money supply is insulated from changes in official reserves by the willingness of foreign central banks to hold nonmonetary U.S. government debt.

---

*Anatol Balbach (1978) describes comprehensively how official reserve transactions impinge—or fail to impinge—on the American monetary base.

In contrast, the supply of *rowa* outstanding responds fully to foreign exchange interventions by ROW bank. Our assumption of perfect capital mobility ensures that ROW bank cannot successfully manipulate A^* to offset these changes.

The equilibrium world money supply arising out of this asymmetrical sterilization procedure can then be calculated by substituting equations 9 and 10 into equation 12 to eliminate B_r in order to get

$$M^w = A/\beta(s) \tag{18}$$

The world money supply now is solely a function of the *domestic* asset position of the Federal Reserve Bank* and of the share of dollars in M^w; it does not depend at all on the domestic asset position of ROW bank.† (In contrast, A^* had an equivalent impact on M^w in the nonsterilization case.) Furthermore, the impact of A on world money increases according to the multiplier $1/\beta$. Suppose the U.S. share in world money β is decreasing perhaps because the other convertible currencies are becoming more important with fewer exchange controls. Then actions by the Federal Reserve to change A are increasingly magnified in their international impact.

This magnified Federal Reserve multiplier by itself need not lead to a loss of international monetary control. If, in the long run, the Federal Reserve calculates the growth in demand for dollars correctly, that is $\Delta M = \beta \Delta M_d^w$, and then increases A commensurately, the world's money growth remains determinate and potentially noninflationary. But the system is hardly "fail-safe" if the Federal Reserve makes even minor miscalculations regarding the growth in demand for dollars.

In the 1950s and early 1960s under the fixed exchange rates of Bretton Woods, a Federal Reserve policy of passive sterilization of foreign official interventions—coupled with monetary policy based purely domestic indicators—could justifiably be called "benign neglect" of the rest of the world (see my 1969 article). First β was probably close to unity because only a limited number of foreign currencies were convertible on capital account so that the dollar dominated the supply of "international money"; and secondly, exchange rates were—by and large—convincingly fixed so that expected fluctuations leading to international currency substitution were minimal.

---

*This result is similar to that of Swoboda (1978), who, however, did not make β an endogenous variable that might fluctuate with s.

†Increases in A^* will result in offsetting decreases in B_r so as to leave the *rowa* money supply unchanged. With A^* fixed, capital flows depend directly on A and β according to $dB_r/dA = (1 - \beta)/\beta$.

However, with managed floating, more volatile exchange rate expectations, and a secular decline of the share of dollars in world money in the 1970s and 1980s, the old strategy of benign neglect is more questionable. Indeed, differentiating equation 18 with respect to the expected exchange rate change, we have

$$dM^w/ds = (-A/\beta^2)(d\beta/ds) > 0 \qquad (19)$$

The supply of world money is now more sensitive to expected changes in exchange rates because β has declined, and because the degree of currency substitution $d\beta/ds$ has likely increased. An increase in expected dollar depreciation causes a multiple capital outflow from the United States, a multiple expansion in the *rowa* money supply—but no offsetting contraction in the supply of dollars because of passive sterilization. These are the simple analytics underlying the two explosions in the world money supply in 1971–72 and again in 1977–78 shown in Table 15.1.

POLICY IMPLICATIONS

Within the context of my simple two-country model of managed floating and perfect capital mobility, the solution to international currency instability is straightforward: the Federal Reserve system should discontinue its policy of passively sterilizing the domestic monetary impact of foreign official interventions. Instead, a symmetrical nonsterilization rule would ensure that each country's money supply mutually adjusts to international currency substitution in the short run, without having official exchange interventions destabilize the world's money supply. Then, long-run monetary control could be achieved by coordinated domestic asset expansion by each central bank: increases in A and A^* that match each country's share of world money, and which, together, just satisfy the demand for M^w at an approximately stable international price level.

However, we do not live in a simple two-country world. In reality, ROW is a hodge-podge of countries whose governments intervene continually and most hold at least some reserves in U.S. Treasury securities. Only a modest number of the 140 countries in the world have currencies that are convertible on current account, and even fewer extend convertibility to capital account transactions. At most, systematic monetary cooperation with the United States can only extend to a very small inner group: those countries which are sufficiently large and stable to offer monies that significantly compete with dollar cash balances internationally. Elsewhere I have suggested (1974; 1980) that Germany, Japan, and the

United States are capable of jointly bringing the world's supply of convertible money under control through a mutual nonsterilization pact *and* agreed-on rates of domestic credit expansion by each of the three central banks. In acting optimally under a continuing world dollar standard, this triumvirate would still follow a monetary policy of benign neglect (passive sterilization) with respect to dollar interventions by other countries.*

A critic might well argue that a more basic problem is "dirty" floating: the continued propensity of central banks to intervene directly despite the absence of official par value obligations. If the governments of industrial countries agreed not to intervene at all in the foreign exchanges, and if each followed fixed domestic monetary growth rules, control over the world's money supply would be secured automatically. Such a nonintervention agreement would seem easier to negotiate than a nonsterilization pact.

Unfortunately, the noninterventionalist solution implicitly presumes that the demand for each national money is stable. But governments in increasingly open economies are unable to risk prolonged upward or downward movements in their currencies (particularly against the dollar) because of (1) the possibility of cumulative currency substitution in favor of or against the national currency (Table 15.1); and (2) the unsettling direct effects that major exchange rate movements have on the domestic economy. For a fiat money without intrinsic value, the direct stabilization of its international purchasing power in the short run may be viewed (possibly correctly) as an important first line of defense in stabilizing its domestic purchasing power in the longer run.

Even in the United States itself, which is a huge, relatively closed economy, expected dollar depreciation and international currency substitution in 1971–72 and again in 1977–78 substantially reduced the demand for dollars. Measured growth in American M1 thus seriously understated the degree of inflationary pressure in the system—pressure that was more

---

*Consider one further caveat to even this partial solution for stabilizing the world's supply of money. Our two-country theoretical model assumed perfect capital mobility. Yet we know that both the German and Japanese authorities have imposed controls on capital movements from time to time. In the presence of current account surpluses or deficits (which was not present in the analytical model presented above), sterilization by the Bundesbank or Bank of Japan may be justified insofar as either is simply acting as an international financial intermediary because normal flows of private capital have been disrupted. Rescinding the assumption of "perfect" capital mobility, however, requires a more elaborate analytical model yet to be developed.

accurately reflected in the "world" money supply series appearing in Table 15.1. The doctrine of "domestic monetarism," where the Federal Reserve system keys on some purely American monetary aggregate such as M1 or M2 and ignores the foreign exchanges, is increasingly inefficient for preventing global inflation or deflation—and for stabilizing American income and prices.*

ADDENDUM: THE GREAT DEFLATION OF 1981–82

Over 1980–81, money growth (M1) slowed down more drastically in Germany, Japan, and Switzerland—countries providing substitute international reserve currencies to the dollar—than did growth in American M1B. True to its doctrine of domestic monetarism, the Federal Reserve system chose to ignore this monetary contraction occurring abroad.

What forced the Swiss, German, and Japanese central banks to let their monetary growth rates fall so sharply? World monetary demand shifted sharply away from their monies (and that of several other smaller countries) toward dollars. On the positive side, it became likely in 1980 that a new "free market" government would be elected in the United States which would have much lower inflation targets. And there was political turmoil in Europe: the threat in Poland of a Russian invasion and the election in France of a socialist government predisposed to expropriate private wealth. The dollar—previously battered in 1977–78—surged upward on the world's foreign exchange markets in 1980–81 and on into 1982. After watching their currencies depreciate quite sharply, these three central banks entered to prevent further price-level disalignment by selling dollars and repurchasing their own currencies, thus contracting that part of world money (M1) denominated in Swiss francs, marks, and yen. There was no automatic offsetting expansion in the American monetary base to accommodate the increased demand for dollars, because of the passive sterilization associated with the normal operations of the world dollar standard.

---

*The doctrine of "domestic Keynesianism," where the government keys on some domestic nominal rate of interest (possibly insulated from the international economy by exchange controls), is likely to be even more inadequate (see my 1979 book and my 1980 article). However, a full treatment of the Keynesian approach requires an analysis of open-economy fiscal policy under the world dollar standard. That is a story for another time.

Thus has speculation in favor of the dollar in 1980–81 imposed unduly sharp deflation on the world economy, just as speculation against the dollar in 1971–72 and again in 1977–78 fueled the two great inflations of the 1970s.

REFERENCES

Balbach, Anatol. "The Mechanics of Intervention in Exchange Markets," *Federal Reserve Bank of St. Louis Review*, February 1978, 60, 2–7.

Bernholz, Peter. "Flexible Exchange Rates and Exchange Rate Theory in Historical Perspective," unpublished, March 1981.

Brillembourg, Arturo T., and Schadler, Susan. "A Model of Currency Substitution in Exchange-Rate Determination, 1973–78," *IMF Staff Papers* 26 (September 1979): 513–42.

Brittain, Bruce. "International Currency Substitution and the Apparent Instability of Velocity in Some Western European Economies and in the United States," *Journal of Money Credit, and Banking*, 13 (May 1981): 135–55.

Friedman, Milton. "The Case for Flexible Exchange Rates," in *Essays in Positive Economics* (Chicago: University of Chicago Press, 1953), pp. 157–203.

Genberg, Hans, and Swoboda, Alexander K. "Gold and the Dollar: Asymmetries in World Money Stock Determination, 1959–1971," unpublished, April 1981.

Girton, Lance, and Henderson, Dale W. "Financial Capital Movements, and Central Bank Behavior in a Two-Country, Short-Run Portfolio Balance Model," *Journal of Monetary Economics* 2 (January 1976): 33–62.

Heller, Robert. "International Reserves and World-Wide Inflation," *IMF Staff Papers* 23 (March 1976): 23, 61–87.

International Monetary Fund. *International Financial Statistics*, Washington, D.C., various years.

Johnson, Harry. "The Case for Flexible Exchange Rates," in *Further Essays in Monetary Economics* (London: Allen and Unwin, 1972), pp. 198–222.

McKinnon, Ronald. "Private and Official International Money: The Case for the Dollar," *Princeton Essays in International Finance*, no. 74, Princeton University, 1969.

———. "A New Tripartite Monetary Agreement or a Limping Dollar Standard?," *Princeton Essays in International Finance*, no. 106, Princeton University, 1974.

———, *Money in International Exchange: The Convertible Currency System* (New York: Oxford University Press, 1979).

———, "Dollar Stabilization and American Monetary Policy," *American Economic Review Proceedings* 70 (May 1980): 382–87.

———, "The Exchange Rate and Macroeconomic Policy: Changing Postwar Perceptions," *Journal of Economic Literature* 19 (June 1981): 531–57.

Marston, Richard. "Cross Country Effects of Sterilization, Reserve Currencies, and Foreign Exchange Intervention," *Journal of International Economics* 10 (February 1980): 63–78.

Mayer, Helmut W. "Credit and Liquidity Creation in the International Banking Sector," *Economic Papers no. 1*, Bank for International Settlements, November 1979.

Meade, James E. "The Case for Variable Exchange Rates," *Three Banks Review* 27 (September 1955): 3–27.

Miles, Marc. "Currency Substitution, Flexible Exchange Rates, and Monetary Independence," *American Economic Review* 68 (June 1978): 428–36.

Swoboda, Alexander. "Gold, Dollars, Euro-Dollars, and the World Money Stock under Fixed Exchange Rates," *American Economic Review* 68 (September 1978): 625–42.

Van Cleveland, Harold, and Brittain, Bruce. *The Great Inflation: A Monetarist View* (Washington, D.C.: National Planning Association, 1976).

16

Exchange Rates
with Substitutable Currencies

D. Sykes Wilford

INTRODUCTION

Economists, analysts, and forecasters have used many different models to explain the movements of the Canadian dollar, as well as predict its future course. The many different approaches, including current account, monetary, interest-rate-differential, and momentum models have been tried, but none has yet proven totally satisfactory. The approach in this chapter will not fill this void, but it is designed to add to the literature and to attempt to move in a new direction. The following analysis is derived from the currency substitution literature first discussed by Boyer.[1] From this literature one knows that for particular countries, especially Canada, demand-side substitution is important in the determination of capital flows and exchange rate movements. New understanding of how a monetary authority should implement policy to meet stated goals is also implied in the work.

To understand why an exchange rate has moved, much less to forecast it, one must understand the behavior of the market forces driving it. The next section describes three such possible models, all within the context of

The author wishes to thank Terry Wiginton for research assistance. Discussions with Bluford H. Putnam and Francisco Comprido were helpful. A version of this paper was presented at the North American Economic and Finance Association meetings in Atlanta, November 1982.

a general monetary model, which could be used to describe the Canadian dollar market. The third section presents estimates of two of the models' reduced forms. Finally, conclusions are drawn in the last section.

GENERAL MONETARY MODELS

The basic monetary model, commonly called the monetary approach to exchange rate analysis, is a subset of the broader set of monetary models of exchange rate determination.[2] We begin with the basic model. Following Humphrey and Lawler, this model assumes that all excess monetary pressures lead to adjustments both in domestic price inflation and in the foreign exchange markets, by a depreciation or appreciation of currency.[3] The model implicitly assumes that currencies are not substitutable in the portfolios of domestic residents or in the portfolios of third parties.[4]

The basic model is outlined in seven equations

$$MC^d = MC^s \tag{1}$$

$$MUS^d = MUS^s \tag{2}$$

$$M^d = yPe^{-i} \tag{3}$$

$$M^s = m \tag{4}$$

where C = Canada; M^d = money demand; M^s = money supply; m = the stock of money created by the monetary authorities; i = short-term interest rate; y = real income; P = price level; and NA = North America, which is the combination of a Canadian parameter, such as money supply, and the same U.S. parameter. Combining 1 through 4, rearranging, and taking the first difference of the log values yields

$$\dot{P} = \dot{M} - \dot{Y} + di \tag{5}$$

where $\dot{X}$ = for all variables means percentage change of X, and
$\quad$ d = differential of X

Or,

$$\dot{P}C = \dot{M}C - \dot{Y}C + diC \tag{5a}$$

$$\dot{P}US = \dot{M}US - \dot{Y}US + diUS \tag{5b}$$

Then, assuming purchasing-power parity, this yields

$$\dot{E} = \dot{P}C - \dot{P}US \tag{6}$$

where E = the exchange rate in Canadian (C) dollar/U.S. dollar

Finally, combining terms *à la* Humphrey and Lawler yields

$$\dot{E} = -(\dot{Y}C - \dot{Y}US) + (\dot{M}C - \dot{M}US) + d(iC - iUS) \tag{7}$$

Alternatively, one may assume that there exists perfect currency substitution.[5] In this case, whether induced from the demand side or the supply side, there would be no change in the rate of exchange between the two currencies.

Following equation 6 then,

$$\dot{E} = 0 \tag{8}$$

and, since 6 holds in the long run,

$$\dot{P}C = \dot{P}US \tag{9}$$

Moreover, under perfect currency substitution on the demand side, a price determination model—where the appropriate money supply is the total money supply in North America—can be derived:

$$\dot{P}US = \dot{M}SNA - (\dot{Y}C + \dot{Y}US) + d(iUS) \tag{10}$$

where d(iUS) = d(iC), and
    MSNA = MUS + MC

There would be no need for currency realignment. Capital would flow into people's portfolios as needed, and quantity adjustments would be sufficient to offset the need for price (exchange rate) adjustments.

Inflation in Canada would in the long run be equal to that in the United States. Since real output would be different, either the rate of increase in domestic money or the velocity of circulation would be different. Or, in a world of perfect demand-side substitutability, the relevant money for price determination should be only North American money. Money would be some linear combination of the supply of money in both the United States and Canada. Thus, the relevant rate of growth in money would be the rate of growth in both U.S. and Canadian money; and the amount of growth which could be supported in each country would depend upon the movement of velocity.

One interesting point in this example—similar to the relationship of Texas to New York—is that the amount of money from the larger North American pool needed to support real activity in one part of the continent would be supplied as needed. In this example, Canada is one part of a larger capital market from which it draws the set of funds needed to support a prescribed level of economic activity. If Canadian activity is substantially higher than that in the United States, funds will flow into Canada from the United States. Thus, the rate of growth of C dollars in the system is of no importance to the rate of economic expansion (or contraction) of Canada or the rate of inflation. From a measurement perspective, it should be noted that if the Canadian economy was clearly growing at a longer-term rate higher than that of the United States, then this would merely mean that the velocity of North American money in Canada would, ex post, grow faster than that in the United States.

The fact remains, however, that the two currencies are not perfectly substitutable; they do move against each other. But the literature does tell us that a model which takes currency substitution into consideration is useful in understanding the monetary relationships in Canada and between Canada and the United States.[6] The third model is of this type. It is first presented in structural form, and eventually a reduced form which can be estimated is derived.*

Following equation 10 and assuming nonperfect currency substitution,

$$\dot{P}C = \dot{P}US + \dot{E} + \dot{\phi} \tag{11}$$

where ϕ represents the scope for currency substitution. Depending on whether ϕ moves toward greater substitutability or lesser substitutability, the currency portfolio effect will tend to cause the C dollar to vary more or less than would be suggested by a model with no currency substitution.

The parameter ϕ can be defined as:

$$\phi = \frac{MC}{MSNA}[A - (MC^e - MUS^e)] \tag{12}$$

where X^e = the expected X, and A is a constant

---

*The general approach that follows is outlined in the sources listed in reference note 6, but differs in that it simplifies the methodology by not utilizing the PPP equation as a more transformation equation to obtain the underlying monetary variables.

The scope for currency substitution will change if expected monetary policy in Canada changes. The scale variable (MC/MSNA) is a measure of the relative size of the Canadian money stock to total North American money.

It should be noted that $(MC^e - MUS^e)$ is likely to be zero most of the time. Only when political events or natural circumstances change the long-run expected monetary policy will $(MC^e - MUS^e)$ not be zero. Still, rewriting 12

$$\dot{\phi} = \dot{MC} - \dot{MSNA} - (\frac{G}{A - G})\dot{G} \qquad (12a)$$

where $G = (MC^e - MUS^e)$

Rearranging 11 and combining 12a yields

$$\dot{E} = \dot{PC} - \dot{PUS} - \dot{MC} + \dot{MSNA} + (\frac{G}{A - G})\dot{G} \qquad (13)$$

The key to this model is the price-determination equation 11 and the exchange rate determination equation 13. These differ from the standard model in several ways. In the long run, prices are expected to move in roughly the same pattern, compensated for by the scope of currency substitution and the movement in the exchange rate. And, in general, the exchange rate is not expected to move enough to realign portfolios unless there is a major shift in policy. The ex post short-run price and exchange rate movements, however, may vary from this long-run trend. Furthermore, the money supplies of both Canada and the United States remain in the equation even if, ex post, G does not change. This results from the fact that the existence of the two currencies in residents' portfolios is a sufficient condition to make the two currencies important determinants of the exchange rate (note, however, that they can be offsetting).

In a simplistic fashion the model may be thought of as an embellished purchasing-power parity (PPP) model of exchange rate determination. But then, this is what most monetary models of exchange rate determination actually are.[7] In this model the embellishments are derived from a view of the world that allows for currency substitution. In the standard monetary model, the embellishment is the use of PPP to make the transformation from price determination to exchange rate determination. In both cases PPP is the bridge between a long-run logical implication of price arbitrage to a more fundamental model of the process that allows prices to differ if the exogenous variables are monetary.

In an effort to highlight the notion that all money in North America is substitutable, we have not considered the fact that both the C dollar and the U.S. dollar are held by third parties as well. These third parties also hold several currencies—the majority of which will not be either U.S. or Canadian dollars—just as Americans and Canadians may hold currencies other than dollars. The model above does not totally take this into account. In an attempt to consider this fact, we can refer to equation 12 and open North America to yield

$$\phi = \frac{MC}{MSNA}[A - G][X] \tag{14}$$

where X = an exchange rate measure

Individuals may hold DMs, C dollars, and U.S. dollars. Suppose an exogenous shock affects the DM/U.S. dollar rate. There would be an incipient buying (selling) of U.S. dollars by the third parties. If there is no change in MC^c, MUS^c or G, there could still be an effect on the C dollar/U.S. dollar rate, unless there existed either symmetrical selling of C dollars and U.S. dollars or perfectly matched symmetrical distribution of buying and selling. That is, suppose only U.S. dollars were sold (bought) by the holders of DM; then there would exist an excess supply (demand) of U.S. dollars vis-à-vis C dollars. If C dollar-holders did not hold this extra supply, the C dollar would change in value. Depending upon the sign of ϕ in relation to E, a third-party selling of U.S. dollars could make the C dollars appreciate or depreciate. Though traditional closed-economy models would argue that a decline in the DM/U.S. dollar rate will lead to a decline in the C dollar/U.S. dollar rate as more U.S. dollars are supplied, this may not be the case. These portfolio-holders, seeing that the two currencies are substitutable, may dump equal amounts of C dollars and U.S. dollars, thereby creating an excess supply of C dollars relative to U.S. dollars. The exchange rate could then move simply as a result of the relative size of the two stocks of money. If portfolio holders consider the two substitutable in their own portfolios, this is the likely result.

$$\dot{E} = \dot{P}C - \dot{P}US - \dot{M}C + M\dot{S}NA + (\frac{G}{A - G})\dot{G} - \dot{X} \tag{15}$$

In either case it appears likely that as the DM/U.S. dollar exchange rate becomes more uncertain, the C dollar would weaken. That is, on net, if third-party activities heightened instability in the C dollar/U.S. dollar rate, uncertainty over the C dollar/U.S. dollar rate would tend to reduce foreign holdings of C dollars relative to U.S. dollars simply because of portfolio consideration of relative size. Thus, the relevant variable is the variability of the rates, not the rate changes themselves.

EMPIRICAL RESULTS

From equation 7 the reduced-form equation for the standard monetary model is

$$\dot{E} = B_0 + B_1(\dot{Y}C - \dot{Y}US) + B_2(\dot{M}C - \dot{M}US)$$
$$+ B_3 d(iC - iUS) + u \tag{16}$$

where u = a stochastic disturbance term,
B_2, $B_3 < 0$, and
$B_1 > 0$

From equation 14 the reduced-form equation is

$$\dot{E} = B_0 + B_1(\dot{P}C - \dot{P}US) + B_2\dot{M}C + B_3 M\dot{S}NA$$

$$+ B_4 \frac{G}{A - G} G + v \tag{17}$$

where v = a stochastic disturbance term,
B_1, B_3, $B_4 > 0$, and
$B_2 < 0$

From equation 15 the reduced-form equation is

$$\dot{E} = B_0 + B_1(\dot{P}C - \dot{P}US) + B_2\dot{M}C + B_3 M\dot{S}NA$$

$$+ B_4 \frac{G}{A - G}\dot{G} + B_5 \dot{X} + w \tag{18}$$

where w = a stochastic disturbance term
B_1, B_3, B_4, $B_5 > 0$, and
$B_2 < 0$

The results of the three sets of regressions are consistent with a model of North American exchange rate determination that is based upon the general guidelines of a monetary model, but which depends upon the consideration of currency substitution. The model that assumes no currency substitution performs poorly by the overall standards of the more general model that considers currency substitution. The F-values, size of the coefficients, and the t-statistics suggest that the proper monetary model of exchange rate determination should be built around the concept of portfolios in North America containing both U.S. dollars and C dollars.

Specifically, regressions for four time periods are reported. Regressions for the total data period, 1971 first quarter (Q1) to 1981 Q4, are reported for the standard monetary model (Table 16.1) and for the currency substitution model that does not consider foreign holders of U.S. dollars and C dollars (Table 16.2). Because of data considerations, regressions that consider third parties (Table 16.3) begin in 1973. The fourth quarter of 1979 is considered a breaking point—owing to the significant change in the direction of U.S. monetary policy—even though the short-time period following 1979 Q4 leaves few degrees of freedom.

The variable G is proxied by a dummy variable that considers political influences on the expectation of the future direction of Canadian versus U.S. monetary policy. Specifically, the Quebec election and the National Energy Plan periods are considered. The variable X is proxied by the mean-adjusted variance of the DM/U.S. dollar exchange rate. The term VARDM is calculated from daily observations on a quarterly basis. All data are quarterly. Regressions are OLS.

In general, the standard model results are not heartening. The coefficients are typically not significantly different from zero and do not appear very stable over the sample period. Moreover, the signs are wrong on the monetary variables. Of particular interest, however, is the coefficient on the interest-rate term. During 1973 to 1979 it was unimportant in explaining exchange rate movements. This was, in general, a period of interest rate targeting by the authorities, which usually found the central banks following market movements along a general trend toward higher rates in both countries. During the period since 1979, however, it became the most significant variable. During this period interest rates moved around substantially and conveyed a great deal of information about expected inflation *and* expected policy.

The results for the model with currency substitution are much better. The corrected R^2s are high, the F-values are high, and the coefficients, for the most part, are well behaved. They tend to be significant and have the correct signs. The key variable is the overall stock of money in North America, resulting from the scale term in the scope for the currency-

TABLE 16.1

PCTEY	Constant	$(\dot{Y}C - \dot{Y}US)$	$(\dot{M}C - \dot{M}US)$	$d(iC - iUS)$	DW	R^2	SER
73IIIP	2.38	-0.24	-0.14	0.62	1.15	.712	2.225
	(1.29)	(-.89)	(-1.21)	(1.95)	Rho=.785		
73III-81IV	4.58	-.60	-0.18	0.71	1.23	.724	2.148
	(2.37)	(-1.89)	(-1.46)	(2.12)	Rho=.762		
73III-79II	6.90	-0.54	-0.38	-0.02	1.31	.759	2.286
	(2.80)	(-1.33)	(-1.81)	(-.03)	Rho=.715		
79III-81IV	0.96	-0.27	0.03	1.06	1.56	.609	1.157
	(.64)	(-.56)	(.26)	(4.05)	Rho=.630		

Note: The terms used in Tables 16.1, 16.2, and 16.3 are as follows:

PCTEY = Annual percentage change in the spot exchange rate (Canadian dollar per U.S. dollar). Source: *International Financial Statistics.*

$\dot{Y}C$ = Annual percentage change in Canadian gross national product at 1975 prices II (quarterly data). Source: *International Finance Statistics.*

$\dot{Y}US$ = Annual percentage change in U.S. gross national product at 1975 prices (quarterly data). Source: *International Financial Statistics.*

$\dot{M}C$ = Annual percentage change in Canadian M3 quarterly data. Source: *Bank of Canada Review.*

$\dot{M}US$ = Annual percentage change in U.S. M3 quarterly data. Source: *International Financial Statistics.*

iC = Canadian long-term Treasury bill rate quarterly data. Source: *International Financial Statistics.*

$\dot{P}C$ = Annual percentage change in Canadian consumer price index (base = 1975). Source: *International Financial Statistics.*

$\dot{P}US$ = Annual percentage change in U.S. consumer price index (base = 1975). Source: *International Financial Statistics.*

$\dot{M}SNA$ = Annual percentage change in combined Canadian and U.S. money supplies quarterly data. Source: *International Financial Statistics.*

$\dot{G}$ = Dummy variable.

VARDM = Quarterly variance of the DM/U.S. dollar spot bid rate divided by the quarterly mean of the DM/U.S. dollar spot bid rate.

TABLE 16.2

PCTEY	Constant	(ṖC - ṖUS)	ṀC	ṀSNA	Ġ	DW	R²	SER
711- 81IV	-4.07 (-3.13)	0.28 (.88)	-0.17 (-2.53)	0.85 (15.15)	1.74 (2.34)	2.01 Rho=.311	.924	1.399
73III 81IV	-2.63 (-1.175)	.15 (.45)	-0.23 (-3.21)	0.82 (12.16)	1.75 (2.24)	2.15 Rho=.394	.925	1.116
73III 79II	-3.84 (-2.10)	0.36 (.87)	-0.16 (-1.84)	0.86 (12.96)	0.58 (.55)	1.96 Rho=.455	.965	.875
79III- 81IV	-2.93 (-1.65)	0.24 (.56)	-0.23 (-3.27)	0.74 (3.66)	3.68 (6.01)	3.19 Rho=.906	.805	.818

TABLE 16.3

PCTEY	Constant	(ṖC - ṖUS)	ṀC	ṀSNA	Ġ	VARDM	DW	R²	SER
73III- 81IV	-4.91 (-3.3)	0.75 (2.28)	-0.17 (-2.66)	0.86 (16.55)	1.45 (2.35)	87.84 (1.94)	1.74	.926	1.11
73III- 79II	-5.28 (-2.79)	0.70 (1.68)	-0.12 (-1.45)	0.89 (15.67)	0.28 (0.31)	52.65 (1.08)	1.48	.959	0.94
79III- 81IV	-5.75 (-1.53)	0.07 (0.11)	-0.22 (-1.85)	0.78 (2.45)	3.06 (2.38)	207.45 (1.46)	2.86	.557	1.23

substitution variable. This is expected under a model of nonperfect currency substitution. Consideration of the third parties holding dollars, by the inclusion of the X variable, improves the regressions. In this more fully specified version of the model the coefficients are close to their anticipated values, the DWs remain well behaved, the t-statistics are strong, and the theory is supported.

CONCLUSIONS

The conclusions from this modeling exercise are straightforward. First, the standard monetary model of exchange rate determination, which assumes zero currency substitution between U.S. and Canadian dollars, appears incorrect. Second, a model of perfect currency substitution is not appropriate for guiding market participants' behavior, but may be considered by the monetary authorities if the alternative is simply to assume that there is no currency substitution. And third, a simple model which begins with the notion that currency substitution is neither perfect nor zero yields a satisfactory explanation of exchange rate determination in North America.

One other point is worth noting. The models do not depend upon difficult or complicated rationalizations of more basic models, nor do they attempt to embellish the existing monetary literature. Rather, they are designed to demonstrate that a very simple model of exchange rates in North America may be used if it is based upon the correct theory of price and exchange rate determination.

NOTES

1. R. Boyer, "Currency Mobility and Balance of Payments Adjustment," in *The Monetary Approach to International Adjustment*, eds., B. H. Putnam and D. Sykes Wilford (New York: Praeger, 1978), pp. 184–98. Other articles on currency substitution are: Lance Girton and Don Roper, "Theory and Implications of Currency Substitution," *Journal of Money, Credit, and Banking* 12 (February 1981): 33–62; D. Sykes Wilford and W. Dayle Nattress, "Economic Integration of North America: Monetary and Financial Integration in North America," *Law and Contemporary Problems* 44 (Summer 1981): 55–79; Marc A. Miles, "Currency Substitution: Perspective, Implications, and Empirical Evidence," in *The Monetary Approach to International Adjustment*, eds., B. H. Putnam and D. S. Wilford (New York: Praeger, 1978), pp. 170–83; Marc A. Miles, "Currency Substitution, Flexible Exchange Rates, and Monetary Independence," *American Economic Review* 68 (June 1978): 428–36, and David T. King, B. H. Putnam, and D. S. Wilford, "A Currency Portfolio Approach to Exchange Rate Determination: Exchange Rate Stability and Monetary Independence," in

The Monetary Approach to International Adjustment, eds., B. H. Putnam and D. S. Wilford (New York: Praeger, 1978), pp. 199–215.

2. For a general discussion of the monetary approach, see Bluford H. Putnam and D. Sykes Wilford, eds. *The Monetary Approach to International Adjustment* (New York: Praeger, 1978).

3. Thomas Humphrey and Thomas A. Lawler, "Factors Determining Exchange Rates: A Simple Model and Empirical Tests," Federal Reserve Bank of Richmond *Economic Review* (May-June 1977): 11–15. Reprinted in *The Monetary Approach to International Adjustment*, eds., B. H. Putnam and D. S. Wilford (New York: Praeger, 1978), pp. 134–46.

4. See Michael Connolly, "The Monetary Approach to an Open Economy: The Fundamental Theory," in *The Monetary Approach to International Adjustment*, eds., B. H. Putnam and D. S. Wilford (New York: Praeger, 1978), pp. 6–18. Also a useful reference on variations in the general model is Michael Connolly and Dean Taylor, "Crawling Pegs and Exchange Rate Crisis," *University of South Carolina Working Paper* (November 1982).

5. For the perfect substitution case, see Wilford and Nattress, "Economic Integration of North America." Miles, in "Currency Substitution: Perspective, Implications and Empirical Evidence," uses Canadian data in a production function framework.

6. See King, Putnam, and Bluford, "A Currency Portfolio Approach to Exchange Rate Determination," and Wilrod and Nattress, "Economic Integration of North America". The proper use of PPP in exchange rate forecasting models is discussed in Wilford, D. Sykes, and Ronald A. Krieger, "Predicting Exchange Rates: A Return to PPP," *International Finance* 14 (July 1979): 7–8. For a further elaboration, see Donald M. McCloskey and J. Richard Zecher, "The Success of Purchasing Power Parity: Historical Evidence and Its Implications for Macroeconomics," in *A Retrospective on the Classical Gold Standard, 1821–1931*, eds., Michael Bordo and Anna Schwartz (Chicago: University of Chicago Press, 1984), pp. 121–170.

7. For a new framework for PPP, see Dayle Nattress and J. Richard Zecher, "The Theory of the Arbitrageur and Purchasing Power Parity." Mimeograph (July 1983).

Part 4

THE POLICY DEBATE

17

The Policy Consequences
of Interdependence

Bluford H. Putnam
D. Sykes Wilford

Economic policy-making is in the midst of a revolution. This revolution is not the product of new philosophies of government or a changed political environment. Rather, the policy-making revolution is the inevitable response to the increasingly interdependent world in which all individuals and countries coexist. To understand the revolution in policy and to interpret the likely direction of future economic policies, a keen understanding of how economies are linked is essential.

The intellectual framework underpinning the monetary approach to international adjustment provides a set of valuable insights into both the capabilities and the limits of macroeconomic policy in an interdependent world. This approach is also the product of a revolution in academic thinking, because it redresses two flaws in more traditional macroeconomic thinking. First, international economics in the 1950s and 1960s focused heavily on trade flows as the primary linkage among nations. Capital flows were often omitted from the analysis or assumed to be a passive function of trade. In the monetary approach, capital flows take their proper place alongside trade flows as key economic links among countries. Second, traditional domestic economic approaches, both monetarist and Keynesian, consistently ignored or greatly underestimated the importance of international linkages. Closed-economy models were often used to support policy decisions which were applied in a distinctly open-economy world with extremely different results than predicted. Again, because the monetary approach to international adjustment takes well-integrated world goods markets and capital markets as basic assumptions, the policy implications are much more robust in today's interdependent world.

In this chapter, three policy issues will be highlighted for the purposes of understanding the capabilities and limits of economic policy in an interdependent world. The policy issues discussed are: (1) the appropriate goals of monetary policy, (2) the importance of long-run policy credibility, and (3) the appropriate world monetary system, that is, the fixed versus floating exchange rate debate.

MONETARY POLICY
IN AN INTERDEPENDENT WORLD

The primary policy lesson from the monetary approach to international adjustment is that there is no such thing as purely domestic monetary policy. Whether monetary policy is implemented by a central bank buying or selling securities in the domestic market or by buying or selling currencies in the foreign exchange markets, the net result is a monetary policy that simultaneously affects domestic and international markets. This point is made explicitly in the monetary approach by its focus on the asset side of a central bank's balance sheet, rather than the liability side.

Most domestic, closed-economy models consider the supply of money as a function of the monetary base and some multiplier representing the leverage in the banking system. This is essentially a liability-side approach since the monetary base is defined as currency and deposits held by banks with the central bank (that is, central bank liabilities). The monetary approach accepts this view, but carries the analysis much further. Assets equal liabilities; any change on the liability side of a central bank's balance sheet must have been accomplished by changes in central bank assets. By dividing the assets into two broad categories—international reserves and domestic assets—and explicitly considering the mechanism by which liabilities are changed, the monetary approach can address a number of issues not covered by traditional approaches.

Foreign Exchange Intervention

For example, can foreign exchange intervention by central banks affect the course of exchange rates? This is a classic issue where closed-economy models either cannot answer the question or answer it incorrectly.

Foreign exchange intervention involves the purchase or sale by a central bank of its own currency for a foreign currency. In the typical case, a country with a depreciating currency will intervene as a buyer of its own currency and a seller of foreign currency. The initial effect on the central bank's balance sheet is a reduction in international reserves (asset side) and a reduction in the monetary base (liability side). If the intervention story ended here there would be an effect on several variables. The decrease in the monetary base could be characterized as a tightening of monetary policy, resulting in a stronger currency.

Usually the story continues, however, with the central bank entering the domestic market to offset the reduction in the monetary base. That is, the central bank sterilizes the foreign exchange intervention's effects on the monetary base by buying domestic assets. Now, the liability side of the balance sheet, on net, is unchanged. On the asset side, the central bank holds fewer international reserves and more domestic assets and the same quantity of total assets. The monetary approach concludes that with total assets and total liabilities unchanged, monetary policy must be unchanged, with no effect on exchange rates.

Had the central bank not sterilized the foreign exchange intervention, then both the exchange rate and domestic monetary policy would have been different. Here, the monetary approach is explicit. Foreign exchange intervention is a tool of domestic monetary policy because it affects the monetary base—unless it is sterilized. The causality runs from the monetary base simultaneously to domestic credit markets *and* the exchange rate. Anything that changes the monetary base will affect both domestic credit markets and the exchange rate. Sterilized intervention, because it involves no change in the monetary base, does not change prices in either domestic credit markets or foreign exchange markets.

Interest Rate Targeting

Another way of illustrating the inextricable link between monetary policy and exchange rate policy is through the effects of a typical open market operation; in this example the monetary base is contracted through central bank sales of domestic assets. This usually is viewed purely as a domestic policy initiative. There are effects, however, simultaneously in the foreign exchange markets. A smaller monetary base implies less inflation in the future and a stronger (or less weak) exchange rate immediately (other factors held constant).

Now, suppose a central bank chooses to target interest rates rather than the monetary base. Events in other countries, then, can have a powerful impact on the exchange rate. If one central bank were to induce a rise in interest rates by a large amount, then other central banks would be forced to make a choice. They must either watch their currencies depreciate (constant interest rates) or tighten their monetary policies to stabilize the exchange rate. For the most part, when the U.S. Federal

Reserve tightened on several occasions during 1980–82, the rest of the world revealed a preference for a relatively easier monetary policy and accepted the potential consequences of a depreciating exchange rate. More important, central banks around the world could not insulate themselves from the U.S. policy shift. Either their economies felt the U.S. policy through the exchange rate or the domestic interest or some combination of the two, but economies around the world had to deal with the U.S. policy shift.

The United States is just as subject to changes in policies in the rest of the world. In the 1976–79 period, the inflation path of the U.S. economy was exacerbated by foreign policy moves geared toward lower inflation. The exchange rate dramatically reflected the policy differences and significantly reinforced the inflationary pattern in the United States. Most traditional, closed-economy models of the United States failed miserably to forecast the high inflation of the weak dollar period, then failed again by overestimating inflation during the strong dollar period of 1980–84.

The monetary approach to international adjustment does not treat an economy differently because of its size or relative percentage of imports to gross national product. As long as world markets are competitive, the United States cannot be treated as a closed-economy island. This realization is the essence of the revolution that is occurring in economic policy-making in the United States. Yes, Virginia, there is a foreign sector and understanding it is absolutely critical to (domestic) policy-making.

POLICY CREDIBILITY AND CURRENCY SUBSTITUTION

The importance of the long-run credibility of economic policy does not surface in most traditional economic models. With the burgeoning literature on rational expectations, however, more attention has been focused on separating permanent policy shifts, which can have profound effects, from temporary ones, which have a muted effect. Still the issue in exchange rate analysis was not accentuated until the basic monetary approach was extended by addressing the issue raised by the substitutability of world monies—currency substitution. This is a portfolio approach to exchange rates and introduces concepts of risk and risk-related behavior into exchange rate determination. The importance of this issue in an interdependent world cannot be emphasized enough.

To understand currency substitution one must think like an international portfolio manager or like a child playing marbles. For example, in your pocket are red and blue marbles and each work equally well for playing various games because the rules do not distinguish between the two colors. You are indifferent to the mix of red versus blue marbles in your pocket, because nothing is at stake in the choice. This represents the fixed exchange world of the 1950s and 1960s. The U.S. dollar was the standard, and an accumulation of dollars (red marbles) was not looked upon as affecting one's wealth position. But in the 1970s the rules changed. Exchange rates were no longer fixed. Red marbles and blue marbles were no longer equals; some games require one color, others the other. In short, the ability to compete now depended upon the mix of marbles or currencies that you were holding. There were real risks and real wealth effects emanating from one's choice of currencies (or marbles). The assessment of these risks could affect one's currency choice and, as a result, affected the exchange rate between two currencies.

In the United States, each Federal Reserve branch bank can issue currency with its own seal. As long as these currencies trade one for one, U.S. citizens are indifferent (if not ignorant) of the mix between St. Louis Federal Reserve dollars and New York Federal Reserve dollars. If ever the possibility of the exchange rate changing occurred, however, indifference (and ignorance) about currency mix would disappear quickly. In this first case, knowledge of exchange rates yields no return—or ignorance has no cost. In the second case, the cost of ignorance and the return to knowledge is very high.

Currency substitution introduces the concept of portfolio risk into exchange rate determination. The ultimate risk involved is the future purchasing power of each currency. As a result, the risk assessment focuses on the long-run commitment each country has to stable prices. Changes in this commitment to stable prices can result in large and swift reallocations of assets within portfolios or in large and swift changes in interest rates and exchange rates.

The transitions of the United States from world economic leader (1950s and 1960s), to a fallen star (1970s), and back to world economic leader status (1980s) illustrates the importance of the currency substitution concept in understanding the role of policy credibility in exchange rate determination. As the commitment of U.S. policy toward price stability eroded in the late 1960s, the first effect was the breakdown of the fixed exchange rate system. Fixed exchange rate systems enforce currency substitutability from the supply side, by central banks' commitment to buy (destroy) and sell (create) their own currency in accordance with a given exchange rate. With the guarantee of supply-side substitutability removed, portfolios had to be readjusted to compensate for the new risks of the floating rate regime. Demand-side substitutability became a critical ingredient of exchange rate determination; risk now mattered.

Demand-side substitutability represents the willingness of those holding (or potentially holding) multicurrency portfolios to adopt a stable mix of currencies. This is where policy credibility plays the key role. One cannot profitably (given the risks) adopt a stable currency mix if policies around the world shift in unpredictable ways. As a country's policies, particularly toward inflation, become less predictable, there is an increased risk that the expected inflation path will not be achieved. Risk and return go hand in hand, and as a result, the markets extract a premium for bearing the increased risk. Effectively, this means that portfolios must be reallocated away from the now riskier currency; the costs of ignorance or indifference have risen.

In the 1970s, the United States' commitment toward stable prices and predictable policies eroded in fits and starts. But with each episode of policy uncertainty, the share of dollars in world portfolios had to be adjusted—downwards—to reflect the greater risks and the decreasing expected usefulness of the U.S. dollar. Without considerations of currency substitutability, most, if not all, economic models of exchange rate determination grossly underestimate the potential for exchange rate shifts when long-run policy credibility is at stake. This was certainly the case in the 1970s as the dollar declined throughout the decade.

The 1980s taught the same lesson in reverse. With the combination of a Federal Reserve committed to low inflation and a president committed to economic incentives, the United States began to reassert world economic leadership. As the commitment to low inflation became more clear, long-run policy credibility was slowly restored. The dollar responded by defying the predictions of traditional models. With the relative usefulness of the dollar enhanced by the reduced risks associated with the United States' newfound commitment to low inflation, world portfolios were adjusted—with the dollar's share rising. This meant that basic price, trade, and interest rate models failed to capture a fundamental portfolio realignment, based upon a reassessment of currency risks which was predicated upon a considerably more credible (read predictable with respect to inflation) long-run U.S. monetary policy.

Another example is the Mexican devaluations of 1976 and 1982. These two cases produced strikingly different results, primarily because of differences in policy credibility which were magnified by currency substitution. The 1976 devaluation came after several years of inflationary policies, and the devaluation was virtually inevitable and widely predicted. But the devaluation came against a backdrop of two decades of peso stability as measured against the U.S. dollar. This legacy of policy credibility was not easily erased, and when the peso was finally allowed to float it roughly redressed the cumulative inflation differential with the United States of the prior 10 years by depreciating from peso/$ 12.5 to peso/$ 20-to-22 range. The absence of appreciable overshooting can be explained by the perception that the new president would restore policy credibility. He appeared to be doing so in 1977 and early 1978. When this perception proved incorrect in the early 1980s the stage was set for another devaluation to redress the inflation differential with the United States. In 1982, however, the peso devaluation was marked by chaotic conditions and a peso dramatically weaker, by a factor of two or more, than inflation differentials suggested. Why? By 1982 policy credibility had eroded and what was left of the peso's demand-side substitutability with the U.S. dollar was obliterated by capital controls and finally the peso-ization of dollar bank accounts in Mexico. The move from fixed exchange rates and perfect supply-side currency substitutability to a floating (read sinking) peso and quite limited demand-side substitutability was associated with a massive realignment of portfolios away from pesos wherever possible. Capital controls, government edicts, and bureaucratic "witch hunts" only made diversification more difficult through quantity changes in stocks of dollar assets. Thus, markets adjusted through massive price changes.

The lessons from the U.S. and Mexican illustrations are obvious: *policy credibility is absolutely essential for exchange rate stability.* Furthermore, policy shifts that either increase or decrease long-run credibility change the risks associated with holding a given currency. This sets in motion portfolio adjustments above and beyond those captured in traditional models. Or from a policy perspective, the lesson is that there is no such thing as policy independence, even under floating exchange rates.

FIXED VERSUS FLOATING EXCHANGE RATES

The contribution of the monetary approach to international adjustment and its most important extension, currency substitution, to the fixed versus floating exchange rate debate has been dramatic, yet inconclusive. That is to say, the monetary approach does not lend itself to a conclusion that either fixed or flexible exchange rates are preferable. Rather, the concepts embodied in the monetary approach have altered the terms of the debate and focus attention more directly on key judgmental issues. Should monetary authorities have discretion in the conduct of policy? How should policies around the world be coordinated, if at all?

These are old questions. To understand how the evolution of the monetary approach has affected these debates, one needs to take a broad view of the fixed versus floating exchange rate controversy. Two perspectives are important—the closed economy view (the United States) and the open economy view (Europe) of much of the rest of the world.

The Debate in the United States and Europe

In the United States, the fixed versus flexible exchange debate has been conducted within the context of one very key and generally accepted assumption: the independence assumption. Monetarists (of the traditional domestic variety) have argued that flexible exchange rates allow each country to adopt its own monetary policy, independent of its trading partners' policies, thereby setting the context for the debate. And, Keynesian economists have generally accepted this concept.

With independence of policy assumed, the debate then focuses on the most appropriate monetary policy for the United States. Broadly speaking, there are three choices:

1. **Discretionary Policy.** Monetary authorities focus their attention on changes in interest rates based on changing economic conditions. Real economic growth is the primary goal.
2. **A Money Stock Growth Rule.** Set into law, and rigidly enforced, monetary authorities focus only on achieving a stable and slow growth in one precisely defined monetary aggregate. Price stability is the key goal.
3 **A Gold Standard.** The monetary authorities enforce a fixed and never-changing price of gold. Again, price stability is the key goal.

As can be seen, this is not a debate about the international monetary system, but a debate about the conduct of U.S. monetary policy, independent of choices made by other countries. Even the third option, the gold standard, would not require other countries to link their currencies to gold. That would be their choice. In short, in the United States the exchange rate debate starts with the question of how monetary policy should be conducted domestically. And as an addendum, the debate allows other countries to choose whether they want the same policy (fixed exchange rates) or a different policy (floating rates).

Among Europeans the assumption of absolute policy independence is never made, for European countries are quite obviously much more dependent on the actions of their neighbors. Still, there are concerns about the degree of policy independence that is possible and desirable. The debate is couched in terms of the tradeoffs: scope for independent action (floating rates) versus the economic benefits of stable international financial markets (fixed rates). These tradeoffs were carefully considered in the construction of the European Monetary System (EMS). This system allows for independent action through irregular parity adjustments and in the interim the EMS enforces exchange market stability.

The Challenge of Interdependence

The monetary approach, and particularly its currency substitution extension, directly challenges the foundation of the debate. By arguing: (1) that there is no such thing as purely domestic monetary policy, (2) that national money stock changes cannot be analyzed in isolation from world economic conditions, and (3) that flexible exchange rates do not yield policy independence, the debate must be reconsidered in both the United States and in Europe.

First, the debate can no longer assume that the results in terms of economic growth or inflation for a given monetary policy are independent of policies around the world. The "rule" versus "discretion" argument must be recast. Now, the debate is one of international coordination versus the costs of exchange market volatility. And in Europe, the conclusion is similar. Interdependence, within Europe and with the United States, has increasingly focused the debate in terms of the costs of exchange rate volatility that is associated with uncoordinated policies. This is, of course, the essence of interdependence.

Expectationalist theories argue that nominal variables adjust to keep real variables more stable. That is, currencies are numeraires and exchange rates are the ratios of these nominal values. With efficient markets and rational expectations, these nominal variables can adjust to policy shifts, leaving real factors relatively unaffected. The key here is that the policy shifts must be anticipated. Then market efficiency and rational expectations render policy shifts impotent. If policy shifts are not anticipated, however, there can be real effects as well as nominal ones. This conclusion focuses the exchange rate debate on the question of whether a fixed or a flexible exchange rate system makes policies more or less predictable.

The contribution of the currency substitution literature is to argue that if policies are not credible or predictable, the risks of policy change will have a large cost. Indeed, one always pays a premium for risk. In this context, the monetary approach to international adjustment and the currency substitution approach do not provide any simple answer. They do, however, force the debaters to answer an important question: which exchange rate regime reduces the risk of unanticipated, destabilizing, and costly policy shifts?

Second, the rules versus discretion debate concerning the conduct of monetary policy is given new importance by the currency substitution arguments. By emphasizing long-run policy credibility, the issue can be seen in terms of contracts. Under a fixed exchange rate system or an international gold standard system, the monetary authorities make a contract to fix the price of their currency to the standard. This contract can increase policy credibility if market participants believe it will be honored for long periods of time. Discretionary systems do not involve such contracts, and almost by definition, policy becomes more volatile. The increase in volatility associated with discretionary policies would be preferable if and only if the monetary authorities correctly anticipated disruptive economic events and moved to minimize them. Traditional monetarists and gold standard advocates have argued that the authorities' ability to do this is lacking and that there will be costly policy mistakes. It is better to stick to a rule. But, what rule is best? Here, the monetary approach challenges traditional monetarist thinking.

Third, domestically based monetary rules may have unanticipated results due to the important failure of traditional monetarist theories to consider international policy interdependence and multicurrency portfolio behavior. If the monetarist assumption of independence under floating exchange rates is rejected, domestic monetarists lose a leg in their case for a money stock rule. Monetarist concerns about rules versus discretion remain valid, but the appropriate rule is questioned.

In sum, the monetary approach to international adjustment has recast the fixed versus floating rate debate in terms of policy credibility, the need for policy harmony internationally, and the costs of volatility. Traditional monetarists have been challenged by the rejection of the independence assumption, but the rules versus discretion debate continues.

The Exchange Rate Regime Does Not Matter

As a final consideration, once one accepts the full implications of policy interdependence, then even the relevance of the fixed versus floating exchange rate debate can be questioned. The choice of fixed versus floating exchange rates may not matter for the achievement of longer-term economic goals such as price stability or economic growth, unless other assumptions are made about policy choices.

Fixed exchange rates merely enforce policy harmony, but the outcome for prices and growth depend on the coordinated policies which are chosen. Flexible exchange rates allow for different policies, but major policy divergences set in motion extremely powerful exchange rate changes. These exchange rate changes tend to discipline the offending country—that is, the country that is out of step in terms of policy choice. Relatively expansionary policies lead to dramatic currency depreciation and inflation, while relatively restrictive policies lead to currency appreciation and potential deflation. As an empirical matter, severe, unanticipated inflation, disinflation, or deflation all appear to have negative correlations with real economic growth.

In sum, either the system provides a set of rules or the market provides penalties. In both cases, fixed or floating, however, the price and income results depend upon the fundamental policies, not upon the exchange rate regime. Hence, the choice of the exchange rate regime does not matter, independent of the set of contracts enforcing policy behavior.

18

Discretionary Monetary Policy and the Gold Standard

D. Sykes Wilford
Ronald A. Krieger

The gold standard question is part of a much wider debate over the advisability of a discretionary monetary policy. Those individuals who believe that monetary policy should be used actively, in attempts to maximize real output and stabilize what they view as an inherently unstable real economy, argue for discretionary monetary policy. This view of monetary policy derives mainly from Keynesian principles, although much of the evidence for the power of monetary policy is a result of monetarist economic research.

Monetarist economics, however, has evolved toward a position that monetary policy is so powerful that it should attempt to be neutral. It views the real economy as inherently stable, so that monetary policy should *not* be discretionary; rather, it should be geared to stabilizing the nominal output of the economy, which would stabilize prices.

The nondiscretionary monetary policy proponents are separated into two camps. One group argues that for long-run stabilization of expectations about monetary policy, it is necessary to move to a "price rule," with the value of money set in terms of a particular commodity. Most proponents of a price rule tend to favor a gold standard. The other group agrees that policy should be nondiscretionary, but argues that the proper way to arrive at monetary control is to move toward a "quantity rule," which would fix the rate of growth of the quantity of money.

WHY GOLD?

Although alternative commodity standards have frequently been proposed, gold has long had an enduring attraction. It possesses those desirable properties of money stressed by earlier writers in economics. It is durable, readily storable, portable, divisible, easily standardized, attractive to the holder, and—most important—relatively scarce. Since it does not perish easily, practically all the gold ever mined is still in existence. Gold therefore retains the attributes that allowed it to emerge as one of the earliest forms of money, and it continues to remain a form of money even in modern society.

The proponents of the gold standard are those individuals who believe that monetary policy should be nondiscretionary and limited by a price rule. They are convinced that the "quantity of money" is an ambiguous concept and, moreover, that if the monetary authorities have the ability to use their own discretion, they will do so. Therefore, a quantity rule will not work. The gold standard, they argue, places a more certain control over the discretion of the monetary authorities.

As indicated above, opponents of the gold standard believe either in (1) discretionary policy or (2) quantity rules for monetary policy. The latter group includes most traditional monetarists. They see the gold standard as a form of price fixing that would place domestic monetary policy somewhat, if not totally, at the mercy of shifts in the world supply of and demand for gold.

THE PRICE RULE VERSUS THE QUANTITY RULE

Under a price rule for monetary policy, the price of gold in terms of the numeraire (dollars) is fixed, and the "rules of the game" are set so that this price remains unchanged. Thus, if there is an excess supply of dollars in relation to the amount of gold in the system at the legal price, these dollars would be turned in at the Treasury for gold, reducing the supply of dollars. This makes the price rule look somewhat like a quantity rule, in that it limits the ability of the monetary authorities to change the quantity of money *significantly*, especially in the long run.

However, a gold standard opens the domestic economy to world events in a broader way than would be the case under a strict quantity rule. A quantity rule implies that the exchange rate and other international elements of the economy are to be totally ignored. Once that rule sets the quantity of money domestically, exchange rates—indeed all international behavior—will change accordingly. In fact, the monetary authorities and the government must be willing to accept *any* exchange rate relationship, if a quantity rule is to be adhered to. The price rule, however, carries specific implications for the determination not only of the price level but of the exchange rate as well, in that the risk characteristics of holding a currency change if that currency is pegged to gold.

HOW A GOLD STANDARD WOULD WORK

Three—and perhaps four—fundamental rules must be adhered to if a gold standard is to allow people to form stable expectations. First, gold must be set at a fixed value in terms of each currency within the gold system. Second, there must be free movement of gold among all regions and countries within the system. Third, all members of the gold system must link changes in their domestic money stocks more or less automatically to the movements in their gold holdings. Fourth, some believe that there must be a degree of downward wage and price flexibility. That is, individuals must recognize that if general prices and wages go up in the near term, in the long run they are likely to come back down.

Adjustment under the gold standard is relatively quick and need not depend upon massive gold flows. This follows from the simple precept that money flows where it is "needed." That is, money demand in a certain area is based upon such variables as wealth, income, price level, and interest rates. Just as domestic money flows to meet changes in the demand for local currency, international gold would flow to meet changes in the demand for international reserves. Thus, under a gold standard, where gold sends the signals for the pricing structure of the world economy, the discretionary ability of central banks would be limited. The amount of money supplied is linked directly to the amount of money that is needed, given long-run expectations that the value of money is set by the quantity of gold.

Domestically, under the gold standard, the stock of money demanded would depend upon how individuals chose to hold money in relation to the stock of gold. For instance, suppose too many dollars were being created, given people's expectations of the price of gold and the value of money. Individuals would then turn in their money at the Treasury to obtain gold. This would reduce the money stock in the United States until the amount of money supplied equaled the amount of money demanded. On an international basis, the argument is very similar. If the world were on a gold standard and an excess demand for money arose in the United States, gold would then flow into the U.S. Treasury until the supply of money increased to equal the amount demanded.

David Hume, writing some 200 years ago, pointed out that the mere fact that gold *could* flow to a country—so that prices would have to adjust—would almost eliminate the need for that gold flow. That is, prices around the world would be arbitraged relatively quickly if there were a discrepancy between, say, the dollar price and a foreign price of any one commodity. Thus, as prices for all commodities are arbitraged around the world under a gold standard, an adjustment would have to take place solely in the stock of money to make it equal to the amount of money being demanded. Prices, as well as interest rates, would be set on the international market; as U.S. wealth increased, given the same supply of domestic money, there would now be a greater demand for dollars, and gold would flow into the United States. If total world output rose while the gold stock remained the same, either prices would fall significantly or the price of gold—relative to the cost of the technology needed to obtain more gold—would shift in such a way as to increase gold production.

INTEREST RATES UNDER THE GOLD STANDARD

Some gold standard proponents have claimed that the gold standard would cause interest rates to fall and remain relatively low. This depends very much, however, upon the price that is set for gold. A price of $600 an ounce, for example, might well be too high. As people exchanged gold for dollars, the money stock would expand and inflation would accelerate. During this period, interest rates would probably rise as people anticipated more-rapid inflation. By the same token, a gold price of, say, $150 an ounce, might be too low, causing deflationary gold purchases and a drastic fall in interest rates.

If the "correct" price of gold were chosen, experience shows that prices would stabilize in the long run and inflation expectations would be lowered considerably, although prices would still fluctuate in the short run. For example, the wholesale price index in the United Kingdom in the early part of the twentieth century was at about the same level as it was early in the eighteenth century. It is reasonable to conclude that long-run inflation expectations were close to zero for this whole period. Thus, the gold standard *could* lead to lower *nominal* interest rates. This does not mean, however, that the gold standard would *necessarily* lead to lower *real* interest rates. History shows that real interest rates in fact varied over gold standard periods; they were both positive and negative at different times.

REAL ECONOMIC ACTIVITY

Proponents have also argued that if interest rates are lowered on the gold standard, this necessarily implies higher output —invalidating the argument for discretionary monetary policy. It is not clear, however, that this will always be the case. Certainly during the 1950s and 1960s, real output in the United States was fairly stable, perhaps even more stable during that interval than over most periods of the gold standard—although a form of gold standard did prevail in the 1950s and 1960s. But it is also true that during the greatest decline in output in the history of this country—the Great Depression—monetary authorities did have some discretion over monetary policy, even though the nation was on a gold standard. The issue of the Great Depression is, in fact, a critical one, in that some people have held it up as an example of what happens when the gold standard breaks down, while others have cited it as an example of what happens when discretionary monetary policy goes astray. Clearly, the debate over the course of real output under a gold standard is yet to be resolved.

But even if the gold standard does not necessarily imply greater output, there still are reasons to consider the gold standard as a desirable policy regime. Inflation expectations will be close to zero under a gold standard, and inflation will be relatively under control. Thus, the central bank will not have to create recessions to fight inflation. On the other hand, however, the ability of the Federal Reserve to use monetary policy to counter a recession caused by, say, the "natural" workings of the business cycle will also be weakened.

It can be argued that by controlling inflation and inflation expectations, the gold standard would make monetary policy neutral, thus reducing the uncertainty associated with that policy. If this is indeed the case, one can also argue that the rate of return for a given amount of investment would be higher in the absence of the uncertainty occasioned by inflation. On the other hand, the uncertainty associated with new gold discoveries (or lack of discoveries) under the gold standard may be just as great as the uncertainty associated with variable inflation expectations. This point is not resolved.

THE "CORRECT" PRICE OF GOLD
UNDER A GOLD STANDARD

The proper price for gold is one that allows restoration of the gold standard without creating inflation or deflation. No one really knows the correct price, which can be found only in a market equilibrium.

Gold has certain characteristics that make it highly desirable as a substitute for certain currencies, but without the problems peculiar to a particular nation. The resultant demand shifts could make the price of gold rather volatile, since the quantity is relatively fixed. Under a fixed exchange rate system, this would be less of a problem. But in today's world of flexible exchange rates, with the price of gold free to fluctuate, finding the proper gold price is indeed difficult. During a period of high inflationary bias and uncertainty about future inflation, the price of gold embodies a risk premium. Thus, the market price of gold in such a period would be higher than it should be were a gold standard to be restored at that time, and going on the gold standard at such a price could entail large inflation risks. Similarly, too low a price would carry substantial deflation risk.

History provides many examples of the effects of mispricing gold. For example, when Britain returned to the gold standard in 1925, it chose a price of gold consistent with the general price level of 1914. This led to deflation and unemployment, a situation no longer acceptable to modern policy-makers. Similarly for the United States, during the War Between the States, the massive issuance of paper money after the gold standard was abandoned led to the doubling of prices. Later, in anticipation of the subsequent restoration of the gold standard at the prewar price, the country was put through a massive deflation to "bring policy under control" as a precondition to returning to gold.

The actual stock of gold held by the Bank of England was relatively low during the period when Great Britain maintained the world gold standard. Present-day stocks are owned mainly by individuals, with the rest held primarily by central banks in Western countries. Table 18.1 presents the estimated gold holdings in the world in the early 1980s. Central banks outside the United States have around 24 percent of the world's gold. Private holdings constitute almost 50 percent of the world's gold stock, either in bullion form or in the form of jewelry. The U.S. government holds nearly 10 percent of the world's gold stock, certainly an amount sufficient to perform the functions necessary to maintain a gold standard.

The amount of gold in existence is important only relative to the price that is set for the gold. What really matters is the stock of gold relative to new supply, given the chosen price. In fact, the present stock of gold is

TABLE 18.1 Estimated Gold Holdings

Central banks other than U.S.	23.9%
Private bullion holdings	23.6%
Jewelry, decorations	22.7%
U.S. government	9.4%
IMF and other international institutions	7.0%
Soviet Union	2.1%
China	0.5%
Undetermined or lost	10.8%

Source: "A Return to the Gold Standard," *Business Week,* September 21, 1981.

huge, relative to new supplies that could come on stream. The leading producers of gold in the world are the Soviet Union and South Africa. But if the Soviet Union produced gold at full potential for the next 100 years, the output would equal the current holdings of the U.S. Treasury. The supply of new gold will emerge slowly, as the price of gold changes relative to prices of other commodities and to the relative cost of gold production. Of course, the possibility that substantial deposits of new gold will be discovered is a risk associated with going on a gold standard.

STABILITY OF A GOLD STANDARD

Opponents have argued that governments or individuals could change their preferences for gold in an attempt to destabilize the U.S. or world monetary systems. It certainly is possible that the Soviet Union could decide to dump an enormous amount of gold into the system, in order to depress the gold price, reduce the amount of dollars in circulation, and create a deflation. However, it is very unlikely that it could do so in a way that could not be detected by the U.S. monetary authorities, who could make adjustments accordingly. Alternatively, members of OPEC could decide to dump their U.S. Treasury bills and buy gold. But it is doubtful that they would have sufficient monopoly power to inflict much pain on the U.S. economy.

Of course, since the two largest producers of gold in the world are South Africa and the Soviet Union, opponents of the gold standard could argue that the United States is subjugating its monetary policy in appearance, even if not in fact, to decisions of those two countries. These political arguments have little economic relevance, but they are likely to be raised in future debate.

GOING IT ALONE

The United States was on a gold coin standard throughout much of the nineteenth centry. A gold coin standard is simply one form of the gold standard, in which coins are minted, circulated, and freely exchanged for dollar bills. Under Bretton Woods the United States was on a "gold certificate standard," in which no coins were minted. Gold certificates freely circulated side-by-side with Federal Reserve notes during most of this period, however, and Federal Reserve notes were backed by gold certificates.

If the United States today were to go on a gold standard unilaterally, the risk characteristics of holding U.S. dollars would become more like the risk characteristics of holding gold. If gold and the dollar were both perceived as a "haven" in times of trouble, the dollar would strengthen relative to other currencies. Many countries could be forced onto a gold standard to prevent the drastic decline of their currencies. Such an implication of a unilateral U.S. move to a gold standard makes that decision very difficult.

The same issue, however, would arise under any form of nondiscretionary monetary policy. That is, if the United States establishes a quantity rule, it must be willing to ignore the impact of the quantity rule on the exchange rate and let the dollar fluctuate. Similarly, if the United States goes on a gold standard, it must be willing to accept the implications of that gold standard for its currency's external value. In both cases, it is likely that there would be an excess demand for dollars and that the value of dollars in terms of other currencies would be bid up. Either way, it is likely that foreign currencies would fluctuate greatly against the U.S. dollar, as political events and economic policies shifted market perceptions.

THE CURRENT STATE OF THE DEBATE

The gold standard question has been relegated to the back burner in the mid-1980s, as both inflation and inflation expectations in the United States appear to have been tamed, to a degree—at least for the moment. Nevertheless, despite the current economic calm and despite the negative report of the majority group on the president's gold commission, the issue has not disappeared. Widespread fears have been expressed that price stability cannot long be maintained in the face of mammoth federal budget deficits and a possible substantial decline in the international value of the dollar.

To gold standard proponents, particularly "supply side" adherents in and out of the economics profession, the overriding issue is not the current inflation rate but the lack of any effective fiscal and monetary discipline in the long run. They argue that the absence of constraints upon the authorities over time has fostered a high level of uncertainty that is affecting financial markets today. Near-term expectations about the long run must be stabilized if financial markets are to provide an environment conducive to continued robust economic growth. The best way to reduce the uncertainty over future monetary policy, in the eyes of gold standard advocates, is to move toward a monetary policy based on a price rule.

Gold proponents are not alone in their alarm over the possible future direction of Federal Reserve policy. However, many Fed critics—even those who see the economy as inherently stable and who oppose a discretionary monetary policy—are unwilling to support a gold standard. Monetarists, in particular, see gold as an unstable commodity and argue that an alternative monetary policy could be designed in such a way as to make money neutral in every way with respect to its influence on the real economy. They maintain that a properly designed monetary regime, without a price rule, would avoid the problem of an inappropriate monetary policy evolving to "protect" the value or quantity of gold.

Although the debate has been more subdued as inflation has receded, gold standard advocates are not likely to let the issue die. They argue that future administrations—and Federal Reserve boards—may someday be in power with a different set of priorities and attitudes. Thus, they avow that even total victory over inflation and stagnation today is no substitute for a gold standard that is permanently and irrevocably in place, constraining the behavior of the monetary authorities over the long run.

19

Refocusing Monetary Theory and Policy

Marc A. Miles

Our collective experience with monetary policy over the last 20 years has been much like our individual experience with the Rubik's Cube. We spy new cubes in the store. They appear so orderly with the little colored squares neatly aligned along each side. We buy one and take it home. But rather than allowing that orderly little cube to rest on the shelf, we feel an urge to experiment, to mess it up. The messing up takes but a minute. We spend the next 20 years, however, trying to put in back in order.[1]

Twenty years ago under the Bretton Woods system there was order in the international money markets. Recent experience had created the expectations that exchange rates would be stable and the interest rates and inflation would be low. People could easily make long-term commitments to production schedules, investment projects, and affordable home mortgages. But then we began to experiment. First the relationship between the dollar and gold was clouded during the period 1965–68. It was severed completely in August 1971. Then in the 1971–73 period the policy of stabilizing exchange rates was shunt aside. Over the next few years governments came under pressure to eliminate any vestiges of interest stabilization policy. Countries were now to try something completely different, something called monetarism. It was to be a policy of economic nationalism permitting, in the words of Milton Friedman, "each country to seek for monetary stability according to its own lights."[2]

Yet, all has not worked according to plan. Current expectations are that exchange rates can ascend or plummet at any time. Interest rates fall, only to rise again. The consensus guess on inflation is wrong as often as right. It is therefore a healthy idea for economists and others to step back and contemplate the last 20 years. It is time to survey our ideas about monetary policy with an objective eye. We must critically reexamine our basic beliefs about the interactions of central banks, money, economic activity, and prices. Where have we gone wrong? What are the crucial keys to getting the sides of the monetary cube quickly realigned and the system back in order? While space does not permit a thorough examination of these questions, a few of the major issues can be raised.

A MISSING COMPONENT—THE GLOBAL MONEY MARKET

A good place to start is with the relevant framework for policy analysis. While the importance of foreign markets is beginning to gain the attention it deserves, most monetary policy discussions in this country look no further than the Golden Gate Bridge or the Statue of Liberty. The United States and its money markets are assumed to exist in isolation. Attention is focused almost exclusively on the Open Market Committee, with all dollars assumed to emanate from that source.

Certainly the United States is large relative to most other countries, and much of its commerce and financial activity is self-contained. But in a world where telecommunication signals can be beamed instantaneously around the world, where space shuttles circle the earth every 90 minutes, and where everything from oranges to Mercedes are dipersed from where they are produced to the far corners of the earth, the importance of individual borders fades. Countries are increasingly interconnected, and any policy that ignores a sizable chunk of the system must be immediately suspect.

There exists no better example of this interconnected economic system than the international money market. Today's money market is a highly technical, highly mobile operation. The latest movements in the money market are sped instantaneously via satellite around the world. Computers of large banks and other corporations continuously monitor interest rate and exchange rate quotations from markets in Europe, America, and Asia for fleeting profit opportunities. In a push of a telex button, millions, or even billions, of dollars can change hands halfway around the world. In this organized world money market, U.S. residents and the Federal Reserve are important participants, and the dollar is an important currency. But the U.S. dollar is only one of the primary monies traded. U.S. residents are only part of the people using dollars. The

Federal Reserve is only one institution supplying liquidity to the global market. Other central banks supply liquidity denominated in other major currencies. Even within the world dollar market, the Fed finds that an increasing number of dollars come from private institutions.

Hence, the U.S. money market cannot be easily isolated. If an individual in the United States wants more money, he has several alternative sources. The money could come from the Fed. But the money could also come from foreign countries or the Euromarkets, and involve dollars or some other currency. Rather than omnipotent, the Fed is but one participant in the competitive, global money market.

A simplified analogy clarifies this point. There are 12 Federal Reserve banks overseeing the regulation of banking institutions in their jurisdictions. Each district bank issues paper money bearing the bank's unique seal. In a sense there are 12 separate monies and 12 separate central banks across the United States. Yet few would consider the Federal Reserve Bank of Dallas capable of implementing an independent monetary policy. The Dallas Fed supplies its own unique dollars. Its region may be one of the largest in the country. But it is still incapable of controlling the number of "Dallas Fed" dollars, much less the total number of dollars, in its district. The reason is that banks and individuals have too many avenues for transferring money to or from any of the other regions. A tightening of monetary policy by the Dallas Fed would create incentives for Texans to shift their loan demands "abroad." Texans would hold more dollars with non-Dallas seals, or deposits in non-Texas banks. Despite the physical and financial size of the Dallas Fed region, it is recognized that the money market is global, incorporating all states. Likewise, the Federal Reserve must contend with the private sector's alternatives in today's global market. In particular, two of these potential avenues, The Eurodollar market and holdings of foreign currency-denominated money, diminish the Fed's ability to control the quantity of money. The global nature of the money market in turn implies that the role of some popular monetary policy signals must be reexamined.

THE EURODOLLAR MARKET

The Eurodollar market can provide a cushion for the private market against the Fed's policy. If the Federal Reserve attempts to reduce the number of dollars in circulation, Eurodollar activity can expand. Domestic borrowers discover that at prevailing interest rates they cannot find as much financing as they desire, so they turn to the Eurodollar market to borrow more for their projects. With higher loan demand, Eurobanks offer slightly higher interest rates to attract more deposits to finance the loans. Eurodeposits expand.

This expansion of Eurodollar financial intermediation does not imply a corresponding decline in domestic dollar deposits. The reason is that while domestic banks are required to hold reserves in only one type of asset—monetary base—Eurobanks have no such requirement. So when a Eurobank has dollars deposited into its accounts, it transfers any monetary base assets back to the home office in the United States. In return the Eurobank receives a deposit at the home office to use as its reserves. U.S. monetary base is unaffected, but the global quantity of dollar deposits rises. So as the Fed attempts to reduce the quantity of deposits created in the United States, the expanding quantities of Eurodollar deposits help to keep the total quantity of dollar deposits unchanged.

An interesting example of how Euromarkets are used to circumvent Federal Reserve policy is the reaction of banks to President Carter's November 1, 1978 attempt to restrict dollar growth. Part of the proposal was a directive by the Federal Reserve doubling the reserve requirements on large CDs from 2 to 4 percent. The change was intended to slow the growth rate of the U.S. money supply. The major effect of the change, however, was simply to switch part of the CD market from the United States to the Eurodollar market. Creating dollar CDs now became relatively more expensive for the home office in the United States, and relatively cheaper for Euromarket branches.

Not surprisingly, the relative amount of large-denomination CDs issued in the Eurodollar market rose steadily in the months following the November 1978 reserve requirement increase. The dollar liabilities of foreign branches of U.S. banks as a percentage of large U.S. domestic market CDs grew from 12.8 percent in November 1978 to 23 percent in August 1979. In October 1979 the Federal Reserve tried again. An additional reserve requirement of 8 percent was applied against CDs of domestic banks above a certain level. This time, however, the Fed tried to plug the Euromarket loophole by simultaneously adding an 8 percent reserve requirement against any additional deposits to foreign branches above a prescribed level. But as before, banks found ways to circumvent these restrictions on managed liabilities.

The new loophole appeared because not only do banks have a choice of whether to raise funds through the parent bank or Eurobranches, but they can choose as well which branch will make the loans. There is no requirement that money raised in the Euromarket be lent again to the U.S. private market through the parent bank. The loan could just as easily be booked directly from the Eurobranch. U.S. banks now found the reserve requirements on liabilities to foreign branches taxing the first lending

percentage

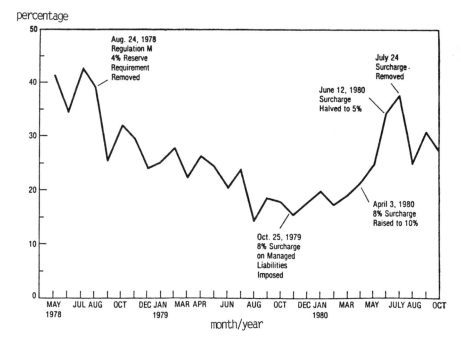

FIGURE 19.1 Foreign Branch Lending: Evading the Costs of Regulation.

Source: Federal Reserve Bulletin (Washington, D.C.: Federal Reserve Board).
Note: Direct lending of foreign branches to U.S. private market as percentage of total foreign branch lending to U.S. Data unadjusted for seasonal variation.

route, but not the second. The reaction was predictable. A greater proportion of funds borrowed through Eurodollar deposits were lent directly to U.S. companies (or their foreign subsidiaries) by the foreign branch (Figure 19.1).

The Euromarket reacted similarly the following March, when the Federal Reserve raised the marginal reserve requirement and widened the range of liabilities to foreign branches to which the marginal reserve requirement applied. Direct lending again rose sharply. Following the elimination of the marginal reserve requirements in July 1980, the proportion of direct lending again decreased.

The Fed, of course, has tried other types of restrictions. Today, not only do CDs and liabilities to foreign branches have reserve requirements, but the same requirements also apply to the direct loans of foreign branches to U.S. residents. If Citicorp's Cayman branch lends dollars to

GM in Detroit, Citibank in New York has to hold noninterest-earning reserves against the loan. Again, however, there are abundant opportunities to circumvent these restrictions. For example, the Cayman branch could lend to a foreign subsidiary of GM, which in turn could lend to the Detroit office. Or GM could borrow from the Cayman branch without receiving a direct loan, say by floating debt on the Euro-commercial paper market.

So the Euromarket is a clear example of how the global market permits banking activity to move beyond the Fed's control. The Fed's influence over the quantity of dollars is clearly shrinking. At the end of 1971 the net size (excluding interbank deposits) of the Eurodollar market was only about $20.9 billion. By 1975 this figure had more than tripled to $63.8 billion. By the end of 1983, it had surged to at least $353.2 billion. This 1983 figure is equivalent to 65.7 percent of M1, and 16.1 percent of M2, and even 13.0 percent of M3.

THE ROLE OF FOREIGN MONEY

The existence of global money markets opens other opportunities to blunt the impact of Federal Reserve attempts to control the growth of money. One of these alternatives is foreign monies. Traditional approaches to monetary policy assume that the Federal Reserve has a captive audience. Individuals and businesses in the United States are assumed to conduct their business only in dollars, so the Fed (from which all dollars are assumed to emanate) can influence the level of business. This assumption, however, is somewhat analogous to the assertion that individuals in Texas use only dollars with Dallas Fed seals, or only deposits from Texas banks.[3] But Texans have a choice. They can borrow from banks in other regions, or use dollars with different seals.

Like the Texans, residents of the United States also have a choice. In the global money market, dollars are only one of several monies that people and institutions use for trading or making investments. They could, for example, conduct their international business in Swiss francs, deutschemarks, or other money assets over which the Federal Reserve has little, if any, direct influence. The idea that Americans would have some of their cash holdings denominated in other currencies is not astounding. Travelers, traders, and people in border areas have always employed foreign monies in their dealings. Furthermore, it is common to assume that bond and equity-holders diversify their portfolios across currency denominations. The purpose of diversification is to reduce risk. One obvious source of risk is uncertainty of exchange rate depreciation, which can potentially inflict capital losses on assets denominated in a given currency. Faced with exchange rate uncertainty, bond and equity owners diversify the currency denominations of their assets, thereby reducing the risk of capital loss. The money diversification argument simply extends this commonsense behavior to the decisions about how to hold money.

This issue of money diversification is discussed elsewhere in this book under the topic of "currency substitution." The basic argument is that as currencies have become more volatile, the incentive to diversify monies has increased. The diversification in turn produces private market flows of money between countries. The theoretical implication is that even with perfectly flexible exchange rates the central bank cannot insulate the domestic money supply from foreign countries. Empirical research indicates that such money diversification may be a significant phenomenon (Miles, 1978; Miles and Stewart, 1980; Brittain, 1981; Laney, 1981; McKinnon, 1982).

SOME MORE CONVENTIONAL ISSUES

What is the Relevant Money Supply?

The existence of the global market raises some serious questions about the assumption of the omniscient, omnipotent Fed. However, the global market is only compounding other doubts about the relevance of the traditional policy approach. For example, a basic assumption is that the Fed effects its policy by varying the quantity of money. But what precisely is this "money"?

The monetary literature abounds with articles trying to define precisely what should be included in a relevant definition of money. Yet, the debate on this fundamental policy point is far from resolved. Ask any two economists, and you are bound to get at least three different answers. But, particularly in the last decade as inflation and regulation have spurred financial innovations, economists have come increasingly to realize that what is used for money in the United States extends far beyond the traditional concepts such as M1 or even M2. Today M1 includes currency in circulation, demand deposits, and other checkable deposits such as NOW accounts and credit union share draft balances. These components are all liabilities of institutions which at least appear to be under the control of the Federal Reserve. Hence the attractiveness of M1 as a policy guide. This is a number that the Fed might be able to influence directly.

There are, however, certainly numerous domestic alternatives to the monetary assets included in M1. For example, there are time deposits, certificates of deposit, money market shares, repurchase agreements, commercial paper, and credit cards, not to mention the global market alternatives such as Eurodollars. These alternatives clearly represent a spectrum of monetary assets which fall less and less under the control of Federal Reserve regulations. Their availabilities are increasingly likely to respond to the demands of the private sector. They provide direct methods for the public to getting around the dollar liquidity policy of the Fed.

Today's M2 is closer to a relevant definition of money than M1. M2 adds to M1 not only small time deposits, but also such assets as overnight repurchase agreements, overnight Eurodollar deposits in the Caribbean, and money market mutual fund shares. But while M2 may be closer to the relevant definition, the newly included assets are simultaneously clearly outside the Fed's control. Is even M2 the relevant definition? Probably not. If overnight Eurodollars at Caribbean branches (included in M2) are relevant, why not overnight Eurodollars at other banks? And why not longer-term Eurodollars? Longer-term Eurodollars at even Caribbean branches do not appear until the broad measure M3. Longer-term repurchase agreements do not appear until M3. Money market funds that belong to institutions also do not surface until M3. In addition, with the current incentives to increase returns and reduce costs in financial markets, financial innovations continue to appear. Such innovations occur because financial markets see a need for the new money instrument. Hence the innovations should be included in any relevant money supply. Yet the Fed typically does not control these assets. Quite likely, the innovation occurred in the first place to avoid a Fed regulation or barrier. Money market funds grew in response to interest rate ceilings. Eurodollar market growth reflected efforts to avoid Regulation Q as well as rising reserve requirements and other Fed-imposed restrictions.

Given these alternative assets, were the Fed, say, to reduce successfully the supply of monetary base in an attempt to reduce M1 (or M2), the private sector could respond with greater use of money market funds, repurchase agreements, and credit cards. The Fed's policy might even successfully reduce M1. But since the relevant definition of money instruments includes more than what is measured by M1, the decline provides a false signal. The decline in M1 is offset by the rise in the alternative instruments. While the Fed, through its limited powers, might alter the relative proportions that the public holds in regulated versus unregulated money, it is unable to control directly the total relevant quantity of money.

What to include in the relevant money supply is an empirical question which may never be resolved to everyone's satisfaction. One empirical criterion which has been suggested is the degree of correlation between a particular definition of money and nominal GNP. By this measure the empirical justification for L (which the Fed clearly does not control) is at least as strong as that for M1. This year's percentage change in nominal GNP, is significantly related to this year's change in L. Statistically there is a percentage point for percentage point change in the two numbers. In fact, the movements in L can even explain marginally more of the variation in GNP than do the movements in M1.

Can the Fed Control Even M1?

Even if the problem of defining money is put aside, are traditional policy approaches likely to succeed? Assume domestic M1 is the relevant money. Are we assured in even that extreme case that the Fed can adequately regulate the "money supply" to achieve its stated policy objectives?

Contrary to prevailing perceptions, it is far from clear that the Fed would be the dominant player in this scenario. Any standard money and banking textbook describes how the reported M1 is the end product of decisions by the Fed, the public, and commercial banks. The Fed attempts to influence M1 through open market operations, minimum reserve requirements and the discount rate. The public affects the level of M1 by choosing how much money to hold in currency versus deposits, and by deciding what proportion of deposits will be transaction versus time deposits. Banks can influence the supply of money by deciding whether to hold reserves over and above those required by the Fed. The textbook then summarizes these various influences in the product of two components: the monetary base, assumed to reflect the influence of the Fed, and the money multiplier, reflecting primarily the influence of the public and commercial banks.

An enlightened book would then go on to question which of the two components exerts more influence over the level of money. Unfortunately, many of the books stop short of this question, assuming instead throughout the remainder of the text that the Fed's behavior "dominates" movements in the money supply. But that relationship has been far from perfect. In fact, historically, swings in the money multiplier have had a significant effect on the movements in money. For example, Cagan's (1965) study of the determinants of the money supply showed that the monetary base and the Federal Reserve's actions were by no means the dominant force determining the course of money. In fact, over the period 1875–1960, the public's ability to vary the amount of currency relative to bank deposits (the currency ratio) accounted for about one-half of the cyclical variation in money. Cagan commented in discussions of cyclical movements, high-powered money and the reserve ratio have generally received all the attention, while the currency ratio has been little noticed. One reason for the differential treatment is that sources of variation in high-powered money and the reserve ratio involve activities of the government and banks—both easy to discuss (and exaggerate)—whereas sources of the variation in the currency ratio involve actions of innumerable holders of money and are, except in panics, obscure. While many students of the money supply have been aware of variations in the currency ratio, the present results highlight their importance, not only in panics but also for all cycles in the money series.[4]

A subsequent study by Laffer and Miles (1977) of the post-war period reinforced Cagan's findings. We found that over months, quarters, and semiannual periods the public's abilities to influence the ratio of currency to deposits and the composition of deposits were far more important than changes in the monetary base for explaining the movements in M1. Not until annual changes did the influence of the monetary base begin to become important. But in most of the years examined, the United States was under the Bretton Woods fixed exchange rate system, which permitted monetary base to flow easily into and out of the country. With integrated global markets, it is quite possible that even these annual changes in the monetary base reflect changes caused by the public's demands as much as Federal Reserve policy. What our results and Cagan's results do, therefore, is seriously question the Federal Reserve's ability to control even M1 with any accuracy.

Some Other Questions

Global markets, domestic money substitutes and the responses of the public certainly raise some haunting questions about recent approaches to monetary policy. They are, however, not the only sources of concern. For example, even if the problems of defining the relevant money supply and controlling it could be solved, other informational problems remain. We would still have to measure accurately the supply of money at a given time. Our track record in this area is far from perfect. The most celebrated mistake occurred in the fall of 1979. The person at Manufacturers Hanover Bank responsible for transmitting the weekly data to the Fed was on vacation. The substitute inadvertently placed some figures in the wrong column and the weekly money supply figures were misquoted by $3.5 billion.

The problems of measurement are exacerbated by the need to correct the data for seasonal patterns and trading day variations. These adjustments are estimates, just like the raw numbers. The opportunities for misleading errors compound. These errors show up as the data are revised. In fact, there is very little relationship between the pattern of period-to-period changes in the initially released data and the pattern in the data after final revisions have occurred. This fact in turn implies that preliminary or first-released data may be of very little use for guiding policies based on historical (completely revised) data.

The seasonal adjustment problem also raises doubts about other essential assertions underlying current policies. For example, causality tests by Sims (1972) and others have probed for evidence of a unidirectional causal relationship running from the money supply to nominal income. However, Feige and Pearce (1979) found that when a Sims causality test was applied to seasonally unadjusted data for money and income, in almost all cases there was an absence of causality. Feige and Pearce found similar results in two other test procedures they examined. They comment, "we are thus led to the conclusion that the empirical results are highly sensitive to the use of seasonally adjusted data. . . ."[5]

WHERE DOES THIS LEAVE US?

The questions about our basic theory of money in turn raise significant doubts about our basic approach to monetary policy. In particular they emphasize the failings of the money supply as an explicit, dependable, direct policy signal which both the Federal Reserve and the public can use with confidence. The impact of giving the money supply a central role in determining monetary policy in our global economy can therefore be summarized in one word—uncertainty.

Money is a yardstick. It is a means of conveying information about the relative and absolute prices of all commodities we purchase or sell. What therefore is of direct concern to most of us is not the *number* of dollars in the economy, but the *stability* of the dollars we hold in our wallets and bank accounts. Is the prevailing yardstick giving us meaningful information for making decisions about not only today, but tomorrow or even a year from now? Thus the uncertainty exists because the monetary authorities fail to guarantee, or even focus their policy on, the value of the yardstick. Instead the world is characterized by guesswork. Businesses and commentators, for example, are busy guessing "Will the money supply be up or down?" "How will the Fed respond to such a change?" and "What is the probable impact of the Fed's reaction?" These questions do not have obvious answers, as witnessed by the money market column of the *Wall Street Journal* where "experts" change their opinions almost daily. The

Fed's policy choices are also full of uncertainties. How big is the money supply? Is that too much money? How much or what type of intervention, if any, is necessary? The potential problems and errors multiply.

The role of the dollar as a yardstick is analogous to yardsticks used in specific industries. Take, for example, shoe sizes. Like the dollar, shoe sizes are an information system, providing a way to compare different pairs of shoes at one time, or over time. A size 10C, for instance, should be almost precisely the same size, regardless of which style shoe is chosen. A size 7B will be shorter and narrower. As long as local shoe sizes remain stable, they are profitably relied upon and used by all.

But suppose the system were not stable. Suppose shoe sizes changed every month. The shoe industry would quickly fall on hard times if shoe sizes fluctuated from month to month, much less day to day. Each month a person wanting shoes would have to have his feet remeasured. Shoes marked as a certain size would also have to be dated. With sizes changing every month, it would be hard for store owners and customers to order pairs of shoes. Ordering would require forecasting what sizes will be on the day the order is shipped. The necessity to forecast repeatedly (not to mention occasionally forecasting incorrectly) raises the cost of using the system. Obviously the worth of such a yardstick declines. At some point people will resort to ignoring the yardsticks completely (I'll just keep trying on pairs until one fits."), developing their own system, or maybe using a more stable foreign system. The industry experiences a period of turmoil, uncertainty, slow growth, and unemployment.

How does the shoe industry avoid such turmoil? It sets up and maintains a basic unit of account, the standard shoe size. Either the government sets the standards and makes sure that the standards are maintained, or a trade group agrees on an acceptable standard. In either case a system for guaranteeing the standard for the market is created. Shoe sellers and consumers then adjust their behavior accordingly. It is the same for money. The basic money yardstick must be determined. Again, the government can set the standard for what its monetary liabilities are worth and make sure the standard is retained. But where the government fails to set the standard directly, the private market settles on the value of the standard.

Under current monetary policy, the government does not set the standard. Instead we are bombarded with quotations about the estimated money supply. To continue the analogy, it is a little like walking in to buy a pair of shoes and being shown all the foot measures in the store. You wonder what the number of measures has to do with buying a pair of 10C shoes. The financial markets face a similar quandary. They desperately desire information about the size of the yardstick. They are shown instead the approximate number of one type of measure sticks. How is this number to be interpreted? Is a certain number of this type of measure sticks directly associated with a specific size of yardstick? Few would claim it is. The Fed is no longer providing the information the market needs.

Given our current situation where neither the government nor a private group is defining the dollar unit of account, how is the market to define or determine the standard dollar and the related dollar prices? Press economists for an answer to this question, and you will find out they are not sure. Some may insist that it has to do with the supply and demand of money. Most of these economists will insist that it has to do with some measure of domestic money supply and demand. With integrated global money markets, however, such an approach is too narrow. A few may have some concept of world money supply and demand. Even here, however, new questions arise. If the analysis includes the relevant world supply of dollars, it is endogenous, responding to the needs of the private sector. But if it is endogenous, so that the relevant world money supply always equals the world money demand, why should there ever be inflation? Conventional monetary thoery does not seem able to answer that nagging, fundamental question.

What is becoming clear is that many questions concerning money and prices remain to be answered. We finally define the relevant money supply, only to run into new problems with explaining inflation under unhinged money. The problems encountered are reminiscent of those faced by the Ptolemaic explanation of the solar system. While putting the earth at the center was a simple, intuitively appealing model, not all the observable data fit the theory. So a more complicated theory was developed, involving circles within circles. More observable facts could be explained, but still not all. It remained for the radical departure of the Copernican system, with the sun at the center of the solar system, to provide a simple alternative theory capable of bringing what we observe better into focus. We still await the economic Copernicus to provide us with an alternative theory of price determination.

REDIRECTING MONETARY POLICY

The problems of current policy in a highly flexible, global money market have been outlined. What are the alternatives? How can the dollar be most efficiently and effectively stabilized in a global economy? My answer has three major points. First, our aproach to monetary policy must be shifted 180 degrees from focusing on the quantity of money to focusing on its price or value. The Fed should agree to adopt appropriate "price rules" where some relevant market prices are stabilized. Under price rules, a target value is chosen for each price, and the Fed's sole guide is to keep that value stable.

A price rule works because the Fed is defining the basic monetary unit of account in terms of something observable. The Fed calls the basic unit of its liabilities the dollar. It then tells the market that these dollar liability units will always be redeemable at a certain price in terms of the observable item. The basic dollar unit now has a specific value. Even better, so too do all the forms of money that are convertible into the basic unit. Bank accounts, Eurodollar accounts, money market mutual funds, and so forth may not be controlled directly by the Fed. But as long as the isuers of these monies define and redeem these accounts in dollars, the Fed is stabilizing the *value* of these monies, too. Immediately we see that the Fed need no longer worry about the quantity of monies it cannot control. Instead the Fed need only concern itself with the value of the money it issues directly, stand ready to define it, and as a result help bring stability to even the monies beyond its direct grasp.

One of the nice qualities of such a policy is that it eliminates most of the current guesswork. Information is transmitted directly through the marketplace (by watching the appropriate commodity or financial quotations) to both the Fed and private sector. Both the Fed and the private sector know what must be done. The Fed knows precisely when to redeem and how much. Any tendency for the target value to move requires the Fed to step into the market. The Fed also knows that it must remain in the market as long as the tendency for movement remains. No elaborate information-gathering or ad hoc policy planning is required. The private sector also knows what to expect. This side of the market is interested in the Fed continuing to "play by the rules." The private market has only to check the targeted value. If, say, spot silver prices are targeted, is the dollar price of silver stable? If the price does move from the target value, does it start moving back? If so, the Fed is doing its job. The public simply watches the commodity tickertape for the latest quotes.

While the Fed is busy assuring the stability of the value of money, the quantity of money takes care of itself. The Fed does not have to worry whether or why money demand has risen or if velocity is stable. If the private sector wants more money, for whatever reason, the Fed will find out soon enough. The dollar price of the target commodity will fall, requiring the Fed to react by buying back the commodity in exchange for money. At the stable target price, the private sector sees that the available money expands and contracts with its needs.

Second, one price rule is not sufficient. At least two price rules are needed. The reason is that there are three prices which we would like to stabilize, the spot price level, the forward price level, and interest rates. People are concerned not only with what they must pay for groceries today. They would also like to know what they will have to pay six months, a year, or two years from now. Using only one price rule, the government could stabilize today's price level or the price level a year from now, but not both. In order to stabilize simultaneously both sets of prices, the Fed would have to carry out two separate price rule intervention mechanisms.

If a policy to stabilize both spot and forward prices were adopted, it would also act to stabilize the third price, the market rate of interest. The ups and downs in interest rates reflect primarily shifts in the expected rate of inflation. The expected inflation in turn reflects how much the market expects the value of the basic dollar unit to depreciate over time. If the spot and forward values of the dollar unit were being directly stabilized, so would the expected change. Hence, interest rates would become stable. The closer the stabilized forward price is to the stabilized spot price, the lower would be the market rate of interest.

Of course the two stabilized prices do not have to be spot and forward prices. The Fed could choose alternatively to stabilize an interest rate and one of the two price levels. For example, the two targets could be spot prices and interest rates on one-year T-bills. Stabilizing these two prices is equivalent to stabilizing simultaneously the price level one year forward. In other words, stabilizing any two of the three relevant prices stabilizes the third.

This discussion of the three price targets illustrates why a return to a simple spot gold standard is not likely by itself to be the panacea some proponents claim. A simple gold standard is a spot price rule. It attempts to stabilize today's price level in terms of gold. Without an additional price rule, however, it does little, if anything, to stabilize either the forward price level or interest rates. Inflation in the near term may fall, but we have no guarantee of what the price level or inflation will be in the longer run. To provide the guarantee, the spot market intervention would have to be combined with intervention to target either the forward price of gold or a market interest rate.

The third point is that ideally the interventions chosen would overcome two objections to a commodity standard, the "terms of trade" problem and the fear that reserves could become depleted. The terms of trade problem is most pronounced when the price of only one commodity is targeted. Say the Fed were stabilizing the spot dollar price of wheat, and for whatever reason, the value of wheat in terms of other commodities were to shift. While dollar wheat prices might remain stable, dollar prices of other commodities and goods would shift up or down. In this scenario, targeting the spot price of wheat does not guarantee stable prices in the spot general price level. The obvious solution is to employ a price rule involving a basket of commodities instead of just one. The broader the basket, the closer the basket approximates the general price level, and the smaller the terms of trade problem. The finite reserve problem occurs as the government's stockpile of the targeted commodity declines. The market begins to fear that the government will no longer be able to stand behind its policy, and the price rule collapses in the ensuing run on reserves. The solution to this problem would be to design an intervention mechanism where the Fed did not actually have to hold reserves.

Elsewhere[6] I have discussed one possible set of price rules which could overcome these problems. One price rule would require the Fed to target and stabilize the interest rate on long-term government bonds. The intervention scheme would direct the open market desk to buy bonds as interest rates rose to the upper limit of the target range, and sell them as the lower limit is approached. The Fed would continue to buy and sell as necessary to keep the interest rate within the targeted band.

The other price rule would require the government to stabilize the price of a futures contract for a broad bundle of commodities. The innovative aspect of this proposal is that the futures contract, like many current financial futures contracts, can be payable in cash rather than the actual commodities. The need for the government to hold commodity reserves is eliminated. The contract would be a promise to pay the cash equivalent of a predetermined weighted average of commodity prices on the settlement date. If the price of the contract rises toward the upper limit of the range, the Fed just creates new ones and offers them on the market at the target price. If the price falls too far, the Fed buys back contracts at the target price. The government could at any moment be long or short in these contracts. The quantity of contracts outstanding is not important, only the stability of the price at which they settle. While this commodity contract does not currently exist, a proposal is currently before the Commodity Futures Trading Commission to permit trading of such a contract on the New York Futures Exchange. The contract would be based on the Commodity Research Bureau's index of commodity futures.[7]

CONCLUSION

The objective of the current discussion has been to point out that there are many unresolved issues surrounding current approaches to monetary policy. Economists have more questions than they have answers. Unfortunately statistical testing does not clearly resolve these questions. There is usually more than one explanation that is consistent with any empirical fact. For example, an economist may observe the money supply rising first, followed by the nominal level of income. We have all been trained to interpret this result as rising money causing a rise in prices or real output. Yet, this result is equally consistent with the alternative scenario that individuals and businesses adjust their money holdings in anticipation of rising prices or real income. The two explanations, however, have very different policy implications.

The number and importance of these basic questions surrounding the prevailing monetary theory and policy raise the serious possibility that policy over the last 20 years has increasingly lost any meaningful orientation. It has been equivalent to flipping the sides of the economic Rubik's Cube randomly. It is therefore time to reassess objectively what we are doing. It is time to search in a new direction for those elusive keys that will put the economic cube back in order.

NOTES

1. This article summarizes some issues to which I devote more detail in *Beyond Monetarism*.
2. Friedman, p. 430.
3. This analogy does not strictly hold because the intervention by the various Federal Reserve Banks to buy and sell at parity dollars with seals from other districts makes these dollars perfect substitutes on the supply side.
4. Cagan, p. 24.
5. Feige and Pearce, p. 530.
6. *Beyond Monetarism*, Chapter 10.
7. See "The CRB Futures Price Index—A 'Basket of 27 Commodities' That May Soon Be A Futures Contract," Commodity Research Bureau, *1984 Commodity Yearbook*, pp. 38–53.

REFERENCES

Brittain, Bruce. "International Currency Substitution and the Apparent Instability of Velocity in Some Western European Economies and in the United States," *Journal of Money, Credit, and Banking* 13, no. 2 (May 1981): 135–55.

Cagan, Phillip. *Determinants and Effects of Changes in the Money Stock, 1875–1960.* New York: National Bureau of Economic Research, 1965.

Feige, Edgar L., and Douglas K. Pearce. "The Casual Causal Relationship Between Money and Income: Some Caveats for Time Series Analysis," *The Review of Economics and Statistics* 61 (November 1979): 521–33.

Friedman, Milton. "The Case for Flexible Exchange Rates." *Essays in Positive Economics.* Chicago: University of Chicago Press, 1953.

Laffer, Arthur B., and Marc A. Miles. "Factors Influencing Changes in the Money Supply Over the Short Term." Economic Study, H. C. Wainwright & Co., Economics, August 18, 1977.

Laney, Leroy O. "Currency Substitution: The Mexican Case." Federal Reserve Bank of Dallas *Voice* (January 1981).

McKinnon, Ronald I. "Currency Substitution and Instability in the World Dollar Standard." *American Economic Review* 72 (June 1982): 320–33.

Miles, Marc A. "Currency Substitution, Flexible Exchange Rates, and Monetary Independence." *American Economic Review* 68 (June 1978): 428–36.

――――. *Beyond Monetarism: Finding the Road to Stable Money.* New York: Basic Books, 1984.

Miles, Marc A., and Marion B. Stewart. "The Effects of Risk and Return on the Currency Composition of Money Demand." *Weltwirtschaftliches Archiv* 16, no. 4 (December 1980): 613–26.

Sims, Christopher. "Money, Income, and Causality." *American Economic Review* 62 (September 1972): 540–52.

BIBLIOGRAPHY

This bibliography has been constructed especially for the researcher interested in the monetary approach to international adjustment. Citations of all studies referenced by the essays in this volume, plus numerous other studies dealing with the monetary approach, have been organized into categories, with identifications of whether the study contains empirical work or not.

The bibliography is divided into two primary parts: monetary approach studies and background references. Within the monetary approach part, there are three categories: fixed exchange rates, flexible exchange rates, and portfolio substitution. Furthermore, studies containing empirical work are marked to indicate which empirical investigations are related to industrial (I) or developing (D) economies. In dividing the bibliography into sections some arbitrary decisions were made. For example, an article by Lance Girton and Don Roper encompassing both fixed and flexible exchange rate regimes fits into more than one section. This example was listed in the fixed exchange rate section. Also, as with any attempt such as this, there are errors and omissions, and the editors apologize for these.

The second part of the bibliography lists background studies that the contributors to this volume found particularly useful. These listings are divided into three categories: historical, purchasing-power parity, and general studies. These sections are not comprehensive in any sense.

A summary of the contents of the bibliography follows:

Monetary Approach Studies

Background References

MONETARY APPROACH STUDIES

Fixed Exchange Rates

Aghevli, B. "Money, Prices and the Balance of Payments: Indonesia 1968–73." *Journal of Development Studies* 13 (January 1977): 37–57. (D)

Aghevli, B., and M. Kahn. "The Monetary Approach to Balance of Payments Determination: An Empirical Test." In *The Monetary Approach to the Balance of Payments*, 275–90. Washington, D.C.: International Monetary Fund, 1977. (D)

Aizenman, J. "The Use of the Balance of Payments as a Shock Absorber in Fixed Rate and Managed Float Systems." *Journal of International Economics* 11 (November 1982): 479–86.

Akhtar, M. A. "Some Common Misconceptions about the Monetary Approach to International Adjustment." In *The Monetary Approach to International Adjustment*, edited by Bluford H. Putnam and D. Sykes Wilford. New York: Praeger, 1978. (See also Chapter 6, this volume.) (I)

Akhtar, M. A., B. H. Putnam, and D. S. Wilford. "Fiscal Constraints, Domestic Credit, and International Reserve Flows in the United Kingdom, 1952–71: A Note." *Journal of Money, Credit, and Banking* 11 (May 1979): 202–08. (I)

Beals, R., and A. Collery. "A Monetary Approach to the Balance of Payments of a Small Country: The Case of Jamaica" 1971. Mimeographed. (D)

Bhatia, S. L. "The Monetary Theory of Balance of Payments under Fixed Exchange Rates: An Example of India, 1951–73." *Indian Economic Journal* 29 (January–March 1982): 30–40. (D)

Blejer, Mario I. "The Short-Run Dynamics of Prices and the Balance of Payments." *American Economic Review* 67 (June 1977): 419–28. (D)

———. "Devaluation, Inflation, and the Balance of Payments: A Short-Run Monetary Approach." *Economic Record* 55 (March 1979): 33–40.

———. "Causality and the Monetary Approach to Balance of Payments." *European Economic Review* 12 (July 1979): 289–96.

Blejer, Mario I., and R. B. Fernandez. "On the Output-Inflation Trade-Off in an Open Economy: A Short-Run Monetary Approach." *Manchester School of Economics and Social Studies* 46 (June 1978): 123–38.

Borts, G., and J. A. Hanson. "The Monetary Approach to the Balance of

Payments." in *Short Run Macroeconomic Policy in Latin America*, edited by Jere Behrman. Cambridge, Mass.: Ballinger, 1979. (D)

————. "The Monetary Approach to the Balance of Payments." Unpublished working paper, Brown University, 1975.

Boyer, Russell S. "Commodity Markets and Bond Markets in a Small, Fixed-Exchange-Rate Economy." *Canadian Journal of Economics* 8 (February 1975): 1–23.

Cobham, D. "Reverse Causation in the Monetary Approach: An Econometric Test for the U.K." *Manchester School of Economics and Social Studies* 51 (December 1983): 360–79. (I)

Collery, Arnold. "International Adjustment, Open Economies, and the Quantity Theory of Money." *Princeton Studies in International Finance* no. 28 (June 1971).

Connolly, Michael. "The Monetary Approach to an Open Economy: The Fundamental Theory." In *The Monetary Approach to International Adjustment*, edited by Bluford H. Putnam and D. Sykes Wilford. New York: Praeger, 1978. (See also Chapter 1, this volume.)

————. "Optimum Currency Pegs for Latin America." *Journal of Money, Credit, and Banking* 15 (February 1983): 56–72. (D)

Connolly, Michael B. and Jose Da Silveira. "Exchange Market Pressure in Postwar Brazil: An Application of the Girton-Roper Monetary Model." *American Economic Review* 69 (June 1979): 448–54. (D)

Connolly, Michael, and Charles Lackey. "Presiones en el Mercado Cambiario de Mexico: 1955–82," in A. Violante and R. Davila, eds., *Mexico: Una Economia en Transicion*. Mexico City: Editorial Limusna, 1984. (D)

Connolly, Michael, and Dean Taylor. "Adjustment to Devaluation with Money and Non-Traded Goods." *Journal of International Economics* (August 1976): 289–99. (D)

————. "Testing the Monetary Approach to Devaluation in Developing Countries." *Journal of Political Economy* (August 1976): 849–59. (D)

————. "Adjustment to Devaluation in a Small Country." *De-Economist* 24 (1976): 319–27.

————. "Exchange Rate Changes and Neutralization: A Test of the Monetary Approach Applied to Developed and Developing Countries." *Economica* 46 (August 1979): 281–94. (I & D)

_____ . "Crawling Pegs and Exchange Rate Crisis." *University of South Carolina Working Paper* (November 1982).

_____ . "The Exact Timing of the Collapse of an Exchange Rate Regime and its Impact on the Relative Price of Traded Goods." *Journal of Money, Credit, and Banking* 16 (May 1984): 194–207.

Courchene, Thomas. "The Price-Specie Flow Mechanism and the Gold Exchange Standard: Some Exploratory Empiricism Relating to the Endogeneity of Country Money Balances." In *The Economics of Common Currencies*, edited by H. G. Johnson and A. K. Swoboda. London: Allen and Unwin, 1973. (I)

Cox, W. Michael. "An Incomplete Information Model of the Monetary Approach to the Balance of Payments." Mimeographed. University of Western Ontario, 1978.

_____ . "Rational Expectations and the Monetary Approach to the Balance of Payments: The Canadian Experience." In *The Monetary Approach to International Adjustment*, edited by Bluford H. Putnam and D. Sykes Wilford. New York: Praeger, 1978. (I)

Cox, W. Michael, and Halbert White. "Unanticipated Money, Output, and Prices in the Small Economy." Mimeographed. University of Rochester, 1978.

Cox, W. Michael, and D. Sykes Wilford. "The Monetary Approach to the Balance of Payments and World Monetary Equilibrium." Mimeographed. 1977. (I & D)

Craig, Gary Alan. "A Monetary Approach to the Balance of Trade." *American Economic Review* 71 (June 1981): 460–66.

Currie, D. A. "Some Criticisms of the Monetary Analysis of Balance of Payments Correction." *Economic Journal* 86 (September 1976): 508–22.

de Macedo, J. B. "Exchange Rate Behavior with Currency Inconvertibility." *Journal of International Economics* 12 (February 1982): 65–81.

Edwards, Sebastian. "The Demand for International Reserves and Exchange Rate Adjustments: The Case of LDCs, 1964–1972." *Economica* 50 (August 1983): 269–80.

Flood, Robert P., and Peter Garber. "Collapsing Exchange Rate Regimes: Some Linear Examples." *Journal of International Economics* 17 (August 1984): 1–13.

Frenkel, J. "Adjustment Mechanisms and the Monetary Approach to the Balance of Payments: A Doctrinal Perspective." In *Recent Issues in International Monetary Economics*, edited by E. M. Claassen and P. Salin. Amsterdam: North-Holland, 1976.

Frenkel, J., and Harry G. Johnson, eds. *The Monetary Approach to the Balance of Payments*. London: Allen and Unwin, 1976. (D & I)

———— . "The Monetary Approach to the Balance of Payments: Essential Concepts and Historical Origins." In *The Monetary Approach to the Balance of Payments*, edited by Jacob Frenkel and Harry G. Johnson, pp. 21–45. Toronto: University of Toronto Press, 1976.

Frenkel, J., and C. A. Rodriguez. "Portfolio Equilibrium and the Balance of Payments: A Monetary Approach." *American Economic Review* 65 (September 1975): 674–88.

Genberg, H. "Aspects of the Monetary Approach to Balance of Payments Theory: An Empirical Study of Sweden." In *The Monetary Approach to the Balance of Payments*, edited by Jacob Frenkel and Harry G. Johnson, pp. 298–325. Toronto: University of Toronto Press, 1976. (I)

———— . "An Empirical Comparison of Alternative Models of Currency Devaluations." *Scandinavian Journal of Economics* 80 (1978): 311–28. (I)

Girton, Lance, and Dayle Nattress. "The Monetary Approach to the Balance of Payments, Stocks and Flows, and Walras' Law." *Intermountain Economic Review* 8 (Fall 1977).

Girton, Lance, and Don Roper. "A Monetary Model of Fixed and Flexible Exchange Rates Applied to the Post-War Canadian Experience." *American Economic Review* 67 (September 1977): 537–48. (I)

Guitian, Manuel. "Credit Versus Money as an Instrument of Control." In *The Monetary Approach to the Balance of Payments*, pp. 227–42. Washington, D.C.: International Monetary Fund, 1977. (D)

Gupta, S. "An Application of the Monetary Approach to Black Market Exchange Rates." *Weltwirtschaftliches Archiv* 116 (1980): 235–52.

Haberler, G. "The Monetary Approach to the Balance of Payments Theory: By Frenkel and Johnson," review, *Journal of Economic Literature* 14 (December 1976): 1324–28.

Hahn, F. H. "The Monetary Approach to the Balance of Payments." *Journal of International Economics* 7 (August 1977): 231–41.

Jager, H. "The Global Monetaristic Variant of the Monetary Approach to the Balance of Payments: An Empirical Study of the Netherlands." *De-Economist* 126 (1978): 342–69.(I)

Johnson, Harry G. "The Monetary Approach to the Balance of Payments." In *Further Essays in Monetary Economics*, 224–41. Cambridge: Harvard University Press, 1973.

_____. "The Monetary Approach to Balance of Payments Theory." In *International Trade and Money*, edited by M. Connolly and A. Swoboda, 206–24. London: Allen and Unwin, 1973.

_____. "The Monetary Approach to the Balance of Payments Theory: A Diagrammatic Analysis." *The Manchester School* (1975): 220–74.

_____. "Money and the Balance of Payments." *Banca Nazionale del Lavoro Quarterly Review* no. 116 (March 1976): 3–18.

_____. "Elasticity, Absorption, Keynesian Multiplier, Keynesian Policy, and Monetary Approaches to Devaluation Theory: A Simple Geometric Exposition." *American Economic Review* 66 (June 1976): 448–52.

_____. "The Monetary Approach to the Balance of Payments: A Nontechnical Guide." *Journal of International Economics* (August 1977): 289–98.

_____. "The Monetary Approach to the Balance of Payments Theory and Policy: Explanation and Policy Implications." *Economica* 44 (August 1977): 217–29.

_____. "Money, Balance-of-Payments Theory, and the International Monetary Problem." *Essays in International Finance* no. 124 (November 1977).

Jonson, P. D. "Money and Economic Activity in the Open Economy: The United Kingdom, 1880–1970." *Journal of Political Economy* 84 (October 1976): 979–1012. (I)

Kahn, Mohsin, S. "A Monetary Model of Balance of Payments: The Case of Venezuela." *Journal of Monetary Economics* 2 (July 1976): 311–32. (D)

_____. "The Determination of the Balance of Payments and Income in Developing Countries." In *The Monetary Approach to the Balance of Payments*, pp. 243–74. Washington, D.C.: International Monetary Fund, 1977.

Keleher, Robert. "Of Money and Prices: Some Historical Perspectives." In *The Monetary Approach to International Adjustment*, edited by Bluford H. Putnam and D. Sykes Wilford. New York: Praeger, 1978. (See also Chapter 2, this volume.)

Kemp, Donald S. "A Monetary View of Balance of Payments." *Federal Reserve Bank of St. Louis Review* 57, no. 4 (April 1975): 14–22. Reprinted in *The Monetary Approach to International Adjustment*, edited by Bluford H. Putnam and D. Sykes Wilford. New York: Praeger, 1978.

Komiya, R. "Economic Growth and the Balance of Payments." *Journal of Political Economy* 77 (January–February 1969): 35–48.

Kouri, Pentti J. K. "The Exchange Rate and the Balance of Payments in the Short Run and in the Long Run: A Monetary Approach." In *Flexible Exchange Rates and Stabilization Policy*, edited by Jan Herin, Assar Lindbeck, and Johan Myhrman, pp. 148–72. Boulder, Colo.: Westview Press, 1977.

Kouri, Pentti J. K., and M. G. Porter. "International Capital Flows and Portfolio Equilibrium." *Journal of Political Economy* 82 (August 1974): 443–67. (I)

Kreinen, M., and L. Officer. "Survey of Empirical Evidence on Monetary Approach to Open Economies." In *Essays in International Finance*. Princeton, N.J.: Princeton University, 1978.

Lachman, D. A. "A Monetary Approach to the South African Balance of Payments." *South African Journal of Economics* 43 (September 1975): 271–83. (D)

Laffer, Arthur. "The Anti-Traditional General Equilibrium Theory of the Rate Growth and the Balance of Payments under Fixed Exchange Rates." Mimeographed. University of Chicago, 1968. (I)

————. "Monetary Policy and the Balance of Payments." *Journal of Money, Credit, and Banking* 4 (February 1972): 13–22.

Laidler, D., and P. O'Shea. "An Empirical Macro-Model of an Open Economy under Fixed Exchange Rates: The United Kingdom, 1954–1970." *Economica* 47 (May 1980): 141–58. (I)

Liviatan, Nissan. "A Disequilibrium Analysis of the Monetary Trade Model." *Journal of International Economics* 9 (August 1979): 355–77.

Lybeck, Johan A., Jan Haggstrom, and Bjorn Jarnhall. "An Empirical Comparison of Four Models of Capital Flows: OLS and 2SLS Estimation of the Branson, Genberg, Kouri and Lybeck Models." In *Modelling the International Transmission Mechanism*, edited by John A. Sawyer. New York: North-Holland, 1979.

Magee, S. "Empirical Evidence on the Monetary Approach to the Balance of Payments and Exchange Rates." *American Economic Review* 66 (May 1976): 163–70.

McClosky, Don, and J. Richard Zecher. "How the Gold Standard Worked, 1880–1913." In *The Monetary Approach to the Balance of Payments*, edited by Jacob Frenkel and Harry G. Johnson, pp. 357–85. Toronto: University of Toronto Press, 1976.

McDermott, J. "Exchange-Rate Indexation in a Monetary Model: Theory and Evidence. *Journal of International Money and Finance* 2 (August 1983): 196–213. (D)

Melitz, Jacques, and Henry Sterdyniak. "The Monetary Approach to Official Reserves and the Foreign Exchange Rate in France, 1962–74." *American Economic Review* 69 (December 1979): 818–31. (I)

Miles, Marc A. "The Effects of Devaluation on the Trade Balance and the Balance of Payments: Some New Results." *Journal of Political Economy* 87 (June 1979): 600–20. (I & D)

Miller, N. C., and S. S. Askin. "Monetary Policy and the Balance of Payments in Brazil and Chile." *Journal of Money, Credit, and Banking* 8 (May 1976): 227–38. (D)

Mundell, Robert A. *International Economics*. London: Macmillan, 1968.

Mussa, Michael. "A Monetary Approach to Balance-of-Payments Analysis." *Journal of Money, Credit, and Banking* 6 (August 1974): 331–51.

————. "Tariffs and the Balance of Payments: A Monetary Approach." In *The Monetary Approach to the Balance of Payments*, edited by Jacob Frenkel and Harry G. Johnson, pp. 187–221. Toronto: University of Toronto Press, 1976.

————. "The Exchange Rate, the Balance of Payments and Monetary and Fiscal Policy Under a Regime of Controlled Floating." In *Flexible Exchange Rates and Stabilization Policy*, edited by Jan Herin, Assar Lindbeck, and Johan Myhrman, pp. 97–116. Boulder, Colo.: Westview Press, 1977.

Myhrman, Johan. "Balance of Payments Adjustment and Portfolio Theory: A Survey." In *Recent Issues in International Monetary Economics*, edited by E. Claassen and P. Salin. Amsterdam: North-Holland, 1976.

Nobay, A. R., and Harry G. Johnson. "Monetarism: A Historic-Theoretic Perspective." *Journal of Economic Literature* 15 (June 1977): 470–85.

Obstfeld, Maurice. "Imperfect Asset Substitutability and Monetary Policy under Fixed Exchange Rates." *Journal of International Economics* 10 (May 1980): 177–200.

———— . "Balance-of-Payments Crises and Devaluation." *Journal of Money, Credit, and Banking*, 16 (May 1984): 159–74.

Otani, I., and Y. C. Park. "A Monetary Model of the Korean Economy." *International Monetary Fund Staff Paper* 23 (March 1976): 164–99.

Polak, J. J. "Monetary Analysis of Income Formation and Payments Problems," in *The Monetary Approach to Balance of Payments*, pp. 15–64. Washington, D.C.: International Monetary Fund, 1977.

Porter, M. G. "The Interdependence of Monetary Policy and Capital Flows in Australia." *Economic Record* 24 (August 1974): 120–50. (I)

Prais, S. J. "Some Mathematical Notes of the Quantity Theory of Money in an Open Economy." In *The Monetary Approach to the Balance of Payments*, pp. 147–62. Washington, D.C.: International Monetary Fund, 1977.

Putnam, Bluford H. "Non-traded Goods and the Monetary Approach to the Balance of Payments." Federal Reserve Bank of New York Research Paper no. 7714, 1976. (I)

Putnam, Bluford H., and D. Sykes Wilford. "Monetary Equilibrium and International Reserve Flows: An Empirical Treatment of the Money Supply Identity Issue." Mimeographed. 1975. (I)

———— . "International Reserve Flows: Seemingly Unrelated Regressions." *Weltwirtschaftliches Archiv* 114 (June 1978): 211–26. Reprinted in *The Monetary Approach to International Adjustment*, edited by Bluford H. Putnam and D. Sykes Wilford. New York: Praeger, 1978. (See also Chapter 4, this volume.) (I)

———— . "Money, Income and Causality in the U.S. and the U.K.: A Theoretical Explanation of Different Findings." *American Economic Review* 68 (June 1978): 423–27. Reprinted in *The Monetary Approach to International Adjustment*, edited by Bluford H. Putnam and D. Sykes Wilford. New York: Praeger, 1978. (See also Chapter 3, this volume.)

Ramanathan, R. "Monetary Expansion, Balance of Trade and Economic Growth." *Economic Record* 51 (March 1975): 31–39. (D)

Rhomberg, Rudolf R. "Money, Income, and the Foreign Balance." In *The Monetary Approach to the Balance of Payments*, pp. 163–84. Washington, D.C.: International Monetary Fund, 1977.

Rhomberg, Rudolf R., and H. Robert Heller. "Introductory Survey." In *The*

Monetary Approach to the Balance of Payments, pp. 1–114. Washington, D.C.: International Monetary Fund, 1977.

Rodriguez, Carlos A. "Money and Wealth in an Open Economy Income-Expenditure Model." In *The Monetary Approach to the Balance of Payments*, edited by Jacob Frenkel and Harry G. Johnson, pp. 222–36. Toronto: University of Toronto Press, 1976.

Rutledge, John. "Balance of Payments and Money Demand." Mimeographed. Claremont College, 1975. (I)

Saidi, N. H. "Expectations, International Business Cycles and the Balance of Payments." *Journal of Money, Credit, and Banking* 14 (August 1982): 327–46.

Swoboda, Alexander K. "Equilibrium, Quasi-Equilibrium, and Macroeconomic Policy Under Fixed Exchange Rates." *Quarterly Journal of Economics* 86 (February 1972): 162–71.

_____ . "Monetary Policy Under Fixed Exchange Rates: Effectiveness, the Speed of Adjustment and Proper Use." *Economica* 40 (May 1973): 136–54.

_____ . "Monetary Approaches to Balance-of-Payments Theory." In *Recent Issues in Monetary Economics*, edited by E. Claassen and P. Salin. Amsterdam: North-Holland, 1976.

_____ . "Gold, Dollars, Eurodollars, and the World Money Stock under Fixed Exchange Rates." *American Economic Review* 68 (September 1978): 625–42. (I)

Taylor, Dean. "Official Intervention in the Foreign Exchange Market, or Bet against the Central Bank." *Journal of Political Economy* 90 (April 1982): 356–68. (I)

Tsiang, S. C. "The Monetary Theoretic Foundation of the Modern Monetary Approach to the Balance of Payments." *Oxford Economic Papers* 29 (November 1977): 319–38.

Tullio, G. "Monetary Equilibrium and Balance-of-Payments Adjustment: An Empirical Test of the U.S. Balance of Payments, 1951–73." *Journal of Money, Credit, and Banking* 11 (February 1979): 68–79. (I)

Van Belle, John J. "Money Illusion and Its Influence on International Adjustment." In *The Monetary Approach to International Adjustment*, edited by Bluford H. Putnam and D. Sykes Wilford. New York: Praeger, 1978.

Whitman, Marina v. N. "Global Monetarism and the Monetary Approach to the

Balance of Payments." *Brookings Papers on Economic Activity* no. 3 (1975): 491–536.

Wihlborg, C. "Interest Rates, Exchange Rate Adjustments and Currency Risks: An Empirical Study, 1967–75." *Journal of Money, Credit, and Banking* 14 (February 1982): 58–75. (I)

Wilford, D. Sykes. *Monetary Policy and the Open Economy: Mexico's Experience.* New York: Praeger, 1977. (D)

Wilford, D. Sykes, and Walton T. Wilford. "Monetary Approach to the Balance of Payments: On World Prices and the Reserve Flow Equation." *Weltwirtschaftliches Archiv* 113, no. 1 (1977): 31–39. (D)

————. "On the Monetary Approach to the Balance of Payments: The Small Open Economy," *The Journal of Finance* 33 (March 1978): 319–23. (D)

————. "Efectos de la Creación de Crédito sobre la Balanza de Pagos en El Salvador." *Caribbean Studies* 17 (July 1978).

Wilford, D. Sykes, and J. Richard Zecher. "Monetary Policy and the Balance of Payments in Mexico, 1955–75." *Journal of Money, Credit, and Banking* 11 (August 1979): 340–48. (D)

Wilford, Walton T. "Some Observations on the Monetary Approach to Balance of Payments and the Third World." In *The Monetary Approach to International Adjustment*, edited by Bluford H. Putnam and D. Sykes Wilford. New York: Praeger, 1978. (See also Chapter 5, this volume.)

Witte, James G., and Barbara Henneberry. "A Monetary-Real Approach to Balance of Payments Theory: Old-New Synthesis for Old-New Problems." Mimeographed. Indiana University, April 1977.

Zecher, J. Richard. "Monetary Equilibrium and International Reserve Flows in Australia." *Journal of Finance* 29 (December 1974): 1523–30. (I)

Flexible Exchange Rates

Akhtar, M. A., and Bluford H. Putnam. "The Exchange Risk and the Demand for Money in Germany, 1972–76." *Journal of Finance* (June 1980): 787–94. (I)

Artus, Jacques R. "Exchange Rate Stability and Managed Floating: The Experience of the Federal Republic of Germany." *International Monetary Fund Staff Papers* 23 (July 1976): 312–33. (I)

———— . "Methods of Assessing the Long-Run Equilibrium Value of an Exchange Rate." *Journal of International Economics* 8 (May 1978): 277–99. (I)

Artus, Jacques R., and Andrew W. Crockett. "Floating Exchange Rates, Rate Management Policies, and the Need for Surveillance." In *Essays in International Finance*, Princeton, N.J.: Princeton University Press, 1978.

Baade, R. A. "A Monetary (Asset) Approach to Exchange Rate Determination: The Evidence since 1973." *Kredit und Kapital* 14 (1981): 341–49. (I)

Barro, R. "A Simple Flexible Exchange Rate Model with Uncertainty and Rational Expectations." Mimeographed. November 1975.

Barro, R. J. "A Stochastic Equilibrium Model of an Open Economy under Flexible Exchange Rates." *Quarterly Journal of Economics* 92 (February 1978): 149–64.

Basevi, G., and P. De Grauwe. "Vicious and Virtuous Circles: A Theoretical Analysis and a Policy Proposal for Managing Exchange Rates." *European Economic Review* 10 (December 1977): 277–301.

Batra, R. N., and S. P. Das. "International Investment and the Theory of Devaluation." *Journal of International Economics* 15 (August 1983): 161–75.

Bhandari, J. S. "A Simple Transnational Model of Large Open Economies." *Southern Economic Journal* 47 (April 1981): 990–1006.

———— . "A Stochastic Macroequilibrium Approach to a Floating Exchange Rate Economy with Interest-Bearing Assets." *Weltwirtschaftliches Archiv* 117 (1981): 1–19.

———— . "Expectations, Exchange Rate Volatility and Non-Neutral Disturbances." *International Economic Review* 22 (October 1981): 535–40.

———— . "A Theory of Exchange Rate Determination and Adjustment." *Weltwirtschaftliches Archiv* 117 (1981): 605–21.

———— . "Informational Efficiency and the Open Economy." *Journal of Money, Credit, and Banking* 14 (November 1981): 457–78.

Bhandari, J. S., and R. L. Tracy. "Exchange Rate and Price Level Determination in a Stochastic Equilibrium Model." *Journal of Macroeconomics* 5 (Spring 1983): 167–84.

Bilson, John F. O., "A Simple Long Run Model of Exchange Rate Determination." Mimeographed. International Monetary Fund, April 1977.

———. "The Monetary Approach to the Exchange Rate: Some Empirical Evidence. *International Monetary Fund Staff Papers* (March 1978): 49–75. (I)

———. "The Current Experience with Floating Exchange Rates: An Appraisal of the Monetary Approach." *American Economic Review* 68 (May 1978): 392–97.

———. "Rational Expectations and the Exchange Rate." In *The Economics of Exchange Rate—Selected Studies*, edited by J. Frenkel and Harry G. Johnson. Reading, Mass.: Addison-Wesley, 1978. (I)

———. "Recent Developments in Monetary Models of Exchange Rate Determination." Mimeographed. International Monetary Fund, 1978. (I)

———. "The 'Vicious Circle' Hypothesis." *International Monetary Fund Staff Papers* 26 (March 1979): 1–38.

———. "Recent Developments in Monetary Models of Exchange Rate Determination." *International Monetary Fund Staff Papers* 27 (June 1979) (I)

———. "The Deutsche Mark/Dollar Rate: A Monetary Analysis." *Journal of Monetary Economics Supplement* 11 (1979): 59–101. (I)

———. "The Speculative Efficiency Hypothesis," *Journal of Business* 54 (July 1981): 435–51.

Bisignano, J., and K. Hoover. "Some Suggested Improvements to a Simple Portfolio Balance Model of Exchange Rate Determination with Special Reference to the U.S. Dollar/Canadian Dollar Rate." *Weltwirtschaftliches Archiv* 118 (1982): 19–28. (I)

Black, S. W. "International Money Market and Flexible Exchange Rates." *Princeton Studies in International Finance* no. 32. In *Essays in International Finance.*, Princeton, N.J.: Princeton University Press, 1978.

———. *Floating Exchange Rates and National Economic Policy*. New Haven: Yale University Press, 1977.

———. "The Effects of Alternative Monetary Control Procedures on Exchange Rates and Output." *Journal of Money, Credit, and Banking* 14 (November 1982): 746–60.

Blejer, M. I. "The Monetary Approach to Devaluation: A Graphical Presentation." *Weltwirtschaftliches Archiv* 113 (1977): 348–52.

Blejer, Mario I., and L. Leiderman. "A Monetary Approach to the Crawling-Peg System: Theory and Evidence." *Journal of Political Economy* 89 (February 1981): 132–51. (D)

Bomhoff, E. J., and P. Korteweg. "Exchange Rate Variability and Monetary Policy under Rational Expectations: Some Euro-American Experience, 1973–1979." *Journal of Monetary Economics* 11 (March 1983): 169–206. (I)

Boyer, Russell. "Optimal Foreign Exchange Market Intervention." Mimeographed. University of Western Ontario, January 1976.

———. "Revaluation and Portfolio Balance." *American Economic Review* 62, 2 (March 1977): 54–63.

Boyer, R. S. "Financial Policies in an Open Economy." *Economics* 45 (February 1978): 39–57.

———."Sterilization and the Monetary Approach to Balance of Payments Analysis." *Journal of Monetary Economics* 5 (April 1979): 295–300.

Branson, W. H. "Asset Markets and Relative Prices in Exchange Rate Determination," *Sozialwissenschaftliche Annalen*, 1 (1977): 69–89.

———."Macroeconomic Determinants of Real Exchange Rates." *National Bureau of Economic Research Working Papers* 801 (November 1981).

———. "Exchange Rate Policy after a Decade of Floating." *National Bureau of Economic Research Working Papers* 909 (June 1982).

———. "Economic Structure and Policy for External Balance." *International Monetary Fund Staff Papers* 30 (March 1983): 39–66.

———. "A Model of Exchange Rate Determination with Policy Reaction: Evidence from Monthly Data." *National Bureau of Economic Research Working Papers* 1135 (June 1983). (I)

Branson, William H., and Hannu Halttunen. "Asset-market Determination of Exchange Rates: Initial Empirical and Policy Results." In *Trade and Payments Adjustments under Flexible Exchange Rates*, edited by John P. Martin and Alastair Smith. London: Macmillan, 1979. (I)

Bryant, Ralph C. "Financial Interdependence and Variability in Exchange Rates." *Staff Papers, the Brookings Institution*, Washington, D.C., 1980.

Burton, D. "Flexible Exchange Rates and Perfect Foresight: The Implications of Domestic Monetary Policy for Foreign Prices and Stabilization Policy." *Weltwirtschaftliches Archiv* 119 (1982): 201–13.

Cathcart, Charles D. "A Monetary Approach to the Exchange Rate in the Short Run." In *The Monetary Approach to International Adjustment*, edited by Bluford H. Putnam and D. Sykes Wilford. New York: Praeger, 1978.

Caves, Douglas W., and Edgar L. Feige. "Efficient Foreign Exchange Markets and the Monetary Approach to Exchange-Rate Determination." *American Economic Review* 70 (March 1980): 120–34.

Clements, K. W. "The Monetary Approach to Exchange Rate Determination: A Geometric Analysis. *Weltwirtschaftliches Archiv* 117 (1981): 20–29.

Collyns, C. "On the Monetary Analysis of an Open Economy." *International Monetary Fund Staff Papers* 30 (June 1983): 421–44.

Connolly, M., and J. da Silveira. "An Application of the Girton-Roper Monetary Model of Exchange Market Pressure to Postwar Brazil." Mimeographed. 1978. (D)

Cooper, Richard N. "Monetary Theory and Policy in the Open Economy." In *Flexible Exchange Rates and Stabilization Policy*, edited by Jan Herin, Assar Lindbeck, and Johan Myhrman, pp. 14–31. Boulder, Colo.: Westview Press, 1977.

Cuddington, J. T. "Fiscal and Exchange Rate Policies in a Fix-Price Trade Model with Export Rationing." *Journal of International Economics* 10 (August 1980): 319–40.

Currie, D. "Monetary Overshooting and the Exchange Rate." *Manchester School of Economics and Social Studies* 52 (March 1984): 28–48.

Djajic, S. "Monetary and Commercial Policy in a Two-Country Flexible Exchange Rate Model with Perfect Capital Mobility." *Journal of Monetary Economics* 12 (September 1983): 399–416.

Dooley, Michael P., and Peter Isard. "A Portfolio-Balance Rational Expectations Model of the Dollar-Mark Exchange Rate." *Journal of International Economics* 12 (1982): 257–76.

Dornbusch, R. "Devaluation, Money an Non-Traded Goods." *American Economic Review* 61 (December 1973): 871–80.

_____. "Real and Monetary Aspects of the Effects of Exchange Rate Changes." In *National Monetary Policies and the International Financial System*, edited by R. Z. Aliber. Chicago: University of Chicago Press, 1974.

_____. "Expectations and Exchange Rate Dynamics." *Journal of Political Economy* 84, no. 6 (December 1976): 1161–76.

_____. "Capital Mobility, Flexible Exchange Rates and Macroeconomic Equilibrium." In *Recent Issues in International Monetary Economics*, edited by E. Claassen and P. Salin. Amsterdam: North Holland, 1976.

_____ . "The Theory of Flexible Exchange Rate Regimes and Macroeconomic Policy." In *Flexible Exchange Rates and Stabilization Policy*, edited by Jan Herin, Assar Lindbeck, and Johan Myhrman, pp. 123–43. Boulder, Colo.: Westview Press, 1977.

_____ . "Flexible Exchange Rates and Interdependence. *International Monetary Fund Staff Papers* 30 (March 1983): 3–30.

_____ . "Exchange Risk and the Macroeconomics of Exchange Rate Determination." In the *Internationalization of Financial Markets and National Policy*, edited by R. Hawkings, R. Levich, and C. Wihlborg. Greenwich, Conn.: JAI Press, 1983.

Dornbusch, Rudiger, and Stanley Fischer. "Exchange Rates and the Currency Account." *American Economic Review* 70 (December 1980): 960–71.

Dornbusch, R., and Paul Krugman. "Flexible Exchange Rates in the Short Run." *Brookings Papers on Economic Activity* 3 (1976): 537–75.

Driskill, Robert A. "Exchange Rate Dynamics, Portfolio Balance, and Relative Prices." *American Economic Review* 70 (September 1980): 776–83.

_____ . "Exchange Rate Dynamics: An Empirical Investigation." *Journal of Political Economy* 89 (April 1981): 357–71. (I)

_____ . "Exchange Rate Overshooting the Trade Balance and Rational Expectations." *Journal of International Economics* 11 (August 1981): 361–77.

Driskill, Robert, and Stephen McCafferty. "Exchange-Rate Variability, Real and Monetary Shocks, and the Degree of Capital Mobility under Rational Expectation." *Quarterly Journal of Economics* 94 (November 1980): 577–86.

Dunn, R. M. "Flexible Exchange Rates an Oligopoly Pricing: A Study of Canadian Markets." *Journal of Political Economy* 78 (January 1970): 146–51. (I)

Edwards, Sebastian. "Floating Exchange Rates in Less-Developed Countries: A Monetary Analysis of the Peruvian Experience, 1950–54." *Journal of Money, Credit, and Banking* 15 (February 1983): 73–81. (D)

_____ . "Floating Exchange Rates, Expectations and New Information." *Journal of Monetary Economics* 11 (May 1983): 321–36.

Fair, Ray C. "Estimated Output, Price, Interest Rates and Exchange Rate Linkages among Countries." *Journal of Political Economy* 90 (June 1982): 507–35. (I)

Flood, Robert P. "Explanations of Exchange-Rate Volatility and Other Empirical

Regularities in Some Popular Models of the Foreign Exchange Market." *Carnegie-Rochester Conference Series on Public Policy* 15 (Autumn 1981): 219–49.

Ford, R. P. "Exchange Rate and Trade Flow Equilibrium in a Stochastic Macro Model." *Canadian Journal of Economics* 15 (May 1982): 294–307.

Frankel, Jeffrey A. "On the Mark: A Theory of Floating Exchange Rates Based on Real Interest Differentials." *American Economic Review* 67 (September 1979): 610–22. (I)

———. "On the Mark: Reply." *American Economic Review* 71 (December 1981): 1075–82.

———. "On the Franc." *Annales de l'INSSEE* (July-December 1982): 185–221. (I)

———. "The Effect of Excessively Elastic Expectations on Exchange-Rate Volatility in the Dornbusch Overshooting Model." *Journal of International Money and Finance* (1983): 39–46.

Frenkel, Jacob A. "Inflation and the Formation of Expectations." *Journal of Monetary Economics* 1 (October 1975): 403–21.

———. "A Monetary Approach to the Exchange Rate: Doctrinal Aspects and Empirical Evidence." In *Flexible Exchange Rates and Stabilization Policy*, edited by Jan Herin, Assar Lindbeck, and Johan Myhrman, pp. 68–92. Boulder, Colo.: Westview Press, 1977.

———. "International Reserves: Pegged Exchange Rates and Managed Float." *Journal of Monetary Economics* 9 (1978): 111–40.

———. "The Demand for International Reserves under Pegged and Flexible Exchange Rate Regimes and Aspects of the Economics of Managed Float." In *The Functioning of Flexible Exchange Rates: Theory, Evidence and Theory Implications*, edited by D. Borgman and T. Saya. Cambridge, Mass.: Ballinger, 1980. (I & D)

———. "Flexible Exchange Rates, Prices, and the Role of 'News': Lessons from the 1970s." *Journal of Political Economy* 89 (August 1981): 665–705. (I)

Frenkel, Jacob A., and J. Aizenman. "Aspects of the Optimal Management of Exchange Rates." *Journal of International Economics* 13 (November 1982): 231–56.

Frenkel, Jacob A., and Michael L. Mussa. "Monetary and Fiscal Policies in an Open Economy." *American Economic Review* 71 (May 1981): 253–58.

Frenkel, Jacob A., and C. A. Rodriguez. "Exchange Rate Dynamics and the Overshooting Hypothesis." *International Monetary Fund Staff Papers* 29 (March 1982): 1–30.

Fry, Maxwell J. "A Monetary Approach to Afghanistan's Flexible Exchange Rate." *Journal of Money, Credit, and Banking* 8 (May 1976): 219–25. (D)

Genberg, Hans. "Effects of Central Bank Intervention in the Foreign Exchange Market." *International Monetary Fund Staff Papers* 28 (September 1981): 451–76.

Genberg, H., and H. Kierzkowski. "Short Run, Long Run and Dynamics of Adjustment Under Flexible Exchange Rates." Discussion paper, GIIS-Ford Foundation International Monetary Research Project. Geneva, June 1975.

Girton, Lance, and Dale W. Henderson. "Financial Capital Movements, and Central Bank Behavior in a Two-Country, Short-Run Portfolio Balance Model." *Journal of Monetary Economics* 2 (January 1976): 33–62.

Girton, Lance, and Don Roper. "The Evolution of Exchange Rate Policy." In *The Monetary Approach to International Adjustment*, edited by Bluford H. Putnam and D. Sykes Wilford. New York: Praeger, 1978.

Gutierrez-Camara, J. L., and H. J. Huss. "The Interaction between Floating Exchange Rates, Money, and Prices—An Empirical Analysis." *Weltwirtschaftliches Archiv* 119 (1983): 401–28. (I)

Hacche, G., and J. Townend. "Exchange Rates and Monetary Policy: Modelling Sterling's Effective Exchange Rate, 1972–80." *Oxford Economic Papers* 33 Supplement (July 1981): 201–47. (I)

Hakkio, Craig S. "Exchange Rate Determination and the Demand for Money." *Review of Economic Statistics* 64 (November 1982): 681–86.

Helpman, E., and A. Razin. "Dynamics of a Floating Exchange Rate Regime." *Journal of Political Economy* 90 (August 1982): 728–54.

Hodrick, Robert J. "An Empirical Analysis of the Monetary Approach to the Determination of the Exchange Rates." In *The Economics of Exchange Rates: Selected Studies*, edited by Jacob A. Frenkel and Harry G. Johnson (Reading, Mass.: Addison-Wesley, 1976, pp. 97–116.

Hoffman, D. L., and D. E. Schlagenhauf. "Rational Expectations in Monetary Models of Exchange Rate Determination: An Empirical Examination." *Journal of Monetary Economics* 11 (March 1983): 247–60. (I)

Hooper, Peter, and John Morton. "Fluctuations in the Dollar: A Model of Nominal and Real Exchange Rate Determination." *Journal of International Money and Finance* 1: 39–56.

Horne, J. "The Asset Market Model of the Balance of Payments and the Exchange Rate: A Survey of Empirical Evidence." *Journal of International Money and Finance* 2 (August 1983): 89–109.

Huang, R. D. "The Monetary Approach to the Exchange Rate in an Efficient Foreign Exchange Market: Tests Based on Volatility." *Journal of Finance* 36 (March 1981): 31–41.

Humphrey, Thomas, and Thomas Lawler. "Factors Determining Exchange Rates: A Simple Model and Empirical Tests." *Federal Reserve Bank of Richmond Economic Review* (May–June 1977): 10–15. Reprinted in *The Monetary Approach to International Adjustment*, edited by Bluford H. Putnam and D. Sykes Wilford. New York: Praeger, 1978. (See also Chapter 8, this volume.) (I)

Isard, Peter. "Factors Determining Exchange Rates: The Roles of Relative Price Levels, Balance of Payments, Interest Rates and Risk." *Federal Reserve Board International Finance Discussion Papers* 171 (December 1980).

Islam, S. "Devaluation, Stabilization Policies and the Developing Countries: A Macroeconomic Analysis." *Journal of Development Economics* 14 (January–February 1984): 37–60.

Johnson, Harry. "The Case for Flexible Exchange Rates." In *Further Essays in Monetary Economics*. London: Allen and Unwin, 1972, pp. 198–222.

Kapur, B. K. "Optimal Financial and Foreign-Exchange Liberalization of Less-Developed Economies." *Quarterly Journal of Economics* 98 (February 1983): 41–62.

Katz, E. "Money-Supply Turbulence and Exchange-Rate Turbulence: Some Empirical Results." *Journal of Macroeconomics* 4 (Fall 1982): 483–88.

Kawai, M. "Exchange-Rate Volatility, Balance-of-Payments Instability and Stabilizing-Destabilizing Capital Flows. *Weltwirtschaftliches Archiv* 118 (1982): 430–42.

Khan, W., and T. D. Willett. "The Monetary Approach to Exchange Rates: A Review of Recent Empirical Studies." *Kredit und Kapital* (1984): 199–222.

Kimbrough, Kent P. "Exchange-Rate Policy and Monetary Information. *Journal of International Money and Finance* 2 (December 1983): 333–46.

_____ . "Aggregate Information and the Role of Monetary Policy in an Open Economy." *Journal of Political Economy* 92 (April 1984): 268–85.

King, David. "Monetary Autonomy and Flexible Exchange Rates." Mimeographed. January 1977.

_____ . "Uncertainty, Flexible Exchange Rates and the Planning Horizon." In *The Monetary Approach to International Adjustment*, edited by Bluford H. Putnam and D. Sykes Wilford, New York: Praeger, 1978.

Korteweg, Peter. "Exchange-Rate Policy, Monetary Policy, and Real Exchange Rate Variability," Princeton University, *Essays on International Finance* no. 140 (December 1980): 1–28.

Kouri, P. J. K., and J. B. de Macedo. "Exchange Rates and the International Adjustment Process." *Brookings Papers on Economic Activity* 1 (1978): 111–50.

Krugman, P. R. "A Model of Balance-of-Payments Crises." *Journal of Money, Credit, and Banking* 11 (August 1979): 311–25.

Levin, J. H. "Devaluation, the J-Curve, and Flexible Exchange Rates." *Manchester School of Economics and Social Studies* 48 (December 1980): 355–77.

Levy, V. "Demand for International Reserves and Exchange-Rate Intervention Policy in an Adjustable-Peg Economy." *Journal of Monetary Economics* 11 (January 1983): 89–101.

Liviation, Nissan. "Monetary Expansion and Real Exchange Rate Dynamics." *Journal of Political Economy* 89 (December 1981): 1218–27.

Martin, J. P., and P. R. Masson. "Exchange Rates and Portfolio Balance." *National Bureau of Economic Research Working Papers* 377 (August 1979).

Mathieson, D. J. "The Impact of Monetary and Fiscal Policy under Flexible Exchange Rates and Alternative Expectations Structures." *International Monetary Fund Staff Papers* 24 (November 1977): 535–68.

McKinnon, Ronald I. "Exchange Rate Instability, Trade Imbalances, and Monetary Policies in Japan and the United States." In *Issues in International Economics*, edited by Peter Oppenheimer. Stocksfield, England: Oriell Press, 1980.

_____ . "The Out-of-Sample Failure of Empirical Exchange Rate Models: Sampling Error or Misspecification?" In *Exchange Rates and International*

Macroeconomics, edited by Jacob A. Frenkel. Chicago: University of Chicago Press, 1984.

Meade, James E. "The Case for Variable Exchange Rates." *Three Banks Review* 27 (September 1955): 3–27.

Meese, Richard A., and K. S. Rogoff. "Empirical Exchange Rate Models of the Seventies: Do They Fit out of Sample?" *Journal of International Economics* 14 (February 1983): 3–24. (I)

Mehta, S. R., and J. R. Moore. "An Analysis of the Balance of Trade of India: 1950–51 to 1976–77." *Indian Economic Journal* 29 (January–March 1982): 16–29. (D)

Mindford, P., M. Brech, and K. Matthews. "A Rational Expectations Model of the U.K. under Floating Exchange Rates." *European Economic Review* 14 (September 1980): 189–219.

Murphy, R. G., and C. Van Duyne. "Asset Market Approaches to Exchange Rate Determination: A Comparative Analysis." *Weltwirtschaftliches Archiv* 116 (1980): 627–56.

Mussa, Michael. "The Exchange Rate, the Balance of Payments, and Monetary and Fiscal Policy Under a Regime of Controlled Floating." *Scandinavian Journal of Economics* 78 (1976): 229–48.

———. "Empirical Regularities in the Behavior of Exchange Rates and Theories of the Foreign Exchange Market." In *Policies for Employment, Prices and Exchange Rates*, edited by Karl Brunner and Allen Meltzer. Carnegie-Rochester Conference Series on Public Policy, vol. 11. Amsterdam: North-Holland, 1979.

———. "A Model of Exchange Rate Dynamics." *Journal of Political Economy* 90 (February 1982): 74–104.

———. "Theories of Exchange Rate Determination." In *Exchange Rate Theory and Practice*, edited by John F. O. Bilson and Richard C. Marston. Chicago: University of Chicago Press, 1984.

Mussa, Michael, and Jacob A. Frenkel. "Asset Markets, Exchange Rates and the Balance of Payments." *National Bureau of Economic Research Working Papers* 1287, March 1984.

Nickelsburg, G. "Dynamic Exchange Rate Equilibria with Uncertain Government Policy." *Review of Economic Studies* 51 (July 1984): 509–19.

Niehans, Jürg. "Exchange Rate Dynamics with Stock/Flow Interaction." *Journal of Political Economy* 85 (December 1977): 1245–58.

Obstfeld, M. "Intermediate Imports, the Terms of Trade, and the Dynamics of the Exchange Rate and Current Account." *Journal of International Economics* 10 (November 1980): 461–80.

———. "Macroeconomic Policy, Exchange-Rate Dynamics, and Optimal Asset Accumulation." *Journal of Political Economy* 89 (December 1981): 1142–61.

———. "Relative Prices, Employment, and the Exchange Rate in an Economy with Foresight." *Econometrica* 50 (September 1982): 1219–42.

Putnam, Bluford H. "Monetary Policy, Interest Rate Targets, and Foreign Exchange Markets." In *The Monetary Approach to International Adjustment*, edited by Bluford H. Putnam and D. Sykes Wilford. New York: Praeger, 1978. (See also Chapter 10, this volume.)

Putnam, Bluford H., and John J. Van Belle. "A Monetary Approach to Afghanistan's Flexible Exchange Rate: A Comment." *Journal of Money, Credit, and Banking* 10 (February 1978): 117–18. (D)

Putnam, Bluford H., and John Woodbury. "Exchange Rate Stability and Monetary Policy: A Case Study." Federal Reserve Bank of New York Research Paper no. 7718 (1976). (I)

———. "Exchange Rates Stability and Monetary Policy." *Review of Business and Economic Research* 15 (Winter 1980): 1–10.

Rasulo, J. A., and D. Sykes Wilford. "Estimating Monetary Models of the Balance of Payments and Exchange Rates: A Bias." *Southern Economic Journal* 47 (July 1980): 136–46. (I & D)

Rodriguez, Carlos A. "Short and Long-Run Effects of Monetary and Fiscal Policies under Flexible Exchange Rates and Perfect Capital Mobility." *American Economic Review* 69 (March 1979): 176–82.

———. "The Role of Trade Flows in Exchange Rate Determination: A Rational Expectations Approach." *Journal of Political Economy* 88 (December 1980): 1148–58.

———. "Managed Float: An Evaluation of Alternative Rules in the Presence of Speculative Capital Flows." *American Economic Review* 71 (March 1981): 256–60.

Sachs, Jeffrey D. "Wages, Flexible Exchange Rates, and Macroeconomic Policy." *Quarterly Journal of Economics* 94 (June 1980): 731–47.

Saidi, N. H. "Fluctuating Exchange Rates and the International Transmission of Economic Disturbances." *Journal of Money, Credit, and Banking* 12 (November 1980): 575–91.

Sargen, Nicholas. "An Empirical Analysis of a Monetary Model of Exchange Rate and Reserve Fluctuations." Mimeographed. November 1975. (I)

———. "Exchange Rate Stability and Demand for Money." Paper presented at the meeting of the American Finance Association, September 1976, Atlantic City, N.J. (I)

Stockman, Alan C. "Exchange Rates, Relative Prices, and Resource Allocation." In *The International Transmission of Economic Disturbances under Flexible Exchange Rates*, edited by J. Bhandari and B. Putnam. Cambridge, Mass.: MIT Press, 1981.

Takayama, Akira, and Y. N. Shieh. "Flexible Exchange Rates Under Currency Substitution and Rational Expectations—Two Approaches to the Balance of Payments." Texas A&M University, manuscript, 1980.

Tullio, G. "The Fluctuations of the Price of Italian Banknotes in Zurich: An Econometric Analysis (February 1973–December 1975)." *Kyklos* 31 (1978): 462–74. (I)

Turnovsky, S. J. "The Effects of Devaluation and Foreign Price Disturbances under Rational Expectations." *Journal of International Economics* 11 (February 1981): 33–60.

———. "The Asset Market Approach to Exchange Rate Determination: Some Short-Run, Stability, and Steady-State Properties." *Journal of Macroeconomics* 3 (Winter 1981): 1–32.

Turnovsky, S. J., and J. S. Bhandari. "The Degree of Capital Mobility and the Stability of an Open Economy under Rational Expectations." *Journal of Money, Credit, and Banking* 14 (August 1982): 303–26.

Vander Kraats, R. H., and L. D. Booth. "Empirical Tests of the Monetary Approach to Exchange Rate Determination." *Journal of International Money and Finance* 2 (December 1983): 255–78. (I)

Vaubel, Roland. "International Shifts in the Demand for Money, Their Effects on Exchange Rates and Price Levels, and Their Implications for the Preannouncement of Monetary Expansion." 116 *Weltwirtschaftliches Archiv* 2 (1981): 1–44. (I)

Wallace, M. S. "The Monetary Approach to Flexible Exchange Rates in the Short

Run: An Empirical Test." *Review of Business and Economic Research* 14 (Fall 1978): 98–102.

Weber, Warren L. "Output Variability under Monetary Policy and Exchange Rate Rules." *Journal of Political Economy* 89 (August 1981): 733–51.

Whitman, M. W. N. "Assessing Greater Variability of Exchange Rates: A Private Sector Perspective." *American Economic Review* 74 (May 1984): 298–304.

Wilson, C. A. "Anticipated Shocks and Exchange Rate Dynamics." *Journal of Political Economy* 87 (June 1979): 639–47.

Portfolio Substitution

Bilson, John F. O. "The Monetary Approach to the Exchange Rate: Some Empirical Evidence." *International Monetary Fund Staff Papers* 25 (March 1978): 48–75. (I)

Bordo, M. D., and E. U. Choudhri. "Currency Substitution and the Demand for Money: Some Evidence for Canada." *Journal of Money, Credit, and Banking* 14 (February 1982): 48–57. (I)

Boyer, R. "Nickels and Dimes." Federal Reserve Board of Governors, Mimeographed, 1972.

———. "Substitutability Between Currencies and Between Bonds: A Theoretical Analysis of Gresham's Law." Mimeographed. University of Western Ontario, 1973.

———. "Currency Mobility and Balance of Payments Adjustment." In *The Monetary Approach to International Adjustment*, edited by Bluford H. Putnam and D. Sykes Wilford. New York: Praeger, 1978. (See also Chapter 12, this volume.)

Brillembourg, Arturo T., and Susan Schadler. "A Model of Currency Substitution in Exchange-Rate Determination, 1973–78." *International Monetary Fund Staff Papers* 26 (September 1979): 513–42.

Brittain, Bruce. "International Currency Substitution and the Apparent Instability of Velocity in Some Western European Economies and in the United States." *Journal of Money, Credit, and Banking* 13 (May 1981): 135–55. (I)

Bronfenbrenner, Martin. "The Currency-Choice Defense." *Challenge* 22 (January/February 1980): 31–36.

Calvo, Guillermo, and Alfredo Rodriguez. "A Model of Exchange Rate Determination Under Currency Substitution and Rational Expectations." *Journal of Political Economy* 85 (May-June 1977): 617–25.

Chen, C. N. "Diversified Currency Holdings and Flexible Exchange Rates." *Quarterly Journal of Economics* 87 (February 1973): 96–111.

Chen, C. N., and T. Tsaur. "Currency Substitution and Foreign Inflation." *Quarterly Journal of Economics* 98 (February 1983): 177–84.

Chetty, V. K. "On Measuring the Nearness of Near-Moneys." *American Economic Review* 59 (June 1969): 270–81.

Chrystal, K. A., N. D. Wilson, and P. Quinn. "Demand for International Money, 1962–1977." *European Economic Review* 21 (May 1983): 287–98.(I)

Chung, J.W. "Substitutability between Currencies: The Dollar versus the Mark and the Yen." *Quarterly Review of Economics and Business* 23 (Autumn 1983): 19–28. (I)

Cox, W. Michael. "The Impact of Substitute Currencies on International Monetary and Exchange Market Equilibrium." Mimeographed. Virginia Polytechnic Institute, 1976.

Cuddington, J. T. "Currency Substitution, Capital Mobility and Money Demand. *Journal of International Money and Finance* 2 (August 1983): 111–33. (I)

Evans, Paul, and Arthur Laffer. "Demand Substitutability Across Currencies." Mimeographed. University of Southern California, 1977.

Frankel, Jeffrey A. 1982. "A Test of Perfect Substitutability in the Foreign Exchange Market." *Southern Economic Journal* 49 (October 1982): 406–16. (I)

Girton, Lance, and Don Roper. "Theory and Implications of Currency Substitution." *International Finance Discussion Papers* no. 86. Federal Reserve Board, 1976. (See also Chapter 13, this volume.)

Hayek, F. A. *Denationalization of Money*. London: Institute of Economic Affairs, 1976.

Kareken, John, and Neil Wallace. "Samuelson's Consumption-Loan Model with Country-Specific Flat Monies." *Staff Report* no. 24. Federal Reserve Bank of Minneapolis. July 1978.

———. "International Monetary Reform: The Feasible Alternatives." *Quarterly Review*, Federal Reserve Bank of Minneapolis. Summer 1978.

King, David T., B. H. Putnam, and D. S. Wilford. "A Currency Portfolio Approach to Exchange Rate Determination: Exchange Rate Stability and Monetary Independence." In *The Monetary Approach to International Adjustment*, edited by Bluford H. Putnam and D. Sykes Wilford. New York: Praeger, 1978. (See also Chapter 11, this volume.)

Klein, Benjamin. "Competing Monies: A Comment." *Journal of Money, Credit, and Banking* 8 (November 1976): 513–19.

Laffer, A. "Optimal Exchange Rates." Paper Presented at the American Economic Association Meeting, September 1976. Atlantic City, N.J.

Laffer, Arthur B., and Marc A. Miles. "Factors Influencing Changes in the Money Supply Over the Short Term," Economic Study, H. C. Wainwright, Economics. August 18, 1977.

Laney, Leroy O. "Currency Substitution: The Mexican Case." Federal Reserve Bank of Dallas *Voice*. January 1981.

Lapan, H. E., and W. Enders. "Devaluation, Wealth Effects, and Relative Prices." *American Economic Review* 68 (September 1978): 601–13.

_____. "Rational Expectations, Endogenous Currency Substitution, and Exchange Rate Determination." *Quarterly Journal of Economics* 98 (August 1983): 427–39.

Lee, C. J. "Capital Movements, Growth, and Balance of Payments." *Journal of Macroeconomics* 4 (Fall 1982): 433–47.

Marston, Richard. "Cross Country Effects of Sterilization, Reserve Currencies, and Foreign Exchange Intervention." *Journal of International Economics* 10 (February 1980): 63–78.

McKinnon, Ronald I. "Currency Substitution and Instability in the World Dollar Standard." *American Economic Review* 72 (June 1982): 329–33. (See also Chapter 15, this volume.)

Miles, Marc A. "Currency Substitution—The Case of the United States." Mimeographed. Rutgers University, 1978.

_____. "Currency Substitution: Perspective, Implications, and Empirical Evidence." In *The Monetary Approach to International Adjustment*, edited by Bluford H. Putnam and D. Sykes Wilford. New York: Praeger, 1978.

_____. "Currency Substitution: Some Further Results and Conclusions." *Southern Economic Journal* 48 (July 1981): 78–86. (I)

_____ . "Currency Substitution, Flexible Exchange Rates, and Monetary Independence." *American Economic Review* 68 (June 1978): 428–36. (See also Chapter 14, this volume.) (I)

Miles, Marc A., and Marion B. Stewart. "The Effects of Risk and Return on the Currency Composition of Money Demand." *Weltwirtschaftliches Archiv* 16 (December 1980): 613–26.

Ortiz, Guillermo. "Currency Substitution in Mexico: The Dollarization Problem." *Journal of Money, Credit, and Banking* 15 (May 1983): 174–85. (D)

Putnam, Bluford H., and D. Sykes Wilford. "How Diversification Makes the Dollar Weaker." *Euromoney* (October 1978): 201–4.

_____ . "Exchange Rate Determination with Currency Substitution." *Business Economics* 15 (May 1980): 16–19.

Rubli-Kaiser, F. "Currency Substitution: A Case for a Counterintuitive Result." *Atlantic Economic Journal* 11 (March 1983): 116.

Sakakibara, E. "Purchasing Power Parity and Currency Substitution." *Economic Studies Quarterly* 30 (December 1979): 202–18.

Spinelli, F. "Currency Substitution, Flexible Exchange Rates, and the Case for International Monetary Cooperation: Discussion of a Recent Proposal." *International Monetary Fund Staff Papers* 30 (December 1983): 755–83.

Tanzi, V., and Mario I. Blejer. "Inflation, Interest Rate Policy, and Currency Substitutions in Developing Economies: A Discussion of Some Major Issues." *World Development* 10 (September 1982): 781–89.

Tullock, Gordon. "Competing Monies." *Journal of Money, Credit, and Banking* 7 (November 1975): 491–97.

_____ . "Competing Monies: A Reply." *Journal of Money, Credit, and Banking* 8 (November 1976): 520–25.

Wilford, D. Sykes. "Exchange Rates with Substitutable Currencies." See Chapter 16, this volume.

Wilford, D. Sykes, and W. Dayle Nattress. "Economic Integration of North America: Monetary and Financial Integration in North America." *Law and Contemporary Problems* 44 (Summer 1981): 55–79.

BACKGROUND REFERENCES

Historical

Alexander, Sidney. "Effects of a Devaluation: A Simplified Synthesis of Elasticities and Absorption Approaches," *American Economic Review* 49 (March 1959): 22–42.

Aliber, Robert Z. "Floating Exchange Rates: The Twenties and the Seventies." In *Flexible Exchange Rates and the Balance of Payments*, edited by John S. Chipman and Charles P. Kindleberger. Amsterdam: North Holland, 1980.

Angell, James W. *The Theory of International Prices.* New York: Augustus M. Kelley, 1965.

Bernholz, Peter. "Flexible Exchange Rates and Exchange Rate Theory in Historical Perspective." Unpublished. March 1981.

Blaug, Mark. *Economic Theory in Retrospect.* Homewood, Ill.: R. D. Irwin, 1968.

Bloomfield, Arthur I. "Adam Smith and the Theory of International Trade." In *Essays on Adam Smith*, edited by Andrew Skinner and Thomas Wilson. Oxford: Clarendon Press, 1975.

Cagan, Phillip. "Determinants and Effects of Changes in the Money Stock, 1875–1960," New York: *National Bureau of Economic Research*, 1985. (I)

Cannan, Edwin, ed. *The Paper Pound of 1797–1821: The Bullion Report.* New York: Augustus M. Kelley, 1969.

Cassel, Gustav. *Money and Foreign Exchange After 1914.* New York: Macmillan, 1922.

———. *The Theory of Social Economy.* New York: Augustus M. Kelley, 1967.

Clements, K. W., and J. A. Frenkel. "Exchange Rates, Money, and Relative Prices: The Dollar-Pound in the 1920s." *Journal of International Economics* 10 (May 1980): 249–62. (I)

Daugherty, Marion R. "The Currency-Banking Controversy: Part I." *Southern Economic Journal* 9 (October 1942): 140–55.

———. "The Currency-Banking Controversy: Part II." *Southern Economic Journal* 9 (January 1943): 241–51.

DeJong, F. J. *Development of Monetary Theory in the Netherlands.* Rotterdam: Rotterdam University Press, 1973.

Eagley, Robert W. "The Swedish and English Bullionist Controversies." In *Events, Ideology, and Economic Theory*, edited by Robert V. Eagly, pp. 13–31. Detroit: Wayne State University Press, 1968.

———. "Adam Smith and the Specie-Flow Doctrine." *Scottish Journal of Political Economy* 17 (February 1970): 61–68.

———. *The Swedish Bullionist Controversy*. Philadelphia: American Philosophical Society, 1971.

Einzig, P. *The History of Foreign Exchange*. London: Macmillan, 1962.

Ellis, Howard S. *German Monetary Theory*, 1905–1933. Cambridge, Mass.: Harvard University Press, 1937.

Fetter, Frank W. *Development of British Monetary Orthodoxy 1797–1875*. Cambridge, Mass.: Harvard University Press, 1965.

Fetter, Frank W., and Derek Gregory. *Monetary and Financial Policy*. London: Irish University Press, 1973.

Fisher, Irving. *The Purchasing Power of Money*. New York: Macmillan, 1911.

Frenkel, Jacob A. "The Forward Exchange Rate, Expectations, and the Demand for Money: The German Hyperinflation." *American Economic Review* 67 (September 1977): 653–70. (I)

———. "Exchange Rates, Prices, and Money: Lessons from the 1920s." *American Economic Review* 70 (May 1980): 235–42. (I)

Friedman, Milton. "The Case for Flexible Exchange Rates." In *Essays in Positive Economics*, edited by M. Friedman. Chicago: University of Chicago Press, 1953.

Friedman, Milton, and A. Schwartz. *A Monetary History of the United States 1867–1960*. National Bureau of Economic Research. Princeton: Princeton University Press, 1963.

Girton, Lance, and Don Roper. "J. Laurence Laughlin and the Quantity Theory of Money." *Journal of Political Economy* 86 (August 1978).

Gregory, T. E. "Introduction" in *A History of Prices*, Thomas Tooke, vol. 1. New York: Adelphi, 1928.

Haberler, Gottfried. *The Theory of International Trade*. London: Hodge, 1937.

———. *A Survey of International Trade Theory*, rev. ed., Special Papers on

International Economics no. 1. International Finance Section, Princeton University, 1961.

Henneberry, Barbara, and James G. Witte. "Variable Gold Parities from a Classical Viewpoint: Hume Versus the Monetarists." Mimeographed. Indiana University, November 1974.

Hollander, Jacob. "The Development of the Theory of Money from Adam Smith to David Ricardo." *Quarterly Journal of Economics* 25 (May 1911): 429–70.

Hume, David. "Of the Balance of Trade." In *Essays, Moral, Political, and Literary* (1752), essay V, part II, reprinted in *International Trade Theory: Hume to Ohlin*, edited by W. R. Allen. New York: Random House, 1965.

————. *Writings on Economics*. Edited with an introduction by Eugene Rotwein, 1955. Reprint. Freeport, N.Y.: Books for Libraries Press, 1972.

Humphrey, Thomas M. "The Monetary Approach to Exchange Rates: Its Historical Evolution and Role in Policy Debates." (See Chapter 9, this volume.)

Jevons, W. Stanley. *The Theory of Political Economy*, 4th ed. London: Macmillan, 1924.

Keynes, John Maynard. "Theory of Money and the Exchanges." In J. M. Keynes, *Monetary Reform*. London: Macmillan, 1924.

————. *A Treatise on Money: The Pure Theory of Money*. London: Macmillan, 1930.

————. *The General Theory of Employment, Interest and Money*. New York: Harcourt, Brace, 1936.

Laughlin, J. Laurence. *The Principles of Money*. New York: Scribner's, 1903.

Letiche, J. M. "Isaac Gervaise on the International Mechanism of Adjustment." *Journal of Political Economy* 60 (February 1952): 34–43.

McKinnon, Ronald I. "The Exchange Rate and Macroeconomic Policy: Changing Postwar Perceptions." *Journal of Economic Literature* 19 (June 1981): 531–57.

Mill, John Stuart. *Principles of Political Economy*. London: Longmans, Green, 1926.

Myhrman, Johan. "Experiences of Flexible Exchange Rates in Earlier Periods: Theories, Evidence, and a New View." In *Flexible Exchange Rates and*

Stabilization Policy, edited by Jan Herin, Assar Lindbeck, and Johan Myhrman, 37–64. Boulder: Colo.: Westview Press, 1977.

O'Brien, D. P. *The Classical Economists*, Oxford: Clarendon Press, 1975.

Ohlin, B. *Interregional and International Trade*, rev. ed., 1933. Cambridge, Mass.: Harvard University Press, 1967.

Pesek, Boris P., and Thomas R. Saving. *Money, Wealth and Economic Theory*. New York: Macmillan, 1967.

Petrella, Frank. "Adam Smith's Rejection of Hume's Price-Specie-Flow Mechanism: A Minor Mystery Resolved." *Southern Economic Journal* 34 (January 1968): 365–74.

Pigou, A. C. "Some Problems of Foreign Exchanges." *Economic Journal* 30 (1920): 460–72.

_____. *Industrial Fluctuations*, 2nd ed. New York: Augustus M. Kelley, 1967.

Protopapadakis, A. "Expectations, Exchange Rates and Monetary Theory: The Case of the German Hyperinflation. *Journal of International Money and Finance* 2 (April 1983): 47–65.

Ricardo, David. *The Works and Correspondence*. Edited by Piero Sraffa. London: Cambridge University Press, 1951.

Robbins, Lionel. *Robert Torrens and the Evolution of Classical Economics*. London: Macmillan, 1958.

Robertson, Dennis H. *Money*. London: Cambridge University Press, 1922.

Rowe, J. W. F. "An Index of Industrial Production." *Economic Journal* 37 (June 1927): 173–87.

St. Clair, Oswald. *A Key to Ricardo*. New York: Kelley and Millman, 1957.

Salter, W. E. "Internal and External Balances: The Role of Price and Expenditure Effects." *The Economic Record* 35 (1952).

Sayers, R. S. "Ricardo's Views on Monetary Questions." *Quarterly Journal of Economics* 67 (February 1953): 30–49.

SeKine, Thomas T. "The Discovery of International Monetary Equilibrium by Vanderlint, Cantillon, Gervaise, and Hume." *Economica Internazionale* 26 (March 1973): 262–82.

Smith, Adam. *An Inquiry into the Nature and Causes of the Wealth of Nations.* Edited by Edwin Cannon. New York: Random House, 1937.

———. *Lectures on Justice, Police, Revenue and Arms.* New York: Kelley and Millman, 1956.

Staley, Charles E. "Hume and Viner on the International Adjustment Mechanism." *History of Political Economy* 8 (Summer 1976): 252–65.

Thornton, Henry. *An Enquiry into the Nature and Effects of the Paper Credit of Great Britain.* New York: Augustus M. Kelley, 1962.

Tooke, Thomas. *A History of Prices,* vol. 4. New York: Adelphi, 1928.

Tullock, Gordon. "Paper Money—A Cycle in Cathay." *Economic History Review* 9 (June 1956): 393–407.

Twain, Mark. *A Connecticut Yankee in King Arthur's Court.* New York: Harper, 1889.

Van Cleveland, Harold, and Bruce Brittain. "The Great Inflation: A Monetarist View." Washington, D.C.: National Planning Association, 1976.

Vickers, Douglas. "Adam Smith and the Status of Theory of Money." In *Essays on Adam Smith,* edited by Andrew Skinner and Thomas Wilson. Oxford: Clarendon Press, 1975.

Viner, Jacob. *Canada's Balance of International Indebtedness 1900–1913.* Cambridge, Mass.: Harvard University Press, 1924.

———. *Studies in the Theory of International Trade.* New York: Augustus M. Kelley, 1965.

Wicksell, Knut. "International Freights and Prices." *Quarterly Journal of Economics* 32 (February 1918): 404–10.

———. *Interest and Prices.* New York: Augustus M. Kelley, 1965.

———. *Lectures on Political Economy.* Vol. 2, *Money.* New York: Augustus M. Kelley, 1971.

Purchasing-Power Parity

Adler, Michael, and Bruce Lehmann. "Deviations from Purchasing Power Parity in the Long Run." *Journal of Finance* 38 (December 1983): 1471–87.

Balassa, Bela. "The Purchasing Power Parity Doctrine: A Reappraisal." *Journal of Political Economy* 72 (December 1964): 584–96.

Barrett, R. N. "Purchasing Power Parity and the Equilibrium Exchange Rate: A Note." *Journal of Money, Credit, and Banking* 13 (May 1981): 227–33.

Blejer, Mario I., and A. L. Hillman. "A Proposition on Short-Run Departures from the Law-of-One-Price: Unanticipated Inflation, Relative-Price Dispersion, and Commodity Arbitrage." *European Economic Review* 17 (January 1982): 51–60.

Bunting, F. H. "Purchasing Power Parity Theory Reexamined." *Southern Economic Journal* 5 (January 1939): 282–301.

Cassel, Gustav. "The Present Situation of the Foreign Exchanges." *Economic Journal* 26 (March 1916): 62–65.

_____. "Comment." *Economic Journal* 30 (March 1920): 44–45.

_____. *The World's Monetary Problems.* London: Constable, 1921.

_____. *Money and Foreign Exchange after 1919.* London: Macmillan, 1930.

Citibank. "Purchasing Power: A Polestar for Drifting Exchange Rates." *Monthly Letter* (November 1973).

Dornbusch, Rudiger. "PPP Exchange-Rate Rules and Macroeconomic Stability." *Journal of Political Economy* 90 (February 1982): 158–65.

Frenkel, Jacob A. "The Collapse of Purchasing Power Parities during the 1970's." *European Economic Review* 16 (May 1981): 145–65. (I)

Genberg, Hans. *World Inflation and the Small Open Economy.* Geneva: Graduate Institute for International Studies, 1975.

_____. "Purchasing Power Parity under Fixed and Flexible Exchange Rates." *Journal of International Economics* 8 (May 1978): 247–76. (I)

Haberler, G. *The Theory of International Trade.* London: Hodge, 1950.

Hakkio, Craig S. "A Reexamination of Purchasing Power Parity: A Multi-Country and Multi-Period Study." *National Bureau of Economic Research Working Paper* 865 (March 1982). (I)

Isard, Peter. "How Far Can We Push the 'Law of One Price'?" *American Economic Review* 67 (December 1977): 942–48.

Jones, Ronald W., and Douglas D. Purvis. "International Differences in Response to Common External Shocks: The Role of Purchasing Power Parity." In *Recent Issues in the Theory of Flexible Exchange Rates*, edited by Emil Claassen and Pascal Salin. Amsterdam: North-Holland, 1983.

Katseli-Papaefstration, L. T. "The Reemergence of the Purchasing Power Parity Doctrine in the 1970s," Princeton University, International Finance Section, 1979.

Keynes, J. M. *A Tract on Monetary Reform*. London: Macmillan, 1923.

King, David T. "Purchasing Power Parity and Exchange Rate Flexibility: 1973–1975." *Southern Economic Journal* 43 (April 1977): 1582–87.

Krugman, P. R. "Purchasing Power Parity and Exchange Rates: Another Look at the Evidence." *Journal of International Economics* 8 (August 1978): 397–407. (I)

Lebon, Jules. "The Real and Nominal Effects of Devaluation: The Relative Price Effects on Exchange Rate Changes." Mimeographed. 1976.

Lee, Moon. *Purchasing Power Parity*. New York: Marcel Dekker, 1976.

Magee, Stephen P. "Contracting and Spurious Deviations from Purchasing Power Parity." In *The Economics of Exchange Rates—Selected Studies*, edited by J. Frenkel and H. G. Johnson. Reading, Mass.: Addison-Wesley, 1978.

———. "A Two-Parameter Purchasing-Power-Parity Measure of Arbitrage in International Goods Markets." In *Trade and Payments Adjustments under Flexible Exchange Rates*, edited by John P. Martin, and Alastair Smith. London: Macmillan, 1979.

McCloskey, Donald M., and J. Richard Zecher. "The Success of Purchasing Power Parity: Historical Evidence and Its Implications for Macroeconomics." In *A Retrospective on the Classical Gold Standard, 1821–1931*, edited by Michael Bordo and Anna Schwartz. Chicago: University of Chicago Press, 1984. (I)

Nattress, W. Dayle, and J. Richard Zecher. "The Theory of the Arbitrageur and Purchasing Power Parity." June 1983.

Niehans, J. "Static Deviations from Purchasing Power Parity." *Journal of Monetary Economics* 7 (January, 1981): 57–68.

Officer, Lawrence H. "The Purchasing Power Parity Theory of Exchange Rates: A Review Article." *International Monetary Fund Staff Papers* (March 1976): 1–60.

_____. "The Relationship between Absolute and Relative Purchasing Power Parity." *Review of Economics and Statistics* 60 (November 1978): 562–68.

_____. "Effective Exchange Rates and Price Ratios over the Long Run: A Test of the Purchasing-Power-Parity Theory." *Canadian Journal of Economics* 13 (May 1980): 206–30. (I)

Richardson, J. D. "Some Empirical Evidence on Commodity Arbitrage and the Law of One Price." Mimeographed. 1977.

Robinson, W., T. R. Webb, and M. A. Townsend. "The Influence of Exchange Rate Changes on Prices: Study of 18 Industrial Countries." *Economica* 46 (February 1979): 27–50. (I)

Roll, Richard. "Violations of Purchasing Power Parity and Their Implications for Efficient International Commodity Markets." In *International Finance and Trade*, Vol. 1, edited by Marshall Sarnat and Giorgio Szego. Cambridge, Mass.: Ballinger, 1979.

Roll, R., and B. Solnik. "On Some Parity Conditions Encountered Frequently in International Economics." *Journal of Macroeconomics* 1 (Summer 1979): 267–83.

Shapiro, Alan. "What Does Purchasing Power Parity Mean?" *Journal of International Money and Finance* (Spring 1983): 295–318.

Thomas, L. B. "Behavior of Flexible Exchange Rates: Additional Tests from the Post-World War I Episode." *Southern Economic Journal* 15 (October 1973): 167–82.

Whitt, Joseph A. "Purchasing-Power Parity and Relative Prices in a Monetary Framework: An Empirical Study." Ph.D. dissertation, University of Chicago (March 1981). (I)

Wilford, D. S. "Price Levels, Interest Rates, Open Economies and a Fixed Exchange Rate: The Mexican Case, 1954–74." *Review of Business and Economic Research* 12 (Spring 1977): 52–65.

Yeager, Leland. "A Rehabilitation of Purchasing-Power Parity." *Journal of Political Economy* 66 (December 1958): 516–30.

General Studies

Aghevli, Bijan B. "Experiences of Asian Countries with Various Exchange Rate Policies." In *Exchange Rate Rules: The Theory, Performance and Prospects of the Crawling Peg*, edited by John Williamson. New York: 1981, pp. 298–319. (D)

Akhtar, M. A. "Demand Functions for High-Powered Money in the United States." Mimeographed. Federal Reserve Bank of New York, 1977.

Akhtar, M. A., and R. Spence Hilton. "Effects of Exchange Rate Uncertainty on U.S. and German Trade," *Federal Reserve Bank of New York Quarterly Review* 9 (Spring 1984): 7–16. (I)

Alexander, Sidney S. "Effects of a Devaluation on a Trade Balance." *International Monetary Fund Staff Papers* (April 1952): 263–78.

————. "Effects of a Devaluation: A Simplified Synthesis of Elasticities and Absorption Approaches." *American Economic Review* (March 1959): 22–42.

Aliber, R. "Speculation in the Foreign Exchanges: The European Experience, 1919–1926." *Yale Economic Essays*, 1952.

————. "The Firm Under Fixed and Flexible Exchange Rates." In *Flexible Exchange Rates and Stabilization Policy*, edited by Jan Herin, Assar Lindbeck, and Johan Myhrman, pp. 177–90. Boulder, Colo.: Westview Press, 1977.

Anderson, L., and Jerry Jordan. "The Monetary Base—Explanation and Analytical Use." Federal Reserve Bank of St. Louis *Review* 50, 8 (August 1968): 7–11.

Argy, V. "Monetarist Models of Open Economies." *Economies et Sociétés* 12 (October–December 1978): 1707–40.

Artus, Jacques R. "Toward a More Orderly Exchange Rate System." *Finance and Development* (March 1983): 10–13.

Artus, Jacques R., and John H. Young. "Fixed and Flexible Exchange Rates: A Renewal of the Debate." *International Monetary Fund Staff Papers* 5 (December 1979): 654–98.

Aschauer, D., and J. Greenwood. "A Further Exploration in the Theory of Exchange Rate Regimes." *Journal of Political Economy* 91 (October 1983): 868–75.

Auernheimer, Leonardo. "The Honest Government's Guide to the Revenue from the Creation of Money." *Journal of Political Economy* 82 (May/June 1974): 598–606.

Balbach, Anatol. "The Mechanics of Intervention in Exchange Markets." *Federal Reserve Bank of St. Louis Review* 60 (February 1978): 2–7.

Barro, R. J. "Rational Expectations and the Role of Monetary Policy." *Journal of Monetary Economics* 2 (January 1976): 1–32.

Barro, R. J., and Stanley Fischer. "Recent Developments in Monetary Theory." *Journal of Monetary Economics* 2 (April 1976): 133–68.

Basevi, G. "A Model for the Analysis of Official Intervention in the Foreign Exchange Markets." In *International Trade and Money*, edited by A. Swoboda and M. Connolly, pp. 107–26. London: Allen and Unwin, 1972.

Bilson, John F. O., and A. W. Hooke. "Conference on Exchange Rate Regimes and Policy Interdependence: Overview." *International Monetary Fund Staff Papers* 30 (March 1983): 185–207.

Black, S. "International Money Markets and Flexible Exchange Rates." *Princeton Studies in International Finance* no. 32, 1973.

Boorman, John T. "The Evidence on the Demand for Money: Theoretical Formulations and Empirical Results." In *Current Issues in Monetary Theory and Policy*, edited by Thomas M. Havrilesky and John T. Boorman. Arlington Heights, Ill.: AHM Publishing, 1976.

Bordo, M., and E. Choudri. "The Behavior of the Prices of Traded and Non-Traded Goods: The Canadian Case 1962–74." Mimeographed. 1977.

Boughton, J. M. "Stable Monetary Growth and Exchange Rates as Policy Targets." *International Monetary Fund Staff Papers* 29 (December 1982): 495–526.

Boyer, R. S. "Optimal Foreign Exchange Market Intervention." *Journal of Political Economy* 86 (December 1978): 1045–55.

Braga, J. C. "Real and Monetary Approaches to Foreign Trade Adjustment Mechanisms in Centrally Planned Economies: A Reconciliation." *European Economic Review* 19 (October 1982): 229–44.

Branson, W. "Stocks and Flows in International Monetary Analysis." *International Aspects of Stabiliation Policies, Federal Reserve Bank of Boston*, Conference Series no. 12, 1974.

Branson, W. H., and Dale W. Henderson, "The Specification and Influence of Asset Markets." *National Bureau of Economic Research Working Paper* 1283 (March 1984).

Brunner, Karl, and A. H. Meltzer. "Predicting Velocity: Implications for Theory and Policy." *Journal of Finance* 18 (May 1963): 319–54.

———. "Some Further Investigations of Demand and Supply Functions of Money." *Journal of Finance* 19 (May 1964): 240–83.

———. "Comment on the Long Run and Short Run Demand for Money." *Journal of Political Economy* 76 (November 1969): 1234–40.

———. "The 'Monetarist Revolution' in Monetary Theory." *Weltwirtschaftliches Archiv* 105 (1970): 1–30.

———. "Money Supply in Process and Monetary Policy in an Open Economy." In *International Trade and Money*, edited by M. B. Connolly and A. K. Swoboda. London: Allen and Unwin, 1973.

———. "A Fisherian Framework for the Analysis of International Monetary Problems." In *Inflation in the World Economy*, edited by Michael Parkin and George Zis. Toronto, Canada: University of Toronto Press, 1976.

Buiter, W. H., and M. Miller. "Real Exchange Rate Overshooting and the Output Cost of Bringing down Inflation." *European Economic Review* 18 (May/June 1982): 85–123.

Cagan, P. "The Monetary Dynamics of Hyperinflation." In *Studies in the Quantity Theory of Money*, edited by M. Friedman. Chicago: University of Chicago Press, 1956.

Cagan, Phillip, and Arthur Gandolphi. "The Lag in Monetary Policy as Implied by the Time Pattern of Monetary Effects on Interest Rates." *American Economic Review, Papers and Proceedings* 59 (May 1969): 277–84.

Campos, Roberto de Oliviera. "Economic Development and Inflation with Special Reference to Latin America." In *Development Plans and Programmes*, 129–37. Paris: Organization for Economic Cooperation and Development (OECD) Development Center, 1964.

Cassese, A., and J. R. Lothian. "The Timing of Monetary and Price Changes and the International Transmission of Inflation." *Journal of Monetary Economics* 10 (July 1982): 1–23.

Chenery, H. B., and M. Bruno. "Development Alternatives in an Open Economy." *Economic Journal* (1962).

Claassen, E., and P. Salin, eds. *Recent Issues in International Monetary Economics*, vol. 2, *Studies in Monetary Economics*. New York: North-Holland, 1976.

Cleveland, Harold Van B., and Bruse W. H. Brittain. *The Great Inflation: A Monetarist View*. Washington, D.C.: National Planning Association, 1976.

Corden, W. M. "The Adjustment Problem." In *European Monetary Unification and Its Meaning for the United States*, edited by L. B. Krause and W. S. Salant. Washington, D.C.: Brooking Institution, 1974.

Cornell,B. "Spot Rates, Forward Rates and Exchange Market Efficiency." *Journal of Financial Economies* 5 (1977): 55–65.

Courchene, T. J. *Money, Inflation, and the Bank of Canada*. Montreal: C. Howe Research Institute, 1976.

Daniel, Betty C. "Monetary Expansion and Aggregate Supply in a Small, Open Economy." *Economica* 49 (August 1982): 267–75.

Dornbusch, Rudiger. "Exchange Rate Economics: Where Do We Stand?" *Brookings Papers of Economic Activity* 1 (1980): 143–85.

_____. "Floating Exchange Rates after Ten Years: Comments and Discussion." *Brookings Papers on Economic Activity* (1983): 79–86.

Dornbusch, R., S. Fischer, and P. A. Samuelson. "Comparative Advantage, Trade, and Payments in a Ricardian Model with a Continuum of Goods." *American Economic Review* 67 (December 1977): 823–39.

Drabicki, J. Z., and A. Takayama. "The Theory of Comparative Advantage in a Monetary World." *Southern Economic Journal* 50 (July 1983): 1–17.

Einzig, P. *The Theory of Forward Exchange*. London: Macmillan, 1937.

_____. *A Dynamic Theory of Forward Exchange*. London: Macmillan, 1962.

_____. *The History of Foreign Exchange*. London: Macmillan, 1962.

Eltis, W. A. "How Public Sector Growth Causes Balance-of-Payments Deficits." *International Currency Review* 7 (January–February 1975): 27–30.

Fabra, Paul. "Un Autre Système Monetaire." *Le Monde* (February 16, 1985), no. 12457, p. 1 and p. 16.

Feige, Edgar L., and Douglas K. Pearce. "The Substitutability of Money and Near-Monies: A Survey of Time-Series Evidence." *Journal of Economic Literature* no. 2 (June 1977): 439–69.

_____. "The Casual Causal Relationship Between Money and Income: Some Caveats for Times Series Analysis." *The Review of Economics and Statistics* 61 (November 1979): 521–33.

Fisher, I. *The Theory of Interest*. New York: MacMillan, 1930.

Frenkel, Jacob A. "The Forward Exchange Rate, Expectations and the Demand for Money: The German Hyperinflation." *American Economic Review* 67 (September 1977): 653–69.

———. "Monetary Policy: Domestic Targets and International Constraints." *American Economic Review* 73 (May 1983): 48–53.

Frenkel, Jacob A., I. Gyltason, and J. R. Helliwell. "A Synthesis of Monetary and Keynesian Approaches to Short-Run Balance-of-Payments Theory." *Economic Journal* 90 (September 1980): 582–92.

Frenkel, Jacob A., and Harry G. Johnson, eds. *The Economics of Exchange Rates: Selected Studies*. Reading, Mass.: Addison-Wesley, 1976.

Frenkel, Jacob A., and Richard M. Levich. "Covered Interest Arbitrage: Unexploited Profits?" *Journal of Political Economy* 83 (April 1975): 325–38.

———. "Transactions Costs and Interest Arbitrage: Tranquil Versus Turbulent Periods." *Journal of Political Economy* 85 (December 1977): 1209–26.

Frenkel, Jacob A., and Michael L. Mussa. "The Efficiency of Foreign Exchange Markets and Measures of Turbulence," *American Economic Review Papers and Proceedings* 70 (May 1980): 374–81.

Friedman, Milton. "The Case for Flexible Exchange Rates." In *Essays in Positive Economics*, edited by M. Friedman. Chicago: University of Chicago Press, 1953.

———. "The Demand for Money: Some Theoretical and Empirical Results." *Journal of Political Economy* 67 (August 1959): 327–51.

———. "*A Program for Monetary Stability*. New York: Fordham University Press, 1960.

———. "Interest Rates and the Demand for Money." *Journal of Law and Economics* 9 (October 1966): 71–85.

———. "The Role of Monetary Policy." *American Economic Review*, 58 (March 1968): 1–17.

———. "The Optimum Quantity of Money." In *The Optimum Quantity of Money and Other Essays*. Chicago: Aldine, 1969.

———. "*A Theoretical Framework for Monetary Analysis*. Occasional Paper 112. New York: National Bureau of Economic Research, 1971.

Friedman, Milton, and Robert Roosa. *The Balance of Payments: Free versus Fixed Exchange Rates*. Washington, D.C.: American Enterprise Institute, 1967.

Genberg, Hans, and Alexander K. Swoboda. "Gold and the Dollar: Asymmetries in World Money Stock Determination, 1959–1971." Unpublished (April 1981). (I)

Gervaise, Isaac. *The System or Theory of the Trade of the World*. Baltimore: Johns Hopkins University, 1954.

Gibson, W. E. "Interest Rates and Monetary Policy." *Journal of Political Economy* 78 (May–June 1970): 431–55.

Girton, Lance, and D. W. Henderson. "Financial Capital Movements and Central Bank Behavior in a Two Country, Short-Run Portfolio Balance Model." *Journal of Monetary Economics* 2 (January 1976): 33–61.

Goodhart, C. A. E. *Money, Information and Uncertainty*. London: Macmillan, 1975.

Grubel, H. G. "The Demand for International Reserves: A Critical Review of the Literature." *Journal of Economic Literature* 9 (December 1971): 1148–66.

Haberler, G. *The Theory of International Trade*. London: William Hodge, 1936.

_____ . "The Choice of Exchange Rates After the War." *American Economic Review* 35, no. 2 (1945): 308–18.

_____ . *A Survey of International Trade Theory*. Special Papers in International Economics 1 (July 1961). International Finance Section, Princeton University.

Halsen, J. A., and J. L. Waelbroeck. "The Less Developed Countries and the International Monetary Mechanism." *American Economic Review* 66 (May 1976): 171–76.

Hamburger, M. J. "The Demand for Money in an Open Economy: Germany and the United Kingdom." *Journal of Monetary Economics* 3 (January 1977): 25–40.

Heller, Robert. "International Reserves and World-Wide Inflation." *International Monetary Fund Staff Papers* 23 (March 1976): 61–87. (I)

Helliwell, John F., and Paul M. Boothe. "Macroeconomic Implications of Alternative Exchange Rate Models." *National Bureau of Economic Research Working Papers* 904 (June 1982).

Humphrey, Thomas M., and Robert E. Keleher. *The Monetary Approach to the Balance of Payments, Exchange Rates, and World Inflation.* New York: Praeger, 1982.

Johnson, Harry G. "Towards a General Theory of the Balance of Payments." In *Readings in International Economics*, edited by Richard E. Daves and Harry G. Johnson. Homewood, Ill.: Irwin, 1968.

———. "The Case for Flexible Exchange Rates, 1969." Federal Reserve Bank of St. Louis *Review* 51 (June 1969): 12–24.

———. *Essays in Monetary Economics.* Cambridge, Mass.: Harvard University Press, 1973.

———. "The Monetary Approach to Balance of Payments Theory and Policy: Explanation and Policy Implications." *Economica* 44 (August 1977): 217–29.

Johnson, Harry G., and A. K. Swoboda, eds. *The Economics of Common Currencies.* London: Allen and Unwin, 1973.

Jonson, P. D., and H. Kierzkowski. "The Balance of Payments: Analytic Exercise." *The Manchester School* 43 (June 1975): 105–33.

Joshi, Vijah. "Saving and Foreign Exchange Constraints." In *Unfashionable Economics*, edited by P. P. Streeten. London: 1970.

Keynes, John Maynard. *Tract on Monetary Reform.* London: Macmillan, 1924.

Klein, Benjamin. "The Competitive Supply of Money." *Journal of Money, Credit, and Banking* 6 (November 1974): 423–53.

Kohlhagen, Stephen W. "The Stability of Exchange Rate Expectations and Canadian Capital Flows" *Journal of Finance* 32 (December 1977): 1657–70.

Kouri, P. J. K. "Macroeconomics of Stagflation under Flexible Exchange Rates." *American Economic Review* 72 (May 1982): 390–95.

Krueger, Anne O. "Balance-of-Payments Theory." *The Journal of Economic Literature* 17 (March 1969): 1–26.

Kudoh, K. "Formation of Expectations and Exchange Rate Dynamics." *Economic Studies Quarterly* 32 (August 1981): 135–45.

Kuska, E. A. "Growth and the Balance of Payments: The Mundell and Wein Theorems." *Economic Journal* 88 (December 1978): 830–32.

Laidler, D. "Some Policy Implications of the Monetary Approach to Balance of Payments and Exchange Rate Analysis." *Oxford Economic Papers* 33 (Supplement July 1981): 70–84.

Laidler, D., and J. M. Parkin. "The Demand for Money in the United Kingdom, 1955–67: Preliminary Estimates." In *Readings in British Monetary Economics*, edited by H. G. Johnson et al. London: Clarendon Press, 1972.

_____. "Inflation: A Survey." *Economic Journal* 85 (December 1975): 741–809.

Lucas, Robert. "Some International Evidence on Output-Inflation Tradeoffs." *American Economic Review* 63 (June 1973): 326–34.

Machlup, F. "Relative Prices and Aggregate Spending in the Analysis of Devaluation." *American Economic Review* 45 (June 1955): 255–78.

Manne, Henry G., and Roger LeRoy Miller, eds. *Gold, Money and the Law.* Chicago: Aldine, 1975.

Mathieson, D. J. "Inflation, Interest Rates, and the Balance of Payments During a Financial Reform: The Case of Argentina." *World Developments* 10 (September 1982): 813–27. (D)

Mayer, Helmut, W. "Credit and Liquidity Creation in the International Banking Sector." Bank for International Settlements, Economic Paper no. 1 (November 1979).

McKinnon, Ronald I. "Private and Official International Money: The Case for the Dollar." In Princeton University *Essays in International Finance* 84 (April 1969).

_____. "A New Tripartite Monetary Agreement or a Limping Dollar Standard?" Princeton University *Essays in International Finance* 106 (1974).

_____. *Money in International Exchange: The Convertible Currency System.* New York: Oxford University Press, 1979.

_____. "Dollar Stabilization and American Monetary Policy." *American Economic Review Proceedings* 70 (May 1980): 382–87.

Melvin, Michael. "The Choice of An Exchange Rate System and Macroeconomic Activity." Arizona State University (January 1985).

Miles, Marc A. *Beyond Monetarism: Finding the Road to Stable Money.* New York: Basic Books, 1984.

Mises, Ludwig von. *The Theory of Money and Credit.* New Haven: Yale University Press, 1954.

Modigliani, Franco, and R. Sutch. "Innovations in Interest Rate Policy." *American Economic Review* 56 (May 1966): 178–97.

Mundell, Robert A. "A Theory of Optimum Currency Areas." *American Economic Review* 51 (November 1961): 509–17.

————. "The Exchange Rate Margins and Economic Policy." In *Money in the International Order*, edited by Carter Murphy. Dallas: Southern Methodist University Press, 1964.

————. *"Monetary Theory.* Pacific Palisades, Calif.: Goodyear, 1971.

Murphy, J. C., and S. K. Das. "Money Illusion and Balance-of-Payments Adjustment." *Journal of Political Economy* 84, no. 1 (February 1976): 73–82.

Nurkse, Ragnar. *International Currency Experience.* Geneva: League of Nations, 1944.

Nussbaum, Arthur. *Money in the Law: National and International.* Brooklyn: The Foundation Press, 1950.

Parkin, Michael. "Price and Output Determination in an Economy with Two Media of Exchange and a Separate Unit of Account." In *Recent Issues in Monetary Economics*, edited by Emil Claassen and Pascal Salin, pp. 74–98. Amsterdam: North-Holland, 1976.

Patinkin, Don. *Money, Interest and Prices*, 2nd ed. New York: Harper & Row, 1965.

Penati, A. "Expansionary Fiscal Policy and the Exchange Rates: A Review." *International Monetary Fund Staff Papers* 30 (September 1983): 542–69.

Phelps, Edmund S. "Inflation in the Theory of Public Finance." *Swedish Journal of Economics* 75 (March 1973): 67–82.

Phelps, E. S., and J. B. Taylor. "Stabilizing Powers of Monetary Policy under Rational Expectations." *Journal of Political Economy* 85, no. 1 (January 1977): 163–90.

Pippenger, John. "Balance-of-Payments Deficits Measurement and Interpretation." *Federal Reserve Bank of St. Louis Review* 55 (November 1973): 6–14.

Polak, J. J. "Monetary Analysis of Income Formation and Payments Problems." In

The Monetary Approach to the Balance of Payments. Washington, D.C.: International Monetary Fund, 1977.

Porter, M. "Capital Flows as an Offset to Monetary Policy: The German Experience." *International Monetary Fund Staff Papers* 19 (July 1972): 395–424.

Putnam, Bluford H. "Controlling the Euromarkets: A Policy Perspective," *Columbia Journal of World Business* (Fall 1979): 25–31.

Rhomberg, R., and H. R. Heller. "Introductory Survey." In *The Monetary Approach to the Balance of Payments.* Washington, D.C.: International Monetary Fund, 1977.

Robinson, Joan. "The Foreign Exchanges." In *Readings in the Theory of International Trade.* Committee of the American Economic Association, pp. 83–103. Philadelphia: Blakiston, 1949.

Rutledge, John. *A Monetarist Model of Inflationary Expectations.* Lexington, Mass.: Lexington Books, 1974.

Sachs, Jeffrey D. "The Current Account and Macroeconomic Adjustment in the 1970s." *Brookings Papers of Economic Activity* 1 (1981): 201–82.

Samuelson, Paul. "An Exact Hume-Ricardo-Marshall Model of International Trade." *Journal of International Economics* (February 1971): 1–18.

Sargent, T. J., and Neil Wallace. "Rational Expectations, the Optimal Monetary Investment, and the Optimal Money Supply Rule." *Journal of Political Economy* 83, no. 2 (April 1975): 241–54.

Schadler, Susan. "Sources of Exchange Rate Variability: Theory and Empirical Evidence." *International Monetary Fund Staff Papers* 24 (July 1977): 253–96.

Shafer, J. R., and B. E. Loopesko. "Floating Exchange Rates after Ten Years." *Brookings Papers of Economic Activity* (1983): 1–70.

Shone, R. "The Monetary Approach to the Balance of Payments: Stock-Flow Equilibria." *Oxford Economic Papers* 32 (July 1980): 200–9.

Sims, Christopher. "Money, Income, and Causality." *American Economic Review* 62 (September 1972): 540–52.

Smith, Vera C. *Rationale of Central Banking.* London: P. S. King, 1936.

Sohmen, E. *Flexible Exchange Rates.* Chicago: University of Chicago Press, 1969.

Spencer, Roger W. "Channels of Monetary Influence: A Survey." Federal Reserve Bank of St. Louis *Review* 56 (November 1974): 8–26.

Spraos, J. "The Theory of Forward Exchange and Recent Practice." *The Manchester School of Economics and Social Studies* 21 (May 1953): 87–117.

————. "Speculation, Arbitrage and Sterling." *Economic Journal* 69 (March 1959): 1–21.

Stein, J. L. "Monetary Growth Theory in Perspective." *American Economic Review* 60 (March 1970): 85–106.

Stockman, Alan C. "Risk, Information and Forward Exchange Rates." In *The Economics of Exchange Rates—Selected Studies*, edited by J. Frenkel and H. G. Johnson. Reading, Mass.: Addison-Wesley, 1978.

————. "A Theory of Exchange Rates Determination." *Journal of Political Economy* 88 (August 1980): 673–98.

Swoboda, Alexander. "Exchange Rate Regimes and European–U.S. Policy Interdependence." *International Monetary Fund Staff Papers* 30 (March 1983): 75–102.

Tanner, J. E., and V. Bonomo. "Gold, Capital Flows, and Long Swings in American Business Activity." *Journal of Political Economy* 76 (January–February 1968): 44–52.

The CRB Futures Price Index. "A 'Basket of 27 Commodities' That May Soon Be a Futures Contract." *Commodity Research Bureau*, 1984 Commodity Yearbook, pp. 38–53.

Thompson, Earl. "The Theory of Money and Income Consistent with Orthodox Value Theory." In *Trade Stability and Macroeconomics*, edited by George Horwich and Paul A. Samuelson, pp. 427–51. New York: Academic Press, 1974.

Thorn, Richard S., ed. *Monetary Theory and Policy*. New York: Random House, 1966.

Tobin, James. "Commercial Banks as Creaters of Money." In *Banking and Monetary Studies*, edited by Deane Carson, pp. 408–19. Homewood, Ill.: Irwin, 1963.

————. "A General Equilibrium Approach to Monetary Theory." *Journal of Money, Credit, and Banking* 1 (February 1969): 15–29.

Tosini, Paula. "Learning Against the Wind: A Standard for Managed Floating." *Essays in International Finance* no. 126. Princeton, N.J.: Princeton University, December 1977.

Triffin, Robert. "National Central Banking and the International Economy." *Review of Economic Studies* 14 (February 1947): 53–75.

————. "Jamaica: Major Revision or Fiasco?" In "Reflections on Jamaica," *Essays in International Finance* no. 115. Princeton, N.J.: Princeton University, April 1976.

Turnovsky, S. J. "Monetary Policy and Foreign Price Disturbances under Flexible Exchange Rates: A Stochastic Approach." *Journal of Money, Credit, and Banking* 13 (May 1981): 156–76.

Van Belle, John J. "Money Illusion and Its Influence on International Adjustment." In *The Monetary Approach to International Adjustment*, edited by Bluford H. Putnam and D. Sykes Wilford. New York: Praeger, 1978.

Vaubel, Roland. "Free Currency Competition." *Weltwirtschaftliches Archiv* 113 (October 1977): 435–59.

Viner, Jacob. *Studies in the Theory of International Trade*. New York: Harper, 1937.

Wilford, D. Sykes. "Politica Monetaria en Mexico: Examen Retrospectivo y Perspectiva." In A. Violante and R. Davila, eds., *Mexico: Una Economia en Transicion*. Mexico City: Editorial Limusna, 1984.

Wilford, W. T., and R. Moncarz. *Essays in Latin American Economic Issues*. New Orleans: Division of Business and Economic Research, Louisiana State University, 1970.

Williamson, Jeffery G. *American Growth and the Balance of Payments 1820–1913*. Chapel Hill, N.C.: University of North Carolina Press, 1964.

Willms, Manfred. "Controlling Money in an Open Economy: The German Case." *Federal Reserve Bank of St. Louis Review* 53, 4 (April 1971): 10–27.

Wyplosz, C. A. "The Exchange and Interest Rate Term Structure under Risk Aversion and Rational Expectations." *Journal of International Economics* 14 (February 1983): 123–39.

Yeager, Leland B. *International Monetary Relations: Theory, History, and Policy*, 2nd ed. New York: Harper & Row, 1976.

Zecher, J. Richard, C. Burrows, and L. McGregory. "Determinants of the Australian Money Supply Since 1950." Paper presented at Congress of Australian and New Zealand Association for the Advancement of Science, August 1972.

INDEX

ABOUT THE EDITORS
AND CONTRIBUTORS

EDITORS

Bluford H. Putnam is vice-president and senior economist with Morgan Stanley and Company. Putnam has edited two books on international financial markets, and his writings on international finance have appeared in both the business press and in academic journals such as the *American Economic Review, Journal of Finance,* and *Journal of Money, Credit, and Banking.*

Prior to joining Morgan Stanley, Putnam was a senior partner at the corporate finance consulting firm of Stern Stewart and Co. He was also a vice-president and economist at Chase Manhattan Bank and an international economist at the Federal Reserve Bank of New York.

Putnam, who earned his Ph.D. in economics at Tulane University, has served on the adjunct faculties of the business schools of Columbia University, University of Pennsylvania, and New York University.

D. Sykes Wilford is a vice-president and economist with the Chase Manhattan Bank. Wilford's newest responsibilities in the Corporate Economics Group are special products development and the presentation of international finance marketing and training seminars to bank officers, major corporate clients, and foreign government officials. Previously he was responsible for interest rate and exchange rate forecasting. Before joining Chase, Wilford was an economist with the Federal Reserve Bank of New York.

Wilford, whose main research interests are monetary economics and international finance, has published in such journals as the *American Economic Review, Journal of Money, Credit and Banking,* and the *Journal of Finance.* He has also both authored and edited several books. Wilford, who earned a Ph.D. in economics at Tulane University, has lectured at several universitites.

CONTRIBUTORS

M. A. Akhtar is assistant director of research at the Federal Reserve Bank of New York. He has served as a consultant to the Bank for International Settlements and has taught at various universities and colleges. Akhtar has published in macromonetary economics, history of economic theory, and international economics in such journals as *American Economic Review, Oxford Economic Papers*, and *Journal of Finance*. He received his Ph.D. from the University of South Carolina.

Russell S. Boyer received his Ph.D. in economics from the University of Chicago in 1971, writing his thesis on growth and the balance of payments. He has been at the University of Western Ontario since that time and is currently an associate professor in the Economics Department. During years of leave, he visited Carnegie Mellon University and the London School of Economics. His research interests continue to be in international financial economics, recently emphasizing stabilization policies in open economies. His articles have appeared in journals such as *American Economic Review* and the *Journal of Political Economy*.

Michael Connolly is a professor of economics at the University of South Carolina. He has held previous teaching positions at the University of Florida from 1972 to 1978 and at Harvard from 1968 to 1972. His articles have appeared in the *American Economic Review,* the *Journal of Political Economy,* the *Quarterly Journal of Economics,* and the *Journal of International Economics,* among others. He holds a B.A. from the University of California at Berkeley and an M.A. and a Ph.D. from the University of Chicago.

Lance Girton, who holds a Ph.D. in economics from the University of Chicago, is a professor of economics at the University of Utah. He was an economist in the International Finance Division of the Federal Reserve Board from 1970 to 1978. Girton has acted as a consultant to the financial industry and the World Bank. He has taught at Michigan Technological University, George Washington University, and the Pennsylvania State University. His articles on international monetary theory and finance have appeared in several leading journals.

Thomas M. Humphrey is a vice-president and economist with the Federal Reserve Bank of Richmond, where he writes for and edits the bank's *Economic Review*. His research interests are in monetary theory and in history. He holds B.S. and M.A. degrees from the University of Tennessee and a Ph.D. from Tulane University. He is the author of *Essays on Inflation* (4th ed., 1984) and the coauthor (with R. E. Keleher) of another book, *The Monetary Approach to the Balance of Payments, Exchange Rates, and World Inflation*. His articles have appeared in *Cato Journal, Journal of Money, Credit, and Banking, Southern Economic Journal*, and *History of Political Economy*.

Robert E. Keleher, a graduate of the University of Illinois, Northern Illinois University, and Indiana University, was an economist at First Tennessee from 1974 to 1976. Currently he is a research officer and senior financial economist at the Federal Reserve Bank of Atlanta, where he specializes in monetary and regional studies. He is also the coauthor (with Thomas M. Humphrey) of *The Monetary Approach to the Balance of Payments, Exchange Rates, and World Inflation*.

David T. King is regional treasurer and chief economist for the Midwest at Citicorp. Before joining Citicorp, he was chief of the industrial economies division at the Federal Reserve Bank of New York and an administrator of the monetary and fiscal policies division at the Organization for Economic Cooperation and Development. King holds a Ph.D. from Tulane University and a B.A. from Southern Methodist University. King's main research interests are international monetary policy and exchange rate analysis. He has published articles on these topics in the *Southern Economic Journal* and *Columbia Journal of World Business*.

Ronald A. Krieger is an economist and economics writer/editor in Washington, D.C. He holds a B.A. in economics from the University of Colorado and an M.S. and Ph.D. in economics from the University of Wisconsin. His earlier positions included economist with the World Bank; assistant professor of international economics at the graduate school of international studies, University of Denver; senior economist in the Economics Department of Citibank; economics editor of *Business Week*; Chairman of the Department of Economics at Goucher College; and vice-president and director of economic publications for the Chase Manhattan Bank. Krieger is the author of a number of articles on domestic and international economic policy.

Thomas A. Lawler is currently a financial economist with the Federal National Mortgage Association. His major responsibilities include working on Fannie Mae's economic and interest rate forecasts, writing for the weekly publication *Money and Capital Markets*, and analyzing and evaluating the pricing of various mortgage products. Previously, Lawler was a vice-president with the Chase Manhattan Bank. He holds a B.A. and an M.A. in economics from the University of Virginia.

Ronald I. McKinnon is a professor of economics at Stanford University, which he joined in 1961 after receiving a Ph.D. degree from the University of Minnesota. He has acted as a consultant to the International Monetary Fund, the Organization of American States and several foreign governments. He is the author of several books on the international monetary system and on the financial structure of less developed countries, research interests which are continuing at the present time. McKinnon has published numerous articles in *American Economic Review, Journal of Political Economy*, and the *Journal of Money, Credit, and Banking*, among others.

Marc A. Miles is currently an economist with H. C. Wainwright & Co., Economics, on leave from Rutgers University where he is an associate professor of economics. Previously, Miles was a research economist in the balance of payment division of the Federal Reserve Bank of New York. Miles holds a B.A., M.A., and Ph.D. from the University of Chicago, as well as an M.Sc. from the London School of Economics. His articles have appeared in *American Economic Review, Journal of Political Economy*, as well as in the *Wall Street Journal* and *New York Times*. He is the author of three books. His most recent, *Beyond Monetarism: Finding the Road to Stable Money*, is published by Basic Books.

Don Roper received his Ph.D. from the University of Chicago. He served as an economist in the international finance division of the Federal Reserve Board of Washington, D.C. from 1969 to 1975. He has taught at the University of Stockholm, the University of Illinois, Tulane University, and the Australian National University and was a professor of economics at the University of Utah through 1985. He is currently director of the Center of International Economic Studies at the University of Colorado at Boulder. His research specialty is the foundations of monetary theory and international monetary history, with articles appearing in *American Economic Review, Quarterly Journal of Economics*, and *Journal of Political Economy*.

Walton T. Wilford is professor of economics and finance and chairman of the Economics and Finance Department at the University of New Orleans. He has held academic positions at the University of Georgia and the University of Idaho, and prior to affiliating with UNO in 1968, served for several years as an economic adviser with the Department of State, Agency for International Development in Central and South America. Wilford's academic interests are economic development and public finance. Journals to which he has contributed include *Economic Development and Cultural*

Change, Economic Inquiry, Economic Letters, Journal of Developing Areas, Journal of Finance, the *National Tax Journal,* the *Review of Economics and Statistics, Weltwirtschaftliches Archiv,* and *World Development.* Wilford's Ph.D is from Southern Methodist University, and he is currently serving as president of the North American Economics and Finance Association.

J. Richard Zecher, who holds a Ph.D. in economics from Ohio State University, is senior vice-president and chief economist at Chase Manhattan Bank. From 1968 to 1978, he taught economics, first at the University of Chicago and then at Tulane University. He took two leaves of absence from Tulane to work in Washington, D.C., first as senior staff economist at the president's Council of Economic Advisers in 1974–75, and then as chief economist at the Securities and Exchange Commission from 1976 to 1978. He served as dean of the College of Business Administration, University of Iowa, from 1978–1981. He has served as a consultant to financial firms and to the U.S. Treasury, and currently is a member of the board of directors of the Chicago Board Options Exchange. His teaching and publication interests have included econometrics, domestic and international monetary policy, financial economics, and the economics of regulation.